A Problem of Presence

A Problem of Presence

BEYOND SCRIPTURE IN AN AFRICAN CHURCH

Matthew Engelke

UNIVERSITY OF CALIFORNIA PRESS

BERKELEY   LOS ANGELES   LONDON

University of California Press, one of the most
distinguished university presses in the United States,
enriches lives around the world by advancing scholarship
in the humanities, social sciences, and natural sciences.
Its activities are supported by the UC Press Foundation
and by philanthropic contributions from individuals and
institutions. For more information, visit www.ucpress.edu.

University of California Press
Berkeley and Los Angeles, California

University of California Press, Ltd.
London, England

Library of Congress Cataloging-in-Publication Data

Engelke, Matthew Eric.
    A problem of presence : beyond Scripture in an African
church / Matthew Engelke.
        p.   cm. — (The anthropology of Christianity ; 2)
    Includes bibliographical references (p.   ) and index.
    ISBN 978-0-520-24903-5 (cloth : alk. paper)
    ISBN 978-0-520-24904-2 (pbk. : alk. paper)
    1. Masowe weChishanu Church.   2. Masowe, Johane.
I. Title.

    BX8095.E54   2007
    289.9'3—dc22   2006023890

Manufactured in the United States of America

16 15 14 13 12 11 10 09 08 07
10 9 8 7 6 5 4 3 2 1

This book is printed on New Leaf EcoBook 50, a 100%
recycled fiber of which 50% is de-inked post-consumer
waste, processed chlorine-free. EcoBook 50 is acid-free
and meets the minimum requirements of ANSI/ASTM
D5634-01 (Permanence of Paper).

In memory of my father,
Edwin Paul Engelke, Jr.

CONTENTS

ILLUSTRATIONS

ACKNOWLEDGMENTS

THE FIELDWORK FOR THIS BOOK was funded by a Fulbright-Hays Doctoral Dissertation Research Abroad Fellowship and the Graduate School of Arts and Sciences at the University of Virginia. During fieldwork in 1999, I was hosted by the Department of Religious Studies, Classics, and Philosophy at the University of Zimbabwe. In Zimbabwe, I wish to single out the staff at the National Archives, who helped me to locate important materials. Several of the chapters in this book were originally written during a dissertation write-up grant from the Department of Anthropology at the University of Virginia. At the London School of Economics, Charles Stafford allowed me to rearrange my teaching commitments so that I could have a solid stretch of time in which to complete the book manuscript.

I have had a number of excellent teachers. Jean Comaroff and James Fernandez shaped my initial interest in the Friday apostolics when I was an undergraduate and supervised my B.A. thesis on African churches. Leslie Bessant played a formative role in this project too. In graduate school, my Ph.D. committee chair, Richard Handler, provided sound advice, clear insights, and unflagging support. My other committee members—Roy Wagner, Ellen Contini-Morava, and Cynthia Hoehler-Fatton—have each enriched my understanding of anthropology, religion, and Africa. At the University of Virginia, I also benefited from the input of other professors, especially Dell Hymes, Joe Miller, Ben Ray, and Edie Turner. During the year I spent at Kenyon College while completing the thesis, Rita Kipp, Howard Sacks, and Dave Suggs were very supportive.

A number of friends and colleagues have read one or more of the chapters, in some form, at some point over the past six years. They include Catherine Alexander, Catherine Allerton, Laura Bear, Maurice Bloch, Erica Bornstein, Judith Bovensiepen, Eleanor Culley, Jeffrey Feldman, Stephan Feuchtwang, Maia Green, Deborah James, David Maxwell, Danny Miller, Amy Ninetto, Johnny Parry, Charles Stafford, and Matt Tomlinson. Conversations with a number of people over the years, especially Fenella Cannell, Keith Hart, Chenjerai Hove, John Tresch, and Dick Werbner, have also been helpful. Most especially, however, I would like to single out Isabel Mukonyora in this regard.

I have had the benefit of comments from audiences at Cambridge University, Goldsmiths College, Kenyon College, the London School of Economics, Oxford University, St. Andrews University, Swarthmore College, University College London, and the University of Illinois at Urbana-Champaign, as well as at several conferences.

Several people read the whole manuscript in its final stages, some of them more than once. They have each offered generous comments, advice, and engaged critiques. Joel Robbins, series editor, has been a good friend and interlocutor. Webb Keane and Johannes Fabian read the manuscript for the University of California Press, and each has given advice and support in other contexts. Terence Ranger has helped to shape this project from the beginning. Michael Scott's thoughtful comments provided important insight. Harry West has probably read what is here in more forms than anyone else and has always had something important to say.

I wish to thank several people at the University of California Press. Stan Holwitz, Randy Heyman, Jacqueline Volin, and Sheila Berg have been very helpful. As a member of the UC Press Board, James Clifford offered appreciated support.

I am fortunate to have supportive friends and family. My mother has always offered encouragement and even came to Zimbabwe. My grandfather Joe Jeff Wilcox inspired an early and long-lasting interest in books. I have dedicated this book in loving memory of my father. My wife, Rebecca Nash, has given the most to this project at every step of the way. Our daughter, Harriet, arrived just before I finished the first major draft of the manuscript, and I look forward to sharing this book and stories of Zimbabwe with her.

My greatest thanks go to the Zimbabweans who invited me into their lives, many of whom have become lasting friends. While almost none of the apostolics asked me to withhold their names, I now think it is prudent to do so, given the current political situation in Zimbabwe and given the fact that the Friday churches have sometimes been caught up in those politics, despite the desires of many congregants. So, except for the prophets, all of whom are public figures, I have used pseudonyms for the friends and interlocutors who appear in these pages. In addition to the people I name, there were dozens of others who gave generously of their time and themselves and without whose help I could not have completed this work. A number of other people in Zimbabwe, or who work on Zimbabwe, were instrumental in the realization of this project, including David Bishau, Moreblessings Chitauro, Norbert and Wilbert Fero, Albert Hororo, Mike Matsosha Hove, Philip Mufanechiyah, Solomon Nkiwane, Sara Rich Dorman, Juliet Thondlana, and Yvonne Vera. The Makonye family adopted me as their own from the outset and have been unconditionally supportive ever since. The input of Lazarus Chidaushe, who conducted a significant amount of the research with me, is evident on every page of this book.

Parts of this book have appeared elsewhere. A slightly different version of chapter 2 was originally published as "The Early Days of Johane Masowe: Self-Doubt, Uncertainty, and Religious Transformation," in *Comparative Studies in Society and History* 47, no. 4 (2005): 781–808 (Cambridge University Press). Chapter 7 appeared earlier as "Sticky Subjects, Sticky Objects: The Substance of Healing in an African Church," in *Materiality,* edited by Daniel Miller (Durham, NC: Duke University Press, 2005). A small section of the introduction and most of chapter 5 come from the article "Text and Performance in an African Christian Church: The Book, 'Live and Direct' in Zimbabwe," *American Ethnologist* 31, no. 1 (2004): 76–91, copyright © 2004 by the American Anthropological Association. The material from these articles is reused here with permission.

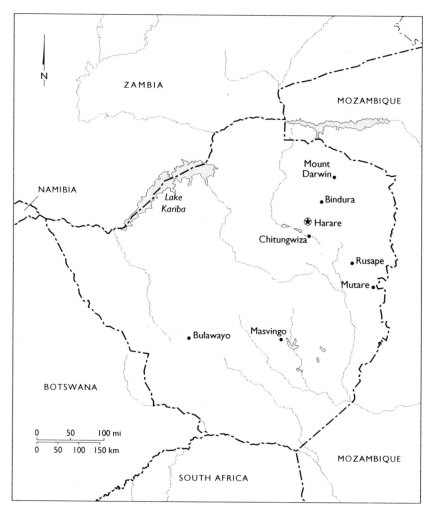

Zimbabwe

Introduction

ON THE OUTSKIRTS OF CHITUNGWIZA, the city of townships just south of Zimbabwe's capital, Harare, there is a place called Juranifiri Santa (the "place of healing") where people gather to pray. The heart of Juranifiri Santa is a clearing of ground amid rubber and msasa trees. On any given weekend, when attendance at the prayer site is highest, up to a thousand people might be gathered. Wearing white robes that stretch to their ankles, the congregants look like a cloud that has settled to earth. The men and women sit separately, facing one another in half circles. Some of these people do come for healing, both spiritual and physical, which is offered by the Holy Spirit through a human prophet. Most, however, are regular congregants who are not in need of healing but travel to the site from throughout Chitungwiza and Harare in order to hear the Word of God.

Juranifiri Santa is a congregation of the Masowe weChishanu Church, or Friday Masowe Church, so called because it recognizes Friday as the Sabbath.[1] The Friday church was first inspired in the early 1930s by a man named Shoniwa Masedza. Born in the area of Gandanzara, in the Makoni District, Southern Rhodesia, Shoniwa was the son of peasant farmers who tried to earn a living as a migrant laborer. One southern winter, while working for a shoemaker near Salisbury (as Harare used to be known), Shoniwa became very ill. It was 1932, and he was no more than eighteen years old. During his sickness, Shoniwa was visited by the Holy Spirit and transformed into Johane Masowe, or John of the Wilderness—Africa's John the Baptist. The Holy Spirit told Johane that he had been sent from heaven to preach the Word of God in Africa. Since that time a number of groups laying claim to Johane's name, inspired by his words and deeds, have grown up in the groves, fields, and empty spaces of Zimbabwe. One of these groups is the weChishanu Church, a loosely defined network of perhaps one hundred thousand people, who meet each week in places such as Juranifiri Santa throughout the country.

Johane's weChishanu followers refer to themselves as apostolics *(vapostori),* a designation used by several other churches in southern Africa as well. But as the "Friday apostolics" are quick to tell you, there is something distinct about them, something that makes them unlike other apostolics and indeed other Christians. They are, as they say, "the Christians who don't read the Bible."

Among the many Zimbabweans I met who consider themselves devout Christians, learning that I was studying a group of Christians who do not read the Bible often sparked an incredulous, even hostile, reaction. In the eighteen months I spent among the Friday apostolics, there were occasions on which their rejection of the Bible was couched in terms that seemed intended to elicit these kinds of reactions. One of the more memorable involved reference to the Bible as something other than a book. It comes from a sermon by the Masowe prophet Madzibaba Godfrey Nzira, delivered in 1999 at Juranifiri Santa.[2] Nzira's reputation as a healer often outpaced the content of his preaching, and there were always some visitors to Juranifiri Santa who did not know they were among "the Christians who don't read the Bible." On the occasion in question, a newcomer got up to express his gratitude for the help he had received from Nzira in dealing with his afflictions. He cited a passage from the Gospel of Luke to bolster his point. The man was unaware that he had done something wrong, but elders in the congregation immediately asked him to stop. He sat down, looking dejected and confused. Later in the service Nzira delivered a sermon, in the course of which he made the stark pronouncement that in this church there is no need for the Bible. "Here," he said, "we don't talk of Bibles. What is the Bible to me? Having it is just trouble. Look, why would you read it? It gets old. Look again. After keeping it for some time it falls apart, the pages come out. And then you can take it and use it as toilet paper until it's finished. We don't talk Bible-talk here. We have a true Bible here."

Nzira's remarks are a useful place to begin this book. They touch on the central concern of the Friday apostolics: they have what they consider an *immaterial* faith. Following Johanna Drucker, by *immaterial* I mean "that which is insignificant in its materiality" (1994, 14). In expressing his disapproval of the Bible, Nzira is emphasizing its materiality. It is this quality that gives his images their force. The apostolics want a relationship with God that is not dependent on things such as books. They want a faith in which things do not matter, because they understand things as a barrier to faith. They want a faith in which God's presence is, instead, immediate. Or, as they often say, "live and direct."

LIVE AND DIRECT

In place of Scripture, the Friday apostolics say, they receive the Word of God live and direct from the Holy Spirit. This phrase is intended to capture the sense of presence that is the cornerstone of their faith. As I propose later, the specificities of "live and direct" faith can be compared to what I will refer to as the "liberal" traditions of Protestantism, like those of the German theologians of *Glaubenslehre* (see Troeltsch 1991) or, even more broadly, the Quakers (Bauman 1983). First, however, to understand what is unique about the approach of the Friday apostolics to divine presence, it is useful to have some background on how they fit into the larger picture of apostolic Christianity in southern Africa.

When I told people in Zimbabwe that I was studying the Masowe apostolics, they almost always replied by saying something like, "Oh, those are the people in white robes who meet under the trees."[3] They said this because most apostolic Christians do in fact wear white robes and meet under trees, for reasons I explain later. These notable features make apostolic churches highly visible: particularly in Zimbabwe's cities, it is difficult not to notice when hundreds of the congregants are gathered in a field by the side of the road. Despite this outward similarity, however, and despite the fact that apostolic Christians can be recognized with ease, Zimbabweans do not always know much about the histories of the individual churches. In a sense, the apostolic groups are the same. They are united in their commitment to living like the apostles—to having an experience of Christianity as vibrant and alive as when Jesus walked the earth. For the Friday apostolics, this commitment is marked in part by what is emphasized in their name. They observe Friday as the Sabbath because, they say, "that's the day Jesus died." Just as they mark his death, however, they take great comfort in what they see as the present work of the Holy Spirit. The emphasis on the power of the Holy Spirit as a source

Figure 1. An apostolic in his church garments, Chiweshe District, 1999. Photo by Matthew Engelke.

of both healing and salvation is another common denominator in the apostolic churches.

And yet, in other respects, the vibrancy of apostolic churches can be radically different, and the groups do not appreciate being lumped together. The Friday Masowe, for instance, are often confused with the Saturday Masowe, known formally as the Gospel of God Church, who are also inspired by Shoniwa-Johane and in fact worked with him closely until his death in 1973.[4] But there are a number of important differences between the Friday and Saturday groups. The Saturday Masowe live together in self-contained communities; the Friday Masowe do not. The Saturday Masowe have well-established church hierarchies and institutional offices; the Friday Masowe do not. The Saturday Masowe reject the use of biomedicine; the Friday Masowe do not (although they once did).

Another apostolic church is the Church of John Maranke. Like Shon-iwa-Johane, Maranke claimed inspiration from the Holy Spirit and built up congregations throughout south-central Africa on the basis of that inspiration and the powers of healing it conferred. In what follows I develop comparisons of these apostolic churches in more detail. For now, the point I want to emphasize is that of all the apostolics in southern Africa, the Friday apostolics are the only ones who reject the Bible and the only ones who have developed this specific understanding of a live and direct faith as marked by its immateriality.

The specific texture of live and direct faith has been formed against the backdrop of colonial history. Johane Masowe's denunciation of the Bible was, in part, a political critique. In the Makoni District, where Shoniwa-Johane grew up, missionaries emphasized "literacy and literature as a key dimension of the 'richness' that Christianity would bring to an impoverished people" (Ranger 1999a, 198). That impoverishment was understood as both spiritual and material. Books were presented as the answer. But as several anthropologists have shown, books have also often served as tools of subjugation. Throughout colonial Africa, for instance, "education was vital in creating and maintaining [the] symbolic power" (Fabian 1986, 74) of mission and state. The Bible, a key source of this power, bore "the essence of white might" (Comaroff and Comaroff 1991, 229). By the early 1930s, as the Southern Rhodesian authorities consolidated the power of white settlers, literacy and the book had become highly charged instruments of struggle. Soon after he began his mission, as an act of political defiance, Johane told people to "burn their Bibles" because, he said, they came from "men with black hearts."[5]

Today the Friday apostolics still question the Bible because of the extent to which it has been used as a political tool of subjugation. As one church elder put it, "We learned that we could not trust the whites or their book." He told me that missionaries often said one thing, the Bible another. Polygamy, for example, was roundly condemned by the missionaries, but it was not condemned in the Bible. In addition to this, the elder suggested that "history is written by the victors, and there is this problem with the Bible. It is a record of what the Europeans want others to know." This remark is representative of the views I heard expressed and contributes to the thesis about white might; from another perspective, however, it suggests a more complicated relationship with text-based knowledge. History may indeed be written by the victors, but there is a contradiction in the elder's understanding. According to his remarks on polygamy,

Africans know they cannot trust the Europeans' Bible in part because of what they read in it.

This contradiction does not exist in other African independent churches, including apostolic ones. In most such churches the authority of the Bible is understood to be independent of missionaries and is appropriated through an active embracement of it. For example, at the Maranke Church, one of the largest apostolic churches in Zimbabwe, I regularly heard as many as a dozen Bible readings in a four-hour service. Members of the congregation would sometimes follow a preacher's reading by pulling out their own copies of Scripture and reading along. Some would get lost in the text, either by carrying on in the book or chapter from which the reading was drawn or by turning to other chapters and verses that echo the message of the original selection. The Maranke apostolics would not deny that the written word is a powerful tool for political manipulation or that missionaries have sometimes used the Bible in duplicitous ways. But their approach to the text is more representative of what one finds in African Christian independency (see, e.g., Comaroff 1985; Jules-Rosette 1975; Muller 1999; Sundkler 1961). Close reading has become a means of empowerment. Christians in the independent churches are often the strongest advocates of Bible knowledge and Bible-based faith. They make Scripture their own by using it to reinforce their visions of what constitutes an authentic Christianity. What this pattern of appropriation suggests is that the position of the Friday apostolics has extrapolitical motivations. If the problem was simply the prevention of textual abuse, we might expect the Friday apostolics to have become close readers. This is not to dismiss the politicoreligious dynamic of their rejection, but we cannot rely solely on a "white might" argument to make sense of their position. I should also mention here that the Friday apostolics do not reject literacy per se; indeed, reading is a valued skill (see note 11).

Politics is important in their rejection of the Bible, but it is not the whole story. More frequently, the Friday apostolics told me they reject the Bible because of its irrelevance to their lives. Apostolics often say the Bible is "stale." They think of the Bible as a historical record that is not always relevant in today's world. What makes it stale, then, is that it's "out of date," like an old newspaper. "The Bible was written two thousand years ago, up in Palestine," one friend of mine said. "There is nothing wrong with that culture, but it is different from ours. It's not so much that the Bible is wrong; it's not. The Bible is the Word of God, but it is not always relevant to the needs of Africans today. We are facing new problems—AIDS, witchcraft, and other African problems—that must be addressed in new ways." For him, referring to the Bible in this context as the "Word of God" was not an assertion of Christian Truth. It was not a theological claim but a historical one—a point I examine in more depth in chapter 5. In any case, my friend did not suggest there was anything wrong with knowing what happened "up in Palestine" two thousand years ago, but he was confident that what matters most is the Holy Spirit working now, live and direct.

Coupled with the claim of the Bible's irrelevance is a more far-reaching concern with the written word as a medium of religious inspiration. Apostolics draw attention to the Bible for what to them it clearly is: an object. The Bible is an artifact, a thing. As such, it does not inspire them. Whereas many Christians treat the materiality of the Word as epiphenomenal, or as in service to its spiritual ("immaterial") significance, the Friday apostolics understand the materiality of texts as a defining quality—something that cannot be separated from its other qualities. Referring to Christianity as a "religion of the Book" is problematic for them, because in effect they deny that books can be spiritual.

In summing up these discussions, we might say the Friday apostolics are concerned with what Johannes Fabian calls "the terror of the text" (1991b) in his work on the Jamaa religious movement within the Catholic Church in Zaire. Among the Jamaa texts produced terror for two overlapping reasons. First, they were signs of colonial authority and administration, for example, pass books and work papers (cf. West 2003). Second, they represented the routinization of religious authority. This second sense of terror was "the terror of habit and ritualistic pedantry" as represented in the "notebook and pencil" dictates of the Catholic Church (Fabian 1991b, 69). Like the Jamaa, the Masowe weChishanu are wary of the written word's potential to do harm. For them, texts are dangerous. They deaden faith; they take the spirit out of things; they are, quite literally, physical obstacles. When Friday apostolics say "the Bible is a record of what Europeans want others to know" or "the Bible is stale," they are expressing the terror of the text. This terror is felt both politically and theologically, and it threatens the immediacy of what they understand as a live and direct faith.

Rejecting the Bible is not the only way in which the Friday apostolics exhibit a commitment to live and direct faith. Their regard for spiritual immediacy as an immaterial quality is expressed in several other ways. Thus, for them, meeting to pray in open fields has this theological significance and is indexed by the very name of the prophet from whom they take their cues. In Shona the word *masowe* refers to a "wilderness" or an "empty space" (Mukonyora 2000; Werbner 1985). Today the Friday apostolics do not primarily emphasize Johane Masowe's position as a John the Baptist figure; in fact, they do not baptize at all.[6] It is, rather, coming together in "the wilderness" that matters most to them, and for which Johane, as a man of the wilderness, is remembered. Church sites are "empty spaces." Apostolics mark this emptiness by leaving behind the trappings of this world. They take off their shoes and jewelry and carry no money. They maintain no altars and have neither hymnbooks nor liturgies. They do not build houses of prayer or commission stained-glass windows. There is no Eucharist celebration. All of this is a move toward what they understand to be the enactment of an immaterial faith—one that is insignificant in its materiality. As prophets can sometimes be heard to sing as they lead the congregation, it is these conditions that create the possibility for the live and direct. "Come here, I am near," they sing. "Come here, I am near."

The articulation of and emphasis on immateriality is also expressed through the concept of *mutemo,* which translates roughly from Shona as "law" but which the apostolics use to refer to "knowledge" as well. Mutemo is the set of guidelines and dispositions according to which an apostolic ought to live. Some people who explained the concept to me emphasized that mutemo is "not written on tablets." In other words, mutemo should not be thought of as fixed, like a written text. This accounts in part for the injection of epistemological meaning: "knowledge" keeps mutemo-as-law fluid. And yet, though mutemo may not be written on tablets, it involves strict adherence to the Ten Commandments. (It was this, I think, that prompted apostolics to emphasize the limits of text-based analogies.) Mutemo involves other acknowledgments and prescriptions too, often referred to as "the basics" of faith. These include abstention from alcohol and tobacco, observance of Levitical food taboos, abstention from sexual intercourse and consumption of meat on the Sabbath, offering of prayers to God at set times during the day, commitment to testifying about one's sins in front of the congregation, and commitment to ridding the world of witchcraft and, more generally, much of what the apostolics call "African custom" or "African culture." This last point is one to which I return—both later in the introduction and throughout the book. As my friend Shimmer put it when he explained church membership to me, "In Masowe, there's no being half Christian and half outside. If you're in, you're in." To have the basics of mutemo is to speak like Shimmer—to inhabit a Christian language (cf. Harding 2000; Luhrmann 2004). Mutemo is a set of laws, but it is also a way of knowing and a process of becoming. Mutemo is never complete, either in its prescriptions or in its potentials. It is in this sense that it has, for its adherents, an immaterial quality.

With respect to spiritual healing, another important aspect of live and direct faith, the Friday churches are like most other African churches. As the academic literature makes abundantly clear, spiritual healing is a major activity within these congregations (see esp. Schoffeleers 1991). One point often emphasized in the literature is that African Christian healers are considered effective because they take seriously what their congregants understand to be the root causes of illness, chiefly witchcraft and the breakdown of social relationships (with both the living and the dead). The Friday apostolics emphasize this understanding too. Through live and direct interventions into the problems faced by Africans, their prophets manifest the presence of God.

However it is reflected, the notion of live and direct faith has to be seen as a key aspect of apostolics' understanding of Christianity. It is the concept through which they make arguments about how Christianity should be practiced. In these arguments there is a significant stress on the difference between a "material" and an "immaterial" faith, the latter of which is the only proper faith. Of course, what counts as material and immaterial is argued for, not given. As this book shows, the designation of these qualities are contested—within the history of Christianity, within colonial and postcolonial Africa, and within the Friday churches. But as defined in their terms, the Friday apostolics want a faith in which things do not matter.

The concept of live and direct faith also provides a fitting point of entry to the theoretical issues that animate this study. I outline these issues in the next two sections. In the first I explain what I understand as a core paradox of Christian thought, the simultaneous presence and absence of God. Live and direct faith is the Friday apostolics' engagement with that paradox, which I refer to in this book as the "problem of presence."[7] Simply put, the problem of presence is how a religious subject defines and claims to construct a relationship with the divine through the investment of authority and meaning in certain words, actions, and objects.

In the second section I connect the problem of presence to the study of semiotics and, in particular, the relationships between language and material culture in culturally grounded modes of signification. Building on the work of Jerome McGann (1991, 1993) and Drucker (1994, 1998), I stress the way in which the materiality of a text plays a central role in how and what it signifies. The materials of which it is composed, the layout, the style of the print, the inclusion of illuminations or illustrations, the quality of its condition—these are just some of the ways in which materiality can matter. In conjunction with these textuality studies, I build on the work of anthropologists making arguments about how "the material" is understood as such (Miller 1987, 2005b; Thomas 1991) and what these understandings can tell us about the ways in which words and things are valued in a given "semiotic ideology" (Keane 2003, 2007; Parmentier 1994). A semiotic ideology is an argument about "what signs are and how they function in the world" (Keane 2003, 419; cf. Parmentier 1994, 142). This notion, developed in the work of Richard Parmentier and Webb Keane, is helpful for understanding the problem of presence in the Masowe Church. In suggesting why, there are two points I want to highlight. The first is that, in communication, the significance of material culture is not always subordinate to that of language (see Miller 1987, 95–98). Too often semiotics has been tied to a model of language as that which is "meaningful" and of material culture as that which is "practical" (Parmentier 1997, 43; cf. Irvine 1989). What Parmentier and Keane want to stress is that the meaning of a sign is related to its materiality.[8] The second point is that the very categories of words and things—of what they are and of whether what they are is fundamentally "material," "immaterial," or both—are made, not given. As Keane (2007, 5) points out, "in their material and formal properties, and in the ways in which people have responded to those properties, words and things have an incorrigibly historical dimension." In other words, what is considered material or immaterial in one semiotic ideology might not be considered such in another.

Thus Nzira's pronouncement that the Bible is trouble because it can fall apart is a clue to the semiotic ideology that underpins his faith. He is arguing, according to the principle of what we might call a "live and direct semiotics," that as an object the Bible is not a sign of the divine, much less its re-presentation. He is suggesting that the materiality of the Bible prohibits it from functioning properly as a sign of the divine. In the analysis of texts, then, we need to consider how their material qualities figure in an understanding of what they can represent. "All writing has the capacity to be both looked at and read, to be present as material and to function as the sign of an absent meaning" (Drucker 1998, 59). Words are never simply "ideas"; they are ideas anchored to and expressed through things in the material world. That "thing" may be the human voice, or it may be a set of stone tablets, but it is, somehow, a medium and thus, in some sense, material. The words and things of representation are mutually constitutive, and we cannot divorce the significance of a sign from its material qualities because, as Jerome McGann stresses, "language is always materialized and embodied in one way or another" (1991, 144). One task of the anthropologist is to explain how such materializations make sense in any given semiotic ideology. Another is to uncover how the logic of any given semiotic ideology allows for things to make sense at all. These tasks are precisely what the Friday apostolics' rejection of the Bible prompt us to consider. Live and direct faith is an assertion, at the theological level, that mediums matter. To claim, as Nzira did, that the Bible is trouble because it can fall apart is to claim that its materiality is antithetical to divine presence.

Situated in the more general notion of a semiotic ideology, the problem of presence is a problem of representation and authorization. This book, then, is not only about "the Christians who don't read the Bible"—as interesting, I hope, as the case may be to those who study religion. It is also about how language and material culture function in modes of signification, the dynamics of which have too often suffered theoretical neglect.

THE PROBLEM OF PRESENCE

It is only recently that Christianity seems to have sparked an interest in the broad comparative discussions that have long taken place elsewhere in the anthropology of religion (Cannell 2006; Engelke and Tomlinson 2006; Robbins 2003b; 2004, 27–34; Scott 2005).[9] Joel Robbins, for example, points to the anthropology of Islam as an area of research that has been able "to develop a set of shared questions to be examined comparatively" (2003b, 192) in a way that anthropologists studying Christianity have not. Of course, not all anthropologists would claim that broad comparative discussions are necessarily productive. And even in self-consciously labeled "anthropology of Christianity" studies there is debate over how to balance the specificities of ethnography and theology with the generalities inherent in a comparative project (Scott 2005). I join those who call for getting an anthropology of Christianity "off the ground" (Robbins 2003b, 191), not to deny the dangers in comparison, but because comparative questions allow us to ask "what it means for people to be Christian" (Cannell 2006, 5) in a manner that the social scientific study of Christianity has not always facilitated. Conviction of faith is difficult to measure or present; nevertheless, I came away from my fieldwork with a clear sense that Christianity is something Friday apostolics take very seriously. Indeed, they regularly informed me that Christianity is "serious business," an engagement that was evident in a number of ways. The Friday apostolics understand Christianity as their own and as something beyond them with which they must engage. Because of this—because Christianity is cultural (Robbins 2004, 30–34; cf. Cannell 2006)—I want to ask if we can locate any central dynamics of Christian thought and, if so, how they are manifest in practice.

I propose that one of the central dynamics of Christian thought is the paradoxical understanding of God's simultaneous presence and absence. This paradox poses what I am calling the problem of presence and allows us to situate the practices of the Friday apostolics within the scope of Christian history. It also allows us to investigate presence and absence as aspects of semiotics.

For the sake of the argument, I want to sketch the paradox of God's simultaneous presence and absence in as broad a sense as possible. I turn first to the work of Paul Ricoeur, whose late reading of Genesis, formulated in dialogue with the theologian André LaCocque, articulates the foundation for the paradox in broadly Christian terms. What is more, because Ricoeur's work occupies a central place in modern hermeneutics, it is relevant to the more general semiotic issues I want to raise.

To begin with, I would argue that while the details may differ from tradition to tradition Christianity is premised on a notion of absolute difference. The two fundamental indicators of this difference are the doctrine of creation and the fall. Above all, it is important to note that for Christians, heaven and earth are creations of the creator. The first difference, then, is between God the creator and that which he has created. God is not, like everything else, a creation. And so in this difference there is also, notably, as Ricoeur wants to highlight, a separation. As Ricoeur puts it, "The first meaning the creature has owing to the fact of being created is to exist at a distance from God" (1998, 39). Yet this distance is not in itself a troubling one. As Ricoeur says, it is the second kind of difference—that precipitated by the fall—that brings about "a qualitative change affecting the very meaning of separation" (1998, 41). In the Garden God spoke to humans directly; he shared an intimacy with them. So the distance that existed in the Garden was of a special kind, because it signaled a special relationship between God and Adam and Eve. It was "an unknown relation between God and the rest of Creation" (Ricoeur 1998, 41) whose quality was both unmatched and unique. The expulsion of Adam and Eve from the Garden of Eden brings about the second kind of difference and with it, a new distance. The second distance does affect the intimacy with God, in large part because it affects the nature of communication.

Most notably, the fall alters the nature of language. After Eden the "era of suspicion is opened," as Ricoeur puts it, and "a fault line is introduced into the most fundamental condition of language, namely, the relation of trust" (1998, 42). This fault line makes communion—and with it, a sense of presence—an uncertainty.

Ricoeur's reading of Genesis is marked by the care with which he differentiates the two meanings of difference. As a Christian the differentiation is important for him because the existence of the first distance (even if now lost) secures the possibility of holy communion. As a philosopher the differentiation is important because the second difference provides the human sciences with their subject matter. Whether or not one understands the "era of suspicion" as a religious condition, it is certainly, inasmuch as communication is marked by imperfection, a human one. In Ricoeur's hermeneutics, what "suspicion" means is that social intercourse is always marked by a degree of uncertainty.

If, as events, creation and the fall layered the meanings of difference (and distance), for the Christian those meanings are changed by the event of Jesus Christ. As David Tracy puts it, Christ is "the decisive re-presentation in both word and manifestation of our God and our humanity" (1981, 218). While Tracy is a Catholic theologian, to the extent that he recognizes Christ as presence this is an ecumenical point. Simply put, Christ closes the distance created by the second difference. He does not restore the world to its prelapsarian relation, but he allows for—indeed, he is—proximity to the divine.

It is with the passing of Christ that the problem of presence gets set in its Christian mode. How is God present? This is a central Christian question, to which the answer is Christ. And yet, with his passing, the answer becomes conditioned by an absence. Christ is the definitive presence; what comes after him is only ever a mediated one.

As others have recently stressed (Cannell 2006, 14–18; Milbank 1997b, 171–93), Hegel has been one of the more influential philosophers to articulate the stakes of absence. For Hegel, the transcendence of the Christian God is his defining—and overriding—feature. Hegel accordingly devotes considerable attention to the notion of presence in the lectures he delivered on the philosophy of religion, and to how Christians might have it. Consider this comment from the lectures of 1827:

But in the hearts and souls [of believers] is the firm [belief] that the issue is not a moral teaching, nor in general the thinking and willing of the subject within itself and from itself; rather what is of interest is an infinite relationship to God, to the present God, the certainty of the kingdom of God—finding satisfaction not in morality, ethics, or conscience, but rather in that than which nothing is higher, ‒ the relationship ‒ to God himself. All other modes of satisfaction involve the fact that they are still qualities of a subordinate kind, and thus the relationship to God remains a relationship to something above and beyond, which in no sense lies present at hand. (Hegel 1985, 322)

Hegel thus argues that in "the spiritual community" of Christianity "immediate presence has passed away, and the community itself is formed with the passage of the sensible presence of Christ to the presence of God in the Spirit" (Hodgson 1985, 32). It is through the Holy Spirit that Christians are connected to the divine.

In Hegel's work the properties of presence are defined in terms by which the evidence of presence shifts from a kind of material ("the sensible presence of Christ") to immaterial ("the presence of God in the Spirit") register. This does not mean God cannot be present in *some* material form; the work of the Spirit is carried out in the world and is thus manifested through material channels (the body, religious artifacts, etc.). And yet for Hegel there is something definitive about the sensible presence of Christ that cannot otherwise or elsewhere be found.

Hegel's philosophy of Christianity is marked by "the pathos of Christ's absence" (Milbank 1997b, 183). That pathos manifests itself, in part, through the uncertainty with which Christians must embrace other signs of presence. The danger is in attributing the qualities of "sensible presence" to these other signs. In this Hegel's work bears the mark of the Reformation. He is not an iconoclast, but he expresses concern with the adequacy of things as properly of the Spirit: "The Holy as a mere thing has the character of externality; thus it is capable of being taken into possession of by another to my exclusion; it may come into an alien hand, since the process of appropriating it is not one that takes place in the Spirit, but is conditioned by its quality as an external object. The highest of human blessings is in the hands of others" (Hegel, in Brown 1981, 86). Hegel's criticism is the Protestant's argument, based on the idea that the holy should never be a "mere thing" mediated by "the hands of others" but an inner experience. For Hegel, "[the] proper way to preserve sensible presence [of Christ] is to let it pass away, because by its very nature it is singular and momentary and cannot be repeated but only remembered. Means of repeating and prolonging it are readily available when needed (relics, holy images, etc.), but they engender an illusion and the spiritual community should have no need of them" (Hodgson 1985, 32).

According to Hegel, presence is preserved through the Holy Spirit, even though the spiritual community cannot have the certainty of sensible presence. As Milbank points out, Hegel's description of the Holy Spirit is, after all, as "the divestment of all immediacy" (Hegel, in Milbank 1997b, 186). This is a description suggesting that the pathos of Christ's absence is always still there.

I should acknowledge that many Christians might find Hegel a poor spokesman for their faith. It might sound odd to most Christians to hear their religion as characterized by a pathetic absence, the point of their faith, after all, being the confirmation of God's presence in their lives through the sacrifice of his son. Many Christians might argue that "sensible presence" as Hegel defines it is not the point. For a Catholic, for instance, the Eucharist could be called a *very sensible presence* of a different kind. As Milbank points out, theologians such as Jean-Luc Marion argue that the Eucharist is a *more* meaningful presence, as "it is precisely in his ascended distance that Christ gives himself to us in the yet more intimate form of assimilable eucharistic food" (1997b, 184). But even more generally, God might be recognized as present in any sacrament, or through the works of the Holy Spirit, or through grace, or through an "inner light," or in an apparition, or on a pilgrimage, and, of course, in the Bible, or even a "live and direct" faith among Christians who do not read the Bible. Indeed, Christian language is defined not by the coldness of God's distance but the comfort of his proximity. *Come here, I am near,* as the Friday apostolics sing—even as they are the church that mark themselves according to the day Jesus died.

For an anthropology of Christianity, however, Hegel's concerns draw useful attention to the hesitations, ruptures, and gaps that exist between the language of presence and the dynamics of a lived faith, in which that presence is often uncertain. In fact, these hesitations, ruptures, and gaps are recognized by most theologians—as well as Christian philosophers such as Ricoeur. As Tracy says, Christians are only ever dealing with, at best, "relatively adequate expressions of the Christ event itself"; for Tracy, Christians must always undertake the "risk of interpretation" (1981, 249). Even in theology (perhaps especially in theology) presence is a problem. For the Friday apostolics, the risk of interpretation emerges out of their simultaneous emphasis on the death of Jesus and the promise of a live and direct connection to God. As in whatever form Christianity takes there is, to borrow Peter Brown's insightful phrasing, a "carefully maintained tension between distance and proximity" (1981, 88). It is out of this tension that the problem of presence emerges.

In Christian thought the tension between distance and proximity is often maintained through a careful differentiation between words and things. Certain words and certain things—defined as such according to specific semiotic ideologies—become privileged channels of divine apprehension. Indeed, how God's presence is rightfully mediated through language and objects is an issue over which Christians have often disagreed. What bridges heaven and earth? How does God become present? Below I address these questions through a series of overlapping discussions on the mediatory significance of the Bible.

Writing and Speaking as Mediums

It would not be too much to say that Christianity and the Bible are inseparably related. This proposition has tenacity even when we break Christianity down into its major Catholic, Protestant, and Eastern Orthodox historical formations. It has tenacity even when we break these down further into subsets—charting the often stark differences among Protestant churches, for example, or certain Catholic orders that have operated in sub-Saharan Africa in recent centuries. It will not have been surprising that people in Zimbabwe reacted to the Friday apostolics with confusion and consternation. One Roman Catholic priest told me that the apostolics are primitive; they clearly did not understand what Christianity is if they had rejected its Scripture. This man, a native Shona speaker, was a figure of some standing in the local Catholic community. But the denigration did not come only from "main-line" churches. The Maranke apostolics, for example, viewed their Masowe brethren condescendingly, secure in their book knowledge where the Friday apostolics were not. And a high-ranking official in a Pentecostal church told me that the idea of claiming to be Christian and then berating someone who brought a Bible to a church service was unthinkable. "What madness," he said.

However, the Friday apostolics are not the first Christians to question the importance and qualities of writing. Their arguments allow us to highlight a long-standing precedent of the spoken word as a privileged channel of communication with God. The medium through which a Christian receives the Word is often key to how the problem of presence is approached.

The earliest Christian communities in the Roman Empire were reacting in part to what they saw as the constraints of Scripture. Paul's evangelism did not rest on, or end with, the Law. God had made himself present through the son, and this had implications for the significance of the Book. The historian Brian Stock offers a useful summary of the antitextual politics in context:

> When Christianity made its appearance, it did so in a world that assumed a large degree of literacy as the norm. Yet its spokesmen maintained that they were in direct dialogue with God. The gospels are filled with metaphors that extol the Word. These expressions were deliberately contrasted with one extreme of the literate mentality in the Hellenistic world, Judaism. Christianity met Roman literacy on a similar level. Just as the Christian "spirit" took the place of the alleged Jewish "letter," so it rose to the challenge of what was due Caesar by disenfranchising Roman civilization through a new form of discourse. (Stock 1990, 3)

In conversation and in interviews the Friday apostolics developed a similar narrative about the vibrancy and relevance of their live and direct approach. Christian missions were religious and political institutions in need of reform, caught in the trappings of the text (a new version of letter over spirit, as it were). When confronted with the criticism that they cannot be Christians because they reject the Bible, the apostolics respond by saying things like "Jesus and his apostles didn't need the Bible." They insist they are revitalizing the Christian mission. They see themselves as taking up the enthusiasm of the earliest converts and reclaiming the direct dialogue with God.

Of course, Christianity did not remain an "oral faith" (Stock 1990, 3), or, as it is often characterized, a religion of the downtrodden (Merdinger 1997, 3–27). By the late fourth century, the time of Saint Augustine's conversion, Christianity had become the official religion of the Roman Empire, the Church was firmly established, and the canonical texts of the New Testament were coming into place. Even in the established Church, however, the boundaries between the written and the spoken word were not settled, and an understanding of their representative qualities and potentials even less so.

It was Augustine who helped to effect a major shift in Christian reading practices and, with it, an understanding of what the written word represents (Stock 1996). Throughout most of the *Confessions* Augustine discusses his experience with and understanding of written texts as most literate ancients would have: in his world "'to read' meant to listen" (Hampl

1997, xviii). Texts were used in oral performances. But just as Augustine underwent a religious conversion, so too did he rethink the potentials of the book. It was in the garden at Milan that Augustine first considered the possibility of reading silently, to oneself. There he would watch Bishop Ambrose, who spent much of his time reading but not reading out loud: "When he read, his eyes would travel across the pages and his mind would explore the senses, but his voice and tongue were silent" (Augustine 1997, 99 [bk. VI, iii, 3]). This style struck Augustine as strange and unfamiliar. It produced a "sense of wonder," according to Nicholas Howe, in "a man who believed that the way to truth was through the written word as performed or interpreted within a community" (1993, 60). Silent reading thereafter became an increasingly productive mode of apprehension. Augustine's argument amounted to the proposition that in Christian reading "sounds cease but meaning endures" (Stock 1996, 75). He helped to make the written word valuable not because of its potentials in an oral performance but because it was *there,* as a physical thing, and could be taken up in silent contemplation by the individual reader.

Stock's work emphasizes that the emergence of Christianity in the ancient Mediterranean world as a religion of direct dialogue with God was shaped by a particular set of relations to the "literate extremes" of Judaism and the Roman Empire. But just as the qualities of the written word have shifted in Christian histories, so too have they shifted in other traditions. Judaism, for example, may have presented the early Christians with an extreme of literate mentality, but that "mentality" is also always in flux. Drawing attention to Jewish evaluations of the text is therefore useful, for two reasons: it places Christianity in a wider historical context, enriching the scope of this book's inquiries; and the Friday apostolics' religious imagination is shaped by a close attention to and interest in Judaism. In fact, the apostolics would often claim a connection to what they call "Jewish culture." They express an affinity for Jewish culture because Jesus was a Jew.[10] They also have a sense that African culture and Jewish culture are more closely connected than either is to European culture—a connection they prize even as they want to move away from many aspects of African culture. As if to stress this connection, some even referred to Christian churches as synagogues. In addition, as I discuss at length in chapter 5, prophets in the Friday churches are said to speak "ancient Hebrew" when filled with the Holy Spirit (although this is *not* the ancient Hebrew known in history). This ritual language is a highly valued index of God's presence and a prophet's legitimacy. And, as I mentioned earlier, the apostolics adhere to Levitical food taboos.

According to Daniel Boyarin (1993), the literate mentality of Judaism might best be defined by the qualities of the spoken word. His argument is that in biblical Hebrew the concept of reading *(miqra)* is understood as a speech act; it is "oral, social, and collective" (1993, 11). Boyarin points to a number of places in the Old Testament in which the root *qr'* (from which *miqra* is derived) suggests this, including Deuteronomy 31:11: "When all of Israel come to appear before the Lord, your God at the place which he shall choose, *read* this Torah in the presence of all of Israel, in their ears. Gather together the People, the men, the women and the children and the stranger within your gates, in order that they hear and in order that they learn and they fear the Lord your God and watch to perform all of the words of this Torah" (quoted in Boyarin 1993, 13; Boyarin's emphasis). In this and in other examples Boyarin argues that "the usage indicates an oral act, an act of the speaking of language" (1993, 13). Moses wrote down the Law (the Torah), but it had to be brought to life; its authority was instantiated through the spoken word.

However language is highlighted or defined as "religious," the examples here suggest that the medium of its transmission plays a role in the definition of its authority. Taken together these cases point to a long-standing concern in Judeo-Christian traditions about how the relationships between the written and the spoken word are defined by practices of reading—whether silently, out loud, or not at all. At stake in each is how God can be approached or made present through certain material representations. In some modes of signification the "immediacy" of speech takes precedence; in others, it is the "durability" or "accessibility" of writing. Regardless of the specific valuations, however, they lead us to the conclusion that words and their mediums cannot be taken for the same thing. In Judeo-Christian traditions it often matters whether a message is conveyed by voice or on the page—whether the voice or the text is considered primary or privileged. What I want to suggest is that in the context of these discussions it is possible to emphasize the Friday apostolics' rejection of the Bible as a rejection of the argument that the written word can create what religious language ought to—"a condition of possibility for the experience of the divine" (Keane 1997a, 48). Live and direct faith is a religious sensibility in which the voice takes precedence. It reminds us that Scripture is never a priori evidence of religious truth; the conditions it creates to advance that truth take place in specific semiotic ideologies in which speaking, writing, and other channels of communication become differently valued. What the written word signifies, then, and how it does so, cannot be taken for granted.[11]

Protestantism and the Problem of Presence

That Augustine was a reader had important implications for the place of Scripture in the historical development of Christianity (Stock 1996). But reading is not all Augustine did with the book. As the historian of religion Harry Y. Gamble (1995, 238) tells us, Augustine's remedy for headaches was to place the Gospel of John under one's pillow at night. Like other ancients, he understood the divine in writing to be "a power that belonged to words, but no less to the books in which they stood" (Gamble 1995, 241). As things, the books of the Bible can be effective in themselves.

This dual character of Scripture is another aspect of the problem of presence worth investigating. As part of a semiotic ideology, it is the claim that the Bible's significance cannot be reduced to the register of either word or object. The Bible is a sign that does not conform to such brute categorizations, just as the Word cannot be reduced to the register of either written or spoken. This emphasis on the Bible's materiality is also a good indication of how presence can be indexed in and through physical objects. Here I focus on how this dual character of Scripture has been articulated within certain trends in Protestantism. I begin with a brief consideration of sixteenth-century iconoclasm, then move on to sketch the gradual differentiation between "liberal" and "conservative" Protestant theologies, which helps us to make sense of how the Bible has been understood in colonial and postcolonial Africa. My aim is to suggest how these trends can situate the apostolics' live and direct faith, at the formal level, as an engagement with the problem of presence.

As Hans Belting remarks, because the Word is paramount in any Christian theology, this begs an important question about presence through other representations: "the question of whether God has established other means of encountering him besides the word" (1994, 465). For the most extreme Protestant Reformers—those driven by iconoclasm—the answer is no.

The Reformation taught the dominion of the word, which suppressed all the other religious signs. Christianity had always been a revelation through the word but now the word took on an unprecedented monopoly and aura. After all, the new preachers had only the word of Holy Scripture and no other authority in practicing a religion without the institution of the church. They wanted, as it were, to rediscover the primal sound of the word, free of all the dross and errors of papism, and to teach it to the congregations. "For on words rests all our ground, protection, and defense against all errors and temptation," as Luther says in his Large

Catechism. "The kingdom of God is a kingdom of hearing, not of seeing," he announces in another place. (Belting 1994, 465)

As in any religious movement, the iconoclasm that sprang up in early Reformation Europe was not always a coherent project: it was driven sometimes by theologians and sometimes by congregations; sometimes it was carried out with a kind of moderation and sometimes to the point of an incoherent and unwitting hypocrisy (Aston 1988; Belting 1994, 458–90; Koerner 2002; Phillips 1973). But in general the destruction of religious images in sixteenth-century Europe was driven by a concern with what they could legitimately represent and by the dangers inherent in their misrepresentation. As things, images were problematic. As one English reformer put it, in a more extreme articulation of this point, "nothing spiritual can be present when there is anything material and physical" (Edwards, quoted in Aston 1988, 13).

This is an extreme articulation because it demands the impossible. It rests on a differentiation of the spiritual and material that would have to deny the existence of the physical world as God's creation. (Because the world is God's creation, surely it stands as a sign of "the spiritual"?) But as an impossible statement, it tells us something important about how the categories of the spiritual and the material come into play. In the semiotic ideology of an iconoclast, in other words, the Bible was not significant in its materiality. As the Word, it is that against which "mere things" like images were pitched. The Bible was different from a crucifix or religious painting because language did not share their material qualities. The Word did not engender illusions, and the Bible, as a providential presence, was properly "spiritual" and not "material" or "physical." What Protestantism brought about was an increased emphasis on Scripture, and with it, language, as a kind of immaterial presence.

One effect of the increasingly positive disposition toward language was a shift in attention away from the figure of Christ and toward Scripture. "And symmetrical with the thinning of Christocentricity," as Milbank tells us, "was the loss of ecclesial mediation. When the individual 'directly' confronted the text, the text's finite and self-sufficient denotation *(sola scriptura)* found its equivalent in the internalisation of meaning within the private conscience" (1997a, 95). In this context, then, a qualitative difference between letter and spirit became unfixed. The immaterial qualities of the written word have helped to shape debates over the nature and authority of Scripture ever since. This is not the kind of live and direct relationship with

God that the Friday apostolics are advocating, but it is a kind of "live and direct" faith nonetheless—a return to the kingdom of hearing.

Immateriality, however, is an inherently unstable lure. As the Reformation settled in the wake of its iconoclastic purges, for example, images regained a foothold—if not as signs of presence, then at least as *not* signs of absence or obfuscation. In England, where some of the most destructive purges took place, Henry VIII tempered his church's position by calling for the distinction between the "abused" and "unabused" images (Phillips 1973, 202; see also Aston 1988, 234–44).[12] Luther also recognized that religious images as such were not the problem: the problem was their misuse. Images became dangerous when they were understood to be something other than what the Reformers claimed. As the art historian Joseph Koerner reports, this middle ground on their significance was eventually recognized as the only viable position: "the supreme irrationality is not to venerate images but to imagine that it is the images that cause their own abuse" (2002, 178). Ironically, iconoclasm created the objects of its own scorn. Nothing could draw more attention to mere things than to assault their thing-ness. "How material was materiality shown to be when, as sometimes occurred, a saint's effigy was decapitated by the town's executioner?" (Koerner 2002, 179).

After the sixteenth century Protestant theologies moved in what might be recognized as two directions. Both have been marked by concerns with materiality as a quality that can matter, and both have tackled these concerns through engagement with the Bible. But the conclusions drawn have been distinctly different. For "liberal" theologies, the Bible became an important guide, yet only that. In some of the more radical liberal theologies, there are even hints that in an ideal faith it is a guide one could do without. In liberal theology the materiality of the Bible became recognition of its historicity, which signals both its human crafting and, in this era of suspicion, the limits of human understanding. For "conservative" theologians, on the other hand, the Bible often became not only a guide but also the destination. The Bible is the unshakable bedrock of faith and something that, as the Word, cannot be separated from God. In the most stringent of these faiths, the materiality of the Bible became presence of the divine—not representation, but presence; not sign, but actuality.

A defining feature of liberal Protestant theologies is an emphasis on the role of interpretation in the understanding of Scripture. In these traditions the meaning of the Word is not self-evident; it has to be discerned by the reader. This hermeneutic approach reached full flower in the work of Friedrich Schleiermacher. His starting point was that understanding is not possible without interpretation; meaning does not assert itself. More than this, the meaning of a text becomes "estranged" outside the original context of its creation. Interpretation, in other words, is defined by the tension between distance and proximity and is motivated by the effort to relieve it. Hans-Georg Gadamer puts it thus: "Everything that is no longer immediately situated in a world—that is, all tradition, whether art or the other spiritual creations of the past: law, religion, philosophy, and so forth—is estranged from its original meaning and depends on the unlocking and mediating spirit that we, like the Greeks, name after Hermes: the messenger of the Gods" (1989, 165).

Schleiermacher wanted nothing less than to understand the intention of an author and the world in which that author's work had been produced. His hermeneutics is based on "an apprehension of the 'inner origin' of the composition of a work, a re-creation of the creative act. Thus understanding is a reproduction of an original production" (Gadamer 1989, 187). Notice the tension between distance and proximity here. What Schleiermacher wants to do is close the distance through the act of interpretation and therefore regain, inasmuch as it is possible, that which is original. As Vincent Crapanzano points out, however, the implication of Schleiermacher's position is that a text "can never be understood immediately" (2000, 10). It is only through interpretation—that "mediating spirit"—that we can reach understanding. There is, then, no transparent relationship between truth and Scripture that makes itself known. In hermeneutics reading is a historical project that can be marked by an unsettling distance and absence.

Where liberal theologians place an emphasis on interpretation, conservatives tend to emphasize revelation. In many conservative theologies, the meaning of the Word *is* considered self-evident; it does *not* have to be discerned by the reader (that is to say, its meaning does not *depend* on the reader). In such "Bible-based" Christianities the divine is often considered present in the book. This position on the Bible has its roots in Luther's idea of sola scriptura, although it developed not in Germany but in the United Kingdom and, especially, in the United States. Between 1910 and 1915 the California businessmen Lyman and Milton Stewart spearheaded a group of "Fundamentalists." They published a series of pamphlets called *The Fundamentals.*

The pamphlets dealt with the key issues of the inerrancy, inviolability, and authenticity of the Bible, but with much else as well. The authors of *The*

Fundamentals attacked German biblical criticism, contending that the ancient Hebrew records must be authentic, since God had chosen the Jews as the people to hear and convey His message. They stressed that recent archaeological findings, or some of them at least, tended to confirm the accuracy of biblical history. As one of the authors, William G. Moorhead, put it: "Ancient Judaism has one supreme voice for the chosen people, and its voice was prophetic. . . . If any man deny the inspiration of the Old Testament, sooner or later he will deny that of the New." (Katz 2004, 313)

Fundamentalist or "literalist" churches can cover a significant patch of theological ground. Conservative Protestantism is not a coherent whole, and literalism is not a fixed idea (Coleman 2006; Harding 2000, 61–82). Generally, however, Christians in these conservative churches "are committed to the inerrancy of Scripture and they resist, often passionately, any theology that departs in their eyes from the teachings of Scripture" (Crapanzano 2000, 34). The fundamentalists take Luther's idea of sola scriptura to its most radical conclusion: in their vision of faith the Bible offers "internal affirmation of its own authority" (Crapanzano 2000, 59).

It is interesting to note that conservative Protestants often stress the materiality of the Bible. The fundamentalist churches, for example, acknowledge and embrace this materiality by putting it to theological work. Actual Bibles can matter to actual people. For the fundamentalists with whom Crapanzano worked in Southern California, carrying the Bible around with them and taking pride in its physical condition (ideally worn from reading) "marked their total commitment to it and the truths, the stability, the guidance, and the discipline it gave them" (Crapanzano 2000, 54). For the conservative Christian, the Bible is often as much presence as representation. In semiological terms it is the sign without a divide—"the coalescence" of signifier and signified in which the "Bible as book is to biblical truth as God's word in its materiality is to God's truth" (Crapanzano 2000, 56).

Although the Bible is central to liberal theologies as well, there is an important sense in which Schleiermacher and others have tried to push beyond Scripture. They have done this in part, I want to argue, by suggesting that the materiality of the Bible can be a barrier to reaching Christian truths. This excerpt from Schleiermacher's second speech in *On Religion* captures this point:

> Every sacred writing is in itself a glorious production, a speaking monument from the heroic time of religion, but, through servile reverence,

it would become merely a mausoleum, a monument that a great spirit was once there, but is now no more. Did this spirit still live and work, he would look with love, and with a feeling of equality upon his work which yet could only be a weaker impress of himself. Not every person has religion who believes in a sacred writing, but only the man who has a lively and immediate understanding of it, and who, therefore, so far as he himself is concerned, could most easily do without it. (Schleiermacher 1958, 91)

"Having religion" is not measured by knowing the Book, still less by material possession of it. Having religion is having that which lies beyond the object, that of which the object is a "weaker impress." As Ernst Troeltsch characterizes it, "Schleiermacher locates the essence of religion in the basic human disposition toward the divine, and the presence of the divine in the human. On the human side, this presence takes the form of absolute dependence, which is also a feeling of divine, sustaining power" (1991, 14). Religion, then, is a feeling and in that sense not a thing. It is not objectlike—produced by a cold reasoning—but a "lively and immediate" understanding. For Schleiermacher, "the barrier to reason and understanding . . . is to be overcome by *feeling*, by an immediate, sympathetic, and con-genial understanding" (Gadamer 1989, 191). His suggestion is that authentic Christianity is experienced, not grasped, either cognitively or physically—that its qualities are immaterial in the sense that they cannot be located outside of that experience as an object of knowledge. The opposition in play here is between sensation and apprehension, in which the former is superior because insignificant in its materiality. It is not that feelings are not material but that they are not so in the way a book is.

Troeltsch, one of Schleiermacher's most influential supporters, developed more views along this line. In Troeltsch's work the Bible is significant but not plenary. It should not be understood as "the insuperable limit to Christianity" (1991, 15). What I want to emphasize here is how, in making these remarks, Troelstch evaluates the Bible according to its material qualities. He calls the Bible "the Lutheran Pope" and he faults both Catholics and Protestants for a wayward emphasis on things: "One side turns to the pope and the church, the other to the Bible, but both sides turn to a clearly circumscribed object" (1991, 18).

Troeltsch's vision of Christianity is a striving toward the lively and immediate understanding of the divine, an understanding that is "beyond the Bible" (1991, 15). He wants to develop a faith in which the written word is only ever a point of departure. In this regard Troeltsch looks positively on Catholicism, which he sees as "much more practical and realistic than Protestantism" because it "recognizes that the gospel is only a germ from which everything else has sprung" (1991, 30). This is not to suggest that Troeltsch points to any given church as more realized than any other. Indeed, in his view the history of Christianity "has not been a process of adulteration, but of becoming" (1991, 30–31). And when religion is cast as a process of becoming it is resisting the pull of the clearly circumscribed object, of rendering the spirit a mere thing.

The concept of immateriality is a useful one for liberal theologies because of the extent to which it bolsters a resistance to what I will call *thingification.* This is an awkward term, but I am using it to distinguish it from the more expected term, *objectification,* and, in the process, to disentangle the latter from the conceptual weeds to which it has long been attached. As Hegel might have used the term, for instance, objectification is something that liberal theologians could actually endorse. And as both Schleiermacher and Troeltsch acknowledge debts to Hegel, this should indeed be borne in mind. While objectification has been primarily understood as a negative experience of separation, especially after Marx, in Hegel's work it was "used to describe a dual process by means of which a subject externalizes itself in a creative act of differentiation, and in turn appropriates this externalization through an act which Hegel terms sublation *(aufhebung)*" (Miller 1987, 28). In Christian theology this kind of objectification becomes a way in which God manifests his presence. For liberal theologians, this is a positive experience. So *objectification* is not the best word to describe that which liberal theologians want to guard against.

What they want to guard against is in fact the more commonplace understanding of objectification—the one characterized by "a lack of agency and even motion, a distancing from the world, a lack of self-recognition, [or] an abuse of others" (Keane 2007, 10). Although this is what many academics mean when they use the word, doing so tends to crowd out its other potentials and functions. As Daniel Miller (1987, 2005a) and Keane (2007) have argued, we cannot (or at least should not) rest our understanding of the concept of objectification wholly on this negative base. Even without taking Hegel or theology onboard, it is important to recognize that objectification can be a positive experience, or at least not a negative experience. "Objectification"—simply—"describes the inevitable process by which all expression, conscious or unconscious, social or individual, takes specific form" (Miller 1987, 81).

By rechristening the negative understanding of objectification "thingification," I want to shift attention away from the subject-object relationship in the most general sense and toward a particular understanding of that relationship in which the object in question becomes recognized as problematic. In this I am following Bill Brown (2001), who (after Heidegger and others) emphasizes that one function of the concept "thing" is to account for what does not fit into a coherent ordering of objects. A thing is often "the entifiable that is unspecifiable" (Brown 2001, 5). If we know what an object is, we name it; if not, it becomes a thing and, as such, dangerous. In other words we are forced "to confront the thingness of objects when they stop working for us" (2001, 4). I want to suggest that this is a useful distinction for understanding how the material gets configured within the Christian imaginations discussed here. What is dangerous in these imaginations is not the object per se but the possibility of its becoming a mere thing—an object that "stops working" or never did so in the first place. When the qualities of immateriality are present in an object—as marked by the Spirit, or a particular power, or a kind of feeling—it cannot become clearly circumscribed, or merely a mausoleum. Thingification, then, is the process through which the object is divested of "immateriality."

The two trends in Protestant theology sketched here are intended to serve, at the formal level, as yardsticks for this ethnography. Throughout the book I argue—sometimes explicitly, sometimes implicitly—that the Friday apostolics articulate a vision of Christianity that fits within the liberal traditions. The concept of immateriality is central to their notion of live and direct faith because of the work it does in helping them to distinguish material things from one another. Emphasizing what is immaterial, and what is not, is a way of claiming that "some things are more material than others" (Rowlands 2005, 80). To say that the apostolics want a faith in which things do not matter is not to say that they are renouncing the world. It is, rather, to suggest that they are making specific claims about how God becomes present through words, objects, and actions that exist within a hierarchy of significative and expressive forms. The semiotics of live and direct faith hinge on the assertion of immateriality (that which is insignificant in its materiality).

The discussions in this section have covered a good deal of ground—no doubt too quickly and with insufficient attention to the details of Christianity in sociohistorical formation. What I hope to have made clear is that the problem of presence can be used as a thread with which to tie together Christianity's formations at the theoretical level. An important way in which Christianity's semiotic ideologies are shaped is by the language of presence and absence. Words and things are enlisted as the mediums for that language. And yet how these words and things are defined—and then conjoined or kept apart—often differs. What counts as material or immaterial, what makes materiality or immateriality valuable, and whether those valuations stand as bridges or barriers to the experience of the divine are, in the end, the stuff of historical and theological contestation. What unites them is the organizational quality of a carefully maintained tension between distance and proximity according to which God's presence can be recognized.

SEMIOTIC IDEOLOGIES

In her wide-ranging study of the concept, Hanna Fenichel Pitkin defines *representation* in the most general sense as "the making present *in some sense* of something which is nevertheless *not* present literally or in fact" (1967, 8–9; also cited in Keane 1997b, 237n2). Pitkin goes on to discuss the paradox this creates: how can something be present and not present or present in something else—and thus recognized as present through its absence? She suggests that "there is no need to make mysteries" because we can say that the presence is "nonliteral" (1967, 9). At the same time she does not want to sideline the concept's social valuation and use. In a Christian rendering, for example, the presence in a representation might in fact be considered literal. Indeed, as the preceding section suggests, the problem of presence often hinges on whether or not the representation is considered literal—that is, on whether it is a re-presentation (a making present again) or a representation (a making present but only *in some sense*). Struggles over the significance of an image or a text are struggles over how the divine can be recognized as present. Similarly, Catholic and Protestant disagreements on transubstantiation can be said to hinge on questions of representation as literal or nonliteral presence. Clearly, then, to define representation is not enough, because it skirts these social, semiotic, and metaphysical loadings. "What we need," Pitkin concludes, "is not just an accurate definition, but a way of doing justice to the various more detailed applications of representation in various contexts—how the absent thing is made present, and who considers it so" (1967, 10).

Understanding how an absent thing is made present, and who considers it so, is the broader conceptual issue behind Christian formulations of the problem of presence. The problem of presence, in other words, is a religious current in the larger and more turbulent stream of the semiotic ideologies through which relations in the world are mediated and defined. Keane, again, defines a semiotic ideology as the "basic assumptions about what signs are and how they function in the world" (2003, 419). Parmentier describes it as "a culturally determined, historically grounded set of interpretive standards" (1994, 142). To say, as Nzira did, that the Bible is trouble because it can fall apart is to argue that texts, as material objects, are not signs of the divine; according to "live and direct semiotics," they neither represent nor re-present God. To say, as Troeltsch did, that the Bible is the "Lutheran Pope" is to suggest that both humans and books can share qualities that limit a genuine spirituality. These are ideological assertions about what signs are and how they function. The study of semiotic ideologies is useful, then, because it draws attention to the modes of signification that become privileged in a given sociohistorical field, and, in particular, to how words and things are intimately bound up with one another in those modes. Through a focus on semiotic ideologies we learn about "the sorting out of proper relations among, and boundaries between, words, things, and subjects" (Keane 2007, 4). In this section I outline broader discussions in the study of semiotics that allow us to make further sense of the basic assumptions about what signs are and how they function in a live and direct faith.

It was not so long ago that Daniel Miller could say "our understanding of material culture is rudimentary in the extreme" (1987, 1). In the study of signs the attention to things has indeed paled in comparison to the attention to language. Miller's argument is that this imbalance is due to the false security that objects provide; we tend to assume that objects "imply a certain innocence of facticity" (1987, 106).

Several scholars have highlighted the word/thing imbalance by tracing it to the work of Ferdinand de Saussure (Drucker 1994; Irvine 1989; Keane 2003). Saussure's science of semiology is, they point out, based on the sign-as-concept.[13] Saussure, as is well known, "produced the framework for a linguistic theory that removes language from its social embeddedness" (Parmentier 1994, xiii). What is pronounced in Saussure, then, and what has fueled the tendency to regularly reassert the difference between words and things is the separation of language from the material world. Judith Irvine argues that Saussure's formulation of this difference has often been taken for granted because "it was consonant with ideas already having a long history in the Western intellectual tradition—most particularly the separation of mind from body" (1989, 248). He is not, therefore, the originator of the imbalance. It figures as well, for example, in several of the Christian theologies touched on above (see also Milbank 1997b, 84–120). Rather, what is notable about Saussure is the compelling way in which he made the case. Saussure tapped into some of the most deeply ingrained Western assumptions about the difference between an idea and an object—in which the former is immaterial, the latter material; the former meaningful, the latter mediatory (cf. Parmentier 1997, 43–44).

Saussure maintained the word/thing separation in part by defining language as that which is spoken. For him, then, the written word is only ever a representation of speech. Writing is not the proper object of linguistics: "The spoken word alone constitutes that object" (Saussure 1983, 24–25). In this respect, Drucker (1994, 13–21) tells us, Saussure accepted the general assumptions of his contemporaries, many of whom theorized language with little regard for the difference between the written and the spoken word. Even more, the object of study in semiology is not an object at all (in the everyday sense) but a system of differences and, thus, immaterial ideas. Saussure's approach is therefore problematic precisely because it "implies *immateriality*, that which is insignificant in its materiality, to which nothing of linguistic value is contributed by the form of written inscription which serves merely to offer up the 'words' in as pure and unmediated a form as possible" (Drucker 1994, 14).

Drucker is critical of Saussure for accepting the implications of immateriality, because it made semiology a "metaphysical proposition" in which "all signification was predicated on a fundamental assumption of the simple fact of *being*" (1994, 38, 35). Language, however, does not simply exist. In this Drucker reinforces Jacques Derrida's argument in *Of Grammatology*, picking up in particular on his point that Saussure was wrong to understand writing as derivative of speech (see esp. Derrida 1974, 30–44). Where Drucker wants to expand on Derrida is in her insistence that "the mere and actual materiality of signifying forms" (1994, 38) demand more attention. Her work, which focuses on Dadaist and Futurist typography, suggests that it is impossible to ignore the material dimensions of written language: "The inherent physical properties of stuff function in the process of signification" (Drucker 1994, 45; see also McGann 1993 on modernist typography).

After Saussure, there have been major students of language, such as Roman Jakobson and Mikhail Bakhtin, who have gone on to demonstrate the importance of materiality in the process of signification. Still others, like Derrida, tried to move beyond the word/thing framework altogether. But there remains in social scientific analysis, in part because of Saussure's legacy, a tendency (1) to assume language exists on an ideational plane; and (2) to reaffirm (implicitly if not explicitly) the Western default distinctions between what is material and what is immaterial (Irvine 1989; Keane 2003). These tendencies have in no small measure hampered the development of a semiotics in which material culture plays a key role. In Saussure we have what Miller calls "the humility of objects" (1987, 85–108). The written word, as artifact, humbles itself (or is humbled) before that which it transmits. It is this assumed quality of humility that allows semiology to do what Drucker observes: offer up words as pure and unmediated. As a semiotic ideology, semiology is indeed a metaphysical proposition. Saussure overlooked how materiality matters. An object may imply an innocence of facticity, but this is "quite illusory" because "the object is just as likely as the word, if not more so, to evoke variable responses and invite a variety of interpretations" (Miller 1987, 106; see also Thomas 1991). When the object in question is also, in some part, a linguistic sign—as it is in any text—this point becomes especially apt.

Since the 1970s the work of the pragmatist philosopher Charles Sanders Peirce has become increasingly important to anthropologists interested in the theory of signs. The linguistic anthropologist Michael Silverstein (1976, 1979) and the sociocultural anthropologist Nancy Munn (1986) developed arguments about meaning and value that drew from Peirce's work and which have become key points of departure for others. I want to highlight Peirce as I round out the discussion of semiotic ideologies and bring the focus back to the Friday churches. This is because Peirce's theory of signs, called "semeiotic," has been central to anthropological arguments that words and things are often intimately connected to one another in modes of signification.[14]

The most important aspect of Peirce's semeiotic in this context is that materiality is central to his doctrine. This is not simply a recognition of what I have been stressing thus far—that the materiality of words functions in the process of signification—but also that words are not all that signify. Indeed, Peirce was concerned with more than language, highlighting in his work that there were three aspects of signs, each of which has a different kind of material relation to the world. The relations can be iconic, indexical, and symbolic. These signs have "presentative characteristics" (Liszka 1996, 37) based on, respectively, an assumed or asserted similarity, contiguity, and convention. (I say "assumed or asserted" because the relation of a sign to its object has to be produced. According to Peirce, "A sign does not function as a sign unless it be understood as a sign" [in Parmentier 1994, 4]). If the presentative characteristics are based on similarity, the sign is an *icon*. Icons are likenesses, in some way, of the objects they represent. Peirce says that icons therefore communicate ideas "directly" (1955, 106). Examples of icons are photographs, maps, and paintings. If the presentative characteristics are based on contiguity, the sign is an *index*. An index "is in dynamical (including spatial) connection both with the individual object . . . and with the senses or memory of the person for whom it serves as a sign" (Peirce 1955, 107). An index points to something. The pointing-to can also involve (or imply) causality. An example of such an index is the weather vane; in this case "the index is caused by the object it represents" (Liszka 1996, 38). So if the wind is blowing east, the weather vane points east; that is, the index (the weather vane pointing east) is caused by the object (the easterly wind). If the presentative characteristics are based on convention, the sign is a symbol. This is probably the closest element in Peirce's work to Saussure's, because a symbol is arbitrary. A sign is a symbol when "just what it does represent lies in nothing but the very fact of there being a habit, disposition, or other effective general rule that it will be so interpreted" (Peirce, in Liszka 1996, 39). Words—like *cat* and *flower*—are symbols in the English language because their meanings are agreed on (more or less) by English speakers. Icons and indexes, on the other hand, are not wholly arbitrary because they are defined, at least in part, by the qualities of their materiality. The wind does not need agreement in order to blow, and the weather vane, as an indexical sign, does not contribute to it doing so.

Why is recognition of the material relations of signs important? In this book it is important because the apostolics demand attention to those material relations, but more broadly still, because it allows for the analysis of relations in what we might call "the real world" (i.e., the sociohistorical fields in which semiotic ideologies operate) and "reality" (i.e., "that which is as it is apart from any and all thought about it" [Parmentier 1994, 23]). Semeiotic has a much easier time incorporating the stuff of ethnography than does semiology. Peirce's doctrine of signs is grounded in processes that "entail sociability, struggle, historicity, and contingency" and puts paid "to the facile but commonplace claim that to take things as 'signs' is to reduce the world to discourse and its interpretation, to give in to the totalizing imperative to render all things meaningful" (Keane 2003, 413). "Peirce offers the possibility that meaning is more than a question of mental decoding, since semiosis is an open-ended process in which each moment of interpretation alters the field for subsequent interpretations" (Parmentier 1994, xiii). That field, moreover, is often conditioned by the material qualities of the sign, independent of human agents. This is in part what the apostolics want to emphasize about the Bible. Nzira's warning that it can fall apart is a recognition that material things are subject to forces beyond the apostolics' control—that what things mean, and what they can be used for, is neither settled nor certain, not only because different communities argue over meanings and uses, but also because things themselves are subject to the vicissitudes of physical existence (cf. Keane 1997b, 31). Peirce's work can help us to account for the materiality in and of signification. Read in this light, Nzira's remark that the Bible could be used as toilet paper is not so much a disparagement of its message as an anxiety over the significance and stability of the medium.

For any semiotic ideology, "before an object of signification can be specified, something must first be specified as a sign. And in the process, its objects must be determined to be objects" (Keane 2003, 423). If we want to understand the claims behind live and direct faith, we have to explore how words and things are defined and evaluated in the Friday apostolics' understanding of Christianity. As I hope to show throughout this book, theirs is a semiotic ideology in which the tension between distance and proximity is maintained through a careful consideration of what things can and cannot (re)present. Most things, by virtue of being so, are always *mere*. Or, at least, they ought to be so.

BACKGROUND OF THE STUDY

Having finished the initial consideration of the theoretical currents that shape my analyses of the Masowe apostolics, I want to make some brief remarks on the contexts of my fieldwork. My research was carried out in Zimbabwe over eighteen months during a seven-year period (February–May 1993, June–August 1996, January–December 1999). Most of it was conducted in Harare and Chitungwiza, although it involved a number of lengthy trips to other parts of the country, especially to those areas where the Friday apostolics have had a long presence. From July 1996 the Juranifiri Santa congregation in Chitungwiza became the primary site of my research. I chose Juranifiri in part for a practical reason: Nzira and the elders were open to my being around. Understandably, not all congregations wanted a resident anthropologist. Juranifiri was also attractive because it was clear by 1996 that Nzira was becoming an influential, though not uncontroversial, prophet whose ministry would allow for a productive exploration of the tensions that shape the Friday message. Friends in other congregations around Harare were always quick to confirm this.

I attended between two and six services at Juranifiri each week. Services lasted up to eight hours on the weekends and were rarely shorter than five hours. When not at the church site *(sowe),* I met with members of the congregation in their homes or, if they held formal sector jobs, on their lunch hours or the end of a day's shift. Throughout 1999 several apostolics came to my flat in Harare—including Godfrey Nzira, who came for dinner one evening with a small retinue of his elders and close family. While the majority of my time was spent focusing on the Juranifiri Santa congregation, I also attended the services of other groups in the Harare area, most notably, a congregation called Afgate in the suburb of Highfield (with whose elders I worked during all three of my field trips to Zimbabwe). Several contacts in these other congregations became close friends. We did not attend church together on a regular basis, but they became important interlocutors on church matters. Maintaining relationships with other congregations was important to me because I did not want a myopic focus on Juranifiri Santa. The trips I took outside the Harare area—also meant to complement the experiences at Juranifiri Santa—usually lasted two or three days and involved attending a major Friday service, conducting interviews, and gathering oral histories. In 1999 I gathered materials in the National Archives of Zimbabwe on the first few years of Johane Masowe's movements to complement the oral historical work. When I could, I attended services at other churches and met with local Christian figures in Harare.[15] On all three trips to Zimbabwe I met with spirit mediums and *n'angas* (African healers). One of these spirit mediums became a close contact and friend.

My partner, Rebecca Nash, herself an anthropologist, spent four months in Zimbabwe in 1999. She attended the Sunday services at Juranifiri Santa each week and often accompanied me to meet with apostolics on social visits. As I discuss in more detail in chapter 4, Rebecca was instrumental in helping me to gain a better perspective on the dynamics among women at Juranifiri Santa, dynamics that the apostolics—who maintain a discourse of equality—did a good job of preventing me from investigating in any depth. (I was able to get closest to men in the church, and many of them said there was no need for me to talk to women because men and women are the same.) Lazarus Chidaushe, a seasoned researcher who had worked with several well-known scholars (Allan Isaacman, Paul Berliner, Erica Bornstein) before we met, was initially my Shona tutor at Ranche House College in Harare, but from March to December 1999 we worked together on this research project on a daily basis. He was instrumental in its realization.

My Mazda 323 five-speed hatchback, Nokia 5100 cell phone, and Marantz PMD 201 tape recorder were also essential during fieldwork. The car got me (and Lazarus) around in prompt fashion, the cell phone helped me to coordinate meetings, and the tape recorder allowed Lazarus and me to gather interviews that we could mull over after the fact.

During the apostolic church services, these fieldwork tools had to be put aside. The apostolics' commitment to immateriality in faith had less than desirous effects on my data collection at the *masowe* (church sites). No books—not just the Bible—can be brought into an apostolic space of worship. Neither can any instruments for recording what went on: pens, notebooks, tape recorders, cameras, or videocameras. I was subject to the same conditions of experience as everyone else. Had I been scribbling, my friends would say, or peering into a viewfinder, I could not have concentrated on the live and direct message. Like those who clutter their services with Gospel readings, or turn to Bible passages in an effort to confirm what a preacher has said, I would miss the condition of possibility for an experience of the divine were I to attend to anything other than what is live and direct. What is presented on ritual speech here, therefore, is based on my recollections, as well as those of Lazarus and, on a few occasions, two colleagues from the University of Zimbabwe, Bella Mukonyora and David Bishau, who accompanied me to services. During fieldwork, I kept a small green notebook in my car, and after leaving a church session I would try to produce useful "mnemonic jottings" (Emerson, Fretz, and Shaw 1995, 31–35) that could be written up into full notes later—usually that evening. I was especially eager to capture key words and phrases that speakers used and any new songs we heard, made easier by the fact that ritual speech often involved repetitions (see chapter 5). Lazarus also took notes, which we compared with mine to extract a clearer sense of what speakers said and how they said it.[16] Lazarus provided me with invaluable copies of his notes, totaling several hundred pages, when I left the field.

Chitungwiza is a city with a registered population of more than 320,000, according to the Zimbabwe Statistical Office's 2002 Preliminary Census. The actual number of people living there is undoubtedly much higher. Chitungwiza is located about thirty kilometers south of Harare and was developed in the 1950s to provide accommodation for African workers in the capital. Chitungwiza was "planned in the spirit of apartheid" (Schylter 2003, 16)—a spirit that still lingers in structural and economic terms. Since Zimbabwe's independence in 1980 Chitungwiza has spread northward and Harare has spread southward—the southern areas of Harare being some of the poorest and also where much of the industry is located—such that, by the time I conducted the bulk of my fieldwork, they formed a massive urban complex. Many of the people I knew who lived in Chitungwiza worked in Harare (or spent time looking for work in Harare). The Juranifiri Santa congregation drew people from all parts of the urban area as well as from the Seke communal lands that surround Chitungwiza.

Almost all the apostolics in Harare and Chitungwiza are native Shona speakers, as are roughly 80 percent of Zimbabweans. I also knew native Ndebele, Venda, and Chewa speakers in the church, all of whom could speak Shona too. Like many Bantu languages, "Shona" is in part a product of colonization and missionization; it was crafted into a standard over the course of several years. There are five major dialects of the Shona language: Zezuru, Korekore, Ndau, Manyika, and Karanga. While most of the apostolics did not usually speak in terms of these "tribal" or "ethnic" identities, it was not unheard of to do so. People who called themselves Zezuru, for example, sometimes joked, usually good-naturedly, that the Korekore were simpleminded because Korekore speakers come from relatively remote areas in the country's northeast. The point here is not to dwell on the discourses of tribalism or its inventions but to draw attention to the fact that the urban centers in Zimbabwe stretch the already well-worn notions of "community" and "culture." I found no such unified objects in Harare or Chitungwiza and doubt I could have regardless of where the study had been based. I want to suggest, however, that the Friday churches form communities for themselves and must, moreover, be taken seriously as culturally Christian. But this is only one aspect of the apostolics' relations with others and one another.

"African Culture"

I ought to clarify something about the language of relations, because they are crucial to how the apostolics define themselves. One way apostolics mark their difference from nonapostolics is by using a language of strategic essentialisms. References to "African culture" and "African custom" were made by my informants on a regular basis in sermons, church lessons, and informal conversations. As I argue throughout the book, this language is a key to the apostolics' project of distancing themselves from those aspects of their "Africanness" considered antithetical to Christianity. In this they resemble the Pentecostals studied by Birgit Meyer (1998, 1999) in Ghana and, more recently, the Seventh-day Adventists studied by Eva Keller (2005) in Madagascar. Like these other Christians, the apostolics want "to make a complete break with the past," a phrase that Meyer's (1998) informants often used to describe their concern with "Africanness." If the apostolics sometimes spoke of the differences between a Zezuru and a Korekore speaker, they also spoke broadly and with more conviction about certain aspects of African culture that *all* Africans were said to share and from which in most respects they must retreat. For the most part, this had to do with "traditional religion," including the consultation of traditional healers (though not all healers would identify themselves as "religious" practitioners). It also involved the characterization of what were understood to be typically African dispositions, none of which was very flattering. Thus, according to the apostolics, if left to their own devices Africans will tear apart their communities through jealousy and distrust. Africans are also considered lazy in the apostolic ideal type. Moreover, what makes Africans jealous, distrustful, and lazy is their adherence to traditional religious practices, especially "ancestor worship" and the consultation of spirit mediums, healers, and, worst of all, witches.

Throughout this book, I do not use these terms as my own analytic categories, and I do not take the characterizations of African dispositions as given. These are important labels and concepts because of their centrality to the ethnographic texture, but they should not be taken as normative.

Similar to the Seventh-day Adventists in Keller's study (2005, 169–78), the Friday apostolics construct pictures of "traditional religion" and "African culture" that often bear little resemblance to what people who would identify themselves as traditionalists recognize. For one thing, the apostolics tend to lump together practices and practitioners that traditionalists see as distinct; holding a ritual to honor one's ancestors, for example, is considered a far cry by most traditionalists from consulting a witch (and no one in Zimbabwe, at least no one I knew, would ever willingly admit to consulting a witch in the first place). Like the Adventists, the apostolics construct a "disembedded notion of 'religion'" (Keller 2005,

177) that reflects a specific set of Christian concerns with ordering the spirit world into that which is of God and that which is not. More than many Christians in Zimbabwe, and more than most traditionalists, the apostolics make a concerted effort to separate what is Christian (in their view) from what is not Christian. These efforts do not always succeed and are not always honestly made, but that does not make them insignificant.

So what do traditionalists recognize as their "culture," and, more specifically, their "religion"? There might be as many answers to this as there are self-identified traditionalists, and a host of other answers by Zimbabweans who would not necessarily think or care to label themselves traditionalists, Christians, both, neither, or more. Nevertheless, given the strength of the apostolics' discursive constructions it will be useful to provide something of a counterpoint here. Throughout this book I develop a number of specific discussions on the questions of culture and custom, including the role of spirit mediums, the work of healers, and the importance of the ancestors. In the next several paragraphs, however, my aim is to provide background remarks to be kept in mind for the later discussions.

If you ask most Shona-speaking Zimbabweans about traditional religion, they will likely emphasize some combination of the following three things: the centrality of the ancestors, the importance of mediums and healers, and the dangers of witchcraft. Occasionally, you might be told about Mwari, the remote Shona "high god" creator. But Mwari is so rarely invoked by people, and so rarely contemplated, that it would be a mistake to overemphasize it.[17] You might also be challenged—as happened to me in a handful of instances—on the validity of your question, since the (disembedded) concept of religion does not necessarily make sense in traditionalist terms, being, as it is, a Christian importation. But even those who challenge you on the validity of your question might well go on to discuss, in light of their caveats, ancestors, mediums, healers, and witches.

For many Shona-speaking Zimbabweans, patrilineal ancestors *(midzimu;* sing., *mudzimu)* play a central role in everyday life, overseeing the course of social and moral relations within the patriline and beyond. Ancestors are invisible but not absent or, in a sense, departed. This sense of continuity and connection has led one anthropologist to characterize the patriline as "an organic and spiritual unity" (Murphree 1969, 41). Indeed, the difference between the living and the dead is in many respects one of degree and not kind. What the ancestors reflect is the hierarchy of relations within the patriline, in which those elder are more august and authoritative. This hierarchy shapes the flow of communication. Thus the living approach the dead through those closest to death (the elders), and the dead intervene in the affairs of the living through those closest to life (usually the first three generations of ancestors).

Ancestors can play a significant role in shaping the fortunes and misfortunes of the living. If a family has a "good" year (a bumper harvest, success in work or schooling, a marriage, the birth of a child), this is taken as evidence that they have shown proper respect to their ancestors. Respect is earned through remembrance in everyday thoughts and deeds but more important through the occasional offering in ceremonies of this-worldly goods, especially millet beer. If a family has a "bad" year (a failed harvest, a serious illness), it is likely because the ancestors have been offended by not receiving the proper respect. The ancestors do not automatically offer comfort and aid to the living; they are demanding and to a certain extent fickle and unpredictable.

In addition to midzimu, most Shona speakers recognize the existence of *mhondoro,* the "tribal" or "royal" spirits (also called "lion spirits"). Mhondoro are figures with societal and not just familial significance. They play a central role in political events and are more powerful than midzimu. Some mhondoro, such as Nehanda and Chaminuka, have widespread reputations and influence. During Zimbabwe's liberation war, for example, these and other lion spirits served as major sources of inspiration and authority in the struggle throughout Zimbabwe (Lan 1985; Ranger 1982, 1985; see also Kriger 1992). Most mhondoro, however, have influence within more well defined territorial areas (Spierenberg 2005). One of their main functions, beyond playing a role in politics, is to provide rain. Like the ancestral spirits, mhondoro are demanding and can withhold rain if the people in their territories do not accord them the proper respect.

Relationships between the living and the spirits are fostered, maintained, and negotiated through the activities of spirit mediums. A family suffering misfortune may seek help from a medium, who intervenes on their behalf to facilitate communication with the spirit responsible. In many cases the medium will try to get the spirit to speak through a member of the family in the hope of hearing why the spirit has been angered and what might be done to rectify the situation.

Mediums have spirits of their own—or, rather, the other way around, for spirits choose their mediums. Mediumship is not something one can decide to pursue. It requires learning, but that process can begin only after a person is chosen as a host. There are several kinds of spirits that work through mediums. The most common are healing spirits and ancestral spirits who have some kind of sociopolitical influence or stature (albeit not as great as a lion spirit) or some kind of special "talent." The mhondoro also have mediums, which are known as mhondoro as well. Mhondoro mediums differ from other mediums in some respects: they are not consulted for healing, and they are also often not chosen from within the spirit's own lineage. This is especially the case in the central and northern areas of Shona-speaking country (Bourdillon 1987, 264). These mediums must be strangers (vatorwa) to the dominant chiefly lineage. As Kingsley Garbett (1969, 117) notes, this is because the mediums often need to mediate in sensitive political disputes, so they must be "without kinsmen or local interests."

The n'anga—"traditional healer" or "diviner"—is distinct from the spirit medium. Most Zimbabweans I knew used it as a catch-all label for figures who dealt with the influences of spirits in people's everyday lives. N'anga do this through the use of "traditional medicine" (muti) or divining dice. Medicine is used to cure afflictions or to ward them off in the first place, whereas divination is used to help people chart some course of action in life. As a catch-all label, n'anga glosses over important differences between such figures, the most important of which is that not all traditional healers will claim that they act on the authority of, or in conjunction with, spirits. In any case, some general points about healers—broadly conceived—can be made. First, healers are neither good nor bad per se. Unlike mediums, who are understood to have a certain duty to a community or family, a n'anga might use his or her skills and powers for good or ill. This leads on to the second point, which is that n'anga act on their skills and powers not on their own accord but because people ask them to do so. They are paid in cash or goods for their services. While n'anga ought only to accept clients seeking help for themselves or their kin, there are plenty of unscrupulous healers who for the right price will use their skills to harm, not heal. If a person wants to derail someone in some way, he or she can buy muti from a healer to do it. Because of this ambiguity, n'anga are often treated with caution, unless they are known to have sterling reputations.

Witchcraft, the third major topic people bring up when they talk about traditional religion or African culture, might not be called a religious activity, except insofar as witches rely on spirits and spiritual creatures. Witches round out the moral spectrum in the spiritual field being set out here. If mediums are good and healers only debatably so, witches are recognized as unrepentantly evil. While in some cases there is evidence that a person can be recognized as a witch and not be considered threatening

(Bourdillon 1987, 179; Murphree 1969, 57), among the Zimbabweans I know witches were described as evil for evil's sake and as characters to steer clear of. No one is safe with them, least of all their kin.

As many anthropologists who work in Africa have reported, witchcraft is a topic that people are reluctant to talk about in any detail because intimate knowledge of witchcraft might be taken as a sign that the person is himself or herself a witch. Nevertheless, it is possible to get a general sense of Shona speakers' understandings of witches by weaving together the overlapping impressions.

Some people told me that the majority of witches are women. Others said this is not true, or is at least no longer true. There was more general agreement on the point that witchcraft runs in families. Although it is possible for a person to choose to become a witch through apprenticeship, these "trained" witches are not as powerful. "True" witches (i.e., those who inherit their witchcraft) are made so by evil spirits that possess and work though them. Like other spirits, these evil spirits demand certain things of their hosts—not millet beer but human flesh and blood. Indeed, witches are thought to crave human flesh, especially the flesh of children. Witches are said to gather in groups at night to raid fresh graves or even kill people. Witches also use familiars, such as baboons and mysterious creatures, to do their bidding. These familiars often help witches to gather human body parts and other things (including certain roots and plant leaves, glass shards, and money) to concoct poisons.

In addition to eating people and sometimes killing them, witches are understood to simply want to cause trouble and harm—especially to those among whom they live. Thus if a person is suffering misfortune of some kind, it may be because of an upset ancestral spirit, but it might just as well be the doing of a witch. Witches, then, add to the unpredictability and fragility of social and moral relationships.

While witches are a source of major concern for many Zimbabweans, the suspicion that people were consulting witches to conduct witchcraft on their behalf was an even larger one. As I understood it during my research, there was a sense that witches are one problem and witchcraft another. Ordinary people were thought to be exacerbating the witch situation by paying them (in money or blood) to "fix" their friends and enemies. The motivation was understood to be jealousy: Someone has someone else bewitched because he or she is jealous of that someone else's success—perhaps in work or a harvest yield or in having several children. The dangers of a jealous disposition—and the sense that Africans are prone to such a disposition—was not specific to the apostolics. I return to how the concept of jealousy is linked to witchcraft, especially in chapters 4 and 7. But there is, I believe, a more general need for Africanists whose work has focused on witchcraft to plumb the nature of these conceptual relations in more depth (for exceptions, see Ashforth 2005, 63–87; West 2005). Among Zimbabweans at least, talk of witchcraft and talk of jealousy come together.

These sketches of what nonapostolics might characterize as the key aspects of "traditional religion" or "African culture" are rudimentary. Fuller accounts of how they both intersect with and diverge from the apostolics' conceptions and constructions are presented throughout this book. In the meantime, there are three points to hold in mind. First, the difference between spirits and the living is one of degree and not of kind. In an important sense spirits and people occupy the same social world. While spirits have powers and capabilities that people do not have, this has to do in large part with the processual dynamics of advancement through an overarching hierarchical order. Second, although there is "one world," the proper relationships between spirits and the living are difficult to maintain. Effective communication with the spirits is very difficult to achieve—in part because spirits are fickle and to an extent unpredictable, in part because they do not often communicate with words but rather through acts, and in part because it is not always easy to tell which spirit (ancestral or evil) is doing what or why. And third, things—millet beer offerings, traditional medicines, divining dice, even human flesh—play a central role in mediating and articulating the many kinds of relationships that people have with spirits.

Zimbabwe's Politics

Zimbabwe is probably better known for its farmlands than its cities. The country is often (if not always recently) referred to as the breadbasket of southern Africa. The rich tracts of arable land that stretch out across the Zimbabwe plateau have been planted with maize, tobacco, cotton, oranges, and, in the lowvelds, sugarcane. The fertile land drew a substantial settler population to Southern Rhodesia in the 1920s and 1930s. With enticements from the government, white settlers arrived to seek a living. Not all, of course, were successful. The novelist Doris Lessing (1994) makes this clear in her autobiography; her parents moved the family to Southern Rhodesia in 1924 after a visit to the Empire Exhibition in Wembley but soon realized "the enticements of the Empire Exhibition had little to do with reality" (1994, 50). Some farmers did become successful and, especially after Zimbabwe's independence (ironically), very rich. The settlers were aided immensely by the Land Apportionment Act of 1931, which reserved a vast majority of the best farmland for the tiny minority of whites. In 1931 there were an estimated one million Africans in Southern Rhodesia and 48,000 white settlers. The Land Apportionment Act displaced hundreds of thousands of local people; it reserved 48 million acres for the 48,000 whites and 29 million acres of poorer quality for the one million Africans (see Meredith 2002, 111–31; Palmer 1977).

Land provided a major idiom in Zimbabwe's War of Independence (ca. 1966–80) as both spiritual and economic resource. The mhondoro "tribal spirits" became key actors in and symbols of the Chimurenga, or struggle (Kriger 1992; Lan 1985; Ranger 1985). According to the information I was able to gather, the Friday apostolics as a church did not play a significant role in the war. In many areas of the country fighting disrupted their ability to congregate. But they claimed not to have aligned themselves with the guerrillas and spirit mediums, even tactically. I often sensed a strain in conversations about the war, however, because most apostolics were by no means in favor of Ian Smith's Rhodesian Front. They also stressed that the only time apostolics ought to mix "religion and politics" (and this was a break with mutemo) is when prevented from freely congregating to pray, as was often the case in the war.

Zimbabwe's Chimurenga left "unfinished business" all around and on several fronts (see Hammar, Raftopoulos, and Jensen 2003). By the late 1990s the farmlands were still largely in the hands of white commercial farmers, except for what had fallen into the hands of the postcolonial politicians. The economy was struggling under the impact of neoliberal World Bank and International Monetary Fund "structural adjustment" programs. On top of this the country was being, and still is, devastated by HIV/AIDS. The country's position on these and other matters was never much helped by President Robert Mugabe or his ruling party, the Zimbabwe African National Union—Patriotic Front (ZANU[PF]). Mugabe has a brutal and totalitarian record, the evidence for which stretches back to the early 1980s (Alexander, MacGregor, and Ranger 2000). Since 2000 he has increasingly tightened his grip. In February of that year his authority was challenged in a referendum to amend the constitution. An opposition coalition called the National Constitutional Assembly (NCA) spearheaded a successful "no" vote campaign that deprived Mugabe of the freer hand the new constitution would have given him. It was around this time that

ZANU(PF) began their now-infamous land resettlement programs, which resulted in the haphazard and violent seizure of many commercial farms. It was a brutal process, and the Western media has often picked up the stories of white farmers killed by farm squatters (sometimes called "war veterans"). Less often reported—as the anthropologist Blair Rutherford (2001, 245–52; 2004) has carefully shown—are the violent effects on the hundreds of thousands of displaced African farmworkers and their families. Since 2000 and the farm invasions Mugabe has continued to clamp down on his opponents, real and imagined. The state has shut down the free press; intimidated, tortured, and killed members of the Movement for Democratic Change (MDC; the main political opposition party, although as of this writing in organizational disarray); rigged (as of this writing) three elections; purged the judiciary of independents; withheld food from communities not firmly behind the ruling party; and much else. Because of Mugabe's brutalities, Zimbabwe was suspended from the Common- wealth in 2003.

Signs of this political and economic turmoil were in the air during my fieldwork. In the closing months of 1999 the NCA's constitutional cam- paign came as an early warning. The MDC was formed in September of that year. Many of my friends and informants (inside and outside the church) had a sense that political trouble and some measure of socioeco- nomic turmoil were on the horizon. The processes that led to the events I am glossing were palpably under way throughout the main year-long com- ponent of my research. If the apostolics were in fact successful at keeping religion and politics separate during the 1970s, this was more difficult in the 1990s. Regardless of any commitment to immateriality, it has been dif- ficult for the apostolics to keep their "empty spaces" empty.

The constellation of materials and impressions I was able to gather on the Friday apostolics can be spread into a wide arc, but they cluster dis- tinctly around two main subjects: the church's history and the day-to- day dynamics within the Juranifiri Santa congregation. As will become clear throughout this study, "church history" (an apostolic term) is not a settled subject, and Juranifiri Santa is not, in everyone's view, a repre- sentative congregation. Like most anthropological studies, then, this one faces the difficulties of shifting scales and of what it can claim to present. My aims are to present the church history in a form that has widespread resonance and to highlight those aspects of religious practice at Juranifiri Santa both similar to and different from other congregations. There is no absolute in the analysis or definitiveness to the conclusions. But I prefer to see this in a positive light rather than as a predicament: like astute anthropologists, the apostolics have an aversion to thingification. It does not fit their faith either.

OUTLINE OF THE BOOK

This book can be roughly divided into two parts. The first part focuses on the reception and use of the Bible in its colonial and postcolonial contexts. Chapter 1 is a broad overview of how the Bible has been understood as a tool of both subjugation and liberation in Africa, especially after the mid-nineteenth century. It sets a context for understanding Johane Masowe's political and theological objections to Scripture, as well as the kind of semiotic ideologies against which the Friday apostolics pose their own. Chapters 2 and 3, based on archival and oral historical research, chart the development of apostolic ideas from Johane's early work in the 1930s up through several prophets still preaching today. What these chapters provide is a sense of the distinctive history behind the apostolics' live and direct approach to Christianity.

The second part of the book focuses on the ritual and everyday life of the Masowe apostolics, in particular, among congregations in the urban centers of Harare and Chitungwiza. It begins, in chapter 4, with portraits of "ordinary members," providing detail on the concepts and practices of mutemo through which they define themselves as Christian—often in contrast to those still considered under the sway of "African culture." Chapters 5 through 7 address three aspects of apostolic ritual: sermons, songs, and acts of healing. Each chapter contributes to the overall picture of what constitutes a live and direct faith and the way in which the Bible's absence plays a role in that faith. These chapters bring us back, along various paths, to how the apostolics claim to instantiate their relationship with the Holy Spirit without textual mediation.

The conclusion returns to a discussion of the vignette that opens the introduction. Reading back, I suggest that Nzira's comparison of the Bible with toilet paper speaks in its own profound way to the problem of presence that has shaped Christian religious practice since its emergence in the ancient Mediterranean world.

ONE

Up in Smoke

Humility, Humiliation, and the Christian Book

The simple reading and study of the Bible alone will convert the world.
The missionary's work is to gain for it admission and attention, and
then let it speak for itself.

ISAAC HUGHES

IN OCTOBER 1999 I INTERVIEWED Gaylord Kambarami, general secretary of the Bible Society of Zimbabwe (BSZ), an ecumenical organization that traces its roots to the British and Foreign Bible Society,
established in 1804. Many churches operating in Zimbabwe, including
several independent churches, support the BSZ. Kambarami estimates
that since 1980 the BSZ has distributed over three million copies of
Scripture, or about one Bible for every four Zimbabweans alive today.
Based on these figures alone and discounting distribution by individual
churches (to say nothing of copies handed down from one generation
to the next), there should be at least one Bible in every Zimbabwean
household, Christian or not. I suggested to Kambarami these were impressive statistics, but he was not satisfied. His goal, he told me, is to
put a Bible into the hands of every Zimbabwean. "The Bible transforms
people's lives," he said. "When you read that book, somehow something
takes change in you."

Kambarami shared a number of stories collected from thirty years of
work to convince me of this fact. One of these stories has stayed with
me, both for the pleasure Kambarami expressed as he told it and for the
unusual manner in which it demonstrates a certain kind of investment in
the power of the book:

In 1995 I went to the Murewa rural areas to distribute copies of the Shona New Testament. In one village, a headman refused to take it. He said he couldn't stand the Word of God. I said, "Why?" And he said, "Because it pollutes people." So he refused to buy it. I told him that he could have it and just give it to someone else. He said he could only accept it if I allowed him to use the pages of the New Testament for smoking purposes. In the rural areas, you know, people use newspaper and whatever else they can find to roll their cigarettes. I said, "Fine, on one condition: read each page before you smoke." He accepted this, because he was literate. So I left the book with him and didn't think about it very much after that. Then, in 1997, I took a return trip to Murewa area. We had a convention there under a big tent. I was invited to speak, and I told the people how this book could change people's lives. Now, the same man whom I had given the New Testament to smoke was in the audience. Before the closing of the service, he stood and said, "Please, let me say a few words to [Kambarami]." He was dressed smart, in a suit. I did not recognize him at first. He said, "This man doesn't remember me; because when I last saw him I was a drunkard. But he came to our village and persuaded me to take the Bible. I told him I would use the paper to roll cigarettes. But I promised to read each page before doing so, which I did. So I smoked my way through Matthew. And I smoked the whole of Mark too. Then I smoked Luke. I started smoking John, but when I came to John 3:16 [For God so loved the world that he gave his only Son, so that everyone who believes in him may not perish but may have eternal life], a light shone in my face. And now I am a churchgoing person. I saw the light."

This is why we try to get people to read the Bible. Even reading it on your own, you can transform yourself. It can transform you. In fact we often say in the BSZ that the Bible reads people. It holds the answer.

The force of Kambarami's story resides initially in the tension provided by the headman, who aims to deny the Word's significance for anything other than facilitating his personal vice. But the tension is soon resolved. We are supposed to recognize the Bible not as hapless object but as humble subject. By going up in smoke—a resonant religious image in the areas where Kambarami and his staff operate—the Bible is sacrificing itself to itself, for the sake of the headman. As the story unfolds the Bible becomes not a representation of the Word but, through a literal inhalation, its presence. That smoke is a key index of the tension is only fitting because it challenges us to define what is central and what is epiphenomenal in this mode of signification. Sending the Bible up in smoke, only to see the light: Kambarami is playing expertly on the difficulty of separating the significance of the Bible from its materiality.[1]

Using Kambarami's story as a point of departure, this chapter focuses on the issues of presence and representation through portraits of six Christians with deep investments in the power of the Bible. Taken together, they provide a picture of the kinds of semiotic ideologies that have had considerable purchase in colonial and postcolonial Africa. In this they exemplify the kinds of Christians the Friday apostolics argue against. Like Kambarami, these Christians suggest that the Bible is a definitive sign through which God's presence is manifested. And like Kambarami, they assume, and sometimes assert, that the materiality of the Bible functions meaningfully in what and how it signifies.

Like Kambarami's headman, Johane Masowe sent the Bible up in smoke, although in doing so he produced a different kind of Christianity. To understand Johane's motivations, we need to understand what the Friday apostolics position themselves against. The six portraits in this chapter comprise a range of examples of how the Bible is made significant as both word and thing, often in a manner that challenges the conceptual separation between word and thing, such that the question of its qualities is not always openly posed. And yet the Bible as a humble subject—which is how it functions in Kambarami's story—ought to be investigated, in light of the role its physical qualities play in the constitution of this status. The portraits in this chapter show that the book-as-object has been central to establishing its authority as the Christian sign, even as the materiality of this sign has often been taken for granted. For this, indeed, is the dual character of any object: "its extreme visibility and its extreme invisibility" (Miller 1987, 108). It is precisely when the Bible's material meaning is *not* taken for granted—and it never is, not uniformly—that we are prompted to consider how the humility of objects can turn into the humiliation of objects. Sending the Bible up in smoke can be either, and much in between.

The first two portraits, of nineteenth-century Protestant missionaries from Great Britain, give us a sense of the efforts to circulate the Bible as widely as possible in early modern evangelical work. Like Kambarami, these missionaries understood the Bible as an agent in itself—something that could reconfigure the world as Christian. The power of the Bible relied chiefly on its introduction: where it was present it could act by "reading" as much as by being read. The second two portraits, of a Zulu Christian prophet and an Acholi Christian medium, make clear that Christian reconfigurations were not always according to missionary expectations. Contrary to the suggestion of Isaac Hughes in the epigraph, there is no such thing as a simple reading and study of the Bible. At the same time (and as Kambarami clearly hopes) Christianity has demanded an engagement with the text. This last point is evident in the second set of portraits but is developed further in the third set, which focuses on two African clergymen, an archbishop in the Anglican Church and a Methodist theologian. For them, the book has a tenacity that provides their theological ground, although the ground for each is distinctly different, as is the nature of the Bible's tenacity.

In what follows I paint in broad strokes. My goal is to provide a general picture of how Christians address the problem of presence through their understandings of the Bible's qualities as a sign. I necessarily leave out some important aspects of what defined African mission fields—the economic dimensions, for example, as well as several social and political ones. When I turn to the ethnography of the Masowe apostolics, some of the aspects left out here come to the fore. The broad-stroked picture omits important theological points too. Thomas O. Beidelman (1974, 1982) has rightly noted that historians and anthropologists have often conflated the approaches and philosophies of missions, assuming that Christianity is a monolithic force and Christians themselves a fairly homogeneous lot. One of the crucial differences to acknowledge here, extending discussions in the introduction, is that Protestants and Catholics "have sharply different views on the religious significance of literacy" (Beidelman 1982, 14). Unlike many of their Protestant counterparts, Catholic missionaries have not, in accordance with Church doctrine, presented the Bible as a sufficient source of faith. For much of the period under consideration, Catholics placed the Bible in the hands of the clergy more firmly than the congregation. What's more, not all Protestant churches have emphasized reading the Bible to the same extent. It has often been cast alongside other indexes such as gifts of the spirit and institutional-specific teachings.

At the same time I want to argue that since at least the 1850s the Bible in Africa has become an increasingly significant index of Christianity that has obscured otherwise obvious confessional distinctions. In fact, according to Norman Etherington (1977), the insistence on Protestant and Catholic difference is not always supported by the historical record. In southeastern Africa, for example, there were nine Protestant and Catholic missions from seven national traditions operating among the Nguni-speaking peoples in the mid-nineteenth century. When each began work there were indeed "marked differences" among and between them; by 1880, however, Etherington tells us, "these variations hardly mattered" (1977, 32, 35). They hardly mattered because missionaries could never define their work by theology alone—if they had time to preach a theology, which was not always the case. African converts and potential converts (to say nothing of colonial authorities) had their own agendas and interests—some pragmatic, some religious. By downplaying historical and theological specificities in this chapter, however, I do not want to deny their existence or reject their importance. Rather, through this temporary suspension of the anthropological sensibility, I want to highlight the discourse of how the Bible has been set apart to lay the groundwork for how the Masowe apostolics approach the Bible in light of its materiality.

If the Bible once defined a paradigm of evangelical Protestantism, it is today something more, something that Christians in Africa have emphasized on their own accord—even, to some extent, in Catholic mission fields and communities.[2] Signs and their circulation are always difficult to control as both objects and ideas (Thomas 1991). The portraits here suggest the Bible has proven a particularly robust and unpredictable sign: robust, in the sense that its presence spread throughout a range of semiotic ideologies; unpredictable, because this was not always according to the plans of those who were spreading it. Even when they are not sent up in smoke, it is important to recognize that "objects change in defiance of their material stability" (Thomas 1991, 125).

PRELUDE TO THE PORTRAITS: THE BRITISH AND FOREIGN BIBLE SOCIETY

"Printing," Martin Luther once wrote, "is the ultimate gift of God and the greatest one. Indeed, by means of it God wants to spread word of the cause of the true religion to all the earth, to the extremities of the world" (quoted in Gilmont 1999, 213). It was the British and Foreign Bible Society (BFBS), progenitor of organizations such as Kambarami's BSZ, that did the most to facilitate the actualization of this "gift," and we cannot present the six portraits without first considering the "scriptural imperialism" (Sugirtharajah 2001, 45–73) Bible societies helped to put into place.

Printing presses were brought to the Cape Colony by the London Missionary Society in 1814 and 1819 (see Bradlow 1987), following on the heels of a concerted effort to provide texts in the emerging mission fields. No organization was more responsible for setting this mandate than the

BFBS. Its "sole aim" was (and still is) "the production and distribution of the Scriptures in the languages of the world" (Fenn 1963, 387). Its advocates were convinced "that the secret of England's greatness was its reading of the Bible" (Sugirtharajah 2001, 53). The BFBS was not a mission society, and none of its editions (all based initially on translations from the Authorized King James version) contained any exegetical material, notes, or comments. Founders of the society worked under the assumption that if the peoples of the world had access to the book that they would want it and that "study and practice would automatically follow" (Howsam 1991, 3).

There was a growing sense in England at the end of the eighteenth century that reading the Bible was the key to salvation and that those without access to it were, in effect, being denied the essence of faith. One clergyman returning to London from Wales, where the poorest subjects were complaining of their lack of access to the text, declared in 1793, "Is there poverty like their poverty, who have not the Bible of God?" (quoted in Owen 1817, 3). His lament was captured in a well-known story from the time—still told today—of a girl named Mary Jones who wanted to buy a copy of the Bible in Welsh. After working hard to save money, she made the long trek to the bookseller's, only to find that there were no copies available. Mary Jones became a symbolic catalyst for the evangelicals. It was unforgivable to deny people's desire—their need—for the book. Mary's story was retold to children throughout the British Isles. "And if for Wales," one evangelist said, "why not also for the Empire and the world?" (quoted in Howsam 1991, 3).

Those sympathetic to the goals of the BFBS tried to suggest an innate desire for the book in the "lower races." John Owen, the Anglican secretary of the society, quoted J. D. Carlyle, professor of Arabic at Cambridge University, who drew on the explorer Mungo Park's observations among West Africa Muslims, to support the argument of this desire. Carlyle wrote in 1803, a year before the BFBS was founded: "According to Mr. Park, the negroes are proud of their literature, and seldom travel without a book slung by their side. Amongst their books he has perceived the Pentateuch, the Book of Psalms, and the Prophet Isaiah. All of these they prize very highly; and such is the general eagerness to obtain them, that he believes no articles would be more saleable in Africa than copies of the Scriptures in Arabic. He has seen a copy of the Pentateuch alone, sold at the price of one prime slave, i.e. about 20 guineas" (quoted in Owen 1817, 157). Carlyle's report asserts a natural, almost unconscious, progression toward

Christianity expressed through African desires to read. And not only did West African Muslims already have a penchant for some of the key texts in the Christian tradition, they were willing to pay dearly for them.

It is worth stressing—certainly here, in light of the focus on materiality—that the BFBS and other Bible societies resist the characterization of the Bible as a commodity. Their underlying principle is the provision of "cheap Bibles" (see Howsam 1991), and none makes a profit. But neither do they encourage giving the Bible away for free, "since people do not value what they get for nothing" (Fenn 1963, 399).[3] This makes Carlyle's report all the more notable. The parallel Carlyle draws between the value of human life and of Scripture is not only a comment on the spiritual worth of the written word, but its desirability as a commodity.[4] It suggests that as part of an emerging ideology of Christianity, commerce, and civilization, the Bible would prove a useful weapon in the abolition of the slave trade. The slave trade might end if there were books to buy instead. In this sense its materiality operated at several levels, indexing it as both the Gospel and a good.

Education was a key goal at mission stations, Protestant and Catholic alike.[5] Indeed, "the domain in which the encounter with mission made its deepest inroads was that of literacy and learning" (Comaroff and Comaroff 1991, 311). Over the course of the nineteenth and early twentieth century, "book knowledge" and "book learning" came to be understood in southern Africa as rooted in Bible study and catechism classes. The Bible's influence in particular now extends well beyond Christian-only discourses. As in the West (Frye 1981; Jasper and Prickett 1999), in Africa (Hofmeyr 1994) it became an integral part of the cultural landscape, providing a well of symbols and allegories that have shaped social, religious, and political life.[6] The theologian John Mbiti has testified in this respect to the influence of the written word: "The Bible is a lived book and a living book, by the community, through the community, and for the community, whose foundation and goal is God. Nowhere else today is the world of the Bible as real or as alive as it is in Africa. Here, it is being experienced, not as a world of two to four thousand years ago, but in many ways as the African world of yesterday, today, and tomorrow. Africa is living in the Bible, and the Bible is alive in Africa" (1994, 38).

Protestant missionary societies established the first schools in southern Africa to bring the Bible "alive" through its reading. The Bible and other religious texts were used as reading primers, further emphasizing the association between literacy and Christian faith. This emphasis on literacy shaped expectations for the "mature" Christian: "The Christian stress on education, expressed in countless schools and colleges which owe their authority to missionary enthusiasm, derives from the conviction that only a literate Christian can fully enter into his faith and that literacy in the community at large is an asset in the propagation of the Gospel" (Fenn 1963, 403). We see this as well in reports from the time. In 1813 Sir John Cradock, patron of the newly formed Bible and School Commission in the Cape Colony, wrote, "The two great pursuits that seem universally, in the present day, to occupy the attention of . . . the civilized world . . . are, the more extensive circulation of the Holy Scriptures, and the solid establishment of such a system of education as will enable the people to reach and behold the divine light contained in those sacred readings" (quoted in Owen 1817, 505). The promise of education, the promotion of literacy, and the vision of Christianity went hand in hand. They were "beginning to make a decisive difference to Africa by 1850" (Hastings 1994, 243). And they were setting the groundwork for an understanding of the Bible as an agent in itself.

VENN, MOFFAT, AND THE TRANSFORMATIVE POWER OF SCRIPTURE

Henry Venn and Robert Moffat were Protestant missionaries with a deep commitment to the power of the written word. Their portraits situate the connections among Christianity, colonialism, and textual authority during the early days of the mission frontier. Each made clear his utmost faith in the transformative power of Scripture. Venn and Moffat saw God's Word as embodied in the physical book. It was as tangible as the thing itself and as fixed as the printed letters on the page.

Venn has been called "the most influential theoretician of mission in the United Kingdom in the nineteenth century" (Shenk 1983, xi; see also Stanley 1990, 66). He was born in London in 1796 to a prominent family in the Clapham Sect, an evangelical group that emphasized the idea of "lived faith" and used their wealth and social position to teach the Word of God through philanthropy. These evangelicals were also "men whose religious life had been transformed by a fresh study of the Bible and who bent their energies to persuading people not only of the truth of the Gospel but the necessity of nourishing their lives at the source of the Gospel in Scripture" (Fenn 1963, 387). In this tradition reading the Bible was an act of liberation and salvation in and of itself. Venn once said that the

Bible "possessed a 'living energy'" (Shenk 1983, 31) all its own, an idea that became a defining characteristic of Venn's missionary vision. It took root in other mission fields too—well beyond those of the Church Missionary Society (CMS)—and resonates in Zimbabwe to this day.[7]

Venn served as clerical secretary of the CMS from 1841 to 1872. (He never worked in Africa.) The CMS is an organization his father, John Venn, had helped to establish in 1799. It is an independent organization of the Anglican Church, a voluntary society responsible for its own fund-raising, recruitment, and strategies. Under Henry Venn's charge, the CMS sought "to send out people, lay or clergy, men or women, to preach the Gospel and spread a knowledge of the Bible" (Hastings 1994, 293). Venn tried to recruit with exacting standards; he "wanted missionaries to be known as people of the Book" (Shenk 1983, 30). "The basis of your teaching," Venn wrote to his recruits, "will be the Bible, the whole Bible, and nothing but the Bible" (quoted in Shenk 1983, 31). Drawing on his upbringing in the Clapham Sect, Venn stressed the idea that the Bible could transform any human being into a good Christian. If an African was taught to read, he or she could find faith. It was a missionary's goal to foster a love of the book through the promotion of literacy. The Bible would take care of most of the rest.

Venn's larger vision of mission work also stressed "native agency," the idea for which he is best remembered and, often, celebrated (Hanciles 2002; Shenk 1983; Williams 1990). Just as Africans should be able to read, so too should they direct their own churches. As Venn put it in an 1861 Minute to the society's members, "It is expedient that native converts should be trained, at as early a stage as possible, upon a system of self-government, and of contributing to the support to their own Native Teachers. . . . It is expedient that the arrangements which may be made in the missions should from the first have reference to the ultimate settlement of the Native Church, upon the ecclesiastical basis of an *indigenous* Episcopate, independent of foreign aid or superintendence" (1971, 68–69). Native agency thus leads to what Venn called "the euthanasia of mission" (see Hanciles 2002). What I want to highlight here is an underlying emphasis on the text in Venn's project of euthanasia. Venn based nineteenth-century missionary work on the assumption that the fixity of the written Word would translate into a fixity of faith, revealing something of the semiotic ideology that fueled his understanding of Christianity. In that ideology the materiality of the Bible is intimately bound up with the Gospel message it conveys. The goal of missionaries was to make themselves unnecessary, to create "a native church nurtured in the theology of the Church of England" (Williams 1990, 49). In this project the Bible would act as a theological security blanket. As J. D. Y. Peel has pointed out in his research on the CMS, its members had no missiology "other than that provided by the Bible itself" (1995, 595). A Christian who read the Bible would be a Christian who read the Bible, regardless of the language in question. The text was thought to "fix the spiritual standard" (Venn, quoted in Sanneh 1994, 40), easing anxiety that Christianity could be compromised by "native culture" and become something less than Christianity as understood by the CMS. A similar logic is evident in Kambarami's story. "Even reading it on your own," Kambarami remarked, "you can transform yourself." Without the benefit of an institutional framework, the Bible is a guarantor of Christian continuity—physical evidence of spiritual justness.

While one biographer has argued that Venn did not intend to "Anglicanize" converts and that he was driven by "the immensely strong conviction that culture and context matter" (Williams 2000, 172), it is clear from his writings that the authenticity of any Christian church was to be determined by his specific brand of Anglicanism. In 1857, for example, Venn made the case against polygamy by turning to the Bible. His logic was almost literalist in tone, as if these were self-evident truths, resistant to other interpretations. "After this review of the Scriptural arguments against polygamy," he wrote in prelude to a lengthy exposition, "there should be no difficulty on the part of Missionaries in plainly stating to the heathen or Mahommedans that the practice is contrary to the will of God" (Venn 1971, 79). There is a tension here that points to a more general aspect of Venn's theory: "native agency" should exist only insofar as it coincides with CMS agendas. Native Christians could govern their own affairs so long as they measured up to the "spiritual standard" set by Venn's reading of the Bible.

The native agency idea also gave rise over time to new group identities. Producing biblical texts in the vernacular contributed to "the 'national' enterprise" (Sanneh 1994, 39–40) in several mission fields. Biblical and other religious texts were some of those that "made it possible for rapidly growing numbers of people to think about themselves, and relate themselves to others, in profoundly new ways" (Anderson 1991, 36). It was well after Venn's death (and the undermining of his program) that these dynamics had their most notable influence. But they became part of a more diffuse ideology of mission that shaped both Protestant and Catholic spheres of operation. In Southern Rhodesia, for example, the most influential nationalists had been educated by missionaries—and many became ministers themselves.[8] As Michael West documents in his study of the African middle class in Southern Rhodesia, "Colonial subjects quickly realized that Western-type education offered one of the few means of rising to a level higher than the one envisaged for them by the European architects of the new social order" (2002, 36). In Uganda, according to Tim Allen, "amongst the Acholi-speakers Catholic history has provided an ideological framework for the formation of a collective identity" (1991, 394), facilitated by the production of a vernacular literature. Religion, writing, and politics have never been far apart; Venn helped to foster their proximity at an important moment of the colonial encounter.

Robert Moffat's mission career brings us closer to my ethnographic focus; his influence reached as far north as Matabeleland, near what is today the city of Bulawayo, Zimbabwe, where Friday apostolics began establishing congregations in the mid-1990s. Moffat too has a paradigmatic status, having been called "the venerable father of the missionary world" by "universal consent" (Morrison 1969, 52). His claims to this title are based more on his perseverance in the field than the widespread influence of his ideas. If Venn was a theorist, Moffat was a practitioner. His portrait rounds out the discussion of mission ideology by highlighting how the creation of vernacular texts and the emphasis on the written word was caught up in the attempt to transform Africans into the subjects of empire. It also provides an example of how a belief in the Bible's "living energy" was coordinated with action in a mission field.

Robert Moffat Jr. was born in 1795 in Ormiston, twenty-six miles from Edinburgh. Though he was the son of a moderately successful salt tax collector, Robert Jr. had little formal schooling in his youth (Bradlow 1987, 5; Comaroff and Comaroff 1991, 83). He learned to read, however, and when he left home "his mother . . . exacted from him . . . a solemn promise to read his Bible every day" (Morrison 1969, 28). Moffat's parents were United Presbyterians. From them he learned that "improvement meant not only industry and thrift"—as demonstrated in the work ethic of his father—"but also good works for those less fortunate" (Comaroff and Comaroff 1991, 82). As a young man he went to Manchester, where he was taken under the wing of the minister William Roby. Listening to Roby's sermons and reading the Bible every day was the extent of his theological education, but he became committed to the idea of devoting his life to mission.

Moffat joined the London Missionary Society (LMS) and set sail for the Cape Colony in 1817. The LMS was founded the same year Moffat was born, 1795, as interest in overseas mission work started to grow in England. Although the LMS was established as an ecumenical mission simply "to further the cause of the Christian gospel," within a decade, and with the founding of other mission societies (such as the CMS), it became dominated by Congregationalists (J. de Gruchy 1999, 2). Moffat seemed drawn to the LMS by its compatibility with the tenets of his upbringing: "The African was to be guided along similar paths, learning to read and reflect, to master the practical arts of civilization, to cultivate and sell his labor, and to see the value of industry and charity" (Comaroff and Comaroff 1991, 83).

Moffat spent most of his life at Kuruman, a mission station at the edge of the Kalahari Desert and "the centre of missionary activity in southern Africa from which Christianity would spread throughout the interior" (Beck 1997, 108). He worked at the station over a period of fifty years, 1820–70. In that time he returned to Great Britain only once, for a five-year period (1838–43). It was on this return visit that he wrote his famous *Missionary Labours and Scenes in Southern Africa* and had his translation of the New Testament in Setswana, which he had worked on for over a decade, published in London. It was also during this trip that he persuaded David Livingstone (his future son-in-law) to join the LMS. When Livingstone left for Africa in 1840, Moffat entrusted him to deliver five hundred copies of the Setswana New Testament to Kuruman. Like Venn, Moffat was committed to the spread of the Gospel in the vernacular. As Cecil Northcott argues, "Moffat's early ambition upon which depended the fundamental success of his mission, was to translate the Bible into Sechuana [Setswana]" (quoted in Bradlow 1987, 3). This ambition was embodied in the work at Kuruman, evidenced most clearly by Moffat's procurement in 1831 of a printing press for the station. On this press Moffat printed more than fifty tracts, hymnbooks, periodicals, and copies of Scripture (Bradlow 1987, 26–35). Kuruman became one of the most important outposts for the dissemination of the written word in southern Africa during the nineteenth century.

Moffat spent the better part of the 1820s learning Setswana. "The acquisition of the language was an object of first importance" (Moffat 1842, 291) to him, as it should be for every missionary. But Moffat often lamented the lack of time he had to pursue the vernacular. He explained why to his European audience in *Missionary Labours:* "After being compelled to attend to every species of manual, and frequently menial, labour for the whole day, working under a burning sun[,] . . . it may be imagined that I was in no very fit condition for study, even when a quiet hour could be obtained in the evening for that purpose" (1842, 292). As late as 1851, after twenty years of operating the press, he wrote in a letter to a colleague, "We are instant in season and out of season in our public duties and in the work of translation, but the progress is slow, very slow" (quoted in Morrison 1969, 46). Even with enthusiasts such as Venn and Moffat, spreading the Word was a long-term proposition.[9]

Reaching the ideal type of Bible-reading Africans involved a series of lengthy steps. The first text Moffat published in Setswana, with Tswana collaborators, was a spelling and grammar book in 1826, which he had printed in London; the first gospel was Luke, in 1830 (Bradlow 1987, 6). But Moffat made clear that collaboration with Africans was not the ideal way to work. Interpreters were always second best to what a missionary could do directly, whether or not the missionary knew the vernacular language well: "A missionary who commences giving direct instruction to the natives, though far from being competent in the language, is proceeding on safer ground than if he were employing an interpreter, who is not proficient in both languages, and who has not a tolerable understanding of the doctrines of the Gospel. Trusting to an ignorant and unqualified interpreter, is attended with consequences not only ludicrous, but dangerous to the very objects which lie nearest the missionary's heart" (1842, 293–94). Moffat's ruminations on translation reveal something of the semiotic ideology that informed his understanding of the Bible. His approach to translation was based on the assumed efficacy of the Word. What mattered to him was the Gospel; "fluency" in Scripture could compensate for language barriers because Scripture could, in a sense, speak for itself. If in theory Venn saw promise in the vernacular, missionaries on the ground never relinquished the idea that they knew best and that the power of the written Word could transcend cultural difference on its own. As Kambarami was to say, "the Bible reads people."

Moffat's assumption points to the discrepancies between the theory and practice of translation, at least in some Protestant traditions.[10] It betrays the power dynamic that was part and parcel of the missionary's ideological agenda. Like other missionary translators, Moffat exerted control over African cultures through the manipulation of language in the production of his texts—even as he might have claimed that the Scriptures themselves were directing his work. But choosing the right word for a translation of Scripture has often had the double effect of promoting "Christian culture" and degrading "native cultures." John and Jean Comaroff (1991, 218), for example, tell us that Moffat used the word *badimo* (in Setswana, ancestors) for *demons* in his translation of Matthew (see also Dube 1999). This has added an indelible negative cast to the word, suggesting an association between "traditional culture" and that which is evil. Ultimately, Moffat "transpose[d] the Bible into a cultural register true to neither [Setswana nor English], a hybrid creation born of the colonial encounter itself" (Comaroff and Comaroff 1991, 218). What Bernard Cohn has argued in his work on the East India Company and British colonization of India holds true in this context as well: like men of commerce and colonial government, missionaries were "invading an epistemological space" and "could explore and conquer this space through translation" (1985, 325; see also Fabian 1986). The "invasion" was also an opening—the creation of something new and not wholly owned by either colonizer or colonized.

Moffat believed that the best way to instill the message of mission was through schooling. In southern Africa preaching was (and still is) a fundamental medium for spreading the Word of God. Hastings has said that what the first missionaries needed "was a good deal of knowledge of the Bible, a great deal of faith, and a strong voice" (1994, 258). As I highlight in later chapters, the spoken word is still alive and well in Africa—and even in the most devout "Bible-thumping" churches. It would be misrepresentative of the character of African Christian faiths to suggest otherwise. But Moffat recognized that "'public preaching in a foreign tongue' was far less compelling than were 'private methods' of conveying the truths of the gospel. And, sure enough, systematic education, with a heavy emphasis on the schoolroom, would replace preaching . . . as the primary medium of moral and intellectual reform" (Comaroff and Comaroff 1997, 72). To this end he established a school at Kuruman, through which he could work toward his ultimate goal—"spreading the Bible to previously illiterate [sic] people, thereby influencing the minds of all men" (Bradlow 1987, 7).

Moffat made regular trips from Kuruman to evangelize in outlying areas. The most famous of these were to see the Ndebele king, Mzilikazi. Between 1830 and 1860 Moffat visited Mzilikazi five times. On the final trip in 1860 he established the LMS station at Inyati, near present-day Bulawayo, with Mzilikazi's support. Moffat's relationship with Mzilikazi is captured from Moffat's perspective in his *Matabele Journals*. He paints a portrait typical for his day of the missionary as hero, layering contrasting images of hardship, boredom, and routine with perseverance, discovery, and evangelical success. Moffat's portrayals of Mzilikazi give us a sense of the ways in which African political figures were beginning to understand the power of the written word and help us to anticipate African responses to the impulse of colonial mission.

In one episode from the third journey, Moffat gives us a sense of how missionaries had managed to reinforce—unwittingly, he seems to think—the idea that writing in itself was an act of God, always associated with the Christian faith:

> Moselekatse [Mzilikazi] sat a considerable time today in my bed with his back to the front of the waggon. He appeared busy looking into the books which lay beside him. Among these were the Bible, Kitto's *Cyclopedia of Biblical Literature* and some numbers of the *Eclectic Review* [a Non-Conformist periodical]. He admits I am wise and has heard that [I] get my wisdom from books. I suppose he was trying his hand to pick up a little. He turned over many a leaf, and the result of his researches was the picture of a parasol in one of the advertising pages of the *Eclectic*. He seemed quite proud that he had found something that he knew; for he had seen an umbrella before. He places all the books he sees in my possession in the category of God's writings, and even when he happens to see me writing my journal he tells those nearest to him that I am at God's writing. As I am a teacher of God he concludes that everything I do in that way must have reference to God. (Moffat 1945a, 278)

Mzilikazi's employment of a "reverse anthropology" (Wagner 1981; see also Guss 1986) is not far off the mark in terms of the book's symbolic capital. It reinforces a more general point I have been stressing: by 1854, when Moffat's third journey was undertaken, there was an intimate association between God's Word and the materiality of books. That Mzilikazi understood the Bible in these terms is testimony to his political acumen, if not his religious interests. Like an increasing number of Africans, Mzilikzai was beginning to recognize written texts as indexes of political and religious power.

On the fourth journey, in 1857, Moffat reinforces Mzilikazi's point that writing and religion should be always already connected. "He had often wondered why I was frequently found looking on a book," Moffat writes. "I said that I had had very little time to do so on this visit, but when I did, it was to get instruction, for though old, I was still learning the things of God and my duty to Him" (1945b, 128). Moffat does not specify which book, or books, he could be "frequently found looking on." He did not have to. The Bible was among them; it was the elemental, unmarked text, the presence of which could be assumed. In the same journal entry

Moffat returns to the impact of the text on Mzilikazi's worldview, this time in relation to its political possibilities. Moffat had failed to visit the nearby groups of Shona-speaking peoples, who suffered at the hands of Mzilikazi's men in attacks and raids. In the journal Moffat intimates that Mzilikazi was coming to understand something of the old adage, "the pen is mightier than the sword," as if he were afraid that Moffat would expose the injustices done to the Shona peoples by writing about them for others to read—by making them objects of knowledge that could be circulated beyond their originary contexts. Moffat writes:

> I expressed my regret, as I had done before, that I had not had an opportunity of visiting a village of the Mashona tribe. [Mzilikazi] tried again to put me off with evasive answers—they were not men worth seeing, they drove away their women from them, etc.—most palpable falsehoods. I replied that I did not care what they did. I only wished to see them in their native towns. He replied, "But you write everything you see and hear." I thought to myself, "the pen and the press, what terrors these are to tyrants!" (Moffat 1945b, 129)

Over fifty years of mission work, Moffat's vision of the political situation of African peoples vis-à-vis the British and the Boers changed considerably (S. de Gruchy 1999). If at times he felt frustrated in his work, sympathizing with those who recognized "the stupidity . . . of savages" (see Bradlow 1987, 3), his sense of Christian social justice placed him in an awkward spot between the colonial and the African. "No missionary . . ." Moffat wrote, "can with any show of Scripture or reason, refuse his pacific counsel and advice, when those among whom he labours require it, nor decline to become interpreter or translator to any foreign power, or to be the medium of hushing the din of war arising either from family interests or national claims" (1842, 207; see also S. de Gruchy 1999, 25). Moffat was well aware that Africans came increasingly to suffer at the hands of white settlers. Moffat, remember, showed sympathy for the Shona at the expense of his friend Mzilikazi. Mzilikazi did not learn to read, and he did not convert to Christianity, but he was astute enough to recognize that the circulation and control of texts would become an integral part of political and social life in the world of his children.

Disseminating the Bible and other texts in vernacular languages shaped local articulations of Christianity in unpredictable ways, a situation missionaries came to understand with greater clarity over the course of the nineteenth century. Venn and Moffat have been lauded primarily for their goals by church historians (if less so by anthropologists), but those who came after them began to disagree with their principles, feeling that vernacularization was leading African Christianity too far astray from European control. By 1900 Venn's CMS had become a different organization. Venn's desire for euthanasia of the mission "was no longer discussed" (Williams 1990, 229). In the last decades of the nineteenth century, the CMS came under the cóntrol of conservative Anglicans unsympathetic to Venn's ideals. Scandals in the Niger Mission, 1880–92, involving the alleged immorality of the native pastorate, fueled the impulses of these Anglican conservatives to wrest control from Africans. "As it was," Sanneh writes, the "CMS permitted the view to harden that Africans were as a race unfit to govern in the church, their lack of moral discipline being something of a natural blemish" (1989, 132).[11] In Moffat's case translating the Bible into Setswana became an unwitting "political decision" (S. de Gruchy 1999, 27) to give the Christian Tswana a sense of authority and legitimacy that made colonial and missionary establishments uncomfortable. Venn and Moffat embodied a tension for missionaries "between their universal humanism and their fear of the degradation of Christianity at the hands of 'others'" (Comaroff and Comaroff 1997, 87). As Sanneh puts it, "The real issue is whether missionaries could successfully perpetuate Victorian values where they also successfully promoted vernacular translation and the literacy that went with it" (1989, 5–6). The answer, I would argue, is no. Missionaries failed to account for an important fact: Africans might read the Bible differently. But to understand this point in any depth, I want to suggest, scholars of mission need also to consider the semiotic principles informing these practices of translation and education. Without due consideration of how the Bible was understood to function in these practices, we elide important questions about the agency invested in the mediums of missionization. Close attention to Venn and Moffat on the Bible suggests that any native agency was thought to be guided by a more powerful one—that the Bible itself was setting the terms of the mission encounter. Moffat's case also suggests that an approach guided by "the Bible, the whole Bible, and nothing but the Bible" was never entirely that. But in figures like Venn and Moffat we find the roots of Kambarami's assertion that the Bible can read people. We find the idea that as a sign the Bible is also a subject. I turn now to look at some African responses to mission and its mediums, men and women who took the Bible and its promises into their own hands, divorcing themselves from missionaries while staying wed to the Word of God.

SHEMBE AND LAKWENA: READING IN THE VERNACULAR

The "success" of missionaries such as Venn and Moffat in bringing the written word to Africans does not mean, of course, that Africans were everywhere reading—still less reading how the missionaries might have liked (Harries 2001; Hofmeyr 1994, 2004). Neither literacy nor Christianity moved as quickly as the influence of textual authority. I alluded to this in the discussion of Mzilikazi. It can be seen as well, from a different angle, in the story of Jim Ximungana, a Swiss Mission convert in Lourenço Marques who established a church and appointed as a preacher a man who did not believe in God but could in fact read (Harries 2001, 418–19). The Bible—and, by extension, all written texts—was identified as a source of power, bearing "the essence of white might" more readily than its role as an elementary reading primer. It is also clear from the historical record that "missionaries often misread any interest in literacy as a sign of religious feeling and a commitment to the values of the mission world" (Hofmeyr 1994, 49). Just as often, it was for the social and political benefits it might bring.

Learning to read in the early days of mission work in any case often entailed disenchantment with the missionary. As I mentioned in the introduction, during my fieldwork, I was told that when Africans first learned to read they picked up the Bible and discovered that missionaries had been lying about a number of things. Polygamy, for instance, has been defended countless times by recourse to the Old Testament, pace Henry Venn. In 1869 David Rood, of the American Missionary Board in South Africa, wrote:

> Native Christians when conversing upon religious topics are I think too apt to let the habit and love of discussion interfere with the simple love to know the truth. I have often noticed this with feelings of regret in the adult classes in the Sunday school. . . . Take such questions as polygamy or the demanding of cattle for daughters when given in marriage, they will go back to the Old Testament history, to Jacob and others, and they will say that they find these customs were approved by God and nowhere in the Bible do they find them forbidden, and they will argue with zeal and boldness. (Quoted in Etherington 1978, 157)

And these were not the only African rereadings:

> With the help of vernacular Scriptures, for example, Zulu Christians
> found sanction for their habit of dressing in skins (Gen. 3:21), and began
> to criticize missionaries for not being properly dressed according to the
> Scriptures. The same criticism was voiced with regard to church services,
> with Africans insisting that missionary churches were unfaithful to the
> Scriptures, which call for dancing and music in worship and praise (Judg.
> 11:35; 1 Sam. 18:6; 2 Sam. 6:14; Ps. 149:3; 1 Chron. 15:16; Lk. 7:32, 15:25;
> Matt. 11:17). As for the custom of singing, Africans found in Scriptures a
> stream in full spate. (Sanneh 1989, 176)

These alternative readings of the Bible and of Christianity inspired a number of African visionaries to take matters into their own hands. "Far from literacy domesticating the savage mind, in many cases its power was appropriated, harnessed, and yoked" (Harries 2001, 417; cf. Goody 1977). Many, such as Mzilikazi and Jim Ximungana, seemed to have little interest in Christianity for itself. But there were an increasing number of Africans who took the missionary message seriously, many of whom became influential Christian prophets and mediums in the newly emerging independent churches.

In many countries, such as Ghana and Zimbabwe, the number of Christians in independent churches matches or exceeds those in the mission churches. I would like to focus the discussion here on two such groups—to fill out the narrative of the Bible's various influences in Africa but also to provide points of comparison for the later, more extensive discussions of the Masowe apostolics. The first example is the Nazarite Baptist Church (NBC) of South Africa, founded in 1910 by the prophet Isaiah Shembe and today having close to one million members. The second is the Holy Spirit Movement (HSM), a much smaller movement led by Alice Lakwena, an Acholi woman in Uganda, that existed for just a short time in the mid-1980s. In the spectrum of Christian independency these movements stand at significant remove from one another. In each, however, the written word has played a central role. Shembe and Alice suggest the way in which Africans have seized on the idea of the Bible as an object with living energy, which as such can be disembedded from the missionary's vision of Christianity.

Isaiah Shembe, a semiliterate, made his living as a wandering preacher and healer. Until 1979, when the Nazarite Baptist Church split over a leadership struggle, it was based at a site called Ekuphakameni (Elevated Place) on the eastern coast of South Africa near the city of Durban. The "loyal" followers of Shembe now congregate at Ebuhleni (Place of Splendor) close to the original headquarters, following a line of leaders descended directly from him. Shembe's teachings have attracted large numbers of women, a phenomenon that other scholars of religion have discussed in their work on African independent churches (see, e.g., Hoehler-Fatton 1996; Mukonyora 1998a). Ekuphakameni became a "place of spiritual and economic refuge for widows, orphans, and those women previously in polygamous marriages whose husbands had converted to mission Christianity" (Muller 1999, xix). The NBC provided a space for those disenfranchised by the competing forces of mission, the state, and "tradition" in the colonial encounter, constituting itself as an alternative "site of bureaucratic power" (Muller 1999, 47).

There is a large academic literature on Shembe and the NBC (Brown 1995; Gunner 1979, 1988; Kiernan 1992a; Muller 1997, 1999). The church has also produced a large body of its own primary texts (see Gunner 2002). For all of that, I want to focus here on the tension Shembe created between the authority of the written and the spoken word, a "complex coexistence" (Gunner 1988, 204) that characterizes Christianity generally.

Shembe did not set out to establish a religious community, but he attracted such a devoted following that he bought the land for Ekuphakameni (with money donated by the people he healed) sometime around 1915.[12] The growth of Shembe's church follows a pattern typical in Christian independency. At Ekuphakameni, after a five-year period of wandering, Shembe established a religious regime framed by a number of concerns: (1) the emerging market economy and growing importance of mission work as exemplified by the influence of writing; (2) the continuing importance of "traditional" rites of passage in the constitution of social life; and (3) the developing culture of African townships, in which traditional and modern lifeways were reworked in secular form. Shembe, then, drew from a range of cultural registers to express his message: "Isaiah's mission was to preach the word of God, as he found it in the mission Bible, to traditional peoples, whom western missionaries had had little success in convincing. Shembe believed that these people could be converted to Christianity and still retain their own cultural ways, many of which were reflected in the Old Testament" (Muller 1999, 25). In this he was perhaps not so different in intent from Henry Venn, although Shembe drew little support from white communities. What backed him in his Christian efforts was the Bible.

Muller argues that "the quintessential issue to which colonial history in South Africa may be reduced, is the contest between the power embedded in the written over the performed or enacted word" (1997, 3). Early on, Shembe recognized ways in which the Zulu Bible could be used to establish his authority at the expense of the white missionaries. "Power, Shembe realized, resided in and with the written word" (Gunner 1988, 204). He drew on narratives in the Old and New Testaments to build a mythic image of the church. He spoke of his followers as Israelites, suffering at the hands of an oppressive regime. He also drew comparisons between the persecution of early Christian communities and his own, citing chapter and verse from the Gospels to reinforce the claim. In this way Shembe was able to build up a "collective consciousness saturated in Biblical mythology" (Muller 1999, 233). Not unlike the CMS in West Africa, Shembe took the Bible as the "supreme paradigmatic history" (Peel 1995, 395). Stressing the similarities between Nguni cultural practices and those in the Old Testament (polygamy chief among them), "Shembe's community 'proved' that in many ways, they were more faithful followers of the Word of God as contained in the Holy Bible than white Christians were" (Muller 1999, 48). Shembe was facilitating the proper functioning of the Bible as a manifestation of the divine.

The influence of the written word is also evident in Nazarite ritual life. At commemorations of the NBC's founding each March, members tell origin stories. One year a woman addressed her audience to explain how at the founding of the church, in March 1910, a star appeared in the sky (see Muller 1999, 69–71). She went on to explain that Shembe interpreted its appearance after hearing a "voice from heaven" and closed her lesson by encouraging Christians to read from certain books in the Bible that paralleled her own. Muller argues that such large-scale public commemorations are part of "a religious discourse deeply embedded in an array of expressive culture . . . and all authenticated through parallel evidence found in the missionary's Bible" (1999, 71).

Women's religious attire has also become a powerful repertoire of signs, both iconic and indexical. According to Muller, "Women have transferred the power and value attached to a central tenet of mission Christian ideology—that Truth is contained in the written word—onto traditional Zulu ritual performance and attire" (1997, 4). The beads women wear, for instance, are referred to as a kind of "writing" that can be "read," based on their configuration, to determine the status of a certain woman's spiritual relationship with Shembe. More generally, women associate their ritual performances—many of which involve strenuous all-night activities, strict taboos, and sacrificing one's duties as a wife and mother—with doing "good deeds" in the name of God. If a woman performs a ritual well, if she lives up to the expectations of a "true" Christian, she is said to be "writing her name in the book of life" (Muller 1999, 119, 184)—or ensuring entry to heaven. For the women of the church, some of whom are illiterate, this is a tangible sense in which they can harness the power of the written word.[13] These performances produce "a discourse of cultural truth equivalent to the value of the written word" (Muller 1999, 231). The implications of this reversal—from text to performance—are important to note. In this example, the binary opposition between the written and the spoken word breaks down through the play of signs in ritual action. Despite the central role of the Bible as an authorizing presence, "Shembe provides a belief system that emphasizes the experiential and visual rather than written evidence" (Muller 1999, 232). The written word is pressed into service through ritual life. Its presence is marked through other tangible signs, to which it has been connected. The beads women wear and the rituals they perform point back to the Bible.

Alice Lakwena's Holy Spirit Movement could hardly be more different from the Nazarite Baptist Church. The movement was short-lived and itinerant; its members promoted violence in pursuit of their goals; it was run by a woman. Like the NBC, however, the HSM capitalized in a number of ways on the power of the written word, a strategy its members recognized as quintessentially Christian.

The story of the HSM reinforces the elementary lesson in social scientific work that religion is never free from the push and pull of social and political life. Alice's movement arose from tensions in the Ugandan civil war in the mid-1980s. The civil war broke out after the Uganda National Liberation Army (UNLA) deposed the infamous tyrant Idi Amin, and Milton Obote, Uganda's onetime president, returned to power. Shortly thereafter Yoweri Museveni challenged Obote's rule. Obote fueled ethnic tensions in the UNLA (the national army) between his own Langi people and the Acholi. This led to an internal coup in which the Acholi, under Bazilio and Tito Okello, toppled Obote and took control of the state in the Ugandan capital, Kampala. This infighting, however, weakened the UNLA to the point that it could not defend Kampala against Museveni's National Resistance Army (NRA). In January 1986 the NRA, under Museveni, took control of state reins, forcing the short-lived Acholi elite out of power. In August 1986 an Acholi woman named Alice Auma declared that she was possessed by a Christian spirit called Lakwena. "She announced in the Acholi language . . . that the spirit Lakwena was fighting to depose the Museveni government and unite all the people in Uganda. She said that . . . she was here to proclaim the word of the holy spirit" (Behrend 1999, 3).[14]

Behrend ties the rise of Alice Lakwena to the misfortune Acholis suffered after their defeat by Museveni. The Acholi became marginalized in national politics. Acholi soldiers were tortured; those who returned to their homes in northern Uganda became "internal strangers" (Behrend 1999, 24; cf. Werbner 1989b, 239). These new "strangers" challenged the authority of the Acholi elders on the strength of their service as soldiers for the nation. The soldiers blamed the elders for their dislocation, appealing to the discourse of witchcraft to explain the Acholi's misfortune. The elders saw the returning soldiers as the source of the Acholi's problems and appealed to ritual proscriptions in an effort to reintegrate the war veterans. According to the elders, the soldiers had not undergone the proper rituals of purification (guns made warfare too indiscriminate) so the spirits of the people they killed in the civil war "tried to avenge themselves on the soldiers or their relatives" (Behrend 1999, 29). Modern warfare had given "tradition" more bite, and the Acholi were suffering for it. The Acholi needed "to establish a new discourse and new practices, in order to dissolve the vicious cycle and put an end to the evil" (Behrend 1999, 30). In her effort to resolve the tensions Alice was drawn to Christianity.

There is sensationalism in the story of the HSM: its woman-warrior leader, the active role of more than 140,000 spirits in their mission to topple Museveni (including a spirit of the kung fu star Bruce Lee), the belief that soldiers rubbed in shea butter were bullet-proof, and accusations against the HSM of murder, rape, and looting on the road to Kampala. According to Tim Allen, Alice "became an international celebrity for a time" (1991, 370), especially in the United Kingdom, where her campaign was chronicled in the newspapers. Yet what interests me here and what Behrend documents so well is Alice's emphasis on the importance of texts for carrying out her mission, in particular, the use of the Bible to establish her authority. Behrend notes, for example, that the HSM was adept at using the media to spread their message; in the initial proclamation of her apotheosis, in fact, Alice "demanded balanced reporting" (1999, 3) from the local and international press (see also Allen 1991, 395). Behrend goes on to catalog the numerous ways in which the written word was used:

Alice and the Holy Spirit soldiers were aware of the power of the mass media, and tried to build up a counterforce to meet it by setting up a Department of Information and Publicity within the HSM. It produced leaflets giving information on the goals of the movement, distributed them among the populace, wrote letters to chiefs and politicians, and also collected information. A radio set was available and a photographer took pictures of prisoners of war, visitors, captured weapons, and rituals. The Holy Spirit soldiers wrote their own texts. They kept diaries; the commanders and heads of the Frontline Co-ordination Team (FCT) drew up lists of casualties, recruitments, and gifts from civilians; they kept minutes of meetings and composed reports on the individual battles. And the chief clerk, Alice's secretary, wrote down what the spirits had to say when they took possession of Alice, their medium. Individual soldiers also noted in school notebooks the twenty Holy Spirit Safety Precautions, rules the spirits imposed on them, as well as prayers and church hymns. And pharmacists, nurses, and paramedics noted the formulas for various medications invented by the spirit Lakwena. (Behrend 1999, 3–4)

The HSM did all this, Behrend argues, as "an act of self-assertion, an attempt to have their truth, their version of the story prevail against others" (1999, 4). Behind the spirits, the written word provided a sense of security; with important items such as the Holy Spirit Safety Precautions written down, there was no excuse for failure. The HSM asserted its authority through the creation and circulation of its texts, which were the assurance of their Christian authenticity.[15]

Alice Auma was born in 1956, the daughter of a catechist in the Anglican Church. In 1948 her father, Severino Lukoya, heard the voice of God while reading a passage from the Book of Isaiah. "God shone a bright light on the open pages of the Bible" (Behrend 1999, 130) and told Severino that he would get married, have many children, and prosper in the church. Severino married Iberina Ayaa. But he became selfish and quickly forgot all that God had done for him. According to one version of the story, one day his wife beat him unconscious. His spirit went to heaven. He saw Jesus with an open book containing all the names of the people on earth. Next to Severino's name the word *love* was written. Jesus took him to God, then to Abraham, David, and Moses. It was decided Severino should live. Before returning to earth, Moses gave Severino a book with the Ten Commandments. Severino was then filled with a number of holy spirits that told him one day they would come to earth and possess his child (Behrend 1999, 130–31). This divine sanction became part of the myth surrounding

Alice; she was Severino's chosen child. The Bible and other holy texts—Jesus' book, Moses' Ten Commandments—grounded her authority before she was even born. As permanent markers of truth, they stood in her stead until the day she became Alice Lakwena to realize their promise.

Lakwena is the name of the spirit of an Italian army captain who died in World War II. He stood at the head of the army of 140,000 holy spirits there to aid Alice and the Acholi in the overthrow of Museveni's government. The HSM's military strategy was simple, and allowed a way around the ritual prohibitions that concerned the Acholi elders. As is often the case in possession (Boddy 1989; Lambek 1981; Lan 1985), in the HSM spirits held agency over the people through whom they worked. "The power of spirits is always borrowed, an alien power; it is granted at the cost of denying oneself" (Behrend 1999, 139). When the soldiers of the HSM went to war, then, it was not they who were fighting but the spirits. In this way Alice's army was able to "wage war without killing" (Behrend 1999, 141) and thus work around rituals of purification that had, in the civil war, proved the Acholi's demise.

The spirit Lakwena was the realization of God's promise to Severino, but even after his arrival the Bible and the written word were accorded prominent places in the expression of HSM Christianity. Behrend suggests that reading and writing were "essentially connected" (1999, 115) with the Acholi understanding of Christian faith. She cites J. K. Russell, according to whom Acholi speakers referred to European missionaries as "readers" (see also Sugirtharajah 2001, 69). As a Christian movement, then, the HSM would always need the inspiration of the text alongside the influence of the holy spirits. Alice stressed "education as the path to salvation and a better world" (Behrend 1999, 157). Positions of leadership in the movement were held by the most educated individuals. For the soldiers, "the Bible became the sign of special status" (Behrend 1999, 157). It had been "the key to the Europeans' power" because "missionaries placed the Book of Books, the Bible, at the centre of their teaching" (Behrend 1999, 148). Now it was to help the HSM overthrow Museveni.

The HSM was soundly defeated by government troops in October 1987, just over a year after Alice took up Lakwena's call to arms. Alice went into hiding in Kenya; today her whereabouts are unknown.[16] She blamed the failure of the movement on the inability of her soldiers to respect the rules the Holy Spirit had set down in the Holy Spirit Safety Precautions—a document every member had access to and which most carried in their school notebooks. The written word may have made the rules clear, and it may have been the key to Christian power. But, as for her missionary forebears, the "fixed text" provided Alice no guarantees.

Independent churches and religious movements in Africa have taken up the text in unpredicted ways. The Nazarite Baptist Church and the Holy Spirit Movement are just two examples. Shembe and Alice did not reproduce Christianities that fit within a missionary mold. All the same, they wrestled with making sense of the Bible's significance in a manner related to some of the dominant evangelical paradigms. Shembe saw himself as giving proper voice to Scripture; Alice expected her movement to be protected by it. For each, then, it was (re)invested as a sign with "living energy." In an unexpected rendering of Isaac Hughes's opinion, it could "speak for itself." The difference between the Victorian missionary and the African visionary is what each heard when it did so.

TUTU, BANANA, AND THE THEOLOGIES OF CRITIQUE

In a postcolonial world where there are more Anglicans in Uganda than in the United Kingdom (Isichei 1995, 1), it cannot be said that "mainstream" religious practice or theology is defined in Western metropoles (Gibellini 1994; West and Dube 2000). "Native agency" is alive and well in what Venn might characterize as a bittersweet victory. And with it, there are struggles over the Bible's qualities as a sign.

The "native agents" I want to discuss are Desmond Tutu and Canaan Banana. Each has expressed strong views about the role of the Bible in Christianity and in African life. Their positions diverge in nearly all respects, but each reaffirms in his own way the centrality of the written word.

Desmond Tutu was born in Klerksdorp, South Africa, in 1931. He was awarded the Nobel Peace Prize in 1984 for his struggles against apartheid. As a young man he trained at a teacher's college and taught in Johannesburg and Krugersdorp before joining the ministry. He was ordained an Anglican priest in 1961 and held a number of positions in the church until his retirement in 1996, including bishop of Lesotho, dean and then bishop of Johannesburg, and archbishop of Cape Town. On a number of occasions throughout his career Tutu has referred to the Bible as the pathway to both deliverance and racial equality in South Africa.[17]

Tutu often tells a story in his speeches and interviews that is popular in South Africa. It goes like this. When the white man came to Africa, he held the Bible in his hand and Africans held the land. The white man said to the Africans, "Let us bow our heads in prayer." When the Africans raised their heads, the white man had the land and the Africans had the Bible. According to the theologian Takatso Mofokeng:

> With this statement, which is known by young and old in South Africa, black people of South Africa, point to three dialectically related realities. They show the central position which the Bible occupies in the ongoing process of colonization, national oppression and exploitation. They also confess the incomprehensible paradox of being colonized by a Christian people and yet being converted to their religion and accepting their Bible, their ideological instrument of colonization, oppression and exploitation. Thirdly, they express a historic commitment that is accepted solemnly by one generation and passed on to another—a commitment to terminate exploitation of humans by other humans. (Quoted in West 2000, 30; see also Engelke 2003, 297)

Throughout his career in the Anglican Church and as chair of the Truth and Reconciliation Commission, Desmond Tutu has been committed to building a South African society based on equal rights and, more generally, the termination of exploitation. But in the meantime he often seems to suggest that in the original transaction with the white man, Africans got the better half of the deal. Just as Mofokeng emphasizes the paradox of liberation-subjugation, Tutu suggests that the Bible contains the key to its own resolution. For Tutu, the paradox is resolved by a turning inward: "This reflection on the Bible is determined by his conviction that liberation is its central theme, its hermeneutical key" (Draper 1996, 222).[18]

Tutu's stance on the Bible can be seen in most of his interactions with the apartheid state. In 1982, for example, Tutu was asked to give testimony before the Eloff Commission, a state-run body established by South African Prime Minister P. W. Botha to investigate the affairs of the South African Council of Churches (SACC), which the government had recognized as an "internal enemy" (Allen 1994, 53). Tutu was general secretary of the SACC at the time. In his statement to the Commission, he began thus: "My purpose is to demonstrate from the scriptures and from hallowed Christian tradition and teaching that what we are as the South African Council of Churches, what we say and what we do, all of these are determined not by politics or any other ideology. We are what we are in obedience to God and in response to the gracious Gospel of his Son our Lord and Saviour Jesus Christ" (1994, 54).

Tutu's strategy was to suggest that as a Christian institution the SACC was not a political body but a religious one and that as such it could not be construed as an "internal enemy" of the state, particularly "by a government which claims to be Christian" (Tutu 1994, 55). He went on: "If anyone were to show me that apartheid is biblical or Christian, I have said before, and I reiterate now, that I would burn my Bible and cease to be a Christian. I will want to show that the Christian Bible and the Gospel of Jesus Christ our Lord is subversive of all injustice and evil" (1994, 56). Tutu's vision of Christianity is not, then, apolitical. As he has said elsewhere, "The God we worship is not a God that is neutral" (Tutu 1994, 158). But the standard against which Tutu measures his "political" activism is set by the Bible.[19] Embodied in a sacred text, the standard is universal. "So," Tutu says, "the Christian must always be critical of all political standards, always testing them against Gospel standards" (1982, 10). In his Eloff testimony he works to resolve the paradox of colonial mission: "The Bible is the most revolutionary, the most radical book there is. If a book had to be banned by those who rule unjustly and as tyrants, then it ought to have been the Bible. *Whites brought us the Bible and we are taking it seriously*" (Tutu 1994, 72; emphasis added).

Six years later Tutu reiterated his claims in a letter to Botha after a turbulent meeting between the two at Botha's offices in Cape Town. The meeting was set up to discuss the sentencing of the "Sharpeville Six," a group of men convicted of murdering a Sharpeville town councillor in 1984. As Tutu left the meeting Botha handed him a letter asking if he and other church leaders answered to God or to political parties, such as the African National Congress or the South African Communist Party. In his reply Tutu said that he was not associated with any political party—that he was a Christian, political only insofar as Christianity was a religion that supported social justice and racial equality. He turned to the Bible for proof: "My theological position derives from the Bible and the teachings of the church. The Bible and the church predate Marxism and the ANC by several centuries" (1994, 147). He then went on to cite passages from 1 Kings 21 and 2 Samuel 12 to reinforce his claim, concluding:

This kind of involvement of religion with politics and the habit of religious leaders to speak to the sociopolitical and economic situation can be attested to as standard practice in the Bible, which provides our mandate and paradigm.

Our marching orders come from Christ himself and not from any human being. Our mandate is provided by the Bible and the teaching of the church, not by any political group or ideology, Marxist or otherwise. (1994, 150)

For Desmond Tutu, the Bible holds the key to both personal salvation and social justice. His arguments are based on a certain Christian lesson—that the Bible transcends culture, that it is bound by neither language nor party politics, and that it sets a universal standard of truth to which all peoples have access. Tutu reads the Bible in this manner as an act of total liberation. So confident is he, so certain that the Bible makes this significa-tion, that he would gladly send it up in smoke if anyone could prove him wrong, if anyone could prove that the Bible is not what he knows it to be.

The late Reverend Canaan Banana had a different take on the power of Scripture, one more closely informed by his understanding of this-worldly politics than Tutu would countenance. Banana was born in Essexvale, Southern Rhodesia, in 1936 and was trained as a Methodist theologian. Throughout the heyday of African nationalism and into Zimbabwe's war of liberation Banana held a number of church and political party posi-tions, including membership on the advisory committee of the World Council of Churches and vice president of the African National Council. In 1977, after serving two prison sentences in Rhodesia for his anticolonial activities, he joined the Zimbabwe African National Union, the earlier incarnation of Mugabe's ZANU(PF). On Zimbabwe's independence, in April 1980, Banana served as the country's president, a position he held until 1987. Although the presidency was at the time a ceremonial post, his appointment was a kind of vindication of his conviction that church and state could freely mix. In his reflections on the role of the church in Zimbabwe's liberation struggle, Banana had little patience for what he saw as the Christian disengagement from the political process: "The Church chose to engage in the theology of silence rather than that of combat, and dialogue at an inappropriate time instead of confrontation. Their theology focused mainly on survival, rather than redemption, and apology rather than protest" (1989, 203).

Banana is less well known on the international stage than Tutu, but in southern Africa he has attracted controversial attention on more than one occasion both before and after Zimbabwe's independence. One of these episodes involved his opinion as a theologian on the role of the Bible in Christian life. In April 1991, while serving as honorary professor of religious studies at the University of Zimbabwe, Banana gave a paper in which he argued for the need to "rewrite" the Bible.

Banana based his arguments on the role of historical contingencies rather than divine plans. He reminded his audience that the canonical texts of the Christian Bible are the product of human decisions—that the books of the New Testament were decided on in the late fourth century in church councils. This suggested to Banana that the Bible should be understood as a tool rather than a foundation of faith. What matters above all is faith in Christ, not faith in a book: "Jesus Christ is not a product of the Bible. He existed before the Bible; the Bible is a product of Jesus Christ. It is a document that tells us about Jesus' life and his saving grace. Let us not forget that most of what Jesus said and did is not recorded in the Bible. The Bible is but a bird's eye view of the life of a great man" (1993, 27). This claim in itself would not necessarily cause alarm throughout the Christian world—even in churches driven by what Sugirtharajah calls scriptural imperialism. Tutu, for example, has always stressed church teachings alongside Scripture in his arguments against apartheid. But Banana goes on to a conclusion that is less well received and in many ways the antithesis of Tutu's:

> Christian church history is a saga of exploitation in the name of Christ, from the subjugation of the European tribes, the crusades to redeem the Holy Land from the infidel, to the subjugation and exploitation of native people in the "new world," to the colonisation of Africa in the great mission thrusts of western civilisation. This history is long, sordid, and deeply sad: the result of the use of the Bible as a justification for exploitation; the self-serving adoption of one group as "superior" to another. In other words, it can be argued that the ideology of racism has its genesis in the Bible. (Banana 1993, 21–22)

And so where Tutu finds a central theme of liberation, Banana finds a template for exploitation. In 1994, just three years after Banana's proclamations, almost one million Tutsis were killed in Rwanda, in a genocide that several anthropologists have argued was set in part within the mythic framework of the Hamitic hypothesis (Mamdani 2001; Taylor 1999). This hypothesis was promoted during the era of colonial rule to naturalize the differences between Hutu and Tutsi, marking the latter as "white" and thus superior to the former. Through a specious reading of Genesis 5, the Tutsi were cast as the children of Ham and therefore descended from Noah. While once considered accursed, the Hamites in this new colonial reading became privileged vis-à-vis the Hutu, who fell outside the biblical genealogy. The Tutsi were "African Caucasians[,] . . . [t]he great civilizers of Africa" (Mamdani 2001, 86). This was used to explain the existence of the Rwandan kingdom—because Africans were thought not to be able to have developed such an "advanced" political system. It also justified the Belgians' preferential treatment of the Tutsi vis-à-vis the Hutu and the Twa. In 1994 Hutu extremists in the *interahamwe* (lit. "work party" but understood as "genocide") used this difference as the chief justification for purging the Rwandan nation of Tutsi: the Tutsi were outsiders who needed to be got rid of. Christopher Taylor is unequivocal on this point: "One of the reasons why people in this area of the world have killed their compatriots by the hundreds of thousands is because of the enduring psychological damage that has been done to them by the Hamitic hypothesis" (1999, 92). Had it happened before his call to rewrite the Bible, Banana likely would have used the Rwandan genocide as another case in point for the corrupted state of the book.

Banana derides the Christian text. But it is important to note that his proposal is for the Bible to be rewritten—not abandoned. His criticism is not of the written word per se but the ways in which a particular text has been abused by historical actors. The Bible as it stands is too far gone. What we need now, according to Banana, is "a more universal Bible," one free from "culture-specific world views" (1993, 17, 30).

Banana has no faith in the Bible as we know it, but he makes clear his conviction that the written word has the potential to foster a more responsible version of Christianity. He wants to "liberate the Bible" from itself, to transform it into a document that can serve as "a unifying element that will help our world to set aside our differences and to learn to live together" (1993, 17, 29). This is a profound and simultaneously perverse confirmation of the message that nineteenth-century Protestant evangelicals worked so hard to instill: in Banana's theology, the written word is a privileged medium. What Banana suggests is that the Bible has an essence and is, in that essence, Truth itself. He expresses doubt that the Bible in circulation today is authentic. What we have been reading is a corrupted version of the Truth, and so the Truth must be re-presented.

That the Bible has been used to justify projects of political and racial domination is a point that Tutu also accepts; he was frequently critical of the Dutch Reformed Church's reading of Scripture as a justification for apartheid. But Banana writes as if hermeneutics, liberation theology, or any number of other traditions that might provide a way out of the "ideology of racism" never existed. His theology has the character of a fundamentalism but a fundamentalism without its proper text. There is, for Banana, a correct way to read the Bible, a just way to read the Bible—only the Bible in question does not exist. Once it does we will be able to "learn to live together" in accord with divine intention. But we cannot read the Truth until its Book is rewritten.

Banana's theology is riddled with holes and contradictions, but it brings us back to the overarching theme of this chapter. Banana's argument reinforces the centrality of a concern for presence in the written word. His association between "Truth" and the Bible, as if the two terms are synonymous, as if there were a Bible-behind-the-Bible, is an idea that frames the chapters that follow. I have already broached this in the introduction. Nzira was at pains to make clear that there is a "true Bible" present in Masowe weChishanu services and that the physical one can be used instead as toilet paper. Having presented several ideas about the significance of the text in Christianity, what remains is to provide some provisional conclusions before turning to the more detailed investigation of the Friday apostolics.

V. Y. Mudimbe has argued that missionaries are "the best symbol of the colonial enterprise" (1988, 47; see also Peel 2000, 317). This echoes Beidelman's observation that "missionaries may be considered the most ambitious and culturally persuasive of all colonialists, attempting social change and domination in their most radical form" (1981, 74). Reading what missionaries such as Venn and Moffat have written, it becomes clear that from their points of view any such projects of social change were not due to them alone but to the books they carried. In their versions of the Christian message—reconfirmed by Kambarami—the Bible is presented as a force unto itself, an agent in the mission fields. When Kambarami says "the Bible reads people" he is making a claim about the object's agency that resonates throughout the portraits presented here. The agency of the Bible permits it a "status of *being* rather than *representing*" (Drucker 1994, 10). And in any such semiotic ideology, that which "is" can move independently of those who put it into circulation. This independence opens onto the possibility of other modes of signification—from those who challenge the status quo, such as Shembe and Alice, to those who occupy positions of authority in erstwhile colonial institutions, such as Tutu and Banana, and wrestle with the transcendent nature of the Word and the instrumental potentials of the written text.

Throughout this chapter I have referred to the unexpected and unforeseen ways in which Africans have taken up the Bible. In doing so, I hope to have shown that there is no such thing as "simple reading" and that the materiality of the Word provides nothing more than an assertion of stable meaning. The portraits here support Nicholas Thomas's point that we cannot take "the 'concrete and palpable' presence of a thing to attest to the reality of that which we have made it signify" (1991, 176). But there is a flip side to the unpredictability and open-endedness of reading. What unites the portraits is the presence of the Bible and the problem of presence in it. Whether it is smoked, burned, translated, performed, iconically represented, read, reread, or even rewritten, it is, in the end, *there;* something to be reckoned with. What is predictable, then, is that in each of the portraits the Bible's materiality is bound up with its significance. It is this materiality—this particular kind of presence—that the Friday apostolics want to consider anew.

TWO

The Early Days
of Johane Masowe

IN 1932 SHONIWA PETER MASEDZA was working for a shoemaker near Salisbury. Shoniwa had come from his home in Makoni, near the border with Portuguese East Africa, in the late 1920s. He had held a number of odd jobs in and around the capital: driving wagons, working as a "garden boy," apprenticing with a carpenter. Just after starting with the shoemaker, sometime around May 1932, Shoniwa fell ill, suffering from "severe pains in the head." He lost his speech for four months and was "unable to walk about." During his sickness, he studied the Bible "continuously." He dreamed that he had died, and in the dream he heard a voice saying he was now Johane Masowe—John of the Wilderness. After his recovery Johane went to a nearby hill called Marimba. He stayed there for forty days, praying to God "day and night" without sleep. He survived on wild honey. Johane was told by a voice, which he believed to be the voice of God, that he had been "sent from Heaven to carry out religious work among the natives." He was told also that Africans must burn their witchcraft medicines and must not commit adultery or rape. After these experiences, Johane no longer suffered from pains in the head.[1]

This narrative of events was related by Shoniwa-Johane to an officer in the Criminal Investigation Department of the British South Africa Police on November 1, 1932. The officer who recorded Shoniwa's testament was interested above all in whether Johane's activities were of a politically subversive nature. The Southern Rhodesian government had an ongoing concern that Africans like this, whom they called "pseudoreligious" or "separatist" figures, might disrupt the political order. In the statement Johane also said that while he hoped in the future to gain acceptance from the Roman Catholic Church, at the time he was not connected with "any other Society but [his] own." The chief native commissioner, C. L. Carbutt, wrote to the premier of Native Affairs the following day that this man, "Shoniwa alias Johane," seemed "quiet and respectful" but should nevertheless be watched closely as he would no doubt "succumb to the temptation of indulging in inflammatory addresses in order to maintain his notoriety."[2] Just what the tenets of Johane's "Society" were remained to be seen, so Carbutt kept a close eye on this new character.

Over the next two years Johane was arrested on at least three occasions, for each of which he served time in prison. He was referred to as everything from an itinerant preacher who did "nothing pernicious" to a "dangerous" charlatan who might threaten the "stability of the state."[3] Depending on the circumstances, Johane would present himself in different lights; by 1934 it was an increasingly negative light in the opinion of the colonial government. The archival records in Zimbabwe and rich scholarship make it clear that Johane and his followers caused confusion and consternation for the colonial regime, established mission churches, and Shona chiefs and headmen. But not enough attention has been paid to the fact that Masowe caused *himself* and his followers a good bit of confusion and consternation as well. If as early as November 1932 Johane was telling the authorities about his "Society," this was a hopeful claim. During the first two years of his preaching (roughly October 1932 to November 1934), Johane was in an ongoing process of articulating his religious message. He did not always know what to say or do, and it is evident from his movements that hearing the voice of God had not made his path clear. A Christian prophet, he nevertheless had to figure out what that meant. Johane was often filled with uncertainty as to how he might carry out his "religious work."

In this chapter I suggest that Johane's uncertainties are a manifestation of the problem of presence. I want to argue that it is often through uncertainty and doubt that a religious subject faces the question of God's remove. During his early days, Johane had an experience of the divine that created a sense of connection to God through the Holy Spirit. While the proximity was empowering and while it fostered, as I argue, certitude in his mission, there was an underlying uncertainty. The proximity to the divine that Johane enjoyed—and that was made possible for others through his coming—did not relieve the difficulties of communion. If here we have the paradigmatic case of a "live and direct" relationship with God, then we also have the first indications of how that relationship takes place in what Ricoeur has called the era of suspicion. In this chapter, then, we see how the problem of presence emerges out of the uncertainties that mark a religious transformation.[4] Even for those to whom God speaks directly—and what could signify presence more definitively than the voice?—there is often a background noise of doubts.

UNCERTAINTY

There are numerous examples in the New Testament that underscore the centrality of uncertainty and doubt in the Christian imagination (John 20:24–28; Matt. 14:31, 27:46), but Augustine's *Confessions* offers perhaps the most elaborate exploration of these feelings. "This much is certain, Lord," Augustine wrote, "that I am laboring over it, laboring over myself, and I have become for myself a land hard to till and of heavy sweat" (1997, 212 [bk. X 16, 25]). Augustine recognizes religion as hard work. For Augustine, a good Christian cannot be comfortable and complacent in what he or she knows. The Christian should be curious and critical: "People go to admire lofty mountains, and huge breakers at sea, and crashing waterfalls, and vast stretches of ocean, and the dance of the stars, but they leave themselves behind out of sight" (Augustine 1997, 206 [bk. X 8, 15]). For Augustine, faith involves what Tracy calls the risk of interpretation. It is a process of critical thinking and apprehension that can bring one closer to God. As such, however, it is full of risks—of disillusionment, frustration, confusion. The *Confessions* is not written to reflect Augustine's life as a seamless narrative; it is full of ruptures that provide the legitimating shape of that narrative. Augustine's conversion is presented as a series of moments in which uncertainty and doubt played a central role in his process of coming to know God—of being able to recognize God as present in his life. And it was, indeed, a process. Becoming Christian had "driven him to anxious self-examination"; Augustine never "allowed himself to be lulled into certainty about what he was really like" (Brown 1967, 163, 179).

Despite such a prominent example as this, it is surprising how infrequently scholars treat uncertainty in the religious subject (Christian or otherwise). By uncertainty, I should clarify that in this context I do not mean "radical challenges to the proposition that life is comprehensible"

(Geertz 1973, 100). This kind of uncertainty has been well studied and, though still subject to debate (Asad 1993; Bloch 1989; Engelke and Tomlinson 2006), is not the primary issue here. Uncertainty *in* the religious subject is something else altogether: It signals the doubts, misgivings, hesitations, and confusions that color life *as* a religious subject. Uncertainty in this second sense relates to "an internally persuasive discourse . . . that is assimilated by the individual and expressed from within" (Lambek 1995, 259). It asks us to consider not simply what someone knows, but on what authority, through what channels, and in which moments. If one prevalent image of the religious enthusiast is one who is comfortable and complacent in the truth, then alongside this we need to consider moments when the "internal discourse" is unpersuasive, or cannot be articulated, or is thrown into doubt. These are the stakes of the risk of interpretation.

Stemming from his work on the Jamaa movement, Fabian (1991a, 1991b) has drawn useful attention to this kind of uncertainty, which he refers to as "negativity." An example of this is the Jamaa concern about the terror of the text. Fabian learned that for Jamaa followers, faith was always haunted by the potentially dangerous effects of writing. Texts could throw the vitality of their faith into doubt because of the "habit and ritualistic pedantry" they fostered. For Jamaa, the "negativity" of faith was expressed through a concern with the mediums of its expression. Here I begin to show how negativity manifests itself in the live and direct ideals of the Friday apostolics. Through an examination of Shoniwa's transformation into Johane Masowe, we gain insight into one way in which the Friday apostolics have come to terms with the problem of presence. From the apostolics' perspective, Johane set the template for how to foster a live and direct faith. He was spoken to by God through the Holy Spirit, and this became a foundational event in setting the terms of how the apostolics understand presence. But as Johane's early days suggest, that presence is always marked by an uncertainty. It is conditioned, in Fabian's terms, by a negativity. Within it, then, we can also see how uncertainty becomes a constitutive element of both religious knowledge and authority. Today this sense of uncertainty—as a quality of the tension between distance and proximity—is a key characteristic of the Friday apostolics' notion of a live and direct faith.

Fabian is one of the few anthropologists to comment explicitly and at length on the fact that "inquiry into self-questioning and self-denial among religious enthusiasts is seldom undertaken" (Fabian 1991a, 118; see also Lambek 1995), although he admits there are exceptions to his rule.

In the history of anthropology he points to Victor Turner's work on liminality and antistructure (Turner 1967a, 1969) as having "kept in touch" with "negativity" (Fabian 1991b, 67n). Turner called liminality a "fruitful darkness" (1967a, 110) in an effort to capture a sense of the productive potentials of moments when the social order is thrown into doubt. More recently two studies of Christian fundamentalism in the United States develop discussions of concepts that might be said to parallel Turner's and that can be defined by the kind of negativity of interest to Fabian. They can also serve as illuminations of the uncertainty Johane might have experienced, even as they represent a more "conservative" theological orientation than what developed out of the Friday message (which in itself should prompt us to consider that the traditions I set out in the introduction are only models, since the Friday message could not be considered conservative when measured against the fundamentalist message.)

According to Susan Harding, for the fundamentalist, the experience of being "convicted by the Holy Spirit" carries with it something like a fruitful darkness. As used by fundamentalists, the term "coming under conviction" describes how the Holy Spirit forces someone to confront his or her sins, accept Christ, and be born again. Coming under conviction is a first step towards conversion in the ideology of Christian fundamentalism. Harding defines fundamentalist conversion as "a process of acquiring a specific religious language or dialect" (2000, 34). The experience of conviction is the moment one first starts to use—or *inhabit*—that language. It is not the sign of certainty, of a newfound faith, but rather of an engagement that may or may not lead to conversion. Harding offers a personal example. After a long and tiring interview with the Reverend Melvin Campbell at the Jordan Baptist Church in Lynchburg, Virginia, Harding climbed into her car and headed back to her motel. On the way she was nearly rammed at an intersection when another car came out of nowhere. She asked herself in that split second, "What is God trying to tell me?" (2000, 33). Reflecting on her reaction after the fact, she concludes, "It was my voice but not my language. I had been inhabited by the fundamentalist Baptist tongue I was investigating" (2000, 33). Harding had come under conviction, a "direct experience of the divine" that threw her into "a liminal state" (2000, 38). She was not born again. Her conviction by the Holy Spirit did not become an internally persuasive discourse. Her direct experience of the divine was only a fleeting presence. But her argument about the power of a religious conviction tells us something important about how, in moments of uncertainty, people ask questions about the presence of God in their lives. Harding's story is a "narrative of negativity" (Fabian 1991a) that grows out of her relationships with people who struggle to close the gap between conviction and conversion.

In Vincent Crapanzano's work on fundamentalism, the most productive pictures of certainty and uncertainty emerge out of his discussions of "sanctification." As fundamentalists understand it, sanctification comes after conviction; it is above all a process, "a spiritual maturing, a becoming holy, a discipline under the guidance of the Holy Spirit" (Crapanzano 2000, 120). Like the "state of confusion" (Harding 2000, 38) that accompanies conviction, sanctification is a process defined by a tension between certainty and uncertainty—which is to say, between a kind of distance and proximity. On the one hand, the fact that someone has been born-again, that she is sanctifying herself, is the sign of salvation. On the other hand, sanctification is never complete. It "continues until death" and can be lost if one does not live according to "continual Bible study, prayer, and the application of biblical precept to one's life" (Crapanzano 2000, 86, 121). As Ted Winter, a pastor in the Grace Brethren Church, said to Crapanzano, "I believe we have certainty, but I can't pretend I'm always certain. There's a living tension in faith, and apparently this tension, this uncertainty, is ultimately good for us, because it is this faith that pleases God" (quoted in Crapanzano 2000, 104). Doctrinally, the root of this uncertainty—this necessary separation from God—stems from the fall (Crapanzano 2000, 91, 165). It is an aspect of the second kind of difference that I framed using Ricoeur's work on Genesis. Uncertainty can thus be seen as an important aspect of the problem of presence; in this context uncertainty is a wrestling with separation. In terms of contributing to the analytic purchase of "negativity," Crapanzano's work on sanctification raises two points. First, even when a subject comes to inhabit a religious language there is always a disconnect between that language and the subject. Second, and importantly for the discussion here, the religious subject can act with certainty and still not understand what that certainty entails. The fruitful darkness in this sense can be likened to having a conviction but not knowing how to act on it. "I'm ready to make a commitment," said Paul Conway, another of Crapanzano's informants. "I don't know what all this includes . . . but I'm ready to make a commitment" (quoted in Crapanzano 2000, 110).

I want to use these discussions of conviction and sanctification as heuristic tools in the analysis of Shoniwa-Johane's religious transformation. This is not to suggest an equivalence between American literalists and Makoni visionaries but rather to underscore the way in which the dynamics of uncertainty can play a constitutive role in the patterning of religious subjectivity. In conjunction with the foregoing discussions, the colonial record and the several discourses produced by Johane's followers can be made legible as a narrative of negativity. The narrative moment in this case lasted two years. Between 1932 and 1934 Johane Masowe was wracked with insecurities. He was an African visionary trying to make sense of his visions in the context of a complicated political and social climate. He was trying to comprehend the voice of God. He was learning to use, if never fully inhabit, a new religious language. At the same time he was trying to master that language toward the end of legitimating his authority and "Society." Johane positioned himself strategically in relation to the state, the mission churches, chiefs, other apostolic figureheads, and even his own "followers." This was not a simple task, and it was not always clear to Johane, much less to those around him, how it should be done.

"A GARDEN WATERED FROM ABOVE": MISSIONARY EXPERIMENTS IN THE MAKONI DISTRICT

A good way to begin Shoniwa's transformation as a narrative of negativity is by looking to the specific forms of the missionary message in the Makoni District, where Shoniwa grew up. In Makoni there was a strong emphasis in the semiotic ideologies of missionaries on the transformative potentials of the Bible as both actor and object. In Gandanzara, Shoniwa's home area, missionaries worked to suggest evidence of connections between the Bible and literacy and economic success and social "progress." Through its introduction, the Bible would take root and bear the fruits of faith and progress.

Gandanzara was a stronghold of the American Methodist Episcopal Church (AMEC) and a notable "centre of Christian literacy" (Ranger 1999a, 197).[5] The AMEC, along with the Catholic missionaries at Triashill and the Anglicans at St. Augustine's and St. Faith's, produced a written vernacular of chiManyika, the local dialect of Shona, by translating the Bible and other religious texts into that language (Ranger 1991, 1999a). Codifying the language in a written vernacular "played a key role in the definition of the Manyika identity" (Ranger 1991, 142), which "was very much a Christian identity—literate, progressive, dynamic" (Maxwell 1999a, 103). Interconfessional relations among the missions and their congregations were often tense, but each emphasized literacy-as-liberation. From the missions' points of view, Makoni was a promising place, and its potentials were being realized with the introduction of the Bible. "We never forget," wrote one American Methodist, "that the primary object of our work is to give the native the Bible and enable him to read it" (quoted in Ranger 1991, 126).

Makoni in this period was described by one missionary as "a garden watered from above" (quoted in Ranger 1991, 133). While Shoniwa spent his youth in this so-called garden, most of the time he was on its outskirts. Gandanzara was an AMEC stronghold, but Shoniwa's parents were Anglicans. In the statement he gave to the police in 1932, Shoniwa said that he received some schooling from the Anglicans at St. Faith's Mission, not far from his kraal. Being Anglican in Gandanzara was, it seems, a difficult matter. Terence Ranger (1981, 21–24; 1991, 125) has shown that rivalries and squabbles between the missions spilled over into dynamics between the people of Makoni. At the outbreak of World War I, for instance, the Anglican congregation of St. Augustine's felt compelled to march on the German Trappists at Triashill (Ranger 1999a, 176–77). Ranger gives a good sense in his work of how, despite the common goal of bringing the Bible to Africans, missionaries were not all one of a kind. Clive Dillon-Malone suggests further that "the presence of such division in white Christianity must have left a strong impression in [Shoniwa's] mind" (1978, 13). All indications, then, "seem to place the [Masedza] family far outside the ranks of the [AMEC] cattle-owning, plough-purchasing clusters who were 'the foundation of progress' in the Gandanzara area" (Ranger 1981, 27). The picture of Christianity Shoniwa-Johane saw as a child suggested it had a fractious and unstable nature. It may be that these instabilities disabused him of the notion—at least for a period during his transformation into Johane—that the Bible was as significant or powerful as missionaries were claiming. It certainly failed to keep them united.

Makoni, like the rest of Southern Rhodesia, hit hard times during the world market depression of the early 1930s. The missionaries and first generation of African converts, however, seemed more concerned with the lackluster response to the missions on the part of the youth.[6] Christianity in Makoni was becoming routinized. Canon Edgar Lloyd, the Anglican priest in charge at St. Faith's Mission, wrote:

The Mission Church has come to the second generation of Christians and begins to manifest many of the weaknesses and inconsistencies of all Mass Movements. . . . Something of the ardour, undisciplined though it may have been, of the earlier converts has been lost. The very emphasis on education primary and secondary . . . and a simple native disposition to take all European ways and manners as necessarily the higher way, have dulled the African spirit. . . . Obedience to social convention is a deeply inherited characteristic not to be questioned by the pagan African. He has carried it so far into his idea of Churchmanship. (Quoted in Ranger 1999a, 179)

And so, as in other mission fields, gains made by missionaries toward achieving their vision of showing the "richness" of Christian life through literacy and education had unintended consequences in Makoni. It took the "spirit" out of the faith that motivated the earliest converts in the established churches. As one African Anglican lamented, "We were taught to read the Bible [in mission churches], but we ourselves never did what the people in the Bible used to do" (quoted in Ranger 1999a, 180). Johane Masowe's early questioning of the Bible might be understood in these terms; today, after all, Friday prophets put emphasis on the spirit and experience, on doing "what the people in the Bible used to do" rather than reading about it in a book. The milieu in which Shoniwa grew up suggests he began facing political and religious questions about what the Bible represented from an early age.

Shoniwa left Makoni in about 1928. In the three years that he held odd jobs around Salisbury it is not clear what else he was doing with his time, although some hints can be gleaned from the archival record and oral historical accounts. It seems he became friendly with a Roman Catholic priest. In his November 1932 statement to the police Shoniwa says he hoped to secure approval for his work from the Catholic Church.[7] There are other indications that Shoniwa was interacting with religious figures. Maxwell, for example, argues that Shoniwa was "caught up in the Pentecostal ambiance" (1999b, 261) of Salisbury. In particular, he took an interest in a preacher from the Apostolic Faith Mission (AFM), Enoch Gwanzura. The AFM would become important to Johane over the next few years.

Shoniwa also found an interest in colonial labor politics. He admits in his November 1932 statement to attending rallies of the Industrial and Commercial Worker's Union (ICU), led by Charles Mzingeli, the young organizing secretary in Salisbury whose influence in labor politics stretched over the next several decades (see Parry 1999). Much of 1929 and the beginning of 1930 were "months of special ferment in urban and industrial politics" (Ranger 1970, 153). In Bulawayo there was a strike by the white workers on the railway that made the colonial administration particularly nervous about ICU activities. Shoniwa attended the ICU's rallies in Salisbury. The message he heard at those meetings addressed a "call for unity, the disillusionment with the failure of the white man to live up to his 'civilizing' professions, [and] the demand for higher wages" (Ranger 1970, 156). Many of the ICU's main concerns later found support among Johane's Saturday congregations; it was the Saturday-based Gospel of God Church that adopted an explicitly anticolonial approach to wage labor through emphasis on economic self-sufficiency (Dillon-Malone 1978).

The early biography of Shoniwa Masedza cannot be treated with finality. But it suggests ideas that shaped his later teachings. Shoniwa had some degree of exposure to both main-line mission and Pentecostal Christianity between Makoni and Salisbury, and many of the ideas that were to define his "Society" can be traced to these experiences. But these experiences and exposures were in flux in the years immediately after his calling at Marimba; a number of ideas were in the air, but their constellation had yet to be determined. At any given time Shoniwa was wrestling with a number of issues: colonial racism, missionary paternalism, denominational factionalism, the influences of literacy, generational tensions, class antagonism, and the world market depression (see Ranger 1981, 1999a). Each contributed to the vocabulary that would later mark Johane's religious language.

THE COMING OF JOHANE

Shoniwa declared in his statement to the police on November 1, 1932, that during the winter months of his sickness he studied the Bible "continuously." But his reception of the Bible becomes a puzzling issue. Because the details of Masowe's statement are so important, I return to and quote at length from it here. When Johane came down from his forty days on Marimba hill, he went to a nearby kraal:

> I began to preach and tell the natives in the compound that I was "John the Baptist" sent by God. . . . I preached to the natives and told them who I was. *I admit telling them that they should burn their Bibles and take up the religion of their forefathers.* I later robed myself in a white robe on which appeared a large red cross. . . . After preaching for three days in the [Nyaweda] reserve I went to see Chief Nyaweda and asked him for his permission to preach in the reserve, this was given to me. I continued to preach until I went to a place on the Hunyani River which I made my Headquarters. By this time I had twelve disciples with me. I had a large following of natives by now. I use[d] to take confessions from either sex.

I did not collect monies from the natives. I did not Baptize. The only thing that I received from them was wild honey and fish. I know Charles Mzengali[.] [H]e is connected with the ICU. I have attended his meetings in Salisbury as a spectator, I did not know him personally at that time. About a week ago [i.e., sometime around October 24, 1932] Charles Mzengali came and visited me at the pool on the Hunyani River where I had headquarters. He did not speak to me but spoke with some of my disciples, who in turn told me that Charles Mzengali approved of my preaching and had foretold the natives that this would happen. I have not seen him since but heard that he would pay me another visit. I am not connected with the ICU or any other Society but my own. I associate myself with the Roman Catholic Church although I have no permission of any representative of this Church to preach to natives on their behalf. It was my intention to gather natives around me and then obtain the necessary authority of the Roman Catholic Church to have a separate native Church. I really do believe that I have been sent from heaven to carry out religious work among the natives. I think that I am "John the Baptist" as the voice told me so. No human being has guided me in my teachings, I am only guided by the voice that I heard when I was staying on the hill for forty days. I have heard the voice since in my dreams. The voice would come to me through a bush that was burning quite near me, when the voice ceased the fire would go out.[8]

This document is kept in the National Archives of Zimbabwe, and we need to acknowledge that archives are never "free of context, argument, [or] ideology" (Dirks 2002, 48). Johane's statement is presented from the perspective of the colonial government. We must be concerned not only with what Johane says but also with why he says it. We must take into account that the document is a transcription of an oral statement probably given in chiManyika and translated into English. It was also likely posed as a series of questions to which he gave answers—not, as it appears, as a lengthy statement. And we must recognize, as Dillon-Malone writes, that "authorities were not interested in the religious motivation which may possibly have been at work in Shona prophets and preachers, nor were they particularly concerned with the possible aspirations and needs which religious movements may have been fulfilling for their adherents" (1978, 25). Uncovering the religious motivations for Johane's message is a task that needs to be addressed.

Dillon-Malone argues that "the picture which emerges from [Johane's statement] is that of a profound religious experience expressed in terms of traditional and biblical imagery and resulting in a firm personal conviction of a call from God to perform a special work among Africans" (1978, 13). Indeed, Johane's illness, dreams, and visions are reminiscent of the process a Shona-speaking spirit medium must endure to assume power, his multilayered allusions to biblical figures (Moses and Jesus, in addition to John the Baptist) and Christian practices and sacraments (confession, baptism) are quite clear, and his bold political assertions are conveniently contradictory (as often suits the purposes of political and religious leaders). But to say that Johane's personal conviction was firm is only part of the story. On the one hand, he was indeed certain of his mission. He uses the language of certainty to proclaim his identity: "I really do believe that I have been sent from heaven to carry out religious work among the natives." And he makes clear the source of his authority: "I am only guided by the voice that I heard." Over the next two years, he spent time in three jails and suffered numerous threats from the colonial authorities, missionaries, white farmers, and Manyika and Zezuru kraal heads and chiefs. It is reasonable to assume that he would not have subjected himself to such abuses and dangers were he not firmly convicted. On the other hand, just how he should articulate his message was not always clear. In this sense his transformation was marked by uncertainty. Like Paul Conway, the fundamentalist described by Crapanzano, Johane was "ready to make a commitment" but he "did not know what all this includes." To understand more clearly the firmness of his conviction, we need to focus on what was at stake in these moments of not knowing what it might include.

A BRIEF COMPARISON OF PROPHETS AND SPIRIT MEDIUMS

I have already connected Augustine and American fundamentalists to Shoniwa-Johane, in part to highlight the benefits of comparison for an anthropology of Christianity. But there are other aspects of anthropological comparison that touch more directly on the nature of Shoniwa's case and which suggest its relevance to the anthropology of religion more generally. Indeed, uncertainty on the part of people possessed by spirits—holy or otherwise—is common in Zimbabwe, as throughout much of Africa. Here I want to describe the early days of a spirit medium I will call Weegirl with whom I worked in Zimbabwe throughout much of 1999. In some respects Weegirl is not like Shoniwa-Johane; most Friday prophets today at least would make a concerted effort to distance themselves from her "traditional" practices. But in assuming their respective positions, prophets and mediums share two concerns: first, a reluctance to accept the spirit; and second, anxiety over how to handle the responsibilities (such as healing or salvation) that might come with this role. For all of the otherworldly help they receive and for all of the new powers at their disposal, these religious figures are still human. They are prone to mistakes. They are not always sure what they should be doing, much less how.

Weegirl, in her mid-forties when we met, lives in an affluent suburb of Harare. She is an active member of the Roman Catholic Church. Her husband is a successful businessman. Weegirl calls herself a spirit medium. Her ancestral spirits bring with them a number of *mashave* (foreign spirits) called *njuzu* (mermaids), widely considered in Zimbabwe to be excellent healers. Weegirl has built up a reputation since the late 1980s as a skilled healer on this account and has had many influential visitors. But Weegirl told me that she did not want to become a spirit medium:

I tried my level best to resist it. It ruined my life. The spirits, especially [my] *ambuya* [grandmother], wanted me to stop going to the Catholic church, but I refused. Eventually we struck a deal, but I am no longer as active in the parish as I once was. And do you know that I have no social life anymore? How can I go out and get my hair done if there is someone waiting here at my house for help?

Figuring out how to hold her consultations was also a problem:

When I first started, I started with consulting in my house. But then when I was alone, I was coughing all the time. I could not stop coughing! It was terrible, you know? I did not know why this was happening. After some time—many months—I got my *sekuru* [grandfather] to say to me, "Why don't you build a round hut?" So, I built this hut behind my house. I put on a thatched roof, just like you see *kumusha* [in the villages] and the spirits liked that. They were very happy, especially my ambuya. Ah, they were good to me after that.

Weegirl casts mediumship as an imposition, and she finds it especially frustrating because she was not told how to go about it. Indeed, ancestral spirits in Zimbabwe do not always make their intentions or desires clear. Weegirl had to negotiate her spiritual life and her social life with the demands of her ancestors. The result was a compromise hammered out over time through trial and error. Like many spiritual figures in Zimbabwe—although in sharp contrast to the "either/or" position of the Friday apostolics—Weegirl did not want to surrender her Christianity. She did not consider it incompatible with the work and demands of the ancestors. And while she won on this point, it was not without compromise. "Effective, articulate, confident, authoritative, socially resonant, and responsible (yet always partly playful and dangerous) possession is," as Michael Lambek judges from his work on Mayotte, "something to be achieved" (1993, 323).

Shoniwa's transformation follows a pattern similar to Weegirl's. According to an account kept by the Gospel of God Church, Shoniwa wrestled over these issues with Jesus:

> Jesus said: "You are to go back to earth to drive away witches and to destroy all medicines *(mishonga)* . . . "
>
> Johane answered: "I cannot do such an important work."
>
> Jesus then said: "You will speak through the power of the one who will help you. I am giving you the power of John the Baptist of Judea who is crying out in the wilderness." (Quoted in Dillon-Malone 1978, 148)

Johane's hesitation and the delicacy of the situation are clearly marked in the Gospel of God Church document that presents this account. The accounts of Shoniwa's transformation that I collected from Friday apostolics emphasize similar points. In each, the idea of Shoniwa being able to "speak" with "the power of John the Baptist" is a crucial concept. It is central to understanding that Johane Masowe—"John the Baptist of Africa"—was always both a man from the Makoni District and a spirit sent from God to Africa.[9] As with Weegirl, we can see the tension between human agency and spiritual imposition. Like Reverend Campbell, even, who told Harding (2000, 44) he was not sure he could live up to God's expectations of him as a preacher, Shoniwa doubted his ability to speak as Johane. This is, of course, a strategy of persuasion (see Harding 2000, 34–38); the reluctance to accept authority is often what makes one more authoritative, as it underscores its seeming inevitability.

Unlike Weegirl, however, Johane was not given room to accommodate another "faith"—at least in the views of those who were to become the Friday and Saturday apostolics. Another notable aspect of the Gospel of God Church document, then, is the opposition it sets up between Christianity and certain aspects of what the apostolics call African culture, represented here by witches and the "medicines" (mishonga) used traditionally. This opposition does not appear to have been clearly articulated in the earliest days of Johane's work. In fact, in some of the police records he sounds like a committed nativist. Within a matter of a few years, however, opposition to African culture became a cornerstone of the apostolic project in both of the main Masowe churches, Friday and Saturday. Out of Shoniwa's transformation into Johane Masowe, the apostolics set up the struggle over spiritual authority as a struggle over the legitimacy of such things as traditional medicines, which as the Gospel of God document suggests were linked by Jesus to witches. One important difference between Weegirl and Shoniwa, then, is that Shoniwa wanted (or was made to want) to "break with the past." As I have suggested, the maintenance of this difference has become a central aspiration of the Friday apostolics and a major motivation for their concern with the semiotic propriety of therapeutic materiel and the spiritual brokers who use it.

Crapanzano might suggest that the Gospel of God document touches on a more general point about agency in many conservative Protestant theologies. Humans are, by their nature, prone to sin—to a "total depravity" (Crapanzano 2000, 91) that would prevent them from carrying out *important work*, as Johane had been asked to do. But this total depravity is not always realized because humans have will. And yet a genuine "free will" in this Christian sense is defined by submission to God's Word. "Salvation," then, "is at once an individual affair and something that requires total submission of an individual to God and His Word" (Crapanzano 2000, 90).

In this light it is interesting to note that whether or not Johane would be successful is not evident in the Gospel of God document. It is not triumphant in tone. Prophets and the Holy Spirit are neither one in the same nor necessarily linked; their relationships do not depend—like those of Weegirl and other spirit mediums—on genealogical ties. Prophets are not always possessed, and when they are not possessed they are no different from other people and can (in theory) make no claims to an inherent authority. In the strict sense, then, Johane Masowe was not a human but a spirit sent by God who spoke through the body of Shoniwa Masedza. As humans, prophets are always learning, subject to their own desires, and forced constantly to negotiate their roles in a religious community with their relationships in the spirit world. Whether they master the language of the spirit—whether they find the "freedom that comes through obedience to God" (Crapanzano 2000, 96)—is an open question. As the next chapter highlights, for the Friday apostolics, this is a "question of leadership."

Before Shoniwa gave his testimony to the police, officers gathered information on him from a number of people who witnessed his preaching in the Hartley District during October 1932. These men and women do not suggest that Johane's "firm convictions" correlated with a stable narrative of thoughts and actions:[10]

Andrea (a man who spoke the Zezuru dialect of Shona): "John the Baptist" preached in the compound of Chipukutu farm. "He preached to the natives whilst I was there and said he had been sent to the natives by God to prepare them to enter the Kingdom of Heaven." The day after, Johane left the farm with a number of the workers and went to the kraal of Ndoro, where he remained for three days preaching "to large numbers of natives who had gathered round." At Ndoro he told them "to adopt the religion of their forefathers, to drink plenty of Kaffir Beer and eat the meat blessed by our forefathers." Johane also said Africans "should burn the religious books of the European as our forefathers did not have books." Next, Johane proceeded to the Hunyani River. He preached every day "in the same strain" and told Andrea to take confessions from the people who had followed them there. Several people "confessed that they had stolen mealies [corncobs] from the lands, that they had been immoral with women, some that they were witch doctors, and several unmarried girls said that they had had sexual intercourse with their sweethearts." Johane told the people who confessed that their sins would be forgiven and that he would baptize them. "At times . . . ," he said, "I saw that 'John the Baptist' preached from a Bible." Johane said the Bible was a gift from a Roman Catholic father in Salisbury.

Msonza (male, another Zezuru speaker): Johane was preaching to people that "he had come from Heaven having been sent by God to preach to the people." Johane had a book with him, but it was "closed." For over two weeks at Hunyani Johane "continued to preach that he was 'John the Baptist' and had been sent by God to preach." Johane preached that Africans should "follow the religion of our forefathers." Africans should "not follow the religion of the churches, as they were against our custom." Johane claimed: "there was no truth in the Bible."

Adzijirwe (a Zezuru woman): Johane said "he had come from Heaven and had been sent by God to preach to the people." People confessed their "sins." Johane "never preached about the White people." No money was collected.

Msodzi (another woman): Johane "said he had come from heaven and had been sent by God to preach to the people." Johane did not preach about white people. Johane "made no mention about the Bible," but did have a book with him; however, "he did not say what it was, neither did he read from it." Johane said he was not collecting money because he had been sent by God.

Kangoma (Andrea's brother): "I spoke to this native and asked him who he was. . . . [H]e told me that he was 'John the Baptist' and had been sent from Heaven to preach to natives that the Kingdom of Heaven was at hand." Johane preached from a Bible. "I know that it was a Bible for I had seen it."

What can we make of these statements? As with Johane's statement, we cannot assume that these men and women told the colonial authorities everything that happened at Hunyani, or, indeed, that they did not simply say what they imagined the police wanted to hear. The witnesses had their own interests to look after, whether or not they were drawn to the message Johane preached. About the only consistency is the claim that Johane said he had "come from Heaven," had "been sent to the natives by God," had "been sent from Heaven." The phrasing is so consistent as to suggest that Johane did, in fact, repeatedly say such a thing, or that maybe the official responsible for transcribing and translating the statements created the regularities.

The keywords are *God* and *Heaven.* Had he wanted to present himself as a spirit medium (like Weegirl), Johane would not have said he was sent by God. While Shona-speaking peoples often acknowledge the existence of a remote "high god," called Mwari (see Murphree 1969, 48–50; see also Bourdillon 1987), Johane's listeners would have expected claims of possession by a powerful "tribal spirit" (mhondoro) had this been a question of mediumship (see Lan 1985, 31–39). The word *Heaven* further disambiguates his claim. There is no conceptual equivalent of *Heaven* in the Shona language; the word most often used, which was pressed into service by missionaries, is *denga,* which means "sky." What denga fails to signify, however, is the difference that *heaven* demands in English. Spirits in "traditional religion" are not transcendent in the way they are in the

Christian imagination; they do not reside in another place. As Murphree has stated, the living and the dead are best described in Shona cosmologies as part of an organic and spiritual unity. While this might be an acceptable description of the relation between the living and the dead in some Christianities—Mormonism, for example (see Cannell 2005)—the difference remains in that a traditionalist in Zimbabwe would not speak of a distinct place called heaven, as such a place would not be thought to exist. For this reason, I argue, Johane's message is a Christian-language message.

But the other claims point to discrepancies and contradictions. Was he preaching from a Bible? Was he telling people to burn the Bible? Was it both? Did he baptize? What was his position on the "religion of the forefathers"? Was he drinking "Kaffir Beer," and toward what end? These might be explained in terms of the various witnesses' desires to safeguard their own positions vis-à-vis the state and/or Johane. But following the argument I have been developing thus far, I want to suggest that perhaps Johane *did* say many or even all of these things. As a man who claimed to have been transformed by a religious experience, Johane was—like Augustine, like Paul Conway, like Weegirl, and like countless other religious figures—finding his feet.

There was no "Friday message" in October 1932, no apostolic worldview. Johane did not even use the phrase "live and direct," so far as the Friday apostolics today know. In subsequent years some of the people who heard Johane's early preaching took up elements of what he said and fashioned something coherent. But it would be a mistake—albeit one often made in the anthropology of religion—to operate on the assumption that religious transformations are accompanied by well-formed ideas. Having just undergone his transformation, Johane was speaking about what he was only just coming to recognize as his "impurity and separation from God," and perhaps the preaching was a way to deal with the "sense that something has to be done about it" (Harding 2000, 38). Johane was familiar with a number of religious idioms, Christian and non-Christian, that might have contributed to his authority. But there is still something inchoate in Johane's message at Hunyani. If the charisma of prophetic leaders is an intersubjective construction (Csordas 1997), then what we have here is a hopeful charismatic fine-tuning his rhetoric (of sin, of heaven, of the Bible, of himself) in a moment of uncertainty as to how he might best proceed.

On October 24, 1932, two Criminal Investigation Department detectives were sent to Johane's camp on the Hunyani River to survey the scenes out of which the above testimonies arose. The next day Johane was hauled in to Salisbury for questioning. Freedom of religious worship was guaranteed by law in Southern Rhodesia, but the question of Shoniwa's connection to Charles Mzengeli was a sensitive issue, and his criticisms of the Bible and Europeans were seen as evidence of a political agenda. And so, while the chief native commissioner was impressed with Shoniwa's polite demeanor during the course of their interview on November 1, he decided the most prudent action would be to break up the Hunyani camp and send Shoniwa back to Gandanzara.

Johane did not stay at home long. He was arrested twice in November for returning to his "headquarters" on the Hunyani River. After his second arrest he was sentenced to three months in jail at hard labor.[11] During Johane's imprisonment, many of the people who had been listening to his message did not stop speaking on his behalf. At the Hunyani camp Johane had chosen twelve disciples to aid him in his works.[12] One of these was Emmanuel Mudyiwa, the man from the Chiweshe District who would become an important figure in the Friday tradition. Mudyiwa continued preaching in Hartley after Johane's arrest until he too was sent home for dangerous "involvement with Baba Johane's 'separatist movement.'"[13]

Dillon-Malone (1978, 18) suggests that after three months in jail Johane began to acquire the status of a martyr to his interested listeners. This would certainly enrich the narrative of his transformation in any Christian register. But the time in jail also turned out to be crucial for the elaboration and clarification of his message. If Johane had become a liminal persona after suffering from "severe pains in the head" in May 1932 and if the preaching sessions at Hunyani capture the betwixt-and-between of his religious language, then jail added another dimension to his position. Time in a cell was time to think; following Turner's model for rites of passage, it could be defined as his "stage of reflection" (1967, 105). Once out, Johane began to build on his initial message by moving more deliberately toward a model of apostolic or Pentecostal faith, a faith modeled on "what people in the Bible used to do." Many of the most visible elements of such a move were already in place at Hunyani, before his incarceration: the designation of "disciples," the donning of white robes, emphasis on the Holy Spirit, and the public confession of sins. These are recognized as important aspects of apostolic Christianity in Africa (see, e.g., Jules-Rosette 1975). But not until after his release, in March 1933, was it clear this was the direction in which Johane was taking his followers. For all of his apparently Christian language, the scenes at Hunyani from October 1932 betray an unease with the content of his Christian message. If he was claiming to have been sent by God to preach to the people about the Kingdom of Heaven, he was also encouraging those around him to drink "kaffir" beer and burn the Bible, neither of which the European missionaries he meant to impress would have found impressive. But jail helped to shape and cement his convictions. Indeed, we might say his conviction by the state strengthened his conviction by the Holy Spirit. It brought him closer to God. It gave him more confidence that he could comprehend God's message. In terms of Johane's emerging religious language, we need to consider "conviction" not only as a kind of religious experience but also as a means of clarifying his course of action and legitimating his authoritative position.

After his first jail sentence Johane's connections with Pentecostal Christianity and the Apostolic Faith Mission grew stronger. The central figure in the next chapter of this story is a white preacher from South Africa named Louis Ludewyk Kruger. Johane's associations with this man sharpen the picture of how Johane saw his so-called Society emerging and reveal the outlines—if only still outlines—of what was to become the Friday message of live and direct faith.

THE APOSTOLIC FAITH MISSION AND
OTHER WHITE-ROBED AFRICANS

The AFM, registered in 1913 by nondenominational missionaries inspired by the 1906 Azusa Street Revival in Los Angeles, flourished in South Africa from its base in Johannesburg. The AFM was not given over to the kind of institutional organization Southern Rhodesian authorities expected in a missionary body. Its ministers, as David Maxwell explains, preached as missionaries "seeking to testify to, and demonstrate the power of, the Holy Spirit" (1999b, 249) without much regard, or interest, for institutional structures. The early AFM was characterized by a number of typical Pentecostal traits: glossolalia, public confessions, and divine healing (Maxwell 1999b, 246). In South Africa it appealed to both Africans and Afrikaners, who suffered most from the development of mining industries in the Rand (Maxwell 1999b, 247; van Onselen 1982). Its preachers had few qualms about "sheep stealing," that is, preying on other churches to win new followers (Maxwell 1999b, 256). This irked other missionaries to no end; in one instance in 1933 the Church of England in Wedza wrote to the government complaining bitterly and in vivid terms that the AFM was luring some of its most loyal members away with unsavory tactics.[14] Such complaints were common in the mid-1930s throughout Mashonaland.

Kruger came to Southern Rhodesia in 1930 to bolster the AFM's presence and reputation. Until that point the AFM there had met with less success than it had in South Africa. Throughout the 1920s there were never more than four (white) AFM families working in Southern Rhodesia at any given time (Maxwell 1999b, 257). The colonial authorities and other mission churches were uncomfortable with the latitude this gave "native" preachers associated with the mission. Africans invested with religious authority by the AFM often worked by themselves, without "European supervision." Regardless, it is doubtful the state would have found much comfort in the management of the AFM's "native ranks" since the preachers, who emphasized speaking in tongues, ecstatic expressions, and disinterest in organization, did not fit the missionary mold. According to Maxwell, "The AFM really let the side down. Its white representatives did not look like missionaries, act like missionaries or even sound like missionaries" (1999b, 256). "I trust that something can be done to stop these people from carrying on their pernicious Teachings," wrote one missionary, "[as] their own leaders seem to have no control whatever over their followers, and there is no telling what it may mean for the future of the natives, if allowed to continue."[15]

Johane probably met Kruger after his release from prison in March 1933. By June 1933 he seems to have established a working relationship with the AFM in a number of districts. On June 26, 1933, in fact, Johane was made a "local preacher on trial" in the AFM by Kruger himself. Johane's preacher's certificate is kept in a file at Zimbabwe's National Archives. It is interesting not least as a suggestive piece of evidence for a commitment of some kind to Christianity, documents having long served as a very specific sign of legitimacy and authority in (post)colonial Africa (Fabian 1991b; Summers 2002, 147–75; West 2003). The certificate says Johane had the authority to "preach the Gospel of our Lord Jesus Christ," "pray for the sick with the laying on of Hands," and "bury the dead" on behalf of the AFM.[16] The extent to which this piece of paper mattered to Johane is hard to say, but it is a useful way-marker for tracing his transformation.

Perhaps not surprisingly, the colonial authorities made little distinction between the flowering of apostolic and Pentecostal groups. Theology was not their forte (see Maxwell 1999b, 262), and the apostolic fashion of wearing long white robes gave them more reason not to think about it.

Charles Bullock, assistant chief native commissioner, wrote that in his estimation all such movements were the same and should be treated "simultaneously."[17] Africans in white robes were Africans in white robes: what difference was there? And while today the apostolic churches in Zimbabwe are rightly sensitive about being lumped together, I do not think details were the chief concern of prophets such as Johane Masowe in the early 1930s. Not just yet. Many apostolics, it seems, saw little reason for making denominational distinctions or choosing one "movement" over another. One police officer makes this clear, writing with apparent exasperation of Africans in the Seki Native Reserve who claimed "association with the Apostolic Church or 'Johane' or both."[18] For most of those listening to Kruger and Masowe, it was not an either/or situation at this time. Despite Johane's certificate from the AFM, these were not institutions at work and he still had no "Society."

CIRCULAR MINUTE NO. 23 AND THE TURNING TIDE

On November 30, 1933, the assistant native commissioner at Wedza complained that "Shoniwa, John the Baptist" was still under "insufficient supervision" by Kruger and that Shoniwa and his followers had "managed to arrogate to themselves supernatural powers and do things in the name of God and religion which, to say the least, are not in conformity with the professed teachings of the sect to which they claim to belong."[19] A month earlier Shoniwa was arrested in Buhera along with three other men, among them Emmanuel Mudyiwa. On November 2, 1933, in Buhera District Court, all four were found guilty of moving without a pass and given one week's intensive hard labor in the local jail.

In 1934 the tide turned against Johane. Even the native commissioners who until that point seemed patient with the presence of his followers (if not always with Johane himself) became more cautious. In part, this was due to an increase in the number of complaints from farmers and missionaries whose works and lives were being disrupted by the often dramatic, and always noisy, apostolic meetings. A. J. Erikson, adjutant of the Salvation Army, wrote to the native commissioner at Goromonzi on March 26, 1934, complaining that the apostolics were "troubling people" by going "into a kind of hysterical trance" and that "their influence on a naturally emotional people may lead to grave consequences at a later date."[20] Less than a month later, on April 17, a white farmer in the Marandellas District wrote:

I wish to report that during the last week or two, meetings purporting to be of religious nature and organized by the Apostolic Faith Mission have taken place on my farm Middlesex Marandellas. This has disorganized my labour and that of my neighbors owing to the fact that the happenings at these meetings are of a most weird nature.

I am informed that the natives present tear their clothes from their bodies and beat their heads on the ground, in other words become quite insane for the time being. You will readily understand this has a most disturbing effect on my labour and that of my neighbors and we will be pleased if some action be taken to put a stop to it.[21]

For the farmer, order was expressed primarily through concern with the disruption of work. The Salvation Army and other missionary bodies were concerned with their own church ranks. Johane represented a threat, as well, to the kraal heads and chiefs, as several of the remarks in the November 1 statement suggest. In a village gerontocracy there was no place for such a young man (Johane was probably about twenty years old at the time). As one kraal head complained, "I wish emphatically for this 'madness' to be forbidden."[22] Farmers, missionaries, even chiefs: all had their reasons to put a stop to apostolic "madness."[23]

The push against the apostolics in government was led by Charles Bullock. Until 1934 the problem native commissioners faced in dealing with prophets and preachers was a legal one. Freedom of religious expression was guaranteed by law, so native commissioners needed to prove that religious movements were political in nature. By 1934 many commissioners began to correspond with the attorney general about how their authority could be used to quell the concerns of the white settlers and missionaries affected by the new movements. By April 1934 Bullock was beginning to push the image of apostolics as a political threat with particular fervor. He wrote a memorandum arguing that the movements "may militate against the state—ultimately if not immediately" and that "what began with religious hysteria [was] now taking a political bias which is anti-European." His suggestion, in the fashion of indirect rule, was to turn to the chiefs (legitimated by the colonial state to begin with), to rely on "powers still lawfully inherent in the tribal system," and to "connect this action with . . . statutory law, so that criminal sanctions [could] be legally enforced."[24] In other words, if the state could get the chiefs to agree (or at least appear to agree) that the "pseudoreligious" movements contravened their authority *as chiefs*, then prophets like Johane could be apprehended not because of their religious beliefs per se but because they were flouting "tradition." The strategy worked. It was adopted by Chief Native Commissioner Carbutt and distributed as Circular Minute No. 23 in May 1934.[25]

When the circular was sent out, Johane was serving his third stint in jail, a two-month sentence in Rusape. Despite mounting opposition, he continued his work after release, often still in collaboration with the loosely defined AFM groupings. By June 1934, in fact, Johane had become such a visible influence in apostolic circles that the commissioner of the British South Africa Police referred to the AFM as an "off-shoot of SHONIWA'S (John the Baptist's) faction."[26] This confusion might have upset AFM officials in South Africa, if not necessarily Kruger. But Circular Minute No. 23 was to have a decided impact over the next two years. By 1936 Johane was little seen, and by 1938 he had moved south to Matabeleland on the first leg of a journey that would take him as far away as Nairobi, eventually as the recognized head of the Gospel of God Church. But throughout much of 1934 Johane was still in the process of articulating his positions.

In late 1934 Johane made what was probably the most important proclamation of his early ministry, a proclamation that brings us back to one of the main themes in this narrative of negativity: the role of the Bible. Sometime around the second anniversary of his appearance in Africa, Johane decided, with a measure of certainty, to accept the Bible as the Word of God. The decision was contentious and divided his followers. Out of this decision emerged the protean forms of the Friday and Saturday apostolics, two groups that have, over the past several decades, interpreted Johane Masowe's message in distinctly different terms.

ORIGIN STORIES

What struck me in my conversations with apostolic elders was their recognition of Johane's initial indecisions and variances. Johane's uncertainty was built into most of the "origin stories" I heard. It was accepted, even expected. As one figure in the Gospel of God Church told me, "Johane weChishanu is the true [church] because when [Johane] came he said pray only on Friday and don't use the Bible." The bishop I interviewed in another Saturday church said the same. "But later," he went on, "Johane asked all people to have Bibles . . . [so they] could understand the Gospel." Elders in Friday congregations concur on the chronology but differ in their interpretation of why Johane took up the Book. According to them, Johane gave in to pressure from his parents, Jack and Effie Masedza, because they could not believe that a Christian leader would reject the written Word. To Anglicans from Gandanzara, especially those of his parents' generation, it would have seemed unnatural. Still others have suggested to me that Johane knew he would face skepticism on his journeys from those who (like his parents) associated Christian salvation so closely with the Bible itself. The Friday elder Julius Sibanda, who worked with Emmanuel Mudyiwa in the 1940s, explained it to me this way during a meeting in 1993:

> In the beginning, Johane told his people to worship on Fridays and not to read the Bible. . . . But in 1934 he told his followers, "If you ever see me reading a Bible, do not follow me. Stay true to my original teachings. A time will come when I will be forced to read the Bible. The people down south [in South Africa] are educated, and they will not follow me unless I let them read that book. This will be fine as long as they follow my message, but you here [in Southern Rhodesia], you must keep my true teachings."

There may well have been this pragmatic motivation for Johane's decision. But it is likely that it grew out of his close work with Pentecostals, who were able to make the Bible-based Christianity Johane knew as a youth more vibrant and attractive. (This is a development that might not have germinated in the same way, for instance, had he continued the "friendship" with the Catholic priest he and his early followers mention.) Though it is a diverse label, Pentecostalism is characterized, like fundamentalism, by an emphasis on the Bible as "a compendium of answers for all significant questions" (Wacker 2001, 71). What is more, according to Grant Wacker (2001, 21–23), one of the defining traits of Pentecostalism is certitude. In Pentecostal and fundamentalist churches the Bible has often provided the material and spiritual bedrock of that certitude—"God's word in its materiality," as I quoted Crapanzano in the introduction.[27] In fact, even Augustine seems to have expressed the sentiment: "To the Bishop of Hippo . . . putting one's trust in God means finding certainty in the Bible" (Stock 1996, 85).

It is not my intention, however, to resolve the differences between Johane's followers. What interests me more is how, in each account, uncertainty and the development of positions over time through a kind of trial and error are central. Whether it was embraced out of piety or pragmatism, the Bible became a focal point in the articulation of Johane's vision and a filter through which to understand the theme of uncertainty as I have outlined it here. Thinking back to the colonial administration's perception of the Pentecostals and apostolics, there is a parallel with what several of the Masowe elders say. The government saw these figures and their followers as disorderly and confused. Some of the most prominent members of Johane's churches might agree with the characterization, at least to a point. The difference is in the attitude toward order and confusion. For colonialists, order was always a preeminent concern. Rather than excise the difficult strands from the narratives of their authority, Masowe elders make it clear that Johane's uncertainties, indecisions, and changes in opinion were nothing, in themselves, to be concerned about. Indeed, in religious narratives "the sense of a constant generation of doubts and qualms about actions, words, and motions is a route to and source of power and authority" (Harding 2000, 103–4). Uncertainty can be used to mark a religious figure's position of power. Authority is generated out of similitude and difference in these narratives: the figure is human, and therefore prone to mistakes, but is also something more, something in this case, for them, closer to the divine.

The tension over textual authority came to a head with Emmanuel Mudyiwa. He was a man who served jail time alongside Johane. He had proven his commitment and emerged as the key proponent of the Friday message to reject the Bible after Johane's decision to take up the Bible and worship on Saturdays. As Amon Nengomasha, former general secretary of the Gospel of God Church, said in a 1977 interview:

> We can speak of Emmanuel. When Baba Johane started the Church at Marimba [Emmanuel] was at Nyamweda. . . . He is one of the first apostolic sect members. Baba Johane had by then not yet decided on which day to rest and pray. Now, they used to observe Friday and gathered on this day and so people took for granted that Friday was the Holy Day. Later on, Baba Johane told his people to observe Saturday as the Holy Day, the day reserved for God. Emmanuel did not want to switch from Friday to Saturday. He insisted that everyone knew that Friday was the day of prayer. . . . Because of this, he left the Church.[28]

Emmanuel and Johane's parting of ways took place in November 1934. Shortly after, in early December, Emmanuel caught the government's attention in dramatic terms as he expressed the immediacy and authority of his mission through a combination (at least as reported) of political bravado and Pentecostal enthusiasm. In Goromonzi he assaulted a native messenger and local kraal head who tried to break up one of his religious sessions. On December 3, 1934, sixty-three people were arrested because of the incident. The situation turned violent when the messenger, who had been sent because of complaints from local residents about the noise the apostolics made each night, asked the apostolics to identify themselves. They continued their activities, which the local native commissioner described in his report as a "mixture of Muhammedan prostrations and Roman Catholic ejaculations." On being asked to identify themselves, the group surrounded the two men, chanting to themselves, closing in, "gyrating faster and faster, some falling down and crawling swiftly around, some moaning and growling like dogs." They began to shout at the native messenger. A scuffle ensued. The messenger ran off, followed by a number of apostolics "making weird noises like lions." The next morning the native messenger returned with reinforcements to arrest the group. When brought before the native commissioner, Emmanuel declared himself "Jesus" and "suddenly ran off muttering, jumped upon a donkey, and rode back to [the commissioner] mouthing some gibberish and shivering." The commissioner's men administered some "stern action" and brought Mudyiwa back to his senses. Mudyiwa said he had been using "'Jesus-talk,' that his work amongst the white-men had finished, and that now he was dealing with black-men." Mudyiwa was tried for the assault and found guilty. Twenty-five young women who were also involved in the assault stated "they had been told that 'John the Baptist' had done his work, now Jesus had come to assume power." The Goromonzi native commissioner who captured this account concluded, "I anticipate that the movement—if such it can be termed—will now fade out; but no doubt the idea will occasion another small movement shortly, each self-styled messiah or apostle endeavoring to take the place of one becoming moribund."[29]

THE PROMISE OF PRESENCE

Goromonzi's native commissioner was not entirely wrong. Since the mid-1930s apostolic groups inspired by Johane Masowe have split on a number of occasions, almost always because of what the apostolics I know have referred to as "the question of leadership"—the issue I turn to in the next chapter. The question of leadership allows us to investigate the problem of presence from another angle, namely, the extent to which the prophet can be understood as a sign of presence. This is certainly what Mudyiwa was suggesting by claiming to be Jesus.

It was in November 1934, more than two years after his initial transformation, that Johane began to act on his certainty, turning his declarations into operations. He now set guidelines for the growth of his society and the realization of his mission. By no means does this suggest his ideas were cast in stone. The churches Johane founded (or inspired) with his Saturday message have undergone numerous changes over the years. But with this decision about the Bible he was beginning to make "particular claims about reality and one's relationship to it" (Harding 2000, 58). That reality was increasingly framed in Christian terms. Johane's split with Emmanuel is the moment his transformation was carried through. It was the moment he found his place in relation to God.

Johane Masowe returned to Gandanzara in 1935. With his Saturday followers he began to build on an image of the self-sufficient religious community. The Saturday apostolics withdrew as far as they could from the colonial economy, establishing their own church fields to support themselves. They did not send their children to government or mission schools and rejected—for the next several decades—the use of biomedicine. But neither, it seems from the annual district reports, did they try to disrupt those around them. Johane remained in Makoni until 1938. In that year the government conducted a centralization survey of the communal areas, prohibiting groups other than families from holding farmland. The Saturday church therefore lost its substantial holding of church fields. "It was this break-up of the communal lands," Ranger has argued, "which precipitated Masowe and his followers into their extraordinary pilgrimage" (1981, 33). From 1938 until his death in 1973, Johane lived in Port Elizabeth, Lusaka, and Nairobi at various "headquarters." It was not until 1947, in Port Elizabeth, that he registered a church with the government officials. The Friday apostolics have yet to register with anyone, and in all these years they have had next to no official contact with their Saturday brethren and still less with their inspirational figurehead.

By folding discussions of Augustine and late-modern fundamentalists in the United States into a chapter about the early days of Johane Masowe I do not mean to suggest that all would share the same understanding of religious transformation. Even if we focus on the work of Harding and Crapanzano, it is clear that not all fundamentalists define or experience conviction and sanctification in the same way. Ted Winter, pastor of the Grace Brethren Church, was, Crapanzano tells us, self-reflexive and ready to discuss his faith, but most of Crapanzano's informants "were so certain of their values . . . that they could not understand why anyone with different values would be angered by their incapacity, their unwillingness, to engage in dialogue or debate" (2000, 99, 325). Harding calls this a "poetics of faith," by which she means that fundamentalist practices of interpretation are based on the firm conviction of "the absolute truth of the Bible" (2000, 88) that does not need to be questioned.

It is often this certainty, pace Augustine's commitment to self-examination, that is used to characterize Christianity. This is in part why I have chosen to focus on fundamentalists in the main comparison, because more than many Christians they stress "the certainty of their theology" (Crapanzano 2000, 23). But certitude, we learn from them, is possible only through the recognition of its absence. Through a process like sanctification, for example, fundamentalists live the exception to their rule. This speaks to a more general issue. As Crapanzano (2000, 126) notes, sanctification mediates the paradox of being *simul justus et peccator*, "at once just and sinful." Christian narratives of transformation are often defined by this dynamic. They depend on uncertainty as the motivation to live as a Christian ought and to create a space in which authority can be constituted. The narratives are marked by "gaps, excesses, and indeterminacies which the faithful must ceaselessly close, suppress, and fix in the name of God" (Harding 2000, 86). But they are never finally fixed. What I am suggesting here is that the tension between certainty and uncertainty is legible as a tension between distance and proximity—of being near God from afar.

Johane Masowe learned how to organize and express his religious mission as he went along. His transformation did not endow him with a special knowledge. He had to learn and craft it. The government, missionaries, farmers, kraal heads, labor union leaders, white Pentecostals, rival visionaries, dedicated followers, and no doubt some curious onlookers provided him with a complex and sometimes contradictory sounding board. And so while convinced of his mission and familiar with the vocabulary on which he might draw, it took him some time to articulate each. Winter used the phrase "become what I am" (quoted in Crapanzano 2000, 103; cf. Bultmann 1956, 182) to characterize his understanding of conversion as a living tension. This phrase captures the dynamic between certainty and uncertainty I have tried to document in the religious transformation of Johane Masowe.

In the early days Johane Masowe did not talk about "live and direct" faith, and there is no evidence of his claiming access to "the True Bible." This kind of language is more recent (though no one could tell me exactly when "live and direct" came into use). It was, rather, certain themes in Johane's early preaching that provided his Friday followers with a point of departure. Emmanuel Mudyiwa and the other prophets inspired by the Friday message understood that message as one shaped by a continuous process of searching. They did not begin with a fixed model of faith and took that as a sign that such fixity is not what Johane had been sent to provide. The Friday message, developed from a range of things Johane said and did in those early days, has, at its core, the concern with becoming. When he came down the Marimba hill in 1932, Shoniwa Masedza was Johane Masowe, but he still had to become what he was. His early days were marked by uncertainty in this living-tension sense. These "negative" aspects of Johane's transformation informed the character of Friday Christianity.

Today what stands out to those who heard a Friday message was the skepticism Johane expressed toward what we might recognize as religious materiel—the Bible, church buildings, "medicines," even money—that stood for something spiritual. It was in a move away from these signs that Emmanuel and other prophets staked their course. Friday apostolics today do not burn the Bible. Yet, apocryphal or not, the story of Johane sending it up in smoke retains a certain force, only bolstered by its ambiguities. Was it a political or pious act? Maybe it was both. But on the banks of the Hunyani River Johane had been able to articulate the promise of something more intimate, something more immediate, than what either missionaries or spirit mediums could provide. Emmanuel and the other Friday prophets have tried to make good on that promise.

THREE

The Question of Leadership

The Friday Message after Johane

"I HAVE NO IDEA WHAT Johane Masowe looked like," said Madzimai Ts-itsi. Lazarus and I had been interviewing Tsitsi and her husband, Madzib-aba Zechariah, for about an hour when she hit on this point. We had been asking the couple about the church's history, something we routinely did in our interviews and conversations. *Church history* is a term the apostolics often use. Not every apostolic claims to know much about it, but most profess an interest in it. Congregants learn about church history from the people who have been around—the "old-timers" in a congregation, as they call them. Old-timers are happy to talk about the history one on one, but on occasion they are asked by prophets and elders to speak about it to the congregation as a whole. After the mid-1930s there is very little in the archives documenting the existence of the Friday apostolics. I wanted to know what happened after Johane: How do we get from Marimba 1932 to Chitungwiza 1999? Answering this question is difficult because apostolics have lived what Steven Feierman calls an "invisible history," for which the written record hangs "like a veil between the historian and the African ac-tors of [the colonial] period" (1999, 186). To learn about church history, Lazarus and I had to ask the old-timers ourselves and listen closely to what they said during services. Most elders today are keen to educate apostolics about their past, but this is not to say they think of the "invisibility" to which Feierman refers as necessarily bad. Staying out of sight during the colonial era allowed the Friday churches to carry on their business with minimum interference from the authorities. But an invisible history is not a nonexistent one, and making this point is becoming increasingly important in today's congregations.

As the Friday apostolics understand it, church history tells them where they "come from" and helps them to stay "on track." These key phrases tell us that, like many other kinds of history, church history is not only a narrative of agents and actions in time and space but also a capsule of cosmology. Histories are, as Greg Dening puts it, "ways of knowing" (1996, 41).

Tsitsi and Zechariah knew a lot about church history. Zechariah is a member of a long-standing church family. His mother had followed Johane's message since 1933, and two of his uncles had been prophets. Tsitsi did not grow up an apostolic—she was raised a Seventh-day Adventist—but she has been an active and influential member of the Warren Park congregation since its founding in the 1970s. Tsitsi, however, is not alone in her "ignorance": aside from the handful of remaining apostolics who moved with Johane, no one in the Friday churches knows what Johane looked like. More than this, however, no one seems to care. This second point was driven home to me just before I left Harare in December 1999. As a token of appreciation I made copies of the only known picture of Shoniwa-Johane (which can be found in the photographic collection at the National Archives) for the apostolics who were most helpful in my research. These gifts were gratefully received, but they left several people amused, wondering what I had learned. The picture was nice to have, said one of my friends, but what could an apostolic do with it? It was just a picture!

Having detailed the early days of Johane Masowe and having just stressed that apostolics like to know where they "come from," it might seem odd to start this chapter with a pair of exchanges that downplay Johane's position. What these exchanges allow us to consider, however, is the relationship between church history and the notion of a live and direct faith. Prophets are a linchpin in this relationship, and their role in the church raises the problem of presence. If I was a bit careless in choosing the picture of Johane as a parting gift, it was not only because of my wrongheadedness. This is because, when apostolics tell history, they ground it in relation to the prophets that have carried them forward—or kept them on track. Indeed, to listen to a couple like Tsitsi and Zechariah relate where they come from is to listen to a genealogy of sorts of the church's leading figures.[1] During interviews, this emphasis always suggested to me that prophets matter, so I thought the picture of Johane

Figure 2. The only known photograph of Johane Masowe, date unknown. Reproduced by permission of the National Archives of Zimbabwe.

was a good idea for a gift. And in a sense I would still want to argue that prophets *do* matter—especially the handful of what apostolics call "major prophets" who came after Johane. But as even the strongest proponents of church history would insist, prophets should only ever matter for what the Holy Spirit does and says through them. A proper rendering of apostolic history is signposted by individuals but driven by their messages, and the latter should always outweigh the former. This is one of the lessons that shapes—or ought to shape—the narratives of the past.

The weChishanu churches have done fairly well at resisting the idolatrous pull of Johane. They display a remarkably consistent apathy for the man. The apostolics do not suffer from the pathos of *his* absence, to adapt Milbank's words. His person, as my exchanges with Tsitsi and Gaylord suggest, sparks little interest. Indeed, *disinterest* in the founding father is a point of pride and something to contrast with the situation in the Saturday churches. In Friday apostolics' eyes, the Saturday churches are cults of personality; the Saturday apostolics place Johane at the center of everything they do, even in death. In 1996, for example, when violence broke out at Gandanzara, where Johane is buried, between two Saturday factions, the Friday apostolics took special note. One group of Saturday Masowe from Zambia had come to exhume Johane's body so they could rebury it at their headquarters in Lusaka. The other group—based there at Gandanzara—refused them. The Zambians were successfully repelled, but in the process four people were killed. The standoff made headlines in Zimbabwe and provided the Friday Masowe with a valuable lesson about the dangers of extolling the man over the message. Their reaction to the tragedy at Gandanzara bordered on Schadenfreude. The violence was interpreted as a vindication of the Friday message, a sign that when Johane went to South Africa he fell "off track" and that the weChishanu had been right to heed his early messages about the dangers of the material. They were right to have picked up on Johane's denunciation of religious things—a denunciation that amounted to a rejection not only of the Bible and African medicines but also of those who claim authority through them. For the Friday apostolics, this means their own prophets as well as witches and spirit mediums. Prophets help to make a live and direct faith possible, but they should not be mistaken as the source of or reason for that faith. What happened in 1996 at Gandanzara was understood by the Friday apostolics as what happens when one does not embrace the logic of dematerialization. The situation among the Saturday apostolics had deteriorated to the point that they were fighting over a dead body. Nothing could be further from what Johane had been sent to relate. Prophets should not receive special burials. To fight over their bodies is to have missed Johane's valuable lessons about live and direct faith. I was told that when prophets die they are "just dead." God's Word is not dependent on any one messenger. To associate it with a specific person—whether living or dead—is to misconstrue the nature of God's presence. It is to indulge in what I have referred to as thingification, because that presence should not be equated with physical bodies.

After Johane, however, the separation of the message from the messenger has proven more difficult to maintain. As I discuss in more detail later, in practice the message often *is* attached to physical bodies, in the sense that some prophets become personally associated with the presence of the divine. The Friday apostolics refer to this difficulty as "the question of leadership." Simply put, a prophet can be wrongfully emboldened by the congregation to assume a position of unique authority or even actively work to convince the congregation that such authority is theirs to claim. Put another way, it is precisely when prophets might be recognized as ultimate leaders that they pose the greatest threat to the realization of their mission.

The question of leadership, then, is another way in which the Friday apostolics grapple with the problem of presence. While they may have been successful in downplaying the significance of the Bible, the significance of prophets has been less easy to tame. In semiotic terms, a prophet is a dangerous and unstable sign. Too often, according to most apostolics, prophets skirt the fine line between messenger and message; too often they assert themselves, or are asserted as, the presence that faith is supposed to manifest. The question of leadership is a question of how the charismatic figure poses the problem of presence.

In this chapter I explore the question of leadership by tracing a "genealogy" of the major prophets. This genealogy, while neither exhaustive nor uncontested, gives form to church history. (The term *church history* was always rendered in the singular, despite its regular contestation.) One goal is to confirm the important argument in the Africanist literature that in order to recover an invisible history we must move beyond the walls of the colonial archive (see, e.g., Miller 1999; Mudimbe 1988). Moving beyond the walls of the archive in this case involved a series of lengthy trips around northern and eastern Zimbabwe. Lazarus and I visited with as many old-timers and major prophets as we could, slowly patching together different aspects of the apostolics' authorized and unauthorized pasts. What we learned is that the network of Friday churches is held together by the acknowledgment of "the Friday message" as paramount. "We are Masowe" and "We are the same" are the kinds of statements of identification we heard most often. But the understanding of the Friday message (the understanding of what constitutes sameness) and the extent to which that message binds congregations to one another could vary greatly. Another goal of providing this genealogy is to show that in recovering an invisible history we begin to see the contours of apostolic cosmology. The telling of history brings its forms, and the ideas that shape and reshape those forms, to the fore. Church history bears the imprint of the apostolics' ways of knowing, giving us a further glimpse into the logic of live and direct faith.

I should stress at this point that if some of the portraits below read as impressionistic, that is because they are, at least by anthropological standards. The details presented here are for the most part (with the exception of those on Nzira) not based on long-term relationships or field site experiences but rather a series of trips throughout Zimbabwe that were meant to provide contexts for my sustained research in Harare and Chitungwiza. Collecting church history any other way would have been difficult; to understand the importance of staying on track we had to do some literal tracking of our own.

EMMANUEL

Zimbabwe's oranges are grown in the Mazoe Valley, a rich tract of land nestled between the hills just north of Harare. This is the kind of place the Southern Rhodesian authorities earmarked through land apportionment in the 1930s. When I was there (before Mugabe's farm seizures) it presented the picture-perfect agricultural scene. The road to Bindura shoots through the valley in a straight line past rows of neatly arranged orange trees. At a few points the orange estates are broken up by crossroads. One of these crossroads leads to Bretten Farm, which is owned by the followers of Emmanuel Mudyiwa. Bretten Farm is named after the white man who settled it some fifty years ago, an early beneficiary of the colonial state's policies. Emmanuel acquired it in the late 1980s (well before commercial farms became major sites of struggle). Since then Mudyiwa's people have been living off the land, farming cash crops to support themselves. They are known today as Mudzimu Unoera, the Respected Ancestor Church (which raises eyebrows in other congregations). But to Lazarus and me they emphasized another connection: "We are Masowe," they said.

We were often told that Emmanuel Mudyiwa is "second from Johane." It was on the basis of his preaching that the Friday message survived Johane's departure. The message took hold slowly in areas around Mondoro and Chiweshe, where Mudyiwa was most able to preach. Like Johane in Gandanzara, Emmanuel had to contend with an increasingly wary state throughout the 1930s. After his run-in with the police in Goromonzi in December 1934, Emmanuel adopted a more cautious attitude. His entrance into the colonial record—marked so dramatically by the "prostrations" and "ejaculations" of his followers—stands in sharp contrast to its fading out. By the late 1930s the annual reports of the native commissioners in areas around Salisbury contain scant mention of any apostolic groups.[2] Emmanuel was still active, only more discreet.

Lazarus and I went to Bretten Farm to ask about Emmanuel's connection with Johane. On our first visit we spoke with five workers from the farm. They wore overalls, woolen caps, and black leather wristbands on their right arms. (We later learned they call the wristbands *denbys,* which "symbolize something unknown." Although similar to phylacteries, no one suggested this similarity.) The farmworkers we met said they could not tell us much about the past because they did not want to "get the history wrong." They said they would speak with the council of church elders and then phone me in Harare to arrange an interview. Two days later I got a call. Lazarus and I went out again the next week to meet with the council. It is not unusual to go through this hierarchical filtering in groups connected to the major prophets, even as hierarchy is something the apostolics explicitly criticize.

On our second visit to Bretten Farm we spent the morning sitting in the shade of a large, unfinished building on the side of a hill, commissioned to serve as Mudzimu Unoera "headquarters." We were attended to by the council of elders, one of whom was Chief Chiweshe, a notable figure in local politics. "The man you are asking about is called Emmanuel Mudyiwa," said the chief. He told us more: "His father was Dzangara, his mother was called Rangu. As a boy, Mudyiwa watched cattle, but he never had to work at it. They would never stray far from him and he could even nap in the afternoon. One day his father and brother found him napping under a tree. They confronted him and asked if a spirit was acting through him. He responded saying, 'I am Emmanuel. I am the son of Mary, killed overseas.'"

For about two decades Emmanuel preached by traveling when and where he could. His family was from the Chiweshe District, but he moved well beyond there. In the 1960s he moved to Seke, south of Harare, which was fast becoming the urban center of Chitungwiza. Emmanuel stayed there for some twenty years, running a brick-making business off Mude Road.

The chief told us that Emmanuel always worked to make the Friday message "stronger." As a consequence and over several decades some of Johane's original pronouncements were altered or abandoned. Johane, for example, had told his followers not to drink alcohol or smoke. Beer and tobacco are, in the eyes of many apostolics I know, African vices—what one uses in "heathen" rituals to call the ancestral spirits, or even practice witchcraft. But Emmanuel did not agree. The chief told us he had learned otherwise through prayer. These prohibitions were unimportant, Emmanuel said, because they distracted apostolics from more serious things, such as learning "how to pray." The prohibitions also made it difficult to gather an interested following, as people were used to these customs; Emmanuel reasoned there was nothing wrong with smoking and drinking if done in moderation.

Emmanuel's changes did not sit well with other Friday prophets, most of whom understood the alcohol and tobacco taboos as central to the success of stamping out witchcraft and "African culture." Chief Chiweshe said that most congregations eventually broke with Emmanuel because of these disagreements. According to the Mudzimu Unoera elders, it was *other* prophets—in particular, a young man named Philip—who began to politicize the faith. By this they meant that prophets questioned Emmanuel's decisions. And yet Emmanuel was only keeping things on track, listening to what he was told by the Holy Spirit. "The big problem," said Chief Chiweshe, "is leadership. Prophets want the power for themselves."

Today, the Mudzimu Unoera Church is run by the council of elders. Due in part to the "big problem" of leadership there are currently no prophets or healers on Bretten Farm. The "respected ancestor" in the Mudzimu Unoera name is none other than Emmanuel, who consolidated power in himself while alive and stalled its transfer, with a measure of success, on his death. "Before he died, Emmanuel said he would come again," said the chief. Emmanuel's answer to the question of leadership was to collapse the difference between himself and God. The Mudzimu Unoera do not recognize other Masowe prophets as legitimate because of Emmanuel's completeness; as second from Johane, he was "Emmanuel the Christ." Far from falling off track, he was the realization of Johane's message.

In keeping with a scriptural program, Emmanuel's followers have prepared the way for his return. They have done this in large part through what Richard Werbner, in an important article on religious organization in African independent churches, has called "innovations in space" (1985, 281). On top of a hill in the farm compound the council of elders showed us what they call "the house of Jesus." It sits in a small clearing with a spectacular view of the Mazoe Valley. It looked to Lazarus and me like a typical middle-class bungalow in a Zimbabwean city: cement brick, painted white, with a wraparound porch, large glass windows fitted with "burglar bars," and a wooden door finished in light brown shellac. Its distinguishing feature is the roof, a cement dome painted a bright, metallic silver. We asked about the unusual roof. The elders said Emmanuel designed the house according to God's plan and that it had a cement roof because God wanted it to be "the most solid house in Africa." We were told it was finished in 1989 just one day before Emmanuel died. For more than ten years the elders had maintained its pristine condition. It had obviously been painted since its construction, as every detail was crisp. The elders told us to go in and look around. There is no furniture inside, giving it a lonely echo. On our visit the floors were being finished in white tile. The walls were painted white. There was a fireplace that jutted out of the wall in the main room like a round brick oven, also covered in white tiles. In the bathroom there was a large white bathtub. The only other thing in the house—besides white sheets hung over the windows—was a large portrait (maybe two feet by three feet), in pencil, of Emmanuel, which leaned against one of the walls in the main room. In the portrait his face is stern and serious, and his eyes seemed to follow you around the room. Later Lazarus told me that looking at the portrait made him dizzy, which it did to me too.

During the course of our conversations and tours, Lazarus and I could hear the faint sounds of a religious service in full swing. The elders had invited us on a Friday, which they still keep as the Sabbath, and business went on as usual around our visit. We joined the service in the early afternoon. The congregants sat under a tree, a short way down the hill from the unfinished building. About forty people were gathered. The men at the service sat on wooden stools facing west, and the women sat on the ground facing east. All the men had denbys on and were carrying bamboo walking sticks. They were dressed in everything from three-piece suits to coveralls. The women wore skirts or sarongs. Many of the people were wearing shoes, which we had never seen before at an apostolic service. But what struck us most was the fact that these people were doing something that we had never seen Friday apostolics do before: dance at church. They marched in place to their own singing. The movements of their arms and legs were stiff—up and down like robots. The songs were punctuated with a deep *hmm-hmm* refrain. They looked like soldiers. Only men spoke, and they did so in an everyday, colloquial voice. "Emmanuel told us how to pray to God. We must continue in his absence to gain entrance to the Kingdom of Heaven," one of them said. Lazarus and I were struck by the Mudzimu Unoera service because if we had not already spoken with the elders, I am not sure we could have guessed the connection to Johane. It was also unusual in that they allowed us to take photographs. Then again, Lazarus mused, it was Friday and no one was carrying the Bible; perhaps we were on to something after all. But without a doubt the Mudzimu Unoera service was unlike any other Friday apostolic service I attended.

In July 1996 I met a reporter, Ray Mawerera, who had written two articles about Emmanuel in 1987 for *Parade* magazine, one of Zimbabwe's popular monthlies. When I told Ray about my research with the Masowe apostolics his eyes grew wide. He smiled and told me that he had "interviewed Jesus." The two articles he wrote describe a service held by Mudyiwa near Mount Darwin in April 1987 (Mawerera 1987a, 1987b). Emmanuel was at the height of his popularity at the time. He had grown rich from his brick-making business. At this meeting more than three thousand people had gathered. Emmanuel, with swollen feet and a closed left eye, looked unwell. He was carried by some of his followers on a "throne" when he addressed the crowds. "His followers call him Emmanuel, the Christ," Ray wrote, "but is he just an old man with a mysterious charisma?" (Mawerera 1987a, 6). "I'm telling you," Ray said to me, "they thought this was real."

Long before Mudyiwa made headlines in the national magazines, most of the other Friday groups had given up on him. "By the mid-1970s we were not hearing about Emmanuel anymore," said Tsitsi. By this, Tsitsi meant that he could no longer be considered on track. But this is not to say that apostolics deny his former importance. Even today he is recognized as a spiritual leader in congregations that otherwise want nothing to do with him. For instance, Lazarus and I heard Madzibaba Gilbert, a prophet in Bulawayo, mention Emmanuel in a sermon. He began with praise, saying that Emmanuel worked with the Holy Spirit for many years and that he was healing and teaching his followers. But the praise became a warning, because Emmanuel became "proud" of himself and told people, "I am Jesus." "This," Gilbert concluded, "was a sad turn of events."

Other apostolics were more specific about Emmanuel's positive legacy. One apostolic in Chiweshe said, "Emmanuel followed Johane, but they parted ways over the Bible. Emmanuel went with the work of God." Over the course of several interviews with Madzibaba Sirus of Juranifiri Santa, I learned how Emmanuel is fitted in to church history as a defender of apostolic principles. Sirus and I always met in his yard under the shade of a tree with a bottle of ice-cold Fanta to split between us. One day he told me that in the late 1930s several prophets gathered at the Nyatsime River, which runs through present-day Chitungwiza. They stayed on the banks of the river for three days, praying to God day and night. On the last evening they saw a shooting star. "Some of the prophets there, who were not local natives, tried to say what the star meant," Sirus said. "But others in the group would not let them, saying,

'Hey, that person is from Malawi, why should we listen to him?' The Holy Spirit spoke through one of the prophets: 'You have refused these foreigners. I am going back to heaven.'" Sirus put down his glass of Fanta and continued: "The next day, Emmanuel said to those gathered, 'I have seen Abraham in a dream taking a bag and going back to heaven. You have all lost track.' Many of the people there forgot about Masowe after that, all except Emmanuel, who kept on with the faith. He would always tell people, 'You must follow what Johane said if you want to go to heaven.' Many people then saw Emmanuel Mudyiwa as their leader. He was healing people with the power of God." The emphasis on openness is a central element of the Friday message. So-called tribal or ethnic affiliations should always fall to the wayside for an apostolic Christian (casual jokes notwithstanding, even though they are sometimes made). Johane came for all Africans—not just the Manyika or other Shona-speaking peoples. Emmanuel's intervention at Nyatsime is remembered as a key moment in the preservation and promotion of this ideal, which most Friday apostolics recognize as their own.

But like Gilbert—and indeed like most apostolics outside the confines of Bretten Farm—Sirus tempered his praise. It was not many years after the prayer sessions at Nyatsime that Emmanuel was thought to have lost track. Here is Sirus again: "It is said that one day in the bush that Emmanuel had a vision. He dreamt that a snake was crawling into his nose—a black snake. It took twelve hours for the snake to slither in. It was a Lucifer-type snake that was possessing him. From then on, he started sleeping with other people's wives. And he had a big party. At the party he served pig and beer. This was totally against Johane Masowe!"

Sirus's claim that Emmanuel betrayed the original teachings of Johane Masowe is part of a widespread sentiment that is not quickly forgotten. But that other Friday apostolics could focus so much attention on "pig and beer" struck the Mudzimu Unoera followers as puzzling. Nevertheless, for Sirus and others, Emmanuel's changes are representative of a more profound undermining of the Friday message. It was a power play, a human decision. As the prophet Lawrence of Marondera told me, "Emmanuel grew disappointed over time, saying, 'I only want what is mine to be recognized.'" The problem with this lament, as I was told on numerous occasions, is that the power of the Holy Spirit cannot be owned; it is not anyone's place to say they must be recognized because of it.

Whether Mudyiwa was the Jesus to Shoniwa's John the Baptist is an irreconcilable difference between the Mudzimu Unoera and other Friday apostolics. For those who do not accept Emmanuel's claims—which is the majority—there is a qualitative distinction between someone speaking with the power of the Holy Spirit (or John the Baptist) and someone claiming to *be* Christ. But for the council of elders at Bretten Farm, Emmanuel simply fit into the church history that Shoniwa-Johane set in motion. After John comes Jesus, and with Jesus, salvation.

PHILIP (AND EUGENIA)

"Third from Johane" is a man named Philip Chigwada. (After Philip, the apostolics do not use ordinal numbers to mark the genealogy of prophets.) Philip, who died in 1993, ran a farm in Chiweshe—not far beyond Emmanuel's farm in the Mazoe Valley. As you approach Philip's place in Chiweshe along the tarred road from Mazoe, the orange trees give way to cotton fields, stretching to the horizon behind well-maintained fences, and then to peasant homesteads. Zimbabwe's colonial history unfolds along this road. In Zimbabwe you know immediately (or did, when I last traveled the roads) when you leave commercial farming areas and enter communal lands. The roads narrow to one lane, and the tar becomes patchy and rough. Chiweshe is one of the more fertile and prosperous communal lands, but even there Philip's farm seems out of place. It stretches out from the base of the Nyota kopje, a striking rock formation inside Chiweshe's southern border. The fields are not the size of a commercial holding, but they are significantly larger than the average communal plots. By the side of the road young men from the farm tend a produce stand with seasonal offerings (bananas, potatoes, maize, and leeks). They are always dressed in white shirts and shorts. Beyond the men at the stand are men and women working in the fields—also dressed in white—and beyond them a row of painted-white huts just at the base of the kopje.

Nyota is now run by Madzimai Eugenia, who was first filled with the Holy Spirit in 1994. Eugenia is the only female prophet I met in a Friday church with any claims to what approximates institutional authority. She is a short, full-bodied woman with round eyes and a peaceful disposition. When she speaks she is quiet and breaks a slight smile. "Philip worked at creating a family," Eugenia told Lazarus and me. "If you come here and accept the teaching, then you are a part of the family."

In Shona, *nyota* means "thirst." At the base of the kopje a freshwater spring provides the Nyota farm with cool, clean water. The water is used by the Nyota "family" to irrigate their fields. Pipes run from the spring to a large water tank, which supplies the fields. This is a major reason that the farm at Nyota has been so prosperous over the past decade. But Eugenia says that the farm's success is due just as much to the hard work that the apostolics put in each day and to the purity of their religious faith: "The Holy Spirit has blessed us for our good work, but this farm is not a miracle. It is the result of our hard labor." In any case, the Nyota farm has garnered a good deal of national attention. In the late 1990s it won an award from a major seed company for the best crop yields. During my fieldwork in 1999, just before the eight o'clock television news each evening, an apostolic from Nyota named Leviticus appeared in a television commercial run by the seed company. "Champion seeds!" the ad ran. Lazarus and I were also shown pictures from the day Thomas McDonald, U.S. ambassador to Zimbabwe during the second Clinton administration, came to inspect the impressive farm setup. We were told the U.S. government had invested money in the construction of the Nyota water tank.

Eugenia and her family met with us on a number of occasions to discuss church history. We sat in one of the huts at the base of the kopje. The floor of the hut was lined with gray wall-to-wall carpeting. The fire pit in the middle, modeled after the standard Shona design, had never been used. To one side near the back wall was a desk made of pressed wood with a high-back, red velvet swivel chair. To the other side near the back wall was a set of shelves. On one of the shelves were displayed several pictures of the apostolics, each covered in plastic wrap. Philip, as an old man, is in one of the pictures, standing in front of a white Mercedes Benz sedan. Eugenia and others (including Leviticus from the television ad) met with us for several interviews in that hut. At the end of each meeting we had butter sandwiches, boiled potatoes with onions, and tea. The trunk of my car was always loaded down with sacks of produce to take back to Harare—much more than I could eat on my own.

Philip's farmstead has been a center of apostolic activity since 1942. It is one of the few places in the Masowe religious landscape (and certainly the oldest) with any fixity. Other places, like Marimba hill, are remembered by the church elders, but none has been inhabited as a lived space of worship like Nyota.

We were told that Philip was filled with the Holy Spirit in 1942. He understood his main task as teaching other prophets how to pray to God. He said that everyone must come to him to be cleansed of evil intentions. He sang a song:

Nyararai vasina ngoni
Munorasa nyika yababa

Those without mercy, silent!
You will not enter the Kingdom of God

Emmanuel was preaching in Mondoro at the time and did not come when Philip called. Philip removed the evil spirits of those who did come and said, "You must remain with me for three years of training." As Eugenia explained it to us, one of the problems with Johane and Emmanuel had been their lack of "training" in how to handle the Holy Spirit. According to her, they began to preach before they were ready: "Johane was 'picked from the road' [i.e., at random]. So, too, was Emmanuel. But they did not learn how to speak with God. Consider Johane: He came and said, 'Let's pray on Friday.' And then, later, he changed it to Saturday!' Or Emmanuel: He told his people they could not drink beer, but eventually they ended up drinking. This was because they were not 'cooked' like Philip. They did not take the time to learn. They were not strong." So Philip himself did not immediately preach but worked with the handful of prophets who joined him to learn how to preach. With them, he climbed to the top of the Nyota kopje. Philip stayed on top of that hill for seven years—until 1949. At least one of the other men, James, stayed for five years. Together they prayed to God each day to ask for guidance. They never came down and learned to survive off of what they could gather by themselves. They slept in the shelter of some rocks. Each day they got on their knees with their arms outstretched. They sang songs, sometimes in the middle of the night. This was their training. Philip was learning how to be a strong and effective prophet. He was listening to the message of the Holy Spirit. Today Philip's dedication is widely admired by Masowe congregations, whether or not they have an active relationship with the Nyota farm. As the prophet Lawrence of Marondera told us, "Hey! This was a serious thing. You can say that Philip really took his faith seriously. He stayed on top of that hill for seven years, and did not come down for lightning, for sun, out of hunger, or to see his family. That is not an easy thing."

When Philip came down from the kopje he had dreadlocks stretching to his knees. People gathered, and he told them that he had been praying for all Africans. He had asked God to send angels to help. The people were surprised to see Philip in such a disheveled state. But before he cut off his dreadlocks, he said, "Can you see this life? This is the life of a dirty African." For his training under the Holy Spirit, Philip had to live like a "dirty African" to complete his transformation. To understand what God could do, Philip had to understand the depths of depravity to which a person could sink. Johane's criticisms of African custom resonated strongly with Philip. The farm he established was to be a model of new African living, a rejection of African ways in favor of order and a godly cleanliness.[3] Philip then cut his dreadlocks, because evil spirits often hide in one's hair (cf. Green 2003, 120–40, on shaving practices among Pogoro Catholics in Tanzania). Today there are several Friday prophets who shave their heads, and some demand that the men in their congregations do likewise.

Eugenia told us that all prophets were supposed to go through an apprenticeship with Philip. He was the shepherd of God's children. He was Peter to Shoniwa's Johane; he had been given "the keys of heaven" and taught "how to pray," she said. Indeed, several prophets come from Philip: Holia of Gombekombe, Admire of Mutumba, Daswis of Guruve, Jacob of Murewa, Paul of Domboshawa. Some of these prophets went on to become influential in their own right. Their congregations still talk about the influence of Philip. They respectfully recall the work that Philip put into teaching them how to pray. Until his death in 1993 Philip was a grounding force for many prophets and congregations. But Emmanuel, for one, did not share Philip's ideas. The two never got along. Emmanuel continued to lay claim to Johane's heritage with some effect, and his mobility in the 1940s and 1950s was as much an asset in spreading the Friday message as was Philip's fixity. Staying at Nyota did not always work to Philip's advantage, however. Some congregations did not go to see him, so his role in church history often pales in comparison to Emmanuel's, even though Emmanuel ended up, by almost all Friday accounts, a failed leader. When I asked Sirus about Philip, for instance, he did not know much. The Juranifiri Santa congregation has had little to do with the Nyota people. "I don't want to lie," Sirus said, "but I don't know much about Philip. When I have asked [the old-timers] about church history, they do not mention him very often, so I am not very much aware."

It may be that Philip came too early. He staked a claim in Nyota as a spiritual center at a time when such centeredness was difficult to maintain for the Friday churches as a whole. In any case, the Friday apostolics at Nyota live a relatively isolated existence from others, going about their business on the farm.

To reach Chiweshe from the Mazoe Valley, you take the Bindura road as it heads up through Glendale. But if you take the northwest fork at the Mazoe growth point (a collection of shops) you end up in the Guruve communal lands. Daswis, who comes from Philip, was born in Guruve. He stayed with Philip at Nyota for his training. In the 1960s he held intermittent jobs in Salisbury, where he helped to establish the first urban-based congregation.

One of Daswis's most vocal admirers is his sister's son, Madzibaba Lawrence. Lawrence—whom I have already quoted in passing—is himself an influential prophet in Marondera, a town about eighty kilometers east of Harare known for its coffee estates and wineries. When we visited him in 1999 Lawrence was the regional head of the ZANU(PF) party and the public relations manager for the town of Marondera. One rainy December day we found him in his office at the ZANU(PF) headquarters, a surprisingly decrepit building on the outskirts of town. The walls inside were unfinished cement and the lights were not working; even the requisite portrait of President Mugabe behind Lawrence's desk was in poor shape. After dealing with some party business, Lawrence took us to his other office in the Marondera Town Hall. The town hall was a much nicer building, but his office there seemed odd too. It was an empty, unwelcoming room. This day job was clearly not the center of Lawrence's life, although we quickly realized there were a number of people who thought it should be. Lawrence had to speak with us between calls on his cell phone and office line while lunching on a curried meat pie, which he washed down with a coke. His lavender shirt and dark blue tie were covered in crumbs by the end of the conversation.

"My uncle was visited by an angel as a young man and told to go see Philip at Nyota," Lawrence said. Daswis was a prophet for more than thirty-five years. He was involved in the training of a number of other prophets, including his nephew. But his two most notable charges were Eriah and Sandros Namwebonde. "A great leader is made evident by his students," Lawrence told us.

ERIAH

Despite the fact that Johane began preaching on the outskirts of the colonial capital, the Friday apostolics gained their primary footholds in the rural areas. That began to change in the early 1970s. (Mudyiwa was living then in Chitungwiza, although most Friday apostolics today discount his presence, because of the extent to which he had turned his religious mission into a personal business.) The real work in the urban areas was initiated by Daswis, even as he moved between town and country. But Daswis did not establish a congregation in Salisbury. He left that to one of his "students." The first prophet to preach regularly in Salisbury was a migrant worker from Malawi named Eriah.

Many of the Africans in Salisbury were migrant workers who stayed in "the locations," places such as Harari (now Mbare) and Highfield, large tracts of land just south of the railway line near the factories and industrial parks. By the late 1960s, with the African population in Salisbury at a height of 280,000 (Barnes and Win 1992, 41), new high-density suburbs were being developed to accommodate the demands of the colonial economy. By the late 1970s even these new suburbs could not cope with the influx of people—refugees from the liberation war, which was tearing through many communal areas, began squatting where they could (Schylter 2003, 16). With these various influxes through the 1960s and 1970s came new streams of thought, politics, and religious organization (Hallencreutz 1999; Pape 1999; Raftopoulos 1999), to which the Friday apostolics added an increasingly vibrant current.

The old housing estates for African workers are still standing in Mbare (or they were; Mugabe began a demolition operation in 2005 that brought some down [see Potts 2006]). They are long, narrow apartment blocks set tightly together, not unlike housing projects in American cities. The streets in these and other high-density neighborhoods are always teeming with people. They are narrow and cramped, occasionally broken up by small plots of maize or gardens where people grow their vegetables. Beyond the apartment blocks large families occupy small houses. The sounds of Zimbabwean pop can be heard on every street. Each block has a tuck shop that sells basic commodities: cooking oil and maize meal, as well as Coca-Cola and freezits (Popsicles) for the children. Almost every house is fenced, or, if the family can afford it, surrounded by a cement durawall. Sometimes bougainvillea hangs from the walls or an archway leading to the front door. In February the sunflowers add an extra splash of color to the cityscapes.

Eriah started the first Salisbury congregation in Highfield, not far from where he stayed. Like Mbare, Highfield has a reputation as a dangerous place (Barnes and Win 1992, 53). As the first prophet settled in a high-density suburb, Eriah was looking to bring much-needed peace to the city.

Throughout the 1970s he preached as he could, sometimes in his home under cover of night (this is reflected on now as an extreme measure). After Zimbabwe's independence in 1980, Eriah began to hold services more regularly in the open fields where they ought to have been held. The congregation he started still meets every week, now at a place called Afgate along a strip of land parallel to the Willowvale Road. The site is called Afgate because it is across the road from an industrial plant with that name.

Many Zimbabweans often told me that Africans from other countries, especially Malawi and Mozambique, are "too spiritual." This was usually understood as a bad thing. The most powerful witchcraft creatures, for example, are often said to come from these countries. At Masowe healing rituals prophets spoke about *zvikwambo* (goblinlike creatures) who had taken the bus from Malawi to Harare's central market, where they planned to wreak havoc on the local population. I return to a discussion of witchcraft creatures in chapter 7. For now, the point is that Eriah is an exception to the foreigner stereotype—at least for many apostolics. He was a *good* Malawian, whose work for the Holy Spirit confirms the value of the inclusive attitude that prophets such as Johane, Emmanuel, and Philip encouraged. The power of the Holy Spirit should always transcend ethnic and tribal boundaries.

Next to Johane, Eriah is probably the least ridiculed prophet in church history. In fact, Eriah can lay claim to something that even Johane could not: he stayed on track, preaching a Friday message until the day he died.

Eriah was a good healer, but he is remembered most for organizing the fast growth of the urban congregations in a practical and even-handed manner. From his base in Highfield, which is still known as the mother congregation of Harare, Eriah engineered the spread of congregations throughout the other suburbs. Since life in Harare provided him with the largest potential following, Eriah used the suburbs to his advantage. If he knew of people coming to Highfield from Mbare to pray, he asked them to start praying in Mbare. They would at first still need guidance from Highfield, so Eriah designated local elders to work closely with him. Often prophets would emerge in these satellite congregations and receive training from Eriah. But if a congregation did not have its own prophet, Eriah was always available to provide spiritual healing. In general, however, the feeling was that congregations should be oriented to serve local areas. By the mid-1970s there were prophets working in Mbare, Warren Park, Sunningdale, and Chitungwiza, all of whom had come from Eriah. The most influential of these was Sandros Namwebonde.

Sandros was born in Guruve, not far from Daswis, and was a close child-hood friend of Lawrence, the politician and prophet in Marondera. Law-rence told me that even as a young boy Sandros had the power of the Holy Spirit. Despite his urban training, then, Sandros maintained links to Daswis as well. In the 1970s, when he was a young man, Sandros came to Salisbury to find work and eventually found a job with a pharmacist at one of Harare's hospitals. For some time he prayed with Eriah in High-field, but when he moved to Chitungwiza Sandros established a congrega-tion, which eventually met by the Nyatsime River, with Eriah's support. By the late 1980s, at the close of Zimbabwe's first decade of independence, Sandros had the largest congregation in the Harare-Chitungwiza area.

In contrast to Eriah's quiet and steady organization throughout the 1970s, Sandros was vocal and fast paced. By the early 1990s he had be-come the first apostolic media persona—a legacy that still bothers several congregations, including Afgate in Highfield. Like Emmanuel, who al-lowed himself to be covered in the pages of *Parade* magazine, Sandros was thought by some elders and fellow prophets to have fallen off track, to have given in to the temptation of placing himself above the Spirit that worked through him.

During the colonial era, particularly at the height of the liberation war, the need to keep out of sight and out of the press was well understood among the Friday congregations. The apostolics knew that in order not to upset the authorities, they had to maintain a low profile (to foster, as it were, an invisible history). They knew what could otherwise happen to them given the plight of Johane's Basketmaker Church. In the early 1960s the authorities in South Africa deported Johane Masowe and the Basket-makers from Port Elizabeth, where they had been living for well over a decade. The Rhodesian government provided them with a small parcel of land in Seke, but it was too far from the markets of Salisbury where they might best earn a living selling their baskets. The leaders of the Saturday church protested strenuously against the Seke settlement but to no avail.[4] Over the 1960s the Basketmakers were welcomed by the new postcolonial governments farther north, in both Lusaka and Nairobi. The community established in Seke has managed to survive, but it never gained vibrancy. The Friday apostolics told me the Basketmakers would have been better off to leave well enough alone. They reasoned that if the Basketmakers had not presented their case in a confrontational manner (at one point in the process of their deportation from South Africa they appealed to Israel for asylum) the government probably would have reconsidered the decision to locate them at Seke. Either way, it was always better for African churches not to give the authorities trouble, because it only ever got in the way of serving God. Tsitsi told me "the strategy after Johane left was that it had to be kept private." Keeping out of the newspapers was only prudent.

Beyond its political expediency, keeping things "private" has a theological dimension. Christianity is a serious matter. If it cannot be reduced to Scripture, it certainly cannot be reduced to a newspaper article or segment on the television news. Even my research—covering eighteen months over a seven-year period—was sometimes suspect for its brevity. "You cannot understand Masowe chop-chop," as one apostolic put it. "This thing takes time." Discretion and privacy have their place whether or not one is contending with a suspicious state.

Sandros had other ideas. Zimbabwe was not Rhodesia, and there were good reasons, in his view, for the church to open itself up. Even in an independent Zimbabwe, where African Christians have greater room to operate on their own terms, the weChishanu have been plagued by negative stereotypes—stereotypes that their recalcitrant privacy only reinforces. Because they do not read the Bible and because they worship in open fields, because they once rejected biomedicine (like the Saturday apostolics), and because they are so easily confused with those who do (like the Maranke apostolics), the weChishanu have suffered to this day from charges of backwardness (even as they fight against a backwardness they perceive in others). Sandros wanted to change these stereotypes.

During my first trip to Zimbabwe, in 1993, I was surprised to open the Zimbabwe *Herald* on March 30 to find the following article:

Church to Set Up $2.5m Centre for Disabled

The Johane Masowe-Chishanu Apostolic Church in Chitungwiza plans to build a $2.5 million centre [at the time, approximately U.S. $416,000] for the church's disabled children.

Addressing more than 5,000 people on the importance of health before spiritual life, the church's national leader, Father Sandros Nhamoyebonde, said the church was working with Chitungwiza General Hospital's occupational therapist to set up the complex. . . .

Father Nhamoyebonde told the meeting that his church had bought land which would be used as gathering sites in Bulawayo, Gweru, Masvingo, and Chipinge.

Most of the apostolics I knew at that point were not happy to see the name of their church in newsprint. The article raised hackles especially because Sandros had encouraged the media coverage. What is more, many found it odd that Sandros claimed to have access to that kind of money and that he would be interested in setting up a permanent institution like a children's center (or for that matter buying land), however noble in principle. It is true that he had worked in a hospital, but he was a Christian prophet, so why go into occupational therapy? And to top it off Sandros sparked ire because he was not the church's "national leader." The Friday groups have no such thing.

And yet some apostolics, such as Gilbert of Bulawayo, have seen Sandros's efforts in a positive light. Echoing claims of the Mudzimu Unoera about Emmanuel, Gilbert told me Sandros recognized that "times change" and that the apostolics had to change with them if the Friday message was to flourish. There are, nevertheless, apostolics who still say that with schemes like his so-called children's center Sandros was not following the path of Johane. Detractors and skeptics aside, Sandros undeniably took his congregation and the Friday message in new directions. Whether or not he had the $2.5 million needed to build his children's center (and no such center was ever built), the very fact that he was willing to promote it in the newspapers was a harbinger of changes to come, albeit changes that have not always been uniformly appreciated.

Sandros died in 1996. Some of the apostolics I spoke with claimed his funeral was attended by more than ten thousand people in the streets of Chitungwiza. I was told the crowds were so large that the police had to direct traffic. Several apostolics told me Sandros died of AIDS because he had fallen off track. Sirus thought that by the time Sandros died he could not be considered a Friday prophet. "I don't know why all those people mourned him," Sirus remarked. "That fact itself proves he was no longer following the path of Johane. It seems to me that, given the evidence, those people at his funeral were more interested in Sandros as a person than they were with the Holy Spirit." For Sirus, the followers of Sandros had confused him *with* the Spirit.

NZIRA

Nzira comes from Sandros. Godfrey Nzira was born in the 1950s and grew up in the Nyamashesha and Mamina areas of the Mondoro communal lands, southwest of Harare. Nzira left school after the second grade. He moved to Chitungwiza as a young man, in the mid-1970s. There he got a job with Chibuku Breweries, which makes a traditional-style millet beer. Nzira worked at Chibuku for over twenty years—long after he became a teetotaling apostolic. Although still relatively young, Nzira retired from Chibuku in 1995 to devote his time to the church. By that point he had built up a congregation that rivaled Sandros's in size.

Like many apostolics, Nzira shaved his head, and he kept it well polished with lotion. His nose and forehead are pointy. Nzira is not a tall man, but this is not something you notice at first. What draws your attention are his eyes, more angular than round—and penetrating even from a distance. His chest is broad and well defined, and he sticks it out as he walks. Nzira's feet are broad and strong. At Juranifiri Santa he stood on them for hours on most days, making his toes puff out like well-stuffed sausages. Outside of church he could be found wearing dapper oxfords and well-tailored trousers. He wore a gold watch that dangled from his left wrist, which he would unconsciously flick around and massage.

In 1975 Nzira's wife, Spiwe, went to Sandros for help with an illness. Nzira went with her. In time Spiwe was duly cured, and together the couple became dedicated apostolics under Sandros's guidance. After a few years Nzira started having dreams that contained prophetic messages about himself and other members at Nyatsime. These dreams—which many prophets have before they are filled and speak out with the Holy Spirit—were interpreted by Sandros. Nzira also sang during the Nyatsime services in a way that forced congregants possessed by avenging and evil spirits to writhe in pain.

Nzira was filled with the Holy Spirit in 1986 on a retreat with Sandros to an island in Lake Kariba, on the border with Zambia. On the island, it is said, he awoke one morning to find a large rock wedged into his back; the rock symbolized the weight of his new mission. Nzira had been given a burden to carry for Africans. He was now a prophet of God, speaking with the power of the Holy Spirit. As a prophet, he was to be called Pageneck.

In the first few years of his preaching Nzira-Pageneck relied heavily on advice from Sandros and the Nyatsime elders. In most congregations, in fact, the elders play an important role in training prophets. One elder told me:

Oftentimes, a prophet—particularly a young [i.e., new] prophet—does not know how to handle the Spirit. We are supposed to guide him. When Pageneck started out, *tsk,* ah, he was young! I saw him. It was not like he is now. Back then, he needed help. In fact, sometimes the *vadare* [elders] are supposed to keep the prophets in line, and make sure that they follow

Figure 3. The author and Godfrey Nzira (right) at the
author's flat in Harare, 1999. Photo by Rebecca Nash.

the rules set down by Johane. Oftentimes, there is human nature comes
and the prophet will fail to follow the rules. Sometimes, even, they forget
themselves and think that they are the real power.

Nzira-Pageneck's burden, symbolized by the rock in his back, was to deal
with the issues raised by this elder—issues faced by all prophets before
him. The elder's comments were made several years after the fact, at a
time when Nzira-Pageneck was nearing the height of his popularity and
authority. But he was not always recognized "like he is now."

On returning to Chitungwiza from the Kariba trip, Nzira-Pageneck
worked solely with Sandros at Nyatsime. But Sandros did not like what
was happening. "He became suspicious," according to Sirus. Some of Sandros's elders were jealous and said, "Hey, do you want to be the leader of
this sowe? Why is it that when you sing the people run away?" Nzira said,
"It is not me, I don't know what is happening." The elders assaulted him,
and Sandros began to sing:[5]

Dominio, dominio, dominio down!

I have come here with thunder!

Thus Nzira was driven away from Nyatsime. Undeterred, he began his own congregation behind a row of tuck shops near his house. In 1989 he moved to the place known as Juranifiri Santa. After their split Sandros and Nzira had little to do with each other, despite the fact that their congregations met only a few kilometers apart from one another.

Nzira's success was secured in part by adopting the outlook of his rival. Nzira did not intend to build a children's center in collaboration with the local hospital, but for spirit-related afflictions he established a "hospital" of his own at Juranifiri, complete with several cement brick, thatched-roof wards. At any given time in 1999 up to thirty people were staying in these wards recovering from different ailments.

To the media-open stance that Sandros advocated, Nzira added a dose of political networking. He was not, like Lawrence, a politician, but he had influential friends in ZANU(PF), not least the commissioner of police, Augustine Chihuri, who sometimes prayed at Juranifiri and who is probably the most well known Friday apostolic in Zimbabwe.[6] Chihuri is certainly the most politically powerful apostolic, occupying a key position in Mugabe's regime. Nzira's combination of media and politics reached its climax after I completed my fieldwork. During the parliamentary elections of 2000, the young and energetic governor of Mashonaland Central, Border Gezi, who was running for the parliamentary seat of Bindura as a ZANU(PF) candidate, gave an address to Nzira's congregation at Juranifiri Santa. Gezi, himself a Friday apostolic, brought the media with him. It was, plain and simple, a political rally intended to mobilize a would-be voter bloc. Other congregations of the church demanded an apology from Gezi. One elder from Nyatsime was quoted in the papers as saying, "We feel offended because Gezi used our church for his own political ambitions" (*Daily News* June 21, 2000; see also the Zimbabwe *Independent,* June 16, 2000; cf. Dorman 2003).[7]

Nzira's role in this political stunt raised serious questions about whether he had fallen off track. These questions were in the air well before the rally, but the media attention only heightened their urgency. And while the *Daily News* quote was provided by an apostolic from Nyatsime, some congregants at Juranifiri Santa were also made uncomfortable by the event. Although I did not get to speak to any Juranifiri elders after the Gezi rally, I can imagine those closest to Nzira saying what they usually said on his behalf: The Spirit works differently through different people. This was not the question of leadership. It was the will of God.

Hwimbo is the uncle of the police commissioner, Augustine Chihuri. It was never made clear to me who he comes from, although the common assumption was Emmanuel. He is, in any case, widely recognized as one of the major prophets because of his success at healing and building up congregations throughout northeastern Zimbabwe. But Hwimbo is different from the other prophets in the genealogy. It was he who broke away from the Masowe path. He is not concerned about having fallen off track because his intention was to change track altogether. Hwimbo does not claim to be Johane's heir but rather the source of something new.

Hwimbo left the Masowe Church in 1996 to start a movement called Vadzidzi vaJesu, or Disciples of Jesus. Since then the "disciples" (*vadzidzi;* lit. "students") have been growing at a quick pace. What Hwimbo did is to shift the emphasis of faith to a more explicit recognition of Jesus, a figure who without doubt receives much less attention than the Holy Spirit in most apostolic congregations. One disciple in Mount Darwin told us what happened:

> Three years ago [in 1996] the church divided into two. Because Hwimbo had prophesized that he had seen a vision with a house, and the house was written with a notice, a surname, and it is said it is the house from which the Holy Spirit comes. And the other members in Masowe did not agree [with Hwimbo], and they broke away from their leader. So they remained Johane Masowe people, known as madzibaba. Those who remained with Hwimbo became Vadzidzi vaJesu, to differentiate between the two. And then the other group, the madzibaba, [they are] still following the teaching of Mudyiwa.

Hwimbo became a weChishanu apostolic—a madzibaba—when he was a young man, soon after Johane left for South Africa. He was filled with the Holy Spirit in 1945. Since then Hwimbo has been building a ministry like his counterparts throughout Mashonaland. Like Philip, he has come to be associated with a particular place, which is called Goora, just beyond the town of Bindura. His influence stretches north from Goora to the Mount Darwin communal areas, which border Mozambique. Since 1996, when he had the vision of the house, Hwimbo's following has, we were told, mushroomed. He has, as always, built his reputation on healing. Like Juranifiri Santa, Goora is a "hospital" for people with spiritual afflictions. When we visited Goora it was abuzz with activity. There were several dozen men and women, most of whom were doing work of one kind or another. Several small structures were being built—mostly one-room cottages that would house the "patients." To the west of this site stands an old farmhouse, painted sky blue. This is where Hwimbo stays.

Lazarus and I sat on the farmhouse porch and spoke with the prophet—an old, steely-eyed man with a white beard and matching robes. Hwimbo began with a repudiation of his counterparts: "I am the leader of all these prophets: Sandros, Nzira, Lawrence, and all others. I gave them the places they are using now. I led them all, but as you know, kids these days, if you give them positions, they do what they want." Hwimbo was certainly no shrinking lily. Not even Nzira spoke with such bravado. Hwimbo was confident of his position and used the repudiation to segue into the heart of the Vadzidzi vaJesu message. Because now, he said, "it's like some of these people are not Christians. They are not worshiping Jesus. Have you heard them sing songs? They always talk about Abraham, Isaac, Moses, Peter. Why? Do they worship them, or Jesus?"

Hwimbo criticizes the Friday apostolics because of the direction of their faith. Their track—the wrong track—has shifted focus away from Christ. And this applies to Emmanuel too. In fact, it applies *especially* to Emmanuel, because of his claims to be the "Jesus of Chiweshe." Hwimbo is the leader of the Disciples of Jesus, but he is nothing more than a disciple himself.

Most of the apostolics in Harare and Chitungwiza are unpersuaded by Hwimbo's critiques. "It's all about leadership that side," said one, referring to the Goora group. "Some of these prophets, well, they just think they can change from Masowe. But you can't just say, 'Oh now, such-and-such.'" His heated reaction was typical. But Zechariah and Tsitsi, it should be said, were cooler.

"We don't have problems with them," Zechariah said. "They are doing their own things, and we are doing our own things, and really—"

Tsitsi interrupted him: "When you really look at it, I don't think they worry about us." She sat with her hands folded in her lap.

"But they don't have Bibles?" asked Lazarus.

"No," Tsitsi answered. "They are just like us."

"So it's a question of leadership," I ventured.

"I should think so," concluded Zechariah.

In the opening section of this chapter I mentioned that the "genealogy" of prophets would be neither exhaustive nor uncontested. In conclusion I want to suggest that these limitations to the church history are not simply a function of academic hedging. For one thing, church history is always limited because—like any other history—it has no agreed on form among its disseminators. While all of the major prophets recognize a common source of inspiration (even Hwimbo, in his way) and while ordinary members like Tsitsi and Zechariah can emphasize how other Friday groups are really "just like" them, there is a considerable degree of difference between what happens at, say, Bretten Farm and Juranifiri Santa; or Nyota and Goora; or Afgate and Nyatsime. The differences are carved out in large part by the question of leadership—that is, the extent to which prophets claim to direct church history toward a conclusion. Or the extent to which they recognize themselves as presence.

But the limitations to church history are more than this—more than political wranglings over who might be the ultimate prophet. They are constitutive elements of apostolic cosmology. There is an important sense in which church history demands to be read as a series of successive failures. The apostolics are aware, perhaps more than most social scientists, "that failure may be a normal or endemic state of relations between religion and society" (Fabian 1991a, 118). One of the key "elements" of the Friday message, an element that seems to persist in spite of occasional efforts at its eradication, is its always-unfolding nature. The sense of immediacy that stands at the heart of Johane's Friday message militates against enduring forms. The failure of any given prophet becomes proof that the Friday message is still relevant. The prophets who fall off track (which is to say, those who stand accused of falling off track) provide valuable lessons about the dangers of conflating human and divine power. They also provide us with insight into how, in a semiotic ideology that highlights the value of immateriality, prophets challenge the commitment to it. Church history is always already framed by the concern with things that Johane set into motion.

I doubt any of the Friday apostolics I know would put an unqualified stamp of approval on the church history as I have presented it here. Not all are prone to factionalism, but those closer to Emmanuel might want his story more positively highlighted, those closer to Philip might want the same for his, and so on and so on. But while it is neither possible nor desirable to construct church history as a stable object, there are, I think, overarching elements and themes of faith to which attention should be drawn. Church history often comes back to a set of key concerns. These include how the apostolics should handle money, politics, media, and the burdens of "African culture." All these concerns become clearer in the remaining chapters, as the book moves into the heart of the ethnography. What I want to highlight for the moment is how the question of leadership is often posed—implicitly and explicitly—in relation to space and place as signs of presence and proximity.

Implicitly, all the major prophets who have proclaimed or implied their plenitude do so through building things. Their "innovations in space"—to draw again on Werbner's insight—are architectonic (cf. Fernandez 1982). A built environment becomes the claim to completion, to a proximity to God that can be seen. Emmanuel erected the most solid house in Africa on a colonial farm; Philip transformed a kopje into a spiritual center; Sandros promised a multimillion-dollar children's center; Pageneck and Hwimbo constructed hospitals of their own. But the certitude of these actions and plans is always challenged by the logic out of which they emerge, a logic that warns against fixing things for good.

Explicitly, the overriding image of faith is a path on which one must travel, a track to which one must keep. Staying on track is of central concern to the apostolics, and the desire to do so motivates the telling and contemplation of church history. But here I have only traced the path and suggested that it continues to unfold despite occasional efforts to direct it toward an end—whether that end is the House of Jesus on Bretten Farm or a "hospital ward" in Chitungwiza. In the next chapter I want to turn attention, broadly speaking, from past to present—to look at "how the past is in the present" (Dening 1996, 44)—through an exploration of the concepts and disciplinary regimes that today mark the apostolic course.

Finally, however, I want to say that the uses of space and place to answer the question of leadership are related to the problem of presence. As these discussions of church history suggest, prophets are always caught up in the problem. They are, inevitably, part of the problem. Whether through their implied plenitude or through the things they build, prophets generate the dangers that a live and direct faith is supposed to dispel. If the Friday apostolics have been relatively successful at resisting the lure of Johane as ultimate, they have not always done without a thingified faith. Indeed, this case gives Max Weber's insightful summation of charismatic appeal—"it is written, but I say unto you"—new meaning. The question of leadership shows how thingification is not only rooted in the tension between letter and voice. Church history prompts us to consider how prophets themselves can become that which a live and direct faith ought to do without. The presences that prophets can become, and the presences they sometimes construct, are not always those of the Friday message.

FOUR

Mutemo in Three Portraits

THE PREVIOUS TWO CHAPTERS ARE held together with minimum reference to the content of the Friday message. In chapter 2 I aimed to make Shoniwa-Johane's transformation legible, and while I tried to highlight those aspects of his preaching that have become the bedrock of a Friday cosmology, we were left with only protean forms. Social scientific clarity is done no favor when we consider that the Friday message is motivated by a specific commitment to immateriality. Nothing and no one should be set in bedrock, and so the message cannot be presented as "fixed." In chapter 3 the shape of things came more clearly into focus; I discussed, for example, something about the language of faith. Faith is a track or path to which one must keep. This track is signposted by sets of prescriptions: what apostolics should and should not do and what they should not eat, drink, or read. Through these prescriptions we begin to see something like "doctrines" or, more shadowy still, "beliefs"—but church history and the question of leadership remind us that not even these signposts are agreed upon by the prophets who claim inspiration and inheritance from Johane. In this chapter, nevertheless, the goal is to give more detail on the form and content of the Friday message—even as the apostolics might want to resist such materializing metaphors. In doing so, I take the opportunity to shift attention away from prophets to explore the dispositions and concerns of apostolics who describe themselves as "ordinary members."

For old-timers and neophytes alike, the concept through which the Friday message gains its expression and relevance is mutemo. The concept of mutemo, as I mentioned in the introduction, is integral to how the apostolics understand faith as live and direct.[1] To recap, *mutemo* is a Shona word usually translated into English as "law" (or "rule") but which the apostolics use to refer to a certain kind of religious "knowledge" as well. Apostolics describe mutemo as the guiding principle in their lives, something that provides both discipline and meaning. It is the concept through which they sense, and make sense of, God's presence. Mutemo was discussed in every Friday congregation I worked with or visited. Elders, in particular, spend a significant amount of time talking about mutemo in their church lessons. Yet on an everyday basis, mutemo is not something most apostolics casually talk about; it is not something that groups of friends will gather together to discuss in each other's homes. Nevertheless, it became clear to me that mutemo can occupy a significant amount of an apostolic's inner attention. When they do speak about it—especially in terms of how it can be known—the language they use focuses on how it "gets into you," comes "from within," and is a "personal thing." Asking about mutemo directly, however, was not always the best way to understand its significance. People would begin to say "That's mutemo" about most everything. Thus their position on the Bible is mutemo; observing Friday as the Sabbath is mutemo; worshiping in open fields is mutemo; the Ten Commandments are mutemo; abstaining from alcohol is mutemo (pace Emmanuel); the fight against witchcraft is mutemo; and so on. Such definitions only strip the term of any specificity. This is not to say that apostolics cannot speak of it revealingly, but to understand mutemo it is best to situate it in relation to particular events and the concerns of particular people. In what follows, I provide portraits of three ordinary members in the Friday churches to show how they talk about and act on mutemo in everyday life, to show how it emerges in the process of its own formation.

MADZIBABA SHIMMER

One helpful way to understand mutemo is through an examination of the apostolics' conversion narratives, which often play a central role in their definition of themselves as Christians (see also Engelke 2004a; cf. Asad 1996, 266). It is through the process of conversion, and the framing of that process in a story, that the religious subject comes to wrestle with mutemo as both a set of laws and a system of knowledge.

The concept of conversion has generated a good deal of heat and light in the social scientific literature. In his recent analysis of this literature, Robbins (2004, 84–88) outlines what he sees as the two main analytic approaches to the subject: the "utilitarian" and the "intellectualist." Simply put, the utilitarian approach suggests that people convert to world religions like Christianity or Islam because of the political and/or socioeconomic opportunities they provide. It is important to stress that in using this term, Robbins is not suggesting that there is "some universal notion of what is valuable" (2004, 85) according to which utility is defined. Here, utilitarianism means only that "in their early approaches to a world religion, people are motivated by their own culturally given goals, not by those that the religion itself posits of the subjects it aims to create" (2004, 85). I outlined hints of this in chapter 1. Jim Ximungana appointed a preacher for the Swiss Mission not because the man was a devout Christian but because he was literate and could serve as an operator for Ximungana in the local political sphere. Mzilikazi, taking a somewhat different approach, never converted to Christianity but understood the potential benefits of allowing Moffat to establish a London Missionary Society station near his court. In these two cases "conversion" is tied up with practical concerns, as defined by an interest in Christianity for what it can provide Ximungana and Mzilikazi as political operators. They suggest that utilitarian motives make for a reasonable argument in understanding the conversion to Christianity, not least in a colonial context.

As several anthropologists point out, however, this approach strips conversion of a religious dimension and sidelines the important question of the religious subject's transformation (Kipp 1995; Robbins 2004, 85–86). Isaac Schapera (1940, 73–81), for example, has documented an early occasion on which Christianity struck its spiritual chord when its utilitarian benefits were not as obvious. He relates that Chief Lentswe of the Kgatla banned *bogadi* (bride-price) after his conversion to Christianity in 1892—a move that was popular with the Dutch Reformed Church but not Lentswe's people. The people eventually prevailed: fifteen years later Lentswe reintroduced the practice after widespread "confusion and dissatisfaction" (Schapera 1940, 75) within his chiefdom. What Schapera shows is how Lentswe's "enthusiasm for Christianity" (1940, 30) proved a risk to his political authority rather than a means of its consolidation.

The example of Chief Lentswe lends credence to the intellectualist approach. Simply put, the intellectualist approach "is built on the argument that conversion allows people to comprehend and live meaningfully in a changed world" (Robbins 2004, 86).[2] Regardless of Christianity's political or economic "practicality," then, it is important to recognize that taking on a religion might alter a subject's understanding of what exactly is "practical" or "right." As Rita Kipp puts it, and as Robbins also shows, converts can "come to see history and their own existential dilemmas through a lens of faith" (Kipp 1995, 879). This is, in many ways, a more useful framework for an analysis of the Masowe apostolics. As I have already argued, Johane's critique of mission cannot be reduced to a political idiom, and I want to stress here that apostolic Christianity does not conform to the blandness of a utilitarian logic. This is not to say that a meaning-centered analysis is ever sufficient in itself.[3] One of the benefits to come out of Robbins's discussion is his attention to conversion as a series of overlapping processes in time, motivated (and driven) by a range of dynamics and claims. Even a meaning-centered analysis must often include a "utilitarian tinge" (Robbins 2004, 86). But when the ethnographic record suggests that faith outstrips functionalism, we need to take it seriously. How my friend Shimmer came to understand and embrace mutemo is a case in point. Here we get a good sense of what an anthropology of Christianity can offer.

In 1991 Shimmer was suffering from severe stomach pains. They made it difficult for him to eat. They kept him awake at night and ruined his concentration. So Shimmer went to see a doctor, thinking he might have an ulcer. But the doctor could not find anything wrong. Shimmer began to suspect that his condition had been caused by some kind of spirit. "You know," he told me, "down here in Africa we've got this problem of bewitching—evil spirits and all that." So Shimmer consulted a n'anga (traditional healer), who charged him an exorbitant fee for some muti (traditional medicine), but the muti did not work. Eventually, his brother's mother-in-law told him he ought to try a prophet she knew of in Chitungwiza called Nzira. She was not a member of his church, but Nzira had helped her in the past and so maybe he could help Shimmer too.

"At that moment," Shimmer said, "I wasn't going to any church. I was just an ordinary person. I used to drink, I use to smoke. I was just a young man." But he thought the prophet was worth a try. Shimmer was not "too spiritual," but he had consulted a few Christian prophets in the past, as well as a n'anga or two. But Shimmer stressed to me that at Nzira's place things were "quite different." The first time he went, for a Saturday healing session, Shimmer was asked with dozens of other people to stand up in groups according to a spectrum of certain ailments. And so he found himself standing amid the congregation with a handful of other people suffering from stomach problems. It made him embarrassed and uncomfortable; his previous interactions with prophets and mediums had always been private affairs. And not only was it somewhat embarrassing to be standing up and revealing his stomach problems in front of strangers, it was also dangerous. To stand up in this way is to articulate the conditions of one's illness in a manner that others can exploit. People ought not to call attention to their afflictions with any degree of specificity because that knowledge can be turned against them. As in many African contexts, Shimmer was raised to think that one should only share the details of an illness with close relatives (cf. Last 1992, 400) and that even this can be cause for concern, since relatives are often the ones who can cause you the most "trouble" (cf. Geschiere 1997, 211–14). What Nzira had asked Shimmer to do made him uncomfortable because it went against his common sense.

Reservations notwithstanding, Shimmer followed the instructions of the prophet and, in due course, the prophet's elders. After standing up with others who suffered from stomach pains, the elders put Shimmer into a queue off to one side of the main congregation. Bolstered by the congregants, who were now singing on behalf of the designated "patients," the people in the queue filed past Nzira, who touched their foreheads as they went by. Shimmer then found himself kneeling on the ground in a row with the other patients. One of the elders gave each of them water to drink out of a wooden bowl. Eventually all the patients were dismissed and told to come back the following morning. By eight o'clock the next morning Shimmer was back at the sowe (church site). That night he had slept soundly for the first time in months. His stomach pains were almost gone. "So, it was like a day and I saw that things were changing. The results were very chop-chop."

Not all patients claim such rapid results, but Shimmer's story of coming to the church is typical. The majority of apostolics first approach the church as "patients." This is an important point to make. Shimmer's story puts the appeal of the church into broader perspective. Spiritual healing is a major activity within the Friday churches, a point I expand on here and in chapter 7. Indeed, it is not the rejection of the Bible that draws someone like Shimmer to a Friday congregation but the promise of healing. Taking "this problem of bewitching" seriously, as Shimmer put it, is often what compels people to consult with African Christian prophets (cf. Schoffeleers 1991). There is, I think, an inevitable (and not necessarily troublesome) "utilitarian tinge" in all this. The African independent churches are valued because of the specific ways in which they address the concerns about witchcraft expressed by those who come to them. Several apostolics told me of their frustrations with the main-line churches to which they once belonged, none of which addressed their concerns about "African problems." A former Anglican, for example, was told that witchcraft and ancestral spirits were superstitions; he met relief for his debilitating headaches only when he consulted a Masowe prophet. The prophet knew the man's ailments could not be traced to physical causes alone, and so he dealt with them accordingly. Friday prophets make good use of healing's instrumental potentials: it is often the first step in drawing someone into a live and direct faith. Apostolic healing is a powerful way in which the Holy Spirit is understood to address African problems in an always relevant fashion.

Shimmer was told his stomach pains were the result of jealousy. This brings us back to the discussion in the introduction. Shimmer was told he had been bewitched by a relative jealous of his success at school. (This is why the medical doctor had been no help.) Like many Zimbabweans I knew, Shimmer saw witchcraft and jealousy as grave dangers to his well-being and indeed the well-being of all Africans. The Friday churches routinely stress these dangers: since the early days, when Johane was first told to rid the world of mishonga (medicines), the eradication of witchcraft and "heathen" religious practices has been a goal. The main problem, as several people pointed out, is that Africans have jealous and cruel dispositions. Left to follow "African ways," Africans will keep themselves mired in destructive relationships. The force of this idea is captured rather starkly in a well-known Masowe song:

Maboyi, maboyi
mweya wetsvino

Kaffirs, kaffirs
the spirit of cruelty[4]

Whenever this was sung at Juranifiri Santa, it provoked uncomfortable smiles and quizzical looks from newcomers to the church. "Maboyi, maboyi," was often sung to complement the lessons of elders and the sermons of prophets that dwelled on the "backward" ways of Africans. As Shimmer once put it to me, "The problem with us [Africans]—instead of striving and saying, 'Why can't I be like him?' we don't think that way. We think the opposite. We say, 'I'll fix you, I'll fix you.'" Some relative had tried to fix Shimmer, and were it not for the Holy Spirit, it might have worked. Shimmer stressed that live and direct Christianity is the key to the transformation of a jealous disposition: "Masowe is trying to teach people not to think that way. That's where the problem starts."

Ira Bashkow argues in his work on the Orokaiva of Papua New Guinea that such "abject talk" (2000, 307) is in no simple way a discourse of self-denigration. But the Orokaiva, like the apostolics, tend to criticize themselves as torn apart by jealousy, a fate that "whitemen" (as the Orokaiva say) do not suffer from—in part because Christianity keeps them from it (Christianity being "whitemen's religion"). The Orokaiva's Christianity is thus "intensely focused" on the eradication of "jealousy and willful desire" (Bashkow 2000, 314–15). I return to a discussion of abject talk in chapter 7, because the nature of Shimmer's remark and songs such as "Maboyi, maboyi" require further contextualization.[5] But the point I want to make here is that Shimmer's remark is an index of the church's concern with genuine change in the religious subject, a "break with the past" that, as I have emphasized at several points so far, characterizes a good deal of Christian discourse in Pentecostal and charismatic churches throughout the postcolonial world (Meyer 1998; cf. Engelke 2004a; Hastings 1976; Keller 2005; Kiernan 1992b; Robbins 2003a).

Although Shimmer's relief from stomach pains came quickly, the subsidence of physical symptoms was only the first step in the process of his healing. It can often take several months for a patient to be cured. During that time, he or she must attend church services on a regular basis. (At congregations such as Juranifiri Santa or Goora—where Hwimbo preaches—this might also involve "treatments" in one of the "hospital wards.") For the first several months after his initial visit, Shimmer went to Juranifiri three or four times per week. He listened to the prophet deliver sermons. He listened to the elders give lessons. He sang with the congregation and began to get to know some of the members. Most important, he continued to queue for "consultations" with the prophet and the administration of the water by the elders. The elders also gave him some pebbles that had been blessed by the Holy Spirit as part of the therapeutic treatment. Shimmer learned that the pebbles and water are called *muteuro,* "prayers." Muteuro is like "God's medicine": they are objects and substances that displace the role of witchcraft medicines and muti in everyday life. Shimmer used the pebbles for several months. He was told to place them in the glass that he used to drink water. I come back to a detailed discussion of muteuro in chapter 7.

Shimmer did not join the church during the course of his treatment. He was still an "ordinary person." He did quit smoking after several months, which pleased the apostolics he had come to know. (The stomach pains had already put Shimmer off drinking.) Shimmer said he began to see that smoking was a "dirty habit" and "not so nice." But he was keen to say that this did not mean he had become a Christian. Indeed, though the elders and congregants with whom he interacted were warm and friendly and encouraged him to act in certain Christian ways, they also maintained a distance. And they did not, Shimmer assured me, try to convert him. It is a chief point in Masowe congregations that apostolics should help everyone who comes to them, regardless of creed. One does not have to become a Masowe apostolic in order to receive the help of the Holy Spirit. Apostolics claim they would rather people be cured of their afflictions and leave than take up the mantle of faith lightly.

Shimmer kept going to Masowe services well after the elders informed him of his treatment's success. During those initial months, Shimmer became convinced that the healing was a result not only of the muteuro but also of a change in his perspective on the world. Something was happening. The sermons, lessons, and songs—everything he had learned—took on an intriguing outline that he wanted to fill in. Drawn to the church by the promise of healing, he began to appreciate the message of the prophets: "What that man [Nzira-Pageneck] used to preach from the Spirit, it coincided with what exactly is written in the Bible. That's [something] that struck me. How come they don't refer to the Bible, but if you read the Bible at home and then you go there it's exactly the same thing? It's not a new thing at all. The difference is that they don't refer to the Bible at all and that the reference is the Holy Spirit. So, that really struck me. I was interested." Shimmer also began to understand the healing as inextricably linked to the tenets of a live and direct faith:

The Johane Masowe people, our faith is in the Spirit and in God. And that Spirit is our reference. Whatever the Spirit says, we follow that. Because, with the Spirit, as opposed to the Bible, the Bible is like history. It tells what happened to people at that time. As opposed to Masowe, it's like I've got a stomach problem right now that I've had for some time, and when it comes to solving my problem in the Bible there's no direct link to my solution today. It's like talking about what happened to other people, but I've got a disease right now that needs some healing. That's when the Spirit comes in. You've got a direct communication with God. And if the prophet is gifted, they can do a prayer and give you some muteuro and you are healed.

There is in these remarks a blurring of the utilitarian and intellectualist logics of conversion. Shimmer makes it clear that Nzira was providing him with a "practical" benefit, although this was not all there was. With his stomach problems gone, attendance at church became a "personal thing" for Shimmer, based on a growing conviction that perhaps he ought to become an apostolic. Shimmer was undergoing what Tanya Luhrmann calls a "metakinetic" process of religious transformation, sparked not only by the Word but also by a learned ability "to identify bodily and emotional states as signs of God's presence" (2004, 519).

Over the course of the next year Shimmer's conversations with the elders became more detailed, covering what apostolics refer to as "the basics" of mutemo. The basics include the kinds of things I have already mentioned in passing: adherence to the Ten Commandments, restrictions against consuming alcohol, observance of Friday as the Sabbath. They also include the more introspective and ineffable aspects of the live and direct faith—an official reminding of what Shimmer would have been learning about during his visits to the church: how "the Spirit is our reference," and so on. Mutemo provides not only a set of behavioral guidelines, but the vocabulary for a religious language. Learning these basics takes time; had Shimmer wanted to become an apostolic any sooner, it is unlikely the elders would have encouraged it. Elders are always cautious in their evangelism. "Because if you want to join there," Shimmer said, "they don't like to hurry you. They like you to take your time, get used to it and know what's required. Then, if you like it, if you can stand it, then you can join." Then again, *liking* the Masowe weChishanu Church is not really the point. Most apostolics do "like" their church—in the sense that they love God and find joy and comfort in Jesus and the Holy Spirit. But there is always a note of caution in such characterizations; apostolics are concerned that too much emphasis on "liking it" might devolve into a shallow or failed faith, such that it comes to resemble liking candy or a nice car. Because in actual fact, I was told by the apostolics on a daily basis, Christianity is hard work. If you give in to its initial appeal, Shimmer said, "normally you won't last. You need to know some basic things, like what you're required to do and what you're required not to do." It is in these moments that anthropologists can document the bleeding of utilitarianism and intellectualism into one another.

So knowing the basics is an important step in the process of an apostolic's conversion. Indeed, mutemo-as-knowledge is not incidental, because no one is permitted to join a Friday congregation on the basis of sincerity or enthusiasm alone. During my research, I did meet a handful of people who expressed their conversion experiences in line with a before-and-after, now-I'm-saved quality. Benetta Jules-Rosette calls this a "moment of specific shock" (1975, 135; emphasis removed) in the religious subject, and it is the kind of narrative that other Christians sometimes employ, such as the Baptists in Virginia studied by Harding (2000, 38–39). There is no effort in the Friday churches to dampen or extinguish such fires, but those who experience these moments must complement the shock with a thorough understanding and acceptance of the basics. The Friday apostolics often criticize other Christians, especially Pentecostals, for accepting members into their ranks with wanton disregard for a "real" understanding of Christianity. At the same time, knowledge alone does not an apostolic make. As I was often reminded, you can know the Ten Commandments and not be a Christian (see Engelke 2006). Knowing something does not necessarily mean you will act on it, and mutemo requires enactment. There is even a strong sense within the church that too much knowledge can be dangerous—a sentiment I have already uncovered. It was the emphasis on Bible knowledge, after all, that drained the mission churches of their spiritual vitality in Johane's day and that continue to plague many independent churches today. In church history too prophets can be found lording their "knowledge" over one another, sparking the question of leadership. To treat Christianity as subject to knowing is to not know what Christianity is. Mutemo, then, is a delicate mix of information and conviction.

Like most apostolics, Shimmer spoke about this mix in both material and immaterial terms. It is very common to hear apostolics say that mutemo is something that "gets into you," as it if were a substance (see Engelke 2004a, 105).[6] But as one *gets* mutemo, one also recognizes the impossibility of its mastery or complete incorporation. Mutemo maintains a resistance to thingification and, ideally, objectification. "Mutemo cannot fit between two covers," as Shimmer put it. "There's nothing like that."

Shimmer approached the elders about becoming an apostolic when he felt the mixture was right. Having absorbed the basics, he was asked to consider a commitment to the church. This commitment is always characterized by an absolute. It was Shimmer who told me that "in Masowe, there's no being half Christian and half outside. If you're in, you're in." With this commitment made, Shimmer was asked, like others in his position, to offer three prayers to God, one each to the Father, Son, and Holy Spirit. These are not the first prayers a neophyte will have said, but they occupy a special role in the transformative process as envisioned by those in the church. The prayers are called *mitumbi mitatu,* a term apostolics use to refer to the Trinity. It translates literally, and somewhat awkwardly, as "three bodies," but for the apostolics mitumbi mitatu has meaning in "deep Shona" (more on this in chapter 5): "the fullness of God," or that which encompasses mutemo. The mitumbi mitatu prayers are not formulaic; they must come "from within," shaped by the force of mutemo as it has been incorporated by the neophyte. For many of the apostolics I spoke to, these prayers are remembered as unique moments of connection with God. They are, we might say, the internal instantiation of a live and direct faith—something not generated by a prophet's work but one's own. Mitumbi mitatu are not the only prayers that can establish this connection, but they are spoken about as the inauguration of the subject as a Christian agent in relationship with the divine.

After his mitumbi mitatu prayers were made, Shimmer was asked to confess his sins in front of the congregation. The concept of sin may or may not be new to apostolic neophytes. Shimmer, for one—having not grown up in a Christian household—did not really think of his wrongdoings in terms of sinful behavior, even if in many ways the moral codes he measured his behavior against matched those of a Christian's (cf. Robbins 2004, 216–19). "Sin" was not an organizing principle in his life before the church, but he articulated his past in that first confession according to the Christian language he was taking on. Shimmer told me that all in all he "wasn't so bad." He had never committed the "major sins," like adultery, murder, or even theft. He had, it is true, participated in "heathen customs," but this was not surprising because many Zimbabweans did. Despite the banality of his transgressions, however, Shimmer found the experience of confession difficult and in stark contrast to the uplift of mitumbi mitatu. Even when one is becoming an apostolic, and thus finding comfort in the Holy Spirit, it is not easy to make oneself so vulnerable in front of others. After the confession Shimmer was counseled by the church elders, who told him how to keep on track in the future.

After his confession Shimmer was—as another apostolic once put it to me—a "full-fledged member" (see Engelke 2004a, 101). All that is left to do after confession is have one's garments made. Shimmer set off to one of the cloth shops run by Asian merchants in Harare's city center to get the materials. In keeping with what he had learned, Shimmer chose moderately priced cotton. To keep mutemo an apostolic's garments must be "plain." They are the material evidence of a commitment to immateriality, to equality and modesty. No one, I was told, ought to stand out in church: no one ought to be able to tell who is rich and who is poor. At Juranifiri Santa, the importance of this principle was often reinforced by reference to Police Commissioner Chihuri. "You can't tell him from the others," Shimmer told me. "Maybe he comes in his Merc [Mercedes Benz], but he'll just be like anyone else. He goes barefoot and puts on his garments." With his cloth in hand, Shimmer asked one of the women in the congregation to make his robes, for which he paid her a nominal fee. After this the robes were taken before the prophet by a child to be blessed by the Holy Spirit. Slipping them on for the first time, Shimmer said, "then it was real."

I met Shimmer in June 1996, on one of my first visits to Juranifiri Santa. By that time he had been a full-fledged member for about four and a half years. A tall and rail-thin young man, he shaved his head after the fashion of Nzira. In his early twenties when we met, Shimmer had not yet married, although he had a steady girlfriend. After finishing his O-level school examinations (which the jealous relative had failed to scupper) he landed a job as a sales clerk in a local record store chain, working in one of the smaller outlets in Harare's city center. To save money he lived with his family, although he planned to get his own place sooner rather than later, probably in Kambuzuma, the high-density suburb in which he had grown up. Shimmer liked to play bass guitar, but with a steady girlfriend, work, and church he found it difficult to find time to practice. Shimmer and I hit it off, probably helped by the fact that we talked about music as much as we did about the church, which allowed us to round out our relationship in a way that does not happen with everyone you meet in the field.

When I returned to Juranifiri Santa in 1999, I could not find Shimmer. After a few weeks I spotted a friend of his at the church, a young man named Clay. I asked Madzibaba Clay where Shimmer had gone. "Go see him in town," he said, and gave me the address of another of the record store branches. I went the next day. As I walked into the store it was clear that Shimmer had moved up in the music retail world. The new branch was marked by the ritzy stamp of South African capital, which had made a notable impact in the city center and Harare's affluent northern suburbs over the course of the mid-1990s. To top it off, Shimmer had been promoted to manager, as his name tag indicated. "Hey . . . ah . . . hey," he said, initiating a multistage handshake that got the better of me. "Hey madzibaba," I said, and we headed out for a coffee break, as is the privilege of managers on sluggish Monday afternoons.

Not having seen Shimmer at the church, I wondered if he had stopped going. But when we met in the shop I noticed that his head was still shaved, giving me the impression that he was keeping up his apostolic practices. Had he just switched to another congregation, I wondered? Somewhere closer to Kambuzuma? It would not have been unusual, given the suggestions Eriah had once made about praying close to one's home. So after catching up with each other's lives, I asked Shimmer where he had been. He looked down at the ground and said with a tisk, "Ah, I haven't been kuMasowe [to Masowe] for some time."

In 1997 Shimmer almost died in a car accident. He was hitching a ride to Chitungwiza on his way to church. Most days, Shimmer took a bus or "combi" (privately run minivan) to the sowe, but for some reason this time he had hitchhiked. Peeling down the Seke Road, somewhere between Harare and Saint Mary's, a tire burst and sent the car flying off into a field. The next thing Shimmer knew he was in the hospital. "I was just lucky to be alive," he said. "That car flipped like hell. The police said we all should have been goners." No one died, but Shimmer sustained massive injuries, including two broken legs and several broken ribs. "I almost bust my spleen," he said. Shimmer spent over three months laid up in hospital, and it was several months after that until he was able to fully walk.

Shimmer understood his car accident as a spiritual problem. Like his stomach pains, that is, the burst tire and his subsequent injuries were not chance occurrences but motivated ones. This time, however, his conclusion on the cause proved more troubling. This was not, he thought, the work of a jealous relative out to fix him. Rather it was his own fault because he had failed to stick to mutemo. Shimmer understood his accident as the result of his shortcomings as a Christian. Why had the accident occurred while he was on his way to church? This was the question that kept popping up in his mind. Why had he hitched a ride, when he usually took a combi or a bus? To Shimmer the accident was a sign of falling off track. The car accident happened, he told me, because he had been "playing around" with mutemo—not sticking to the law. This conclusion was confirmed in his eyes by the fact that, despite the severity of the crash, no one else was badly hurt. This was about him, and him alone.

Shimmer never told me what he meant by "playing around" with mutemo, and I did not feel it was my place to ask. He reported that he was drinking and smoking again, although he never did so around me, and I do not know if he started up before or after the accident. Regardless of the gravity of his transgressions, however, Shimmer's self-diagnosis would not have been accepted by the church. It is not the place of apostolics to explain their own misfortunes. Shimmer should have consulted a prophet, as he had in 1991. Given this, a host of other reasons for the accident ought to have remained in play: it might have been witchcraft again, because even a devout apostolic can be caught in its webs; it might even have been chance, because despite the sociomoral complexity of the world, sometimes things just happen. There were, moreover, indications to suggest that the accident was not a divine "punishment" of any sort. As Clay pointed out to me, Shimmer not only got his old job back after all that time in the hospital—he was promoted. Shimmer also married his girlfriend and was able to move in to his own place, just as he had been hoping when we met in 1996. These were hardly sure signs of falling off track.

At Juranifiri Santa Clay and a handful of elders were aware of Shimmer's situation, but no efforts were made to get him back to the sowe. Clay had remained a good friend and visited him during his recovery. But the church does not maintain a strategy for returning lost sheep to the fold. It was up to Shimmer to present himself at Juranifiri Santa because his return had to be sincere, not forced. As Shimmer himself once told me: "People must worship God from the bottom of their hearts. . . . If I force my brother to join the church, it will be a waste of time. He won't be in the spirit. He's just coming because he's been told to go to church. That normally happens in other churches, like the Roman [Catholic Church]." It would be a mistake, however, to interpret Shimmer's self-imposed absence as an admission of lost faith. Rather, I want to argue, Shimmer felt compelled to stay away from the church precisely because he was committed to it. He never claimed to have lost faith and indeed insisted that he was "genuine Masowe" and "the genuine article." Every time we met during my fieldwork in 1999, Shimmer asked me what was happening at Juranifiri Santa. What had the Holy Spirit said? What had the elders said? What songs were sung? How many people were there? He gathered information like an enthusiastic armchair anthropologist. But, as to an armchair anthropologist, one always felt compelled to ask, why not go himself? "I'm going," he would reply, as if he was already on his way, "it's just a long journey." Clay, for one, was never satisfied with this line, which he was also fed. In his view it was playing too deliberately on the path-to-faith imagery. This is probably true, but it does, I think, express the kernel of Shimmer's intentions. It was clear to me through our meetings that Shimmer still thought about the world through the lens of his faith—that what struck him listening to Nzira-Pageneck in 1991 had changed his sense of himself, now "genuine Masowe." This does not mean, as we can see, that all apostolics maintain the standards of Christian living that mutemo demands. The break with the past that conversion to Christianity is framed by can never be complete (Hastings 1976, 44; Meyer 1998, 339; Robbins 2003a, 230). As in any other social frame, there are no clear boundaries of before and after, even when these boundaries are invested with considerable discursive force. But this is not to say that religious subjects cannot act on breaks as if they exist; indeed, more than pointing to the inadequacy of dichotomies in the analysis of religious subjectivity, Shimmer's case suggests that he was taking the logic of a break seriously. Most notably, perhaps, as his explanation for the car accident and the apostolic practice of not pursuing lost sheep suggest, Shimmer was taking responsibility for his misfortunes rather than explaining them as the result of someone's jealousy. Of course, this is not to say that "personal responsibility" is otherwise an unknown concept among Zimbabweans, or that "jealousy" is a convenient substitute for it. But here we have an example of someone relocating the sources of agency in the world; that in itself would be understood by apostolics as a mark of fulfillment, of a live and direct faith. Shimmer was risking the failure of that faith, and it is in risks like this that actions become significant (cf. Keane 1997b, 22; Sahlins 1985, 143–51). Were he driven by a utilitarian calculus, he might easily have gone back to Juranifiri Santa to receive more muteuro. If he did not want to go there, he could have gone to another prophet, or a spirit medium, or a n'anga. But for Shimmer, becoming an apostolic meant not taking the easy route. It means wrestling with mutemo as a system of knowledge, even as one breaks it and even when it cannot be found in one's words or deeds.

MADZIBABA MARCUS

Like Shimmer, a majority of apostolics first come to the Friday churches as adults, and often as adults facing some kind of difficulty in life. As Shimmer's example should make clear, however, these encounters do not produce born-again experiences—at least not exactly in the way those experiences are normally understood. It should also be noted that most of the people who come to the Friday prophets for help stop attending services after they have received it. Not everyone "gets" mutemo, or feels the personal pull of the live and direct. For everyone like Shimmer who begins to take on mutemo as a personal thing, there will be several others who consider time at the church a practical thing and, after they are gone, not much of a thing at all.

Narratives of conversion are valued by the apostolics as evidence of the Holy Spirit's live and direct influences. They are a way in which God is understood to manifest his presence. Most apostolics who join after receiving help will relate their stories during services, in part as an effort to draw in potential converts. These testimonials are about as public and pointed as Friday evangelizing gets. Yet while the elders encourage people like Shimmer to share their stories, it is not incumbent on all apostolics to mark their faith in such a manner. This is certainly the case for the increasing number of apostolics who grow up in the church—the children of old-timers, like Zechariah, for example, and like his father's brother's son, my friend Marcus.

Marcus has been an apostolic "since day one," as he put it to me. He was born in 1947 in the Chihota Native Reserve, the son of a respected prophet and the grandson of a woman who moved with Johane in the first days of his ministry. Marcus is a good example of how apostolic faith is thought to always unfold. As I learned from him, old-timers might not be expected to undergo marked transformations like Shimmer, but even those born in the Friday churches are always in the process of coming to understand and live up to mutemo.

Marcus is a businessman. He owns a construction firm and a beauty parlor, the latter of which is operated by his wife, Angela. He owns a farm in Ruwa, about half an hour's drive from Harare. He has two secretaries, a slew of "business associates," and a BMW. Each time I returned to Zimbabwe Marcus was in a bigger and better office. In 1993 it was only a dark one-room above a carpet warehouse on Robert Mugabe Avenue. By 1996 he had moved to a brightly lit two-room on the ninth floor of the NCR Building on Samora Machel Avenue (home to the Zimbabwe Stock Exchange). In late 1999 he moved to Coal House, along Nelson Mandela Avenue, to a space probably four times the size of his NCR Building office. Looking back on it now, his office addresses can be read allegorically: in African politics moving from Mugabe to Machel to Mandela is moving up in the world. Marcus's business in the 1990s followed a similar upward trajectory.

Marcus is my second longest standing contact in the church; we met on the afternoon of March 6, 1993. All in all, however, I did not see Marcus as much as I saw most other close friends and interlocutors. But Marcus was very helpful. He was responsible for many of the interviews and meetings I held with the handful of people still alive in the 1990s who had "moved with Johane." Marcus also introduced me to several apostolics in his extended family, including Tsitsi and Zechariah. But I could go long stretches without talking to Marcus. When we did meet it was usually in intense bursts—several times over a few days, often late into the night. These meetings were hit or miss, which I often found frustrating. I calculated at the end of my fieldwork that we only actually met about a third of the time we were scheduled to. I would sometimes spend two hours or more just waiting for him in the foyer outside his office, just to learn that I should come back the next day.

Marcus, who is a long-standing attendee of the Afgate sowe, has been an elder in the church since the mid-1980s. Eldership is a position that deserves more considered attention here, not least because elders play a central role in supporting and teaching mutemo. The Shona word that apostolics use for "elders" is *vadare* (sing., *mudare*), which they have drawn from an aspect of village-level sociality and organization. A *dare,* or court, is the meeting place in a Shona village where headmen gather to resolve conflicts within and settle issues for the community (Bourdillon 1987, 127). Vadare might thus be called "community judges." Elders in the Friday churches serve this function. They are the arbiters for a congregation, responsible for resolving this-worldly issues and disputes between members that do not require the attention of a prophet. This tends to be more important in the rural areas, where apostolics from different homesteads might interact with one another on a daily basis, but it is not a function wholly absent in the cities and towns. As I discussed in relation to Shimmer, elders are also important in the sense that they are responsible for providing council to the congregation. They set the guidelines by which an apostolic ought to live and should themselves serve as models to others.

Congregants are encouraged to approach elders for any questions they might have about mutemo, or indeed any other subjects relating to Christianity or Christian life. And elders are responsible for teaching neophytes the basics of mutemo. In large congregations, such as Juranifiri Santa, it is not unusual during a service for the vadare to take a group of new apostolics off to one side to go over the important first lessons of faith, much like teachers do in other churches during Sunday school, catechism classes, and Bible study groups. Elders are also available at other times to discuss matters of faith, clarify a point, or outline certain aspects of mutemo. Even an apostolic who has been a longtime attendee of the church might have occasion to consult vadare from time to time. If a prophet administers a special kind of muteuro, for example, the elders will teach people how and when to use it, as knowing how to do so is not necessarily based on previous experiences.

One of the ways in which vadare teach people about mutemo is to give lectures, or "lessons," during church services. These lessons can last from five minutes to half an hour, and they may or may not be relevant to what else is going on in the service that day. The following is a point-specific example. At large prayer sites, such as Juranifiri or Nyatsime, people mill about in the shade of nearby trees before services begin. When an elder calls the people to gather in the sowe for the start of a service, people often run up so they can get a good spot at the front, near the prophet. (Some people run not to the front necessarily but to the shade of other trees that falls within the prayer ground, especially in months when the heat of the sun can be difficult to bear.) Such behavior is considered uncontrolled and disrespectful. Self-discipline is understood to be a strong, Christian value. Self-discipline is presented as a bulwark against witchcraft, for example, because witchcraft is spread by desires that go uncontrolled. Indeed, as I suggest later, self-discipline speaks to the apostolics' concern about the control of agencies in the world. In July 1999, after one of these running episodes, and just weeks before an important three-day prayer session called a *misi mitatu* (see chapter 5), a mudare at Juranifiri Santa warned the congregation:

Apparently we need to keep reminding one another about the rules [mutemo] of this place. Please, apostles. You are always doing things which are off track. Why are people always running? It was said [by the Holy Spirit] that apostles must walk nicely to the sowe. But everyone is gathering too fast. It's all of our faults. Ladies and gentlemen, please. We were promised a misi mitatu soon, but don't be surprised if the Holy Spirit now says no because we continue to do the wrong thing. The misi mitatu is for our blessing, so if we miss it, it's our own fault. We are all sick, so let us do the right thing to be blessed.

In this case the mudare is making an example of a specific incident. It is an example of mutemo-as-law, which is one of the more concrete ways in which the concept can be understood. By pointing out how the congregation is falling off track, he is pointing out how an aspect of mutemo has been broken. The mudare wants to reinforce the more general lesson of respect for and obedience to God. In this case mutemo means not only *do not run* but also, and more important, that *we must listen to what the Holy Spirit tells us to do.* In a congregation vadare bear the brunt of telling people to do what they are told. As the example suggests, this is sometimes pitched in relation to the group, such that the wayward behavior of some has ramifications for everyone. On many other occasions vadare stress the importance of mutemo in similarly punitive terms. This elder's lesson emphasized the responsibility of the community to "stick to" mutemo because the well-being of the congregation can be jeopardized by the few. It is up to everyone to stay on track. If mutemo is often about meaning, this example suggests also its more disciplinary dimensions.

Sometimes an elder's lesson makes a more general point and is not inspired by a specific incident. These are usually the longer lessons, planned out in advance of a service. The following suggestion was made in a lesson by an elder at the Afgate sowe in Highfield:

> You know that as apostles we are supposed to pray every three hours. In the middle of the day, this can be difficult if you are at work. It is not always easy to put on your garments and kneel to the east. That is okay, but just remember to stop for a minute, make the sign of the cross three times, and thank God. But at night, you must really be diligent. It is hard to get up at midnight, 3:00 A.M., 6:00 A.M., and so on. Sometimes it is cold out from under the covers! But you must try. And I can make a serious suggestion: drink lots of water before you go to bed, so that in the middle of the night you need to get up and relieve yourself. Then you can pray!

It is not unusual to hear advice like this for a good portion of a church service, and this is the chief way in which the vadare can do their job. Well after they have joined the church and attended the initiatory sessions, apostolics talk about the value of these lessons. And just as aspects of "the law" are reinforced by the threat of God's discipline, there is room for levity when coming up with strategies to keep mutemo.

It is not clear when elders took up a central role in weChishanu religious organization. During the early days, Johane was said to have both "disciples" and "apostles," the former of whom most resemble the vadare, although many of these figures (including Emmanuel) were actually prophets, and today at least the Masowe stress that elders do not go on to become prophets. Eldership is not a stage in prophetic transformation, as dreaming can be. An elder's authority is a human authority. As Marcus explains, the authority of elders can differ from congregation to congregation, but before turning to his thoughts on that matter I want to make a few more general points.

First, elders are not necessarily old. They are chosen by the Holy Spirit regardless of their age and, even, experience in the church. An apostolic may be called at any time to become a mudare. I heard cases of people being chosen as vadare anywhere from three months to seventeen years after becoming Masowe. Not surprisingly, elders are respected members of the community. Many, like Marcus, are believed to be chosen because of their integrity and understanding of mutemo. But an equal number are made vadare because they have "serious problems." "The thing with people who are actually in big trouble," Marcus told me, "is that the prophet wants them to be around as much as possible. And if you are a mudare, you need to be at masowe and close to the Holy Spirit nearly all the time." A number of vadare at Juranifiri fit this bill; they came to Nzira-Pageneck as self-confessed thieves and liars, and he tried to transform them into exemplary apostolics (not always successfully).

Not all elders are men, but only men are called to the position. If a man is married his wife becomes an elder too, and she is responsible for working with the women in much the same way her husband works with the men. In theory women can approach male elders for help or advice, and vice versa for men, but this rarely happens. Male elders are more visible during services in their roles as arbiters, teachers, and witnesses to confession, but there are exceptions to this rule. Madzimai Yvonne, a middle-aged mother at Juranifiri, was well known for her lessons on honesty and diligence in family life. She was a more prominent elder than her husband. Female vadare play their most visible role during healing sessions, during which they work to protect women possessed by evil spirits from harming themselves and others. At Juranifiri they also did much of the cooking for people staying in the hospital wards and had a reputation for their ability to help people work through "mental illness."

Elders serve the prophet as much as the congregation. They see to it that a prophet is not bothered with inconsequential requests as his or her main responsibility is to channel the Holy Spirit. It is up to the elders, then, to make sure that services run smoothly. In the larger congregations this is no mean feat. It took about a dozen vadare, male and female, to run the services at Juranifiri. They had to do several things: call the service to order; direct people who arrived late so as not to disrupt the proceedings; field queries and comments from newcomers who might not know what was going on; police the edges of the congregational circle, where children often migrated to talk to and play with one another; attend to the sick; and attend to the prophet, in whatever manner of ways he might require (this could even involve trips away from the sowe; I once drove with an elder to collect an order of bread from the local bakery for the patients in Juranifiri's wards). During healing services, the range of an elder's responsibilities is even more elaborate. Given all this, it is no surprise that many elders say they are the ones who "run" a congregation. While always quick to point out they are only human, most held the firm conviction that their work was central to the process of maintaining a live and direct faith.

Latent tensions over the nature of an elder's role occasionally surface. In chapter 3 I discussed the friction between prophets and elders primarily in terms of how intergroup dynamics shaped the question of leadership. It was the elders at Bretten Farm who offered criticisms of prophets other than Emmanuel, and it was the elders at Juranifiri and Nyatsime who traded barbs about the relative sanctity of Nzira and Sandros. But such friction speaks to more general concerns about the role of elders in facilitating the potentiality of mutemo. What I want to suggest here is that conflicts and disagreements over what counts as mutemo are, like conversion narratives, useful for tracing its contours. No elder brought this out as clearly as Marcus. In the remainder of this section I want to focus on what he sees as the key issues facing the realization of mutemo today.

I was often struck by the fact that even a prophet's most "loyal" congregants would openly speculate how one day the prophet might fall off track. As humans, prophets are imperfect vessels and might succumb to what Marcus and others call "human nature." Prophets have to live and keep mutemo too, and it is the elders' duty to make sure they do. Marcus was constantly at pains to make this point. It came up in almost every conversation we had about the church, because he sees the possibility of a prophet falling off track as the biggest threat to the future of the church. Elders often said that in the absence of a written doctrine *they* must have the final word on procedure and form, because they are the ones who have been entrusted by the Holy Spirit to teach mutemo. I think Marcus's anxiety clearly parallels concerns over the question of leadership. Prophets are human. God gave humans free will. This free will can be abused, because while a prophet channels the Word of God live and direct, he or she is not divine and can make mistakes. "Power can corrupt," Marcus would often say with a chuckle (he was fond of clichés). During one interview in October 1999, Marcus expressed all of this especially well, echoing Nzira's transformation and pointing out a particular threat to mutemo:

> The thing with prophets is that they are sometimes very young, and the Spirit can descend on them quickly. They do not necessarily know how to follow the rules of the church. We are supposed to guide them, because we are ultimately responsible to the Spirit that speaks through them. The problem is if you get a person who does not know what they are doing, it is possible for them to take things off track without knowing it. So, the vadare are in charge of making sure the prophet upholds mutemo as a person. When he is filled with the Holy Spirit, he will not do anything, or say anything, incorrect. The problem comes when the prophet is not filled with the Spirit. He can say, "I need to charge you $10 for healing." He says this as himself, as a person. And so someone pays him $10. Then it is the Spirit that does the work, and the person makes a material gain. This is wrong. . . . In Masowe we do not charge people for healing. The Holy Spirit does not ask for your money, so why should we? Money is the root of all evil, so they say. There is serious evidence for this. Look at Emmanuel. Do you think it was a coincidence, him making all that money to buy a farm? No. He abused the power of the Holy Spirit for his own ends. That is human nature.

This is another of his favorite clichés: money is the root of all evil. In chapter 2 we learned from the police statements of those present at the Hunyani River meetings in October 1932 that Johane did not collect money from his followers. This is often presented today as a key element of mutemo. Rejection of money (in the religious domain) is a rejection of the material trappings it can produce. I was regularly told that the Holy Spirit gives its blessings freely and that no prophet should take advantage of this by charging people in need. Healing people for free is a point of pride in the church. It is used with some effect to differentiate the Masowe weChishanu from both other apostolic groups, many of which charge a healing fee, and traditional healers (n'angas) who—as Shimmer would want to point out—always seem to charge something.

As a church with no formal institutional framework and little in-practice bureaucracy, there is in fact very little need for money to be collected. This is just how Marcus and most other elders would have it. Indeed, one of the main reasons given for the church's "anti-institutionalism" is the trouble caused by money. When apostolics pass judgment on other

Christians, they often do so with reference to their "materialism." Other Christians spend too much time collecting money to build church halls and cathedrals and not enough listening to and living the Word of God. Only a few fund-raising causes are deemed appropriate among the Friday congregations. If a member of a congregation dies, donations can be collected to help the family. Or if a congregation takes a trip to visit a distant congregation, money will be collected to pay for a bus or lorry rental. In these instances it is the responsibility of the elders to gather the funds. Some congregations keep track of collections by writing them in a ledger book. An elder, perhaps a man who works in banking or finance, will keep the ledger and the collections. The money is never deposited in a bank account because the church is "not like a company." In theory, the collection book is accessible to any apostolic in the congregation—except the prophet. "It is very important," Marcus told me, "that the prophet has nothing to do with the money. This is becoming a problem nowadays, but, really, these are not matters of the Spirit and it is bound to cause trouble."

And trouble there has been. As Marcus suggests, Emmanuel stands out as the paradigmatic "troublemaker" in this regard. He used his religious authority to start a brick-making business, which had nothing to do with the Word of God. But the flow of money has increased elsewhere in recent years, spurred in part by the evangelical strategies of the more popular prophets. Sandros was collecting money to build his children's center, and Nzira did so to run his hospital. Nzira did not demand that his patients pay him (I met several who never did), but he was more than willing to accept "donations" (of money and in-kind payments) from "well-wishers," a practice that many of the other major prophets also followed. What is more, most other congregations—even Afgate, which Marcus sees as having been a consistently successful spiritual center—were being pressured throughout the late 1990s to build toilets at their prayer sites to meet the hygiene standards of the government. Building toilets is expensive and caused a good deal of concern among congregants as to where the money should come from (Engelke 2000b). Marcus and a number of other elders are worried about the encroaching influence of money because it tempts the worst side of what they understand to be human nature. Money and mutemo are incompatible, and as far as Marcus is concerned the situation should never change. At the same time he became increasingly aware throughout the 1990s, especially with the rise of prophets such as Sandros and Nzira, that it might be impossible to stem this tide of materialism.

Marcus was more willing to entertain other changes, however, and there are several he sees as worthwhile because they might help apostolics keep mutemo rather than cause them to fall off track. His attitude toward change is shaped in part by his children, all of whom, he is proud to point out, also attend the church. More than some fathers, perhaps, Marcus takes what his children say about the church to heart. "Some of the things we do," Marcus told me one day, "the children don't understand. And they are asking some good questions." I was curious as to what those questions were. Marcus went on:

Like, "Why can't we record our church music?" Lots of churches sell their gospel music, but as you know it is forbidden to record at Masowe. The thing is we are often complimented because we have such good songs. Even the Maranke now, I think they are recording their music. I tell my kids this is why: because we can't handle money for these things. And yet, at the same time, we don't want to profit from this; the children don't either. What we want is to be able to listen to Masowe verses [songs] at home or in the car. There is nothing wrong with that. My children point these things out to me. Sometimes it takes a fresh perspective to see these things. The music is not so serious, but there are other issues which I am afraid might drive the youth away from Masowe. For instance, why do we pray in the rain? They ask about that all the time. Maybe kids these days are just weak, but then I think to myself, "Well, why do we? Does God want us to get wet?" Of course not! I don't think it matters, but because it has always been that way, the old guys won't budge. Look, my children are educated. They are modern. One of my sons is now at Trinity College in Dublin. He is seeing the world, and when he comes back he asks questions. Good questions.

Change has always been accepted by the Masowe, even as mutemo retains a discursive rigidity and even as congregations criticize each other for "changing things." I have mentioned in passing some stand-out changes, for example, the acceptance of biomedicine.[7] The apostolics today have no objections to such treatment; in fact, they encourage it. At Nyatsime Sandros (a pharmacist's assistant) coordinated a measles vaccination campaign for the infants of mothers in his congregation—a campaign that was featured on the front page of the *Herald* in August 1996. The important point about seeing a doctor is that one must first consult a prophet to determine whether a spirit has brought on the problem. A doctor's medicines will be of no use without the simultaneous intervention of the Holy Spirit.

Biomedicine's adoption, then, is justified on the grounds that the church still diligently supports the spiritual warfare that was Johane's primary concern. But to reject "modern medicine" out of hand is unnecessary.

The church's attitude toward Western-style education has also shifted. Shoniwa had gone to school, but Shoniwa-Johane discouraged it among his early followers in an effort to, as Ngũgĩ wa Thiong'o (1986) might put it, "decolonize the mind." But even by the late 1940s, when Marcus was born, this had changed: "You can't stop evolution. Even in the 1940s, prophets like my father began to realize that while Johane had wanted to sabotage the white man's system, it was to our disadvantage to stay out of school. Consequently, I went to school, and you can see the results around you." We were in his plush office in the NCR Building, sipping on the ice-cold cokes he had pulled out of his mini-refrigerator. "This is why people started going to school," he continued. "Johane had prophesied that blacks would rule this country before the turn of the century, and that began to be interpreted in terms of the need to educate the children so they could run the economy. This was a situation you couldn't stop." Today prophets and elders often devote time during church services to the virtues of education. Nzira, for example, coordinated regular rituals to protect children from spirits that might try to disrupt their concentration during school exams (see chapter 7).

I remember distinctly the first time Marcus got on to the topic of change; I remember it because he raised it in relation to the future of the written word in the church. It was a Saturday evening in April 1993, and he was driving me home after dinner at his place. He said that things would have to change in some respects for the church to keep going, and it is only that some of the "really old guys" won't go for it. Some of them are very stubborn. They never went to school, and they do not realize what is happening in the country or to the church. Marcus wanted to produce an "official" church history—what six years later he would call a "proper constitution" (when Zimbabwe was gearing up for the referendum on its own Constitution), complete with guidelines for mutemo and a list of prophets. In that car ride home, in 1993, he framed the concern with change in terms of the old guys' anxiety about the written word. "We have got to write our history down," he told me. "This is how the world works!" "Mark my word," he said, "in a few years' time it will be okay. People will begin to see that if they don't write these things down, they will lose track of what Johane said." When the old people are all gone, Marcus worried, anyone could say they know what it means to be Masowe, to follow mutemo. "But if we write it down," he continued, "then these things can be preserved."

By 1999 something of what Marcus had predicted was starting to come true. Several prophets and elders, from congregations across the country, met in August to discuss the possibility of setting out a "proper constitution." So far as I know, however, a proper constitution has yet to be drawn up. If it were it would only ever be "proper" for its authors, inevitably supporting the positions of some congregations at the expense of others. Its existence would also contradict the religious principles that inspired it. But in other registers the written word had, by 1999, become acceptable. New kinds of ledgers were being kept—not just those for collecting bus-trip money. Some congregations had begun to keep rolls of their members and lists of other Friday congregations that they considered on track and off track. These lists, while unofficial documents, helped to ease the anxiety of authenticity from the apostolic perspective because they clear up the field of religious politics (or promise to, at any rate). Some elders even told me that they had been instructed by the Holy Spirit to write down what a prophet says after each church service, so that mutemo could be kept track of that way. I never saw such records, and most elders would tell me they never kept them anyway. Indeed, no elder ever admitted to writing anything down: each one I spoke to told me he was afraid of writing down the wrong thing, so he did not write anything at all. Without more information on these documents it is difficult to draw conclusions, even provisional ones, about the ways in which the introduction of "transcriptions" might (re)shape the live and direct ideal. Suffice it to say that the idea of a secret body of texts is not new to the Christian religious imagination, not least in colonial and postcolonial contexts in which the Bible has been such a forceful sign of politicoreligious power (see, e.g., Fernandez 1982, 299–301; Rutherford 2000, 2006).

For Marcus, the benefit of texts was supposed to be practical. What sparked his interest in them is the danger of congregational schisms. He often talked about the proliferation of Friday groups claiming ties to Johane Masowe. This concern went well beyond the claims of major prophets such as Emmanuel and Hwimbo. It was sparked more immediately by intracongregational fights resulting in splits throughout the smaller groups in Harare and Chitungwiza.[8] More than anyone I know, Marcus lost sleep over this fear. "It's crazy," he said. "Anyone can go into a field with white robes and proclaim out loud, 'We are Johane Masowe.' The name has become valuable. People respect it, so if they hear that someone near them is an important Johane Masowe prophet, they flock to the site. But that person could have no idea what it means to be Masowe, or even what mutemo is. None at all!"

Like an ardent nationalist, Marcus sometimes projected a "negative vision" of the church defined by a "pervasive fear of pollution and contamination" (Handler 1988, 47). This vision did not always reflect the situations it was meant to describe. But it was an influential discourse in other church circles. "It's very simple, if you think about it," Marcus told me. "We are becoming a brand name, and that is dangerous. But if you have a brand name, then you need to have recourse to the law to protect it. Would Coca-Cola allow some other company to call their drinks Coca-Cola? No. This is the situation we are facing in Johane Masowe today. We have got to protect ourselves, we have got to protect mutemo." The ironies and contradictions of the situation do not escape Marcus. He realizes that comparing his church to Coca-Cola suggests that Masowe faith is a commodity and that he is, in essence, appealing to the kind of thingification that apostolics most oppose—but only in the hope of preserving the spirit of that opposition. By writing mutemo down, apostolics can then get on with the possibility of living it:

> The thing is, some aspects of mutemo can be vague. This has helped in a number of cases, but I can say now that perhaps it also hurts. Some of the old guys will say that we cannot write things down, and I agree with them in the sense that we are not like Romans [Catholics] or Anglicans. . . . But for these practicalities, we need clarity, and we need to have recourse to a written set of bylaws and rules. Mutemo can be written down, I think. I have never heard the Holy Spirit say otherwise, in all my years of belonging to this church.

"What about the Bible?" I asked. "Will there ever be a need for it?"

"*No way,*" Marcus replied. 'That at least will always be clear.'

As teachers and arbiters of mutemo, elders have an acute sense of its possibilities and limits. The debates over writing as a means of uncovering (and controlling) these possibilities and limits are shot through with contradictions. Even strong proponents of a "proper constitution," like Marcus, recognize as much. The commitment to mutemo-as-law that elders must display only generates new ambivalences about the written word. Marcus knows the "old guys" have a point. If the apostolics were to produce a literature, or even if they were to record their songs, the integrity of a live and direct faith might well be compromised. Despite the ease with which he answered my question about the Bible, the issue of unduly fixing faith remains. To codify mutemo in the written word is to take two risks. The first is the risk of routinization, in which it becomes "stale," like the Bible. The second is the risk of articulation, for how could human beings ever claim to delimit, and thus to signify, the ultimate meaning of mutemo?

MADZIMAI VERA

Although direct questions about mutemo did not always get me far in my research, I was able to have sustained (if diffuse) conversations about it with friends such as Shimmer and Marcus. Marcus, in particular, spent a good deal of his time thinking about mutemo and its future. Even without my anthropological prompting and even if they did not discuss it when they got together, I often got the sense that mutemo occupies the attention of apostolics. Mutemo is a "serious issue." In this final portrait, however, I want to sketch another perspective, because it would be inaccurate to present the apostolic subject as forever caught up in the gravity of faith. While my informants would often stress that Christianity is hard work, there are limits to mutemo's push to contemplation and moments in which apostolics push back.

Vera, a young woman I knew at Juranifiri Santa who wanted to be a fashion designer, is good at pushing back. We only met in May 1999 when my partner, Rebecca, came to Zimbabwe. Rebecca attended the Sunday services at Juranifiri for the next four months. Because men and women sit separately in services, the elders arranged (at Nzira's request) for Vera to sit with Rebecca. Vera was supposed to help Rebecca understand the services. They became friends, and through Rebecca I became friends with Vera too.

Recent studies of collaboration in the field between significant others have problematized the image of the "lone fieldworker" (Fernandez and Sutton 1998; Gottlieb 1995; Handler 2004). Having a partner or children in the field changes one's relationships and helps to shape the production of ethnographic knowledge (Engelke 2004b). Edith Turner, for example, has remarked that the presence of her children in the field during the early 1950s made her and her husband "more human" (Engelke 2000a, 845) in the eyes of the Ndembu (see also Engelke 2004b, 15–23). In a similar way, Rebecca's arrival made me more human in the eyes of the apostolics. Because

I was a young man of marriageable age, they always found it strange that I was living alone.[9] Rebecca's arrival saved me from this awkward condition. My interactions with men at Juranifiri Santa changed as a result. It became easier to talk about everyday things, even with apostolics who were not personal friends. Rebecca's arrival also helped to reconfigure my relationship to women in the church. Before she came, I had only spoken to a few women in any depth and did not know any women I could have counted as friends. This was not for lack of trying; since 1993 I had been asking contacts like Marcus to arrange meetings with women in the church so that I could learn something about their experiences. But I was repeatedly told that "according to mutemo" men and women are the same. There was, therefore, no need to speak to a woman; what she would tell me would be the same as what a man would tell me. Marcus once arranged for me to talk to his wife—but only after I pushed him on it. "Masowe is Masowe if you are a man or a woman," he said.

Before Rebecca arrived, my meetings with women in the church were awkward at best. Things got markedly better after her arrival. At Juranifiri Santa the only place where men and women could interact at length was along the dirt track that wound its way up to the sowe, which sits some two hundred fifty yards off the Seke Road. After Nzira built his hospital wards on the Juranifiri Santa site, he put up some boundary markers around the sowe, including a gate across the dirt track that is supposed to regulate the flow of people into and out of the place. It is around this gate that men and women split off from one another: the men move farther along the track, which ended in a small clearing for parking cars; the women move off along the northern edge of the sowe site, which stretches out parallel to the fenced compound for one of Chitungwiza's municipal water tanks. Men and women mingled at the gate before and after services. Rebecca and I would meet at the gate after the service, which afforded me the opportunity to meet the women who walked out with her. Those brief encounters developed into a handful of relationships over the final six months of my fieldwork. Even so, I was not able to spend much time with women; I did not, for example, sit down to conduct taped interviews with any female apostolics until three weeks before I left the field. If Rebecca had not joined me in Zimbabwe, I doubt I would have been able to collect even this much.

I never interviewed Vera, despite the fact that we ended up spending a good deal of time together. What is more, within a few weeks of knowing her I learned not to ask much about the church. It did not seem to get me anywhere. She would always answer my questions by saying something along the lines of "I don't know." Our friendship revolved around social visits. Rebecca and I would meet her where she lived in Chitungwiza. We would drop by in the afternoons when Vera was watching videos and minding her brother's children. Vera also took us to her parents' homestead in the rural areas for a two-day visit, where we were able to attend a small Friday apostolic service with another of her brothers (neither of her parents was an apostolic).

I have never accepted that "Masowe is Masowe if you are a man or a woman." The church "leadership" is dominated by men, and although power and position are of course not as simple as that, it is hard to make sense of Marcus's claim on this count. In chapter 6, in my discussion of apostolic singing, I question further the erasure of gender. But regardless, I do not have the ethnographic data to develop a sustained argument contrary to Marcus's claim. My friendship with Vera did not provide me with "the woman's point of view." Of course, it never could have—even if she had been a loquacious informant. There could be no such thing as the woman's point of view in the Friday churches, any more than there is a unitary view in any social group anywhere. This is not to say that a gendered analysis of the Masowe apostolics is impossible. The theologian Isabel Mukonyora, who has studied both the Friday and Saturday apostolics, makes a sustained and compelling case that "the religious aspirations of women and ideas about them go a long way to explaining the vibrancy of the Masowe movement as a whole" (2000, 1; see also Mukonyora 1998a). Mukonyora (2000, 15–16) has also focused on the images of masculinity that Nzira built up in several of his sermons that she and I attended together in 1999. But when it comes to my relationship with Vera, and what I learned from her about mutemo, I can only make limited suggestions about its gendered dimensions.

Most of what I learned about mutemo from Vera was filtered through her relationship with Rebecca. If she was reluctant to discuss the concept with me in the anthropological abstract (or even through her own experiences), she was not reluctant to impart what she knew to Rebecca. Each week Rebecca would emerge from the services knowing something more about the basics, and it was helpful to have these confirmations and points of comparison. But the more interesting things I learned about mutemo from their relationship are the things that went unsaid. Rebecca's presence and her relationship with Vera provided me with a critical distance in the context of my own research, a reflexive lens that I did not expect to have.

It was not much, but I tried to make the most of it. I will limit myself here to one example of what I mean by focusing on an aspect of bodily discipline—an aspect that is relevant to both men and women but which was pronounced for me by Rebecca's experiences with Vera.

Vera duly relayed to Rebecca those aspects of mutemo that she needed to know. Most of this related to conduct during church services, since Rebecca's contact with the church was limited primarily to the large Sunday gathering. As I have already discussed in brief—and this is something I return to in the next chapter—bodily discipline is an important aspect of mutemo. It is part of the "metakinetic" realization of faith, one in which the apostolic's agency as a Christian is foregrounded. Rebecca was asked to take on some of its demands, which included, among other things, learning how to sit. Women are subject to more restrictions than men in this regard. Women have to sit with their legs straight out, not crossed or folded, and they must keep their hands in their laps. This is considered a "respectful posture" (and echoes how a woman should comport herself in a "traditional" Shona household). A woman's feet (although purposefully bare) must be covered with a white shawl, and her head must be covered with a scarf. These aspects of mutemo are part of a larger understanding of modesty that apostolic women should embrace—an aspect that prophets and elders often stressed in their sermons and lessons. (Men must also sit "respectfully," but they have more options as to what this entails.)

Conforming to the demands of respectful posture is a physical hardship—for both women and men but especially women. It is very difficult to sit on the ground with one's legs outstretched, hands in one's lap, for a seven- or eight-hour service, with only occasional opportunities to stand up to sing. (I did try.) The demands of posture, then, can have a direct effect on other aspects of one's disposition. Chief of these is listening to what is being said by the elders, the prophet, and, above all, the Holy Spirit. Without doubt, a prophet filled with the Holy Spirit will command the greatest attention; there was often a notable shifting of the mood, for instance, when the Holy Spirit spoke at Juranifiri Santa. But the lessons of elders—and even Nzira on occasion—sometimes fell on deaf ears. As I suggest in the next chapter, church services are often looked forward to, and many apostolics demonstrate a strong devotion to ritual life. But mutemo, in the forms discussed here, can also lead to sore backs and boredom, which do not always lend themselves to the realization of a live and direct faith in ritual action.

Vera, it seems, was sometimes inattentive. Toward the end of a service, when everyone was getting tired, Rebecca told me that Vera would start to talk about going home and eating dinner. Vera, of course, had some liberty to talk because she was responsible for teaching things to Rebecca. This was supposed to involve church matters but as often as not devolved into chit-chat. I was often struck by the amount of nonpious talk that went on at services, especially by what Rebecca could report. But men also talked among themselves, and on more than one occasion I watched men (and many boys) doodling in the smooth sand with their fingers or a small twig, not obviously paying attention to what was being said. The talk and inattentiveness that spring up during a service undercut the gravity of mutemo. Put another way, the demands of mutemo can collapse under their own weight—not necessarily into a struggle of faith, as Shimmer experienced, but rather momentary recognitions that its seriousness cannot always be so serious.

Taken alone, the portraits of Shimmer and Marcus might leave us with a false impression of mutemo. While it is something that motivates devotion and something that helps make a live and direct faith real, their presentations of it tend to fill in gaps that in practice remain open. Vera helped me to understand that mutemo is not always on one's mind and that the metakinetics of faith can run awry. It was the unusualness of our relationship that made this clear—an unusualness that in this case had something to do with gender and that, concomitantly, reinforced my sense that gender is a pertinent issue. But what Vera helped me to understand about mutemo is relevant beyond the analysis of women's positions. In using her as the example here, I do not mean to suggest that women per se are less "serious." Mukonyora (2000), in fact, makes the opposite point and not without justification. My points, simply, are that (a) not all apostolics speak with passion and clarity about mutemo all the time and (b) of those who do not, not all feel lacking because of it. Indeed, even the most "devoted" apostolics—even those who have let mutemo get deeply into them—can get bored, hungry, and tired. Prompting apostolics to talk about mutemo, or listening to the lessons and sermons through which it is imparted, can obscure this point. Vera's portrait brings out some of the dynamics of mutemo that go without saying.

At the beginning of this chapter I said I wanted to take the opportunity in the discussions of mutemo to shift attention away from prophets and toward a more detailed consideration of some ordinary members. But there is an ineluctable pull in my analyses, as there is among the congregations, toward the figure of the prophet. If you ask an ordinary member what is distinctive about the Friday churches, the first thing you are likely to hear is how the Holy Spirit speaks to the people live and direct, and by that they mean live and direct *through prophets* in the action of church services. This emphasis on prophets is a source of both satisfaction and concern, for the reasons detailed in chapter 3. In the analysis of mutemo prophets have not been the main focus, but neither are they far from view. For Shimmer and Marcus, in particular, the presence of the prophet is central to how they talk about mutemo. Shimmer's story was made possible because of the work of the Holy Spirit through Nzira. Marcus's discussions are not as dependent on the good works that come through prophets; he is, rather, concerned with whether or not prophets stick to mutemo themselves so that the works might continue to flow.

It is unlikely that the strong associations between live and direct faith and the figure of the prophet will stop anytime soon. Shimmer spoke articulately about Nzira's sermons as "direct communication with God"; but this line of communication is not all there is, or all there should be. This chapter presents mutemo as another aspect of the Friday faith—that aspect in which the words and deeds of the "ordinary member" play a central role. The incorporation and enactment of mutemo is part of a live and direct relationship with God in which all apostolics can participate. Once mutemo "gets into you," once the Word of God becomes a "personal thing," once you know "what mutemo is," then you can act on and with the Friday message. And learning what mutemo is never stops, because the process of its incorporation is never complete. God's presence is that process.

FIVE

Listening for the True Bible

Live and Direct Language, Part I

I WAS TOLD THAT BEING an apostolic is a "full-time thing." This saying picks up on the commitment Shimmer highlighted in his conversion narrative: one cannot be half Christian and half outside. An apostolic should maintain his or her commitment at all times and in all places. The language of commitment is indeed a common feature of the apostolics' discourse (if not always practice). One of their worries, for example, is the "Sunday Christian"—someone who seems to forget what the Word entails during the rest of the week. The concept of mutemo plays a crucial role in the apostolics' efforts to gauge whether they are falling prey to a part-time faith. Mutemo makes demands on the individual in direct relation to God at all times. Only *you*, after all, can pull yourself out of bed in the middle of the night to offer a prayer. Shimmer's reticence and hesitation about returning to Juranifiri only reinforces this principle. The Friday message is an all-day, everyday message; in order best to understand it, the concept of mutemo had to be filled out in relation not only to church lessons and confessions but also to car rides, car crashes, coffee breaks, and conversations that never were. Lest they become like "Sunday Christians," then, anthropologists studying religion must always look to more than ritual life, the topic to which—having engaged something of the everyday—I now turn.

The Friday churches hold services several times a week. At Juranifiri Santa, for example, services were conducted every day except Monday and almost continually from Thursday afternoon through Sunday evening. The session on Friday is the most important in this three-day stretch but not always the most well attended because many of the congregants had to be at work. None of the Friday prophets I knew in Harare or Chitungwiza forbade their congregants to hold jobs that required them to work on Fridays, as long as those who did could attend at other times. On Wednesday mornings, in fact, there was a service at dawn geared to the employed: it ran just over two hours, as long as someone with a day job in Harare could stay before gambling too much on the cooperation of the commuter buses to get them to work on time. On Thursday evenings some stalwarts at Juranifiri Santa would not go to sleep, opting to stay up all night to sing. This often made for long Fridays, whether or not the singers had to rush off to work or could stay on for the main Sabbath service.

Two activities are regularly singled out by the apostolics when they talk about church services: *listening* (above all, to sermons inspired by the Holy Spirit) and *singing*. On this basis it would not be far off the mark to say that ritual life for the apostolics is shaped by the generation and reception of words. In the next two chapters I want to use discussions of religious language to frame the analysis of ritual, discussions that will elaborate the dynamics of live and direct faith. Live and direct faith is manifested in language and based in part on the apprehension of what Nzira called "the True Bible." As I get in to the analysis of live and direct language, I turn increasingly to what the apostolics imagine the True Bible is.

Christianity is often characterized by its emphasis on language. It has been praised for its "potentiating linguistic spirit" (Schleiermacher 1977, 50), documented for its "extraordinary premium on verbal formulation" (Cameron 1991, 19) and observed as a "religion of talk" (Robbins 2001) and "akin to a verbal factory" (Coleman 2000, 117). As I highlighted in the introduction, this emphasis on language is often sustained by a faith in its revelatory capacities.[1] But it gives Christians as much pause as inspiration. In *Christianity and the Rhetoric of Empire,* for example, Averil Cameron describes how early Christians saw their rhetoric as the road to truth but acknowledged that this truth could not be comprehended through or defined by linguistic signs. "A great deal of Christian discourse is of this kind," she writes. "It necessarily attempts to express the paradoxical, to describe in language what is by definition indescribable" (1991, 156). In this chapter and the next I describe how language is another key medium through which the problem of presence is both articulated and apprehended. God comes to people through words that are voiced: sermons, songs, inner voices, and more. In these registers linguistic communication is a kind of presence. Yet this explicit turn to language brings us back to a point raised in the introduction, about the consequences of the fall. It was after the fall that distance from God became problematic, a distance marked by language and conditioned by what Ricoeur calls the fault line in the truth it once conveyed.

Cameron's comments on language focus on the early Church, but the paradox of what we might call its "perfect inadequacy" is also relevant to the inquiries in this book, even if the architects of Christianity in colonial and postcolonial have not always acknowledged it.[2] In chapter 1, for example, we saw how some of the key Victorian missionaries expressed an unswerving allegiance to the Bible as self-evidently true. It was all they needed—*the Bible, the whole Bible, and nothing but the Bible,* in Venn's memorable refrain. Their motivation was the Word made text, as it were. But the force of nineteenth-century missionary zeal moves quickly over theological questions that other Christians might ask. For instance, is the Bible identical with truth? And if so, is that truth literal or figurative? Hans Frei (1974) has explained that before the eighteenth century the answer to these letter-and-spirit questions often proceeded from a reading of the Bible according to three interdependent assumptions: its historical truth, its narrative coherence, and its religious relevance. *Truth* in this context meant that biblical stories "described actual historical occurrences" that together made up a sacred history; *coherence* was based on the argument that all biblical stories fit into a "single, unitary canon" (made legible through figuration) that expressed the Word of God; and *relevance,* finally, accounted for the text's transcendence, which is to say the recognition that biblical stories described "the one and only real world" in which Christ is always coming (Frei 1974, 2–3). Frei calls this approach precritical interpretation; its legacy is evident today in the fundamentalist and literalist churches studied by such anthropologists as Coleman, Crapanzano, and Harding, but it can offer insight into the Bible-driven agendas of Christians in Africa after the age of Venn and Moffat.

While the kind of theology Frei describes is still very much in play, its dominance was challenged in the eighteenth century. From that point onward, the "liberal" theologians began to argue that the Bible's authority did not emanate from the words it contained but rather from the message behind those words. Frei (1974, 42–46) traces this split in part to the earlier work of Benedict de Spinoza. Spinoza's charge was that "it is one thing to understand the meaning of Scripture and the prophets, and quite another thing to understand the meaning of God, or the actual truth" (quoted in Frei 1974, 44). It is not the words in the Bible that should matter but the religious lessons they convey. Casting this point in the precritical idiom, Spinoza argued that we cannot assume truth, coherence, and relevance are inextricably connected to reveal the meaning of God. The medium (the Bible) is not identical with the message (truth). Spinoza's questioning of what constituted the veracity of the Bible was not a denial that Scripture is the Word of God. In fact, he concluded that "the ultimate meaning of scripture is without question identical with what we know in any case to be religious truth" (Frei 1974, 45). What Spinoza's work questioned, rather, was the nature of the relationship and the manner in which it should be approached. Interpretation took the place of revelation, setting the groundwork for Schleiermacher, Troeltsch, and other liberals. What I want to highlight here is how this tradition can be seen to include the Friday prophets.

The theological intentions of the Friday apostolics run parallel to the Protestant traditions in which the medium is not identical with the message. Johane Masowe's Friday message is, in this sense, a kind of liberal commentary. It gave rise to a series of overlapping discourses in which the Bible has been denied as the generator of faith. There is a difference between biblical text and biblical truth, and as far as the Friday apostolics are concerned most Christians emphasize the former at the expense of the latter. The concept of the True Bible, I show, is based on the separation of Scripture from truth, such that the latter is not dependent on the former. In live and direct language the True Bible is the message, with Scripture only a medium.

THE PROCESSES OF LINGUISTIC DIFFERENTIATION

Apart from the groups on Bretten Farm and at Nyota, Friday apostolics do not live together in tight-knit, place-based communities. It is the church service that draws a congregation together, so I want to begin with a discussion of the ways of speaking (Hymes 1974b) that govern the action of ritual life. Although it is difficult to speak of congregations as distinct speech communities (Gumperz 1972), there are several ways in which the apostolics work to differentiate and aggregate themselves.[3] A congregation might best be described as a community of practice, "an aggregate of people who come together around mutual engagement in an endeavour" (Eckert and McConnell-Ginet, quoted in Hanks 1996a, 221). At Juranifiri

Santa and in other congregations, there are varying degrees of knowledge of, competence in, and commitment to the proceedings. The concept of a community of practice allows us to keep these differences in mind, to recognize that in an event such as a church service there is "participation at several levels" (Lave and Wenger 1991, 98). The community of practice is also useful as an analytic category because it does not privilege speech at the expense of other communicative channels (Bucholtz 1999). Words stand at the center of the next two chapters, then, but this is not to ignore the corporeal and physical dimensions of sermonizing and singing—or the metakinetic aspects of religious practice that the portraits of Shimmer and Vera brought out. For the apostolics, God's presence is not revealed through words alone. Drawing attention to these processes of differentiation is therefore also important in semiotic terms. Through their language and actions, the apostolics make certain semiotic ideological assumptions, creating a group within the group that maintains ideas about "what signs are and how they function in the world."

Speaking at church services is governed by a more formal, restricted code than speaking in everyday circumstances. One example of this formality (common to other Christian communities of practice) is the use of a standardized greeting. Before anyone speaks during a service he or she must say "Happiness be with you" *(rufaro kwamuri)* three times, to which the congregation replies "Amen" each time. This greeting should be uttered with one's hands clasped (right over left) across one's chest. The position of the hands is important because it signals that the salutation is "held" *(kutenda)* by the heart. When someone finishes speaking, he or she might say "Happiness be with you" once more. The speaker makes the sign of the cross three times and then folds his or her hands in a prayer position before the mouth, lightly swinging them in a downward arc to the chest three times. The movements are a sign of propriety, of showing humbleness and respect. These things are said and done three times, once each for the Father, Son, and Holy Spirit.[4]

Apostolics appreciate this kind of formality for a number of reasons. For one thing, it is seen as a good way to restore some integrity to everyday social relations. During my fieldwork, there were often low-level grumblings among the apostolics (and other people) about the decline of manners in Zimbabwe. People were said to be increasingly rude and disrespectful, especially in the cities, signaling a downward trend in morals that was affecting everyone's well-being. The sowe is a space to show people the respect they deserve and provide a model for others to follow.

The modeling often made at least a superficial impact, especially with elderly newcomers to the church. A man once told me that if everyone could "act proper" like the apostolics, there might not be so many African problems. Formality, then, simultaneously plays on visions of decline and progress, ambiguating the value of the past in a way that the effort to otherwise "break" with it might not suggest. In this, we get hints of the positive aspects of "African custom."

Formality of the greeting also gives people at church a confidence boost. I was told that using respect took the edge off speaking up, which is in any case a nerve-wracking experience. As Shimmer said, one of the reasons an apostolic might get up to speak is to confess sins—not an easy thing to do in public. But even when not facing a confession, people would say they were "too shy" to speak up. Indeed, many apostolics would complain about getting butterflies in their stomachs before addressing an audience, no matter how many times they might have done so before. There is nothing unusual in this, but the standardized call of "rufaro kwamuri" seems to make speaking up easier. Rufaro kwamuri invites the presence of the Holy Spirit, and this puts apostolics at ease. But in rules alone there is also often comfort, as if "formality guarantees purposefulness" (Keane 1997b, 91).

In addition to the formal greeting, it is not unusual for significant portions of a service to be conducted in what apostolics call "deep Shona." By this they mean "old-fashioned" language, which, like the greeting, is part of a restricted speech code.[5] Deep Shona is constituted in part by using words that are said to be "long gone." But mostly it involves using more formal terms of address. For example, apostolics use plural pronouns and concords as a matter of course in the sowe (and sometimes outside of it); these terms of address are normally reserved for one's elders, but the apostolics also use them with children—cutting very much against the grain of African custom, even as their reconfiguration of language signals an appreciation for what is old-fashioned.

Deep Shona strikes newcomers rather like Shakespeare's English might strike an American high school student on the first day of English class. It takes some getting used to. Some people told me with enthusiasm that when they first started attending Masowe services they had no idea what the prophets and elders were saying. These were, I think, exaggerated claims. The Shona is not so "deep" as to be unintelligible. But the claims make the point that language in ritual life is consciously marked and that, in keeping with mutemo, coming to understand it is always an ongoing process. It takes work. When I asked about deep Shona in interviews, it often elicited responses such as "You just know it's serious." As one man said, "That language, it's respectful. It cuts deep."

To say that an event is formal is to suggest that it is systematically organized, but this begs the question of when an event is "organized enough" to qualify as formal (see Irvine 1979). What is more, several communicative codes may be used in the same event, often cross-cutting even the relative distinction between formality and informality. At Masowe services, for example, the greetings and deep Shona represent an "increased structuring" where "the discourse is subject to extra rules or some greater elaboration of rules" (Irvine 1979, 774). But this does not preclude the possibility of using more informal discourse in the same events (Irvine 1979, 786). The apostolics employ several colloquialisms in this way. The colloquialisms are explicitly recognized as informal and intimate—something shared by a group of people who identify with one another but not restricted to use in any one setting. A common example of this is the saying "without work" *(hapana basa),* which apostolics use as a term for "bad luck" *(rushambwa).* During healing sessions, *hapana basa* is even used to classify a type of illness. As shown in Shimmer's portrait, prophets call people to be healed according to particular afflictions: stomach pains for one but also headaches, marriage troubles, mental illness, and hapana basa—bad luck (the course of healing sessions is discussed in more detail in chapter 7). In casual conversation, as well, apostolics might respond "hapana basa" when hearing about an unfortunate turn of events in someone's life. To give a mundane example, I once overheard two men at Juranifiri talking before the service began. One of them had apparently lost his keys, and the other man said, "Ah, hapana basa."

Hapana basa is not generally used as a term for bad luck, although most Shona speakers would recognize not having work as a *kind* of bad luck. It is important to say, however, that the apostolics do not use this phrase primarily to index wage labor as a sign of Christian well-being. In the Friday churches material success is not—as we should expect—evidence of piety. What "hapana basa" signals for the apostolics is faith that the Holy Spirit can deliver them from the hardships common to those beset by the jealousies of relatives and the misfortunes of witchcraft. More than an economic connotation, then, the phrase carries a specific, apostolic meaning. Apostolics take "work" primarily to signify the activity of the Holy Spirit, and they appropriate it as such as part of their religious language. It was even something they joked about with me, "testing" me to see if I *really knew* what *basa* (work) meant.

The examples here are brief, but they make the point that there are several ways in which apostolics use language, bodily movements, and speech codes to differentiate themselves from others. The standardized call of *rufaro kwamuri*—completed as much through its physical as verbal articulation—is an example of what Judith Irvine and Susan Gal call the semiotic process of *iconization*, "a transformation of the sign relationship between linguistic features (or varieties) and the social images with which they are linked" (2000, 37). The greeting is both linguistic and imagistic, combining words and actions into a form that is supposed to be an "iconic representation" of the community, "as if a linguistic feature somehow depicted or displayed a social group's inherent nature or essence" (Irvine and Gal 2000, 37). The use of colloquialisms and deep Shona produce similar effects, differentiating apostolics from others. This boundary drawing is even more salient when we consider that most apostolic services are attended by large numbers of nonapostolics, each with varying degrees of familiarity with the church. Within a community of practice there are always gradations in knowledge, competence, and skill (Lave and Wenger 1991). On a basic level, of course, everyone present at a sowe can be defined as "the group" in question. Physical presence is one kind of sociological measure. But through certain ways of speaking the apostolics become a group within the group, shifting the boundaries of belonging from physical presence to cultural practice and semiotic principles.

Formal greetings, deep Shona, and colloquialisms are ways of speaking that anyone can learn. They are aspects of mutemo. For apostolics, using language in this way is about the incorporation and expression of mutemo. Just as apostolics should live their lives according to Christian precepts, so too should they speak a Christian language. This point brings us back to the discussion in chapter 2 about the dynamics of religious transformation. Using Harding's (2000) work on Baptist fundamentalists as a point of comparison, I suggested that Johane came to *inhabit* a religious language—or, at least, always attempted to do so (Crapanzano 2000, 162–66). Similarly, I would argue that the ways of speaking discussed here index the speaker as a Friday apostolic. Knowing how to speak as a Christian is one aspect of achieving a live and direct relationship with God, of closing the distance to the divine.

Within ritual life there is another way of speaking, and another vocabulary, that does not exactly fit this model: what the apostolics call "ancient Hebrew." Some of these ancient Hebrew words are used on a daily basis by the congregation, but it is prophets filled with the Holy Spirit who reveal their meanings and who alone can use them as competent speakers. I should stress that the apostolics' ancient Hebrew is *not* several things. It is not (in any recognizable way) related to the written and spoken forms of Hebrew in known circulation. I gave a list of ancient Hebrew words to a colleague at the University of Zimbabwe who was quick to state that nothing in it looked like the Hebrew he had studied. The Masowe apostolics accepted this point and were not especially troubled by it. But ancient Hebrew is said to be a "proper language" that, while inscrutable to human beings, is spoken by the divine. The only ancient Hebrew words that ordinary apostolics use are a handful of "nouns," although apostolics do not always know what the words mean. Some of the words are well understood, however, and the elders are happy to relate the meanings. *Juranifiri Santa,* for example—Place of Healing—is not a Shona term but an ancient Hebrew one. Apostolics understand it only as being the language of God—as momentary exposure to a language of power and truth.

For the apostolics, ancient Hebrew words are an index of divine presence. Prophets never speak exclusively in ancient Hebrew, but they momentarily code switch into it from Shona when casting out evil spirits from possessed members of the congregation. The following example from a healing session at Juranifiri Santa in May 1999 is typical. A woman is possessed by the spirit of a man who was murdered by her paternal uncle. She is agitated, pacing around the center of the sowe, back and forth, wringing her hands and punching the air. The spirit has exacted retribution for the murder by possessing the woman so she might serve the spirit's bidding. As often happens in these situations, the spirit is said to have "married" the woman (see Engelke 2004a, 95–98). The voice of the possessed woman, then, is not hers but that of the avenging spirit *(ngozi).* Pageneck, the prophet at Juranifiri who fills Nzira, is trying to save the woman from the spirit by casting it out. He stands calmly in place. The spirit in the woman is railing against Pageneck, angry that the Holy Spirit thinks it can recuperate her. There is shouting. The possessed woman yells, "I was murdered, and my wife was murdered too. You [Pageneck] want me to live without a wife, I will not allow it! This woman is mine. I will not let her go." "Hey," Pageneck replies. "Leave! I'm not using earthly tactics in this war. *Trona!* Hey, I said go away!"

The word *trona* is ancient Hebrew. No one could tell me what this word meant, but it was understood as "heavy artillery" in the fight against witchcraft and possession (a practice laden with militaristic metaphors). Only prophets filled with the Holy Spirit use such words. They cause avenging spirits a great deal of discomfort.[6] But they are considered "too much" to be uttered by human beings. Two other common ancient Hebrew expressions are *andrea* and *chrai se mutome,* the latter of which a prophet mutters softly to himself or herself when berated by evil spirits to steel the nerves and gather the strength necessary to respond.

The use of ancient Hebrew words in ritual life was often described to me as evidence of God working live and direct in a congregation. But rather than language to master or inhabit, ancient Hebrew marks the boundary between the human and the divine. It is as much a means of asserting difference as generating a sense of belonging—marking the proper relationship between distance and proximity by reminding the apostolics of God's separation and separateness. Apostolics feel enriched by hearing ancient Hebrew. They talk about it as a privilege to hear. But it unfurls the flag of power that is not theirs to wave. It is an element of live and direct language that establishes a prophet's position of authority and difference from ordinary members. It also reconfigures the provenance of the past, for ancient Hebrew is more ancient even than Hebrew.

Of the several ways of speaking highlighted in this section, deep Shona and ancient Hebrew help to make a final point that enables the transition to the consideration of a prophet's ritual speech. Deep Shona and ancient Hebrew each bring to mind the classic discussion in anthropology of the magical power of words (Malinowski 1965; Tambiah 1968). What role do words play in ritual? As Stanley Tambiah emphasizes, "As long as religion . . . harks back to a period of revelation and insists on the authority of properly transmitted true texts either orally or in written form, its sacred language will contain an archaic component, whether this is represented by a totally different language or other elements of the same language" (1968, 182). The archaic components of Masowe religious language are without doubt central features of ritual life, both for what they do to make the rituals efficacious and to the extent that ritual participants engage in their discussion as such. What I want to suggest here is that deep Shona and ancient Hebrew reinforce a central theological concern within the Friday churches. Rather than ground speech in chapter and verse—rather than use what Nzira disparagingly called "Bible talk"—these communicative codes shift the terms of reference away from Scripture. Deep Shona and ancient Hebrew suggest divine revelation but a period that is not grounded in the Bible. Nothing in the Bible, from the apostolic point of view, has the power of an originary moment. With this in mind, I turn to a more detailed consideration of the ritual speech of prophets. For it is in the context of the congregation as a community of practice, working to substantiate live and direct language, that prophets are able to present the True Bible as something that exists beyond Scripture.

PROPHETS AS PEOPLE

In a typical church service prophets speak only when they deliver sermons or interpret dreams. (Sometimes they initiate songs, but as I discuss in the next chapter this is usually left to congregants.) During healing sessions, prophets also speak with both their patients and the spirits afflicting those patients, as we glimpsed in the example of ancient Hebrew as "heavy artillery." These "battles" can last up to an hour, during which a prophet might carry on as many as a dozen separate exchanges with the possessed, shifting from one to the other as their energies peak and trough.

Most of the time they speak prophets are filled with the Holy Spirit. But they also address their congregations as fellow apostolics—that is, when they are not filled with the Holy Spirit. While neither as common nor as important as hearing the Holy Spirit, what prophets say as themselves is taken seriously.

For example, in the vignette that opens the introduction to this book, Nzira was speaking as himself the day he castigated the man who quoted from the Gospel of Luke. The man inspired Nzira to craft the stark imagery of the Bible as toilet paper because the man crossed a sensitive line in the arena of religious authority. Direct quotation from the Bible is a disrespectful act, especially in a sowe. On the one hand, then, Nzira's reply highlighted the man's outsider status, serving as a reminder to the congregation of the standards of conduct to which they would be held: an apostolic should not talk like that. On the other hand, I would argue, Nzira's reply reveals the threat that exactitude poses to the authority of the prophets. By speaking to the man as an apostolic Nzira was able to present the ideal position on such an issue. "We don't talk Bible-talk here," he said. Nzira's use of the first-person plural made his language open but not necessarily inclusive. Who was the *we* in question? It may or may not have included the man. The deictic grounding *(here)* is also notable. In using it, Nzira was referring to the sowe as a conceptual space—as a place in which the community of practice engaged in the common task of listening to the Word live and direct. Nzira's delivery was meant to create a human bond. His admonition helped to shape the boundaries of the community of practice by defining its standards: to quote from chapter and verse is one thing but to understand the message—to get the True Bible—is another.

PROPHETS AND POSSESSION

To appreciate the importance of ritual speech is to know who is speaking. It has long been clear to sociolinguists that models of communication based on binary oppositions of sender-receiver or speaker-hearer are too imprecise for the task (Goffman 1981; Hymes 1974a). Erving Goffman's triadic model of animator-author-principal presents a more fine-grained set of distinctions that allows us to address issues of agency, authority, and provenance in a manner that binary schemes cannot. His work is useful for understanding the communicative dynamics of apostolic possession. For Goffman, the *animator* is simply "the talking machine, a body engaged in acoustic activity"; the *author* is "someone who has selected the sentiments that are being expressed and the words in which they are embodied"; and the *principal* is "someone whose position is established by the words that are spoken, someone whose beliefs have been told" (1981, 144). Prophets speaking as themselves presents no major issues in this regard; Nzira would be said to occupy all three roles. But when it comes to the analysis of ritual speech in which a spiritual or otherworldly being might be the primary agent, the triadic model is helpful for sorting out the dynamics (cf. Hanks 1996b; Keane 1997b).

In the Friday churches a prophet is the "vessel" through which the Holy Spirit speaks. Following Goffman's model, we would say that the prophet is the animator but not the author or principal of the message. Prophets do not know what is said through them, and they claim no authority over their actions or accomplishments when filled. The Holy Spirit occasionally reinforces this distinction when speaking through a prophet. Take the case of Nzira. When Nzira is filled by the Holy Spirit he is known as Pageneck, which is the ancient Hebrew name of the angel that speaks through him (more on this below). Pageneck—whose cantankerous nature parallels that of his human host—often reminded the congregation of the difference. "I am not a human being," Pageneck said one day. "When people come here, they say, 'I am going to Nzira's place.' Nzira, Nzira. I am not Nzira. This is not Nzira's place. He is a just a human. I am not a human being." For several weeks after he first said this, Nzira-Pageneck repeated it at every service.

The point of Pageneck's message was to remind the congregation that they should not associate Juranifiri Santa with a person: it did not belong to Nzira. In ritual life there is a concern on the part of most prophets and elders that people not come to associate God's Word too closely with a particular human being. We have seen how this played out in chapter 3, where I addressed the question of leadership. From the point of view of several Friday congregations, for example, Emmanuel Mudyiwa fell off track because he tried to claim equivalence with God. It is vitally important as part of mutemo to recognize that the church has no leader other than God. It is precisely when religious authority becomes too closely associated with a person or a thing—when it becomes thingified and thus rendered fixed—that one needs to worry about a compromised faith. This is what happened with the missionaries and their Bible, it happened to Emmanuel, and it can happen again.

The language that Pageneck used to make a point of his difference is notable in several respects. As with the example from Nzira in the preceding section, the deictics *(here / Nzira's place)* ground his words but this time in a more specific sense. Pageneck was restricting the frame of reference to the sowe, and he did so through a transposition—quoted speech that maintains the indexes and deictics of an original utterance—that the congregation found humorous. In this case, the utterance *I am going to Nzira's place* was articulated in a shrill voice, suggesting the ignorance of the author-principal. As Robin Shoaps argues, transposition is interesting because it "occurs when texts are animated in order to access (and evaluate) the point of view they are held up as representing" (2002, 16). Pageneck's evaluation was categorically negative; referring to the sowe as *Nzira's place* struck the apostolics as it should have: it was a foolish thing to say and so said in a foolish way.

Birgit Meyer (1999) has made the point that Christians in Africa often draw a distinction between possession by the Holy Spirit and possession by other spirits. For the Ewe Pentecostals with whom she worked in Ghana, the difference sets a clear boundary between Christianity and "heathenism" (see Meyer 1999, 205). For the Masowe apostolics, these boundaries must also be maintained. The language ideology implicit in apostolic talk about possession reflects the desire to break with the past that I have already touched on in several earlier chapters. One indication of this is that apostolics will never say their prophets are "possessed" *(kusvikirwa)*. They consider *possession* a bad word.[7] *Kusvikirwa* denotes another dangerous and shameful aspect of "African culture" that apostolics must fight against.

Prophets in the Masowe Church are "filled with" *(kuzadzwa)*, not possessed by, the Holy Spirit. I was told that prophets are like jars and that the Holy Spirit is like water. While these similes draw on both African and Christian religious imageries, for apostolics this act of "filling" a prophet represents a significant process that must be distinguished from the normative understanding of possession in both content and form.[8] One point in particular stands out. Being filled by the Holy Spirit is a blessing; it never results in deleterious effects. Apostolics will argue that there is ample evidence other spirits produce no such blessings. On the contrary, even one's ancestral spirits are as likely to harm as to help. I focused in chapter 2 on how after his transformation at Marimba in 1932 Johane was wracked by uncertainties as to how he should carry out his mission. But this was never a doubt about the gift of the Holy Spirit or its meaning. Apostolics today lay claim to a similar certitude and argue that no unbeliever—even the most adept spirit medium—can do the same. Other spirits are capricious and fickle, amoral even. "We have nothing like that," claim the apostolics.

I am interested in developing an analysis of what marks the live and direct faith as distinct, but it is also important to recognize the traditionalist's counterargument here. Christian and non-Christian boundaries are not (let me repeat) clear cut. Apostolics deny any similarity between a prophet filled with the Holy Spirit and a spirit medium possessed by an ancestor or mhondoro (tribal spirit), but I met several spirit mediums who begged to differ. Weegirl, for example, pointed out to me that an apostolic emphasis on the Holy Spirit-as-water was not so different from the way in which she used mermaid spirits (njuzu) to heal the afflictions of her clients. Mermaid spirits come from distant bodies of water, such as the Indian Ocean, and are noted by many Zimbabweans for their healing prowess. Weegirl also remarked on the fact that in what she called "the Shona culture" both the Holy Spirit and mermaids are classed as *mashave,* or foreign spirits. For her, this typological classification is a good way to cut through the rhetoric of exclusivity and privilege that underlies many African Christian discourses. We might also note that one of the names for the Shona high god is Dzivaguru, which means "Great Pool" (Mukonyora 2000, 2–7; Murphree 1969, 49). The point here is not to settle any debates between Masowe prophets and spirit mediums but simply to acknowledge the porous nature of any cosmological system, not least through the evidence and appropriation of language. Even further, I want to note, the extent of the porousness is the grounds for contestation. It is an indication of how semiotic ideologies can clash. In the examples here, the apostolics and Weegirl are not simply interpreting the classes of spirits in different ways; they are arguing over whether the classes are even the same—over whether any one of them is a stable sign.

With two exceptions over six years, I saw nothing in the conduct of a prophet filled with the Holy Spirit that a traditionalist would have recognized as possession. Prophets are not prone to the trances that often mark ancestral presence. In a sense, then, "apostolic possession" is notable because it is not notable. What marks prophets as filled is how they speak and what they say (cf. Placido 2001).

There are two reliable signs that a prophet is filled with the Holy Spirit. The first, to which I have already alluded in passing, is the presence of congregants possessed by ancestral or avenging spirits. The often "violent" behavior of African spirits is taken as evidence of divine presence. Like a brass rubbing—in which the image is made visible by filling in the empty spaces around it—the presence of the Holy Spirit in these instances can be seen through what it is not. The Holy Spirit causes other spirits anguish and pain, forcing them to manifest themselves through the bodies of their hosts (cf. Brown 1981, 108).

In sermons, however, this type of spiritual contrast is almost always missing. But divine presence can still be staked out through bodily and sensorial evidence. The most reliable sign that a prophet is filled with the Holy Spirit when sermonizing is the presence of a man alongside the prophet called the *mumiriri wemweya,* or interpreter of the spirit. Mumiriri wemweya are chosen by the Holy Spirit to speak for the prophet.[9] They can be elected at any time to perform this job and usually do so for a number of years. Ideally there should be twelve mumiriri in each congregation, just as there were twelve apostles (although the actual numbers often differ). Mumiriri are given the gift of being able to "hear what God says." Mumiriri are always men, and, though they are called interpreters, from the perspective of an outsider they more closely resemble human megaphones.[10] The main task of a mumiriri wemweya is to make sure that the congregation can hear the message of the Holy Spirit. I was often told the Holy Spirit "does not like to shout." Prophets do indeed speak softly for the most part when filled, and so it becomes necessary for someone else to project the Word, especially in large congregations. Sometimes prophets also whisper directly into the ears of a mumiriri, so that only he can hear what is said. Audibility and inaudibility are evidence of the tension between distance and proximity.

A mumiriri resembles a megaphone in that he always shouts out exactly what the Holy Spirit utters. There are a few exceptions to this rule, the most common being the way in which a prophet might shorten the formal greetings—saying "rufaro" instead of the full "rufaro kwamuri," the latter of which is what the mumiriri will shout. Prophets are able to build rapport with their mumiriri and work out shortcuts in this way. There are also often signs of affection between the two. Pageneck sometimes put his arm around the mumiriri in a friendly manner. On a few occasions he used the mumiriri as a human prop in a risqué way. But the mumiriri is rarely at ease. He has a serious job to do and is expected to perform to perfection. If he does not—if the mumiriri makes just one mistake, even a stutter—he may be asked to sit down. Pageneck, who could be one of the more extreme prophets, often hit his mumiriri if they failed him.

On those occasions when a prophet momentarily code switches into ancient Hebrew, a mumiriri will not repeat what is said. This limit to reiteration suggests that what a prophet says is always something more than what the mumiriri can reiterate. On a more ineffable level, then, the mumiriri does "interpret," and his inability to repeat an ancient Hebrew word marks his limitations. This limit reminds the congregation of divine difference. Listening to the Word alone does not render truth transparent. But even when a prophet filled with the Holy Spirit is speaking in Shona, his or her words are said to be endowed with meanings not fully accessible to human beings. Perhaps the simplest way of putting it is that prophetic speech needs to be confirmed, that it has an anagogic dimension always inaccessible to the congregation. Someone chosen by God must act as the witness and give the people listening a sense of security by making the words "fully intelligible," inasmuch as that can be done. The task of interpretation involves not only making words meaningful but also, just in itself, the act of repetition.

The presence of a mumiriri creates a moment of conceptual slippage between the prophet as subject and object of authority, entextualizing the ritual speech. Joel Kuipers defines entextualization as "a process in which a speech event (or series of speech events) is marked by increasing thoroughness of poetic and rhetorical patterning and growing levels of (apparent) detachment from the immediate pragmatic context" (1990, 4). Entextualization is a strategy of making what is said more authoritative by suggesting its transcendent, textlike qualities. Similar to what Keane describes in Anakalang ritual speech, entextualization through repetition "stresses the context-free dimensions of language" and "implicitly portrays the particular event and participants as instances of general types" (1997b, 133). Of course neither the written nor the spoken word is, in this context-free sense, fixed. Just as texts are unstable objects of interpretation, so too is entextualized speech. "Like formality in language entextualization must not be reified as a 'thing' with certain inherent properties or states, but treated as a useful analytic concept with which to make sense of ethnographic data" (Kuipers 1990, 5). In this discussion entextualization helps us to make sense of how the live and direct style of a sermon becomes a text-made-immediate, both transcendent and present. The mumiriri is a speaking subject in relation to which the prophet becomes the object of authority—the object that in much other Christian practice is the Bible. This helps to clarify the shift in the source of truth that is central to the analysis. The Bible is sidelined, recognized as neither author nor principal of the divine message.

How something is said and in what kind of environment are also factors in the equation here. Indeed, the physical dimensions of the community of practice play a central role in apostolic entextualizations—in particular, in large congregations such as Juranifiri. While Pageneck sometimes raised his voice over the course of a sermon so that everyone could hear what he was saying (as was often the case when he fought against voluble spirits), this could not be taken for granted. On the days when he remained relatively quiet, the fact that the Holy Spirit does not like to shout produced both frustration and a heightened sense of expectation. It might be impossible for those at the back of a large congregation to hear what a prophet is saying, so the mumiriri's role as animator of the message becomes essential. Regardless of this, however, in principle the possibility of not hearing the prophet should not matter. Whatever the prophet says must always be confirmed by the mumiriri. As long as an apostolic hears the mumiriri, then, he or she is hearing the Word of God live and direct. It would probably make an apostolic uncomfortable to know that a prophet was filled with the Holy Spirit and delivering a sermon *without* a mumiriri. And yet it always seemed to frustrate at least some of the people at the back of Juranifiri Santa's large congregation when they could not also hear the Holy Spirit's message out of Nzira's mouth. This is the kind of thing that prompted congregants to start running when elders called a service to order. Nothing bothered the elders more than such uncontrolled behavior, and it was the subject of many fiery lessons. But congregants always wanted to hear both iterations of the Holy Spirit's message, even though from a more theological point of view it was hearing the mumiriri that mattered, and even though it landed them in trouble with the elders. In sum, the audibility of a prophet filled with the Holy Spirit brings the tension between distance and proximity into sharp focus. It suggests that, on the one hand, apostolics want to hear the live and direct word as "directly" as possible. But on the other hand, there is something unsettling in this, something that the presence of the mumiriri rightfully qualifies. This is why the dynamic is in tension; neither distance nor proximity in itself is a proper relation to the divine. The presence of the mumiriri makes the presence of the Word possible by functioning as the sign of human distance. So presence becomes possible through the recognition of distance.

In his study of biblical narrative Robert Alter (1981) devotes a chapter to "the techniques of repetition," which adds another dimension to the overarching discussion here on the process of entextualization. Alter argues that repetition is central to the religious message of the Hebrew Bible. Repetition is not simply artifice: it expresses "the inescapable tension between human freedom and divine historical plan" (Alter 1981, 113). Repetition throws the provenance of discourse into relief by calling attention to its figural dimensions. Its truth emerges out of its patterning. I would argue that the relationship between the prophet and the mumiriri expresses an analogous tension. Whether or not everyone can hear the message coming out of the prophet's mouth is, in one sense, a logistical issue. But it becomes part and parcel of the problem of presence. Reiteration "translates into a central narrative device the unswerving authority of a monotheistic God manifesting Himself in language" (Alter 1981, 91).

ANGELS AND OTHERS

The presence of possessed congregants and the mumiriri are two ways in which to recognize the presence of God, but the identity of the "speaker" is often thought to be more specific than just the Holy Spirit. For my informants, to say that God or the Holy Spirit had been speaking to them on any given occasion was not always a satisfactory answer, even if this was what mattered most. But that was obvious. They were curious as well about whether or not a particular spirit (such as the spirit of John the Baptist) had been at work. The relationship between God and other "holy" spirits raises an aspect of Masowe cosmology that I have referred to thus far only in passing but which forms a central pillar in the structuring of the True Bible and a live and direct faith. The role of other holy spirits is important because they serve the apostolics as evidence of Scripture's secondary status.

When prophets are filled with the Holy Spirit they are often said to be filled by other spirits as well. Shoniwa Masedza referred to himself as "Africa's John the Baptist" because the spirit of John the Baptist spoke through him on a regular basis. Emmanuel Mudyiwa made similar (if more contested) claims of identification with Jesus. The same holds for Nzira-Pageneck, although this is an uncommon example in the sense that the spirit called Pageneck has no historical precedent. However, the "spirit" in each of these examples does not replace the Holy Spirit; it is possible for both to be at work through the same person. As one elder put it, "The Holy Spirit is a tree, and the other spirits are its branches." In such cases the Holy Spirit is the principal, the other spirits are the authors, and the prophet is the animator of the message.

Apostolics refer to these other spirits as the angels *(ngirozi)*. Their understanding of angels, however, is not entirely like that of most other Christians. Although it should be said, as Harold Bloom (1996, 35–81) makes clear in his generalists' overview, angelology is itself a complicated field, developed to varying degrees of complexity in different Christian and other Abrahamic religious traditions. Although there is not space to offer a point-for-point comparison with some of the more prevalent understandings of angels, I want to provide more detail on how apostolics conceive of them. This is because angels play an important role in the workings of a live and direct faith.

According to the apostolics, angels, like humans, have personalities (Pageneck, we know, can be rough) and talents (he is also good at spiritual healing). Unlike humans, angels are not mortal. I was told they have always existed, although I do not think the apostolics meant to imply that they are, therefore, divine. Indeed, angels were discussed as if they are creations, not extensions, of God. There are more angels than humans know; only some have worked through human beings in the past and built up significant this-worldly reputations. Several of the major characters in the biblical narratives are recognized by the apostolics as angels—including several prophets and kings in the Old Testament and all the apostles of the New Testament. The most powerful angels are used by the Holy Spirit to address specific needs on earth. John the Baptist was the first angel to come to

Africa (through Shoniwa Masedza) because Africans needed an evangelist. Moses is believed to be an angel of guidance, a leader on whom the people can rely to guide them out of difficult situations. The Archangel Michael (a meta-angel, if you will) is a fierce warrior. In Zimbabwe he has fought on behalf of the possessed to rid them of their spiritual afflictions.

According to the apostolics, when we read in the Bible about, say, Moses, we are reading about an angel called Moses—not a man. Moses' part in the Bible is simply an instance of the angel's work through a human actor that was recorded, as the apostolics often say when referring to the world of biblical times, "up in Palestine." Similarly, the angel John the Baptist existed before the man John the Baptist; we know the man who was John the Baptist *as* John the Baptist because of his angel. Since that time the angel has expressed himself through Shoniwa Masedza as well. So to say that Shoniwa Masedza was Africa's John the Baptist is not to say that Shoniwa had in some sense been possessed by the spirit of a man from Judea. It was to say that the angel John the Baptist has worked through both the man from Judea and the man from Makoni. This was a point that elders in particular were keen to stress, because they worried that if misunderstood it could make them look "backward" or immured by the "African culture" they so roundly condemned. As one elder put it, "This is not ancestor worship, hey?!"

There are, again, some notable singularities in how the Friday apostolics understand angels. One not already mentioned but that follows from the points just made is that there are female ngirozi; whereas there are no female angels named in the Bible, the apostolics recognize Ruth and Sarah (for instance) as ngirozi. But what would probably strike most Christians as problematic is the extent to which, through their angelology, the apostolics downplay the significance of the histories the Bible contains (whether or not these histories are accepted as literal). This is in fact the heart of the matter. The distinction between the angel John the Baptist and the man John the Baptist is theologically important because it means that what is recorded in the Bible is not a sacred history but rather a set of types that can be, and are, combined in new configurations according to God's will. John the Baptist is not authenticated in the Bible but in his angelic essence, which is something that transcends the text. A discussion of the ngirozi, then, allows us to see how the apostolics push authority away from Scripture and toward the message (the True Bible) that stands behind it. In a "live and direct semiotics," angels become meaningful signs freed from history.

The anxiety expressed by the elder over being labeled an ancestor worshiper because of the form their angelology takes brings us back to the question of how the apostolics distinguish themselves as Christians. Most apostolics would argue that holding rituals to communicate with one's ancestors—as many Shona-speaking people do—amounts to the worship of false gods. You should not pray to your ancestors; pray only to God. As with several apostolic interpretations of "traditional" religious practice, this one is rejected by the people it is meant to describe. Those with whom I raised the issue pointed out that they do not worship—or even "pray" to—their ancestors. What they do is show ancestors respect in an effort to maintain good relationships between the visible and invisible worlds. For many Shona-speaking people, as I have noted, ancestors are an integral part of social relationships, and they can often intervene (for better or worse) in daily life. They are respected because of their position in a patriline. On spectacularly rare occasions, if there is a grave breach in the social equilibrium, one's ancestors might convey a request for redress from the visible world through a successive chain of past generations until the message reaches Mwari. But this is *highly* unusual, and for a traditionalist it is not a matter of worship at all. "Worship" is not an accurate and relevant description of the relationships between humans and ancestral spirits. I remember one friend putting it in terms of me visiting my grandmother's grave in the United States. He concluded that I would do so out of respect and asked if this meant I worshiped her. I said of course not, and he said that it was the same in Zimbabwe. In turning the argument around, what traditionalists find problematic about Christians (in particular, the apostolic and Pentecostal churches) is the disavowal of the ancestors and their claim to be able to speak to God directly (cf. Keane 1998). Critics of the Masowe apostolics cry hypocrisy; they tend to think of angels simply as ancestors by another name.

Sometimes an angel identifies itself by name in the course of a sermon. Such angelic self-identification is a jolting experience for the apostolics. It is a powerfully intimate thing—something like breaking the frame of implicit difference between the human and the divine, of making the live and direct connection too live and direct. But it helps to convey the religious message. Consider this example. In August 1999 the congregation at Juranifiri held a misi mitatu (three-day prayer session) that drew in several thousand apostolics from throughout Zimbabwe (in fact, as far away as Johannesburg). Over the course of the three days a few thousand nearby residents also turned up, many in search of spiritual healing. Church elders regularly arrange such mass meetings, deemed necessary because elders have to make sure all the congregations "stick to mutemo." The temptation of a congregation to develop its own ways of doing things, above and beyond what the Holy Spirit instructs, is too great. As Marcus explained it, a misi mitatu functions as a system of checks and balances. It is not simply a measure to ensure the proper course for the churches but a strategy of reining in prophets who get too big. Juranifiri's misi mitatu was a particularly charged occasion because in the eyes of some elders Nzira was a prophet flirting dangerously close to the edge of mutemo—of claiming to be superior to other prophets. For Juranifiri to hold a misi mitatu at that time, then, was like a suspect running his own trial. This at least was the opinion of several elders and prophets who did not attend, those for whom the question of leadership was being asked of Nzira.

Even with notable absences the misi mitatu was large by church standards. Prophets from around Zimbabwe spoke, but Nzira-Pageneck undeniably held center stage. Pageneck delivered several sermons. In one of them he made a rare statement of angelic self-identification. Until that point he had been talking about the help that God provides to those in need—fighting witchcraft and the jealousies that fuel family tensions. He said that God can show people the way to heaven *(kudenga)*. Then he said, "Your Bible told you that the Holy Spirit will come. I am the one you heard was coming. Do you know me? Do you know where I come from? I am Peter, I come from the palm *[chanza]* of Moses." I return below to the first pronouncement—"Your Bible told you that the Holy Spirit will come"—but I want to frame it by a discussion of the invocation of the angels. For this is what most struck the congregation. The self-identification at the misi mitatu was received by many informants in a less charged manner than it might otherwise have been. The three-day prayer session was a special event, so the naming seemed reasonable to expect. When I asked what was significant about Peter's presence and his explicit self-identification through Nzira-Pageneck, I was repeatedly told two things: like Moses, Simon-Peter was chosen by God as a leader of His people; and Peter holds the keys to the Gates of Heaven. On these grounds several friends speculated that some apostolics must have been achieving salvation at the misi mitatu, that Peter was "opening the Gates" because the prayer session had been a success.[11] When I told one of the elders who had not attended the misi mitatu what had been said, he scoffed. Clearly this was Nzira—*the man Nzira*—using the good name of Peter (and Moses) to assert his own authority, his superiority. This was the move of an insecure and power-driven man, not a "true prophet."

As with the disagreements between prophets and spirit mediums, I am not in a position to fill out the various arguments over this example. It should remind us, however, that the question of leadership is not confined to church history but arises in ritual practice. It is also a good indication that the sincerity of ritual speech is on occasion doubted (an issue I address in the next chapter). But the point of the example is that the naming of angels in ritual speech is a means of substantiating live and direct faith through the discursive circulation of iconic Judeo-Christian figures. It makes worship biblical without the Bible, because it depends on the interpretive work of the congregation to articulate the angel's importance. These namings are not fit into full narratives, thus eclipsing the Bible's historical coherence. Over the course of a sermon a prophet often builds a sense of the live and direct around nothing more than evocative images. The self-identifications of angels are speech acts grounded in time that simultaneously transcend it. The name of an angel carries with it a set of associations that are emplotted and deployed by the apostolics in an effort to apprehend the True Bible. Peter's self-identification provided a metacommentary on the action of the misi mitatu that—for the "faithful"—grounded Nzira-Pageneck's authority as a divinely chosen guide.

Increasingly, however, angels do not reveal themselves explicitly because revealment leads to the kind of contest that developed over Nzira-Pageneck at the misi mitatu. Shimmer explained it to me: "If I happen to speak with the spirit of Ezekiel, then I am called Ezekiel. But if I go to another church, and I see someone else who says he is speaking with Ezekiel, I'll try to defend myself and say, 'Hey, friend, I am the one who speaks with Ezekiel. You are not Ezekiel.' And then human nature starts. We might fight." Even Nzira-Pageneck did not reveal an identity on most occasions. And he never, in fact, referred to himself as "Pageneck." His elders told me that like other prophets he had no intention of "starting human nature." Besides, they would say, all prophets are the same because they are all filled with the Holy Spirit.

Let me recap these most recent points. Fitting the analysis of angels into the proposed argument runs something like this. The Bible is not identical with the Truth. What is recorded in the Bible might well be, in Frei's reading of the precritical idiom, a series of actual historical occurrences. But for the apostolics, its religious truth emerges in the message, and the message is not dependent on any one set of historical events. Independent of the particular narratives in which they appear, angels bear this message. They are the divine's evangelists, soldiers, healers, and leaders and can always lend themselves to new times and places. They are not mortal and always transcend the particular events in which they play a part. They are—to borrow from Edmund Leach's (1969, 7–9) structuralist readings of the Bible—units of information that can always be recombined. Angels could never be hostage to a narrative. They are not defined by the Bible; rather the Bible is defined by them. Angels are part of the apostolic cosmological apparatus through which the critique of scriptural authority is leveled. Here we see how the semiotic ideology of the Friday apostolics shifts the sources of meaning and authority away from the text and onto the activities and presences of angels.

At this point I want to return to what else Pageneck said when he named himself as Peter. As that example shows, a prophet's message is often grounded in some relation to the Bible. One of the things Pageneck said was "Your Bible told you that the Holy Spirit will come." But *Your Bible (Bhaibheri yenyu)* in this sermon is ambiguous. To whom was the prophet speaking? If to the apostolics—*yenyu* is the plural possessive—he might have meant the True Bible that figures elsewhere in Masowe sermons. If to the nonapostolics he might have meant the Bible, which they could now dispense with—that is, they could get rid of their Bible and embrace the True Bible made live and direct through the coming of the Holy Spirit. Considering the claim as a prophetic fulfilment (X said Y and now Y is true) makes it no less ambiguous. Presented in an indirect manner *(Your Bible told you . . .)* it does have "the authoritativeness of the reliable narrator" (Alter 1981, 67). But it lacks specificity. What Bible says this, and where? The ambiguity works in a community of practice, however, because in its multivalence *Your Bible* speaks to the range of participants. But there were occasions on which Pageneck and other prophets made more restricted references, suggesting a role for historical precedent even as that precedent was meant to be replaced.

Just after the start of every church service a prophet or elder asks if there are any visitors that day from other Friday groups. At Juranifiri Santa there usually were; apostolics are encouraged to call on different congregations in an effort to maintain strong churchwide connections. (Juranifiri received from five to twenty visitors per week, usually on weekends.) One does not have to be appointed to undertake such visits, and even ordinary members can find themselves in the pleasant position of playing ambassador for a day. After a service the visitors might be invited to spend time with a selection of the local elders to share news about happenings in other quarters of the church.

On one occasion this normally pleasant experience went wrong for a visitor. It was Pageneck who invited the guests to introduce themselves, to say where they had come from and why they had come to Juranifiri. About a dozen people stood up. The third or fourth person was a middle-aged man. He said:

> MAN: My name is X. I have come to worship with you here. *[Nervous, stuttering]* I-I- ha-ha-have come to join this sowe from another one in Hatcliffe.[12]

Pageneck's response in this instance only reinforced the insecurity that apostolics face when speaking up. He interrupted the man to ask him a more pointed question.

> PAGENECK: Do you think you will be able to follow us here?
> MAN: Yes, I shall.
> PAGENECK: You won't. I don't have relationships with Galatians [Garatini]. I don't eat with Galatians. Please, sit down.

When the exchange was over none of the other visitors got the chance to introduce themselves. The man in question sat down, and Pageneck began a sermon on how being a good apostolic involves following the Word of God, on living with faith "in the heart."

The reference to Galatians led some of my friends in discussions after the service to suggest that Paul had been speaking through Nzira. Paul could be recognized as an angel at work from context clues; Pageneck did not have to say "I am Paul" because it was known (by some at least) that Paul wrote an epistle to the Galatians. But why Galatians? I asked several apostolics about this incident in the days after. They were quick to point out that Pageneck had not referred directly to the Book of Galatians but to the Galatians as a kind of people. It was both a trivial and a significant distinction that needs to be interpreted with the text of the New Testament in mind.

Galatians is one of Paul's most exhortatory epistles. Having established a church in Galatia, Paul learns that a Jewish-Christian countermission has asserted itself and insisted on the adoption of Mosaic Law and the practice of circumcision. Dispensing with the polite manners that mark his earlier, more assured letters, Paul launches into an angry polemic: "You foolish Galatians! Who has bewitched you?" (Gal. 3:1). With two of his other letters (2 Cor. and Rom.), Galatians betrays a "shaken confidence and a tendency to anger and despair" (Goulder 1997, 488). It was written after a series of setbacks to his missionary work. The epistle is an effort to steer the Galatians back to the Pauline model of Christianity, which is summed up in the first part of Galatians 2:16: "a person is justified not by the works of the law but through faith in Jesus Christ." This verse—the subject of much debate in New Testament scholarship—was referenced by one of the elders I spoke to at Juranifiri about Pageneck's comment to the man from Hatcliffe.[13] (The elder had once belonged to the Seventh-day Adventist Church; he was very familiar with the Bible.) It was clear in our conversation that this elder interpreted "the law" in Galatians as the written word—both Mosaic Law and, by implication, Scripture.[14] He contended that Paul was concerned with showing that Scripture was no longer necessary and referred me (without rehearsing them himself) to an additional four verses: "Now before faith came, we were imprisoned and guarded under the law until faith would be revealed. Therefore the law was our disciplinarian until Christ came, so that we might be justified by faith. But now that faith has come, we are no longer subject to a disciplinarian, for in Christ Jesus you are all children of God through faith" (Gal. 3:23–26).

To call someone a Galatian in the context of the service was to imply that they had betrayed the presence of the Holy Spirit, that they adhered to what no longer mattered. However, the man from Hatcliffe was probably rebuked for more than his personal shortcomings. We know all too well by this point about Nzira-Pageneck's reputation as a polarizing figure. He was not afraid to discredit other prophets and elders just as they discredited him. In this exchange, then, it is important to note that the relationship between Juranifiri Santa and the particular Hatcliffe congregation from which this "Galatian" came was tense. In Pageneck's estimation, the Hatcliffe sowe had fallen off track; they had become like the Galatians in the Bible, ruled not by faith but by adherence to a set of empty (stale?) proscriptions. At the same time, I would argue, Pageneck was reinforcing the apostolic critique of Christianity in its widely practiced form for placing emphasis on the written word. The elder's interpretation of this example was defined by the pragmatic concerns of Juranifiri's operators. But of course ritual can serve both idealistic and practical ends (Keane 1997b, 95; Silverstein 2003, 33–62; Turner 1967b). Inasmuch as apostolics work to create the True Bible through a live and direct approach, we see here also "the purposive activities, of individuals and groups, in pursuit of their contemporary and long-term interests and aims" (Turner 1967b, 264). The mumiriri may objectify what a prophet says into something akin to a text, but a prophet's words can often reach in the opposite direction. Ritual speech is in many respects about detachment, about authority through transcendence. But it is also, always, situated in a particular time and place, caught up in more local power struggles. Getting rid of the book as an object does not resolve this tension. Nor, as we can see in this case, does it erase what is compelling in a historical example.

The elder I spoke with about the imagery of the Galatians was regularly consulted by apostolics with similar inquiries. Like other elders, he offered comments on what prophets said during his lessons, including this one. It should be noted, however, that the specific chapter and verse citations in the Galatians episode were for my benefit as a researcher. He probably would not have cited them to other apostolics in conversation—and certainly did not do so in any church lesson I heard. But the main points he got across to me were consistent with the messages that circulated after Pageneck's intervention. The problem with the Galatians is that they betrayed God's message (and messenger). They allowed themselves to get caught up in religious trappings.

The sense of betrayal and loss was reinforced in a sermon that Pageneck delivered three weeks after the incident with the visitor from Hatcliffe. He built a parallel example that was less graceful but probably accessible to a wider cross section of the congregation. "I cannot have friendships with Galatians," he said. "I do not like people who behave like Adam. What Adam did was wrong, so why would you act like Adam?" Galatians, then, are people who act like Adam. Adam and the Galatians did something they had been told not to do. The betrayal entails a loss and should serve as a lesson for the apostolics to think about. A "Galatian" in the apostolic imagination is someone driven by that most dangerous of things—book knowledge, or knowledge for its own sake. Because what Paul set about to argue is that knowledge is neither the means nor the end of faith. Just as the angels provide a repertoire of blessings, gifts, and inspiration, so Adam and the Galatians offer something—not as spiritual agents but spectral examples.

What would happen to the Masowe weChishanu Church if it was suddenly purged of members who had, at some point in the lives, been devout students of the Bible? As I have mentioned both incidentally and in passing, the Friday church ranks are filled with those who come from the main-line and other denominations. Any Bible study they may have done does not have to be renounced. More generally, of course, one legacy of what Sugirtharajah calls "scriptural imperialism" in the colonial world (see chapter 1) is that biblical motifs, themes, and figures have become part and parcel of popular consciousness (cf. Hofmeyr 1994, 2004). So it is important to recognize that overall there is a fairly high level of Bible literacy in the Friday churches and indeed more generally in Zimbabwe. Without this Bible knowledge—both detailed and diffused—it would be difficult, as the discussions in this chapter make clear, for prophets to ground their authority. In this respect there is a tacit acceptance of the sociological fact that knowledge and practice do not emerge ex nihilo. Indeed, the presence of the Bible is a precondition for its absence—a recognition made especially evident, if only elliptically, in the ritual speech of prophets. As a negative declaration, 'We are the Christians who don't read the Bible' contains a dependency. As this study shows, that dependency is reconfigured through the elaboration of a live and direct semiotics but is always, in the end, there.

A SECONDARY SOURCE

I have presented some of the key ways in which the apostolics instantiate their faith through language and through a semiotic ideology shaped by the action of ritual life. Building on the discussions provided in chapter 4, I have moved on to consider in more detail the coming together of the congregation as a community of practice. We have seen, from another angle, how people like Shimmer, Marcus, and Vera come to inhabit a religious language, a process that is built in part on close attention to ways of speaking.

Live and direct language suggests that the Bible is never more than a secondary source. The Book is always physically absent. But even through words the force of its presence is underdetermined by the denial of any narrative coherence. In their ritual speech prophets never relate the Bible as a set of historical occurrences, literal or figural, sacred or not. This task falls to others in the community of practice who must draw on their Bible knowledge to do so. Prophets might invoke Peter or the Galatians, but these are never more than invocations; narratives are the congregation's tools, and though they often help to make sense of what a prophet says, the authority of the message is not dependent on any one articulation. It is in this sense, returning to the point I made at the outset, that Scripture is only ever an example of the truth. Learning how to listen helps to unlock that truth's potential.

Listening, then, which apostolics so value, is not a passive activity. The congregation plays an active role in the realization of God's message. But ritual speech can be as dangerous as it is uplifting. It can also prompt the question of leadership, running the risk of turning prophets into objects of authority and, thus, compromising the divine relationship. Prophets are mediations too; the authority of what they say is marked by the process of entextualization that takes place in their relationships with the mumiriri wemweya. Indeed, the presence of the mumiriri suggests that the prophet is never enough alone. In this chapter, then, we see again how the prophet is part of the problem of presence. From what I have examined of live and direct language so far, in fact, it might not always seem very live and direct. Nzira-Pageneck is a powerful intermediary; his presence does not so much relieve as reinforce the tension between distance and proximity. Before reaching a conclusion on the effects of the prophets, however, I need to take account of another way in which words become valuable. In the next chapter the focus shifts accordingly to singing.

SIX

Singing and the Metaphysics of Sound

Live and Direct Language, Part II

The question of the sensorium in the Christian economy of revelation is particularly fascinating because of the primacy which this economy accords to the Word of God and thus in some sense to sound itself.

WALTER ONG

SINCE SHONIWA-JOHANE'S DESCENT FROM the Marimba hill, singing has been central to the makeup of apostolic Christianity. Johane's position as a prophet was marked by music well before the articulation of a distinct Friday or Saturday message. It was the singing, in fact, as much as what Johane said, that often got the nascent apostolics into trouble. In a report to the chief native commissioner in Salisbury, the native commissioner at Goromonzi wrote that in the last months of 1934 "singing, shouting and dancing could be heard nightly" from the summit of a hill in the Chindamora Reserve. Local missionaries and kraal heads were complaining most about the noise. If only the "wapostoli" (apostolics) could be more quiet; Kraal Head Marapi reported, "John's disciples had made a practice of trying to interrupt services held by [registered missionaries]" through their nightly auditions. Masawi, a native messenger sent to investigate the meetings, likewise complained, because he could not get the apostolics to quiet down long enough to listen to him: "The din became terrific and my shouts were drowned in the din." To this day apostolic singing generates complaints. Near the University of Zimbabwe, on Arundel School Road, a congregation met for most of the 1990s in a vacant lot. Every Thursday night they would gather until the early hours of the morning, singing for most of the time with little regard for their sleeping neighbors. As one resident made clear, she was not sorry when a house went up on the lot, forcing the group to move elsewhere. She had nothing against the apostolics per se, but at least it put an end to the otherwise endless "racket."[1]

There is something telling in the nature and consistency of these complaints. As far as their neighbors are concerned, a problem with the apostolics has always been their noisiness. Here, as I continue the analysis of live and direct language, I turn more explicitly to singing as the expressive genre through which apostolics make the most noise. Singing helps to call attention to the sonic qualities of language that I have already marked as important but deserve more consideration. Indeed, live and direct language is always more than words. The goal in this chapter, then, is not simply to analyze the song texts of the apostolics' repertoire but also to place that language within a broader discussion of its sonic qualities. For apostolics, the voice is the rightful channel through which God becomes present in language. Building on discussions in the previous chapter, here we learn something more about how, in a live and direct semiotics, the qualities of materiality begin to matter. For apostolics, the voice is taken seriously in both sermon and song as the proper materialization of language, exhibiting what the Slovenian philosopher Mladen Dolar describes in his work on the voice as "the hold in the presence" (2006, 37). It is, for the apostolics, the material of the divine.

I want to suggest, following Steven Feld (1990), that any ethnography of communication must also be an ethnography of sound. In his research on the Kaluli of Papua New Guinea, Feld argues that sound is "a dominant cultural means for making sense out of the Kaluli world" (1990, 84). The Kaluli live in dense forests near Mount Bosavi. In this place where fields of vision are often limited, the soundscapes play a major role in the organization and knowledge of relationships. Feld thus describes how the qualities of sounds play a role in structuring Kaluli social life and cultural expressions. Specific "sound modes" become "embodiments of basic Kaluli concepts of sentiment and appeal" (1990, 24). One of these modes is men's songs of mourning, which are performed in the voices of certain birds to capture the emotional qualities of loss and abandonment (each of which is closely associated with the particular bird). Feld's key insight is that sound is not only a medium of communication but also part and parcel of the message. Sound, in other words, is often invested with significance all its own, acting as more than a vehicle for meaning. In this case that means paying attention to the significance invested in the human voice. For the Friday apostolics, sound is a constituent element of live and direct semiotics. It tells us something about the manner in which a live and direct relationship with God can be nurtured and developed. The human voice is not incidental in that relationship; it functions in a way that other mediums of linguistic communication (such as inscription) cannot.

To understand why live and direct language is important to the apostolics we must also understand the ways in which that language is defined by its sonic qualities. In this respect complaints about the din in Goromonzi and the racket on Arundel School Road draw attention to the sensuous aspects of apostolic religious experience. Noise has a cosmological significance. The audition of words (through singing especially but not only singing) is a constitutive quality of live and direct language. For an apostolic, singing is the privileged medium of the divine. Properly produced, it brooks no barriers. Herein lays a further clue to what the apostolics understand as the shortcomings of texts: the materiality of the Bible is an inadequate one because it cannot produce sound.

MAKING SENSE OF SOUND

In the past twenty years an increasing number of Africanists have turned their attention to the relationship between sound and religious practice. Paul Stoller, for example, began to highlight the relationship after he was told that he would understand Songhay sorcery only if he learned how to hear, because in Songhay epistemology sound "is a foundation of experience" (1984, 561). Stoller (1997) has since gone on to develop a framework for "sensuous scholarship" to challenge the traditional Western academic emphasis on sight (see also Howes 2003, 40–43). Philip Peek also challenges this emphasis. In his work on divination in Nigeria and elsewhere, he argues that in Africa "otherworldly presences or messages are always signaled by acoustic differences" (Peek 1994, 474).[2] This gives new meaning to the characterization of "visible" and "invisible" worlds in the Africanist literature on religion and witchcraft (see, e.g., Kalilombe 1994; West 2005; see also Werbner 1989a). What it suggests is that the *invisibility* of the invisible world is not necessarily the problem. Hearing the invisible may in some cases be more important than seeing it.

These discussions draw attention to an aspect of religious practice that the apostolics would wholly endorse. The Masowe understand themselves to be people of the ear; this is, they say, because they are Africans. Unlike most other African traits, this is not one they try to distance themselves from. In their opinion hearing is the most useful sense for a Christian. Far from impeding their spiritual development, this trait helps the apostolics to realize it.

Because the apostolics appeal to this aspect of their "Africanness," a discussion of Shona language ideology is useful here, at least for what it tells us about sensual "hierarchies." In Shona, for example, the verb *kunzwa*, "to hear," is often used to describe sensations that an English speaker would describe using "taste" and "smell." When I was first learning Shona the emphasis on hearing confused me. I remember learning the verb *kunzwa* in an early language lesson; for the corresponding homework assignment I had to translate a series of sentences in which it appeared. A number of the sentences made no sense in English. I came to the next lesson with awkward translations, such as "Oranges hear good." My teacher had played the trick on purpose; she wanted me to understand this sensual aspect of what she called "Shona culture." On a few subsequent occasions, I noticed that native Shona speakers used the word *hear* in English where they ought to have used *taste*. Kathryn Linn Geurts describes a similar experience from her research among the Anlo-Ewe in Ghana, arguing that these discrepancies are not issues of language fluency but rather indexes of a cultural logic that is "fundamentally aural" (2002, 49). Definitions of the word *sound* in Michael Hannan's *Standard Shona Dictionary* also reveal such an ideology. Hannan lists no fewer than two dozen terms that denote specific kinds of sounds, ranging from "shrill" and "distant" sounds to those "made by green sticks burning," "fatty meat roasting," "running animals," and "heavy rain approaching." Like the Anlo-Ewe, Shona speakers employ a cultural logic that is fundamentally aural.

There is a strong relationship between sound and the spirit world among the Shona-speaking peoples.[3] The basic concept of a spirit, *mweya*, is also the word for "breath" (this is a connection made in other languages too—most notably for my purposes, in ancient Greek). Breath, which is spirit, is the root of speech, and speech is a primary medium through which the ancestors express themselves. During a *bira*, for example, one of the most important "scenes of encounter" (Keane 1997b, 7) with the ancestors, the activity is organized around close listening. A bira is an all-night ritual staged by patrilineal kin when someone in a family is suffering from misfortune, or when a family is in need of guidance from the ancestors (see Berliner 1978, 187–206).[4] Help comes in the form of words: the goal is to get an ancestor to speak through one of the living relatives (usually through the family member suffering misfortune). The register of delivery is highly marked: an ancestor speaks in a high-pitched or low-pitched voice punctuated by unusual grumbles and burps. The sounds they make are definitely not human sounds.

An ancestral spirit might only speak for a matter of minutes during a bira. Getting it to do so, however (which is never guaranteed), usually takes several hours. Music plays a vital role in its calling. The activity leading up to an ancestor's manifestation is dominated by singing, dancing, and the music of the mbira.[5] The mbira, or finger piano, has become the iconic instrument of the Shona, in part because of the success of the musician Thomas Mapfumo, a kind of African Bob Dylan who infuses his compositions with neotraditional mbira parts (see Turino 2000). The ethnomusicologist Paul Berliner (1978) has studied mbira music in Zimbabwe in depth, including *kudeketera,* the song poetry that accompanies it. He shows that mbira music is not simply an aesthetic genre but a key means through which the social order is regulated and redefined. "In the context of the *bira,*" Berliner argues, "the people believe the mbira to have the power to project its sound into the heavens, bridging the world of the living and the world of the spirits and thereby attracting the attention of the ancestors." "The mbira is not just an instrument to us. It is like your Bible," an informant said, addressing Berliner. "It is the way in which we pray to God" (Berliner 1978, 190).

Although the discipline has often expressed an epistemological bias for sight, David Howes makes the point that an anthropology of the senses must be careful not to overcorrect the analysis but recognize instead how "the senses operate in relation to one another in a continuous interplay of impressions and values" (2003, 47; see also Erlmann 2004, 4–5). In this regard we should note two things. First, a sense can have "effects" in different sensual registers. Hearing, for instance, might have "visual" effects. Consider how the apostolics run to the front of the sowe when services are called to order by the elders: they do this so that they might hear what the prophet says when filled with the Holy Spirit. This action—which so irks the elders—might be interpreted as a visible "effect" of sound. Second, "dominant" senses are rarely the only senses. Hearing is a dominant sense in Shona language ideologies and certain ritual practices, but it is not the only sense that matters. At a bira, for example, even a "secondary" sense such as taste can make a difference in the ritual's efficacy. Offering beer to the ancestors is a central component in the proceedings (as it is in many other rituals). Whether or not the beer is strong *(gandure)* or sweet *(maheu)* might influence the outcome. If a family knows which type of beer the ancestor in question prefers, they will offer it as a sign of respect.[6] Not everything, then, is dependent on the qualities and values of sound.

We should be careful not to romanticize or overinterpret Africa as—in Marshall McLuhan's charged words—"the magical world of the ear" (1962, 27–31). But I hope to have suggested the importance of sound and hearing in Shona epistemology. Providing this background is useful because, as I suggested earlier, the Masowe articulate a similar sensorium. Apostolics say that Africans (*all* Africans) are "musical people." With or without McLuhan, this is an essentialism they willingly embrace and deploy. It is also worth noting—as Walter Ong (1967) might want to, in a spirit similar to McLuhan—that what apostolics appreciate most about other Christians is their music. A number of people in the Friday churches have libraries of Zimbabwean, South African, and American gospel tapes. They speak with heartfelt admiration about this music, shedding the reserve they will express toward fellow Christians at other times.[7] These willful associations surrounding sound provide a refreshing contrast to their often more critical attitudes. All in all, music provides a patch of common ground.

There are three points, however, on which apostolics stake the difference of their sensorium and its relation to their spirituality. The first difference is that, unlike an ancestral spirit, the Holy Spirit always reveals itself readily and speaks loquaciously. It never takes longer than a few minutes for the Holy Spirit to "arrive" at a Friday church service. It usually does so of its own accord, but if not, it can be "invited" through singing. Ancestral spirits might never arrive at the ritual sessions through which they are called. If they do it is usually after a strenuous evening of drumming, singing, and dancing that leaves the would-be animator and other participants physically and emotionally exhausted. Once present, an ancestral spirit might not speak for very long—perhaps only five to ten minutes. For the apostolics, this difference in ease of communication is an indication that their relationship with the Holy Spirit in sound is a privileged one.

The second difference has to do with the means of musical expression. For an apostolic, the best music, and the only genuine Christian music—in the sense that it helps instantiate God's presence—is vocal. Like other objects, instruments compromise the integrity of religious practice. This is especially the case with drums and the mbira (which to the apostolics is indeed "like a Bible"). But the apostolics also take the program of their colonial missionary counterparts a step further. Until the 1950s several missionary bodies in Southern Rhodesia banned the use of "African" instruments such as the mbira and the drum because it was argued they could not produce Christian sounds (Axelsson 1974). Not even this is enough for the Masowe. Producing Christian sounds should involve nothing more material than the human voice. As one church elder put it, "All you need is you."

In this second point of difference we have a further clue to how, within their semiotic ideology, the apostolics distinguish between kinds of materiality. The human voice is the proper material channel through which God becomes present. It is live and direct in a way that a written text or musical instrument is not. It is, thus, the medium harnessed with the least mediation. It is less a thing than other things, and a better thing for it. For the apostolics, the voice can thus be cast as immaterial, as "that which is insignificant in its materiality," as Drucker puts it, to the extent that everyone has it. "All you need is you."

This ideological differentiation between sounds produced by humans and sounds not produced by humans is, of course, contestable; not every semiotic ideology might attribute this quality of immateriality to the spoken word. It is nevertheless interesting to note the frequency with which this differentiation is made. In his analysis of poetry readings, for example, Charles Bernstein draws attention to the distinction between "speech sounds" and "material sounds" (1998, 18), the implication being that the former do not exhibit the quality of materiality. Bernstein uses the work of Reuven Tsur to support his analysis, citing Tsur's argument that "there is a marked cognitive difference in the way a listener hears a material sound—say a flapping flag or the pouring rain—and the way she or he hears human speech" (Bernstein 1998, 18).[8] I cannot comment on whether a cognitive-level differentiation between speech and material sounds takes place for the apostolics, but in the details their ideas certainly seem to rely on similar distinctions.

The third point of difference the apostolics make between what they sing and what other people sing is definitional. Apostolic songs are considered so important that the apostolics hesitate to call them "songs" at all. It is only in casual conversation that they refer to them in this way (as I have done in the book thus far for convenience). What one sings in church are not songs but *maverse*, "verses." The apostolics use this term—which is borrowed from the English—with a conscious precision. Drawing on its English-language meanings, apostolics define verses as more than songs in three respects. First, they point out, *verse* is a term used for poetry. Like poetry, maverse are creative expressions that capture "true feelings," whether those of God or the singer. Second, "to verse" means to learn—as in to verse oneself in a certain subject. This is important to acknowledge because singing teaches you mutemo. Last but not least, they highlight that a "verse" is the conventional division for chapters in the books of the Bible. Maverse are better than "chapter and verse" because they come directly from the Holy Spirit. What the apostolics sing is the live and direct Word of God. In sum, then, the word *maverse* is used to signify the creative, instructive, and authoritative potentials of singing.

Verses are said to effect physical and metaphysical changes in the religious subject. Apostolics were constantly telling me what singing "does" to them: "We don't notice the heat when we sing"; "We don't mind the rain when we sing"; "My pains go away when I sing." The diminishment of physical and spiritual discomfort is attributed to the qualities of the sound. Ideally, the louder a verse is, the better. The logic behind this is that volume is a gauge of spiritual presence; the louder one sings, the closer God becomes. When circumstances prevent such joyful noise, however, a quiet hum will do. History has often played a role in conditioning the apostolics' volume. Between the 1930s and the 1990s—both "loud decades"—the Friday groups often had to keep quiet, just as they had to keep out of sight. Today the likeliest situations in which apostolics will temper their singing is at the workplace: my informants who worked in offices told me they would hum verses quietly to themselves throughout the day so as not to disturb their colleagues. What this suggests, I think, is how the act of audition is meaningful in itself. This is not to say that apostolics do not consider the words to what they sing, as I soon discuss. And it is not to deny the premium they place on singing at high volume. But the sound of music has an irreducible core, even when the song text is reduced to a hum.[9] There are, in fact, two verses that have no words—that are, even at their loudest, amplified hums. "Hmm, hmm, hmm" is one; "Ye, ye, ye," the other. This is not deep Shona or ancient Hebrew; there are no hidden meanings here. The verses are just sounds. For apostolics, there is something about the human voice in song to God that serves as a vehicle for God's presence—that indeed *is* God's presence. Singing, as a certain kind of sound, conveys that presence in itself.

WHERE VERSES COME FROM

Verses come from God. They are composed in heaven by the angels. Whatever the apostolics sing is attributed not to their creative talents, then, but to divine inspiration. While there are an infinite number of verses in heaven, only some of these—no more than several hundred, all told—are known on earth. Each has been passed down by the Holy Spirit through members of the church in moments of inspiration.

Inspiration for a new verse can grip any member of the church at any time but usually occurs in one of two ways: during a service or in a dream. When someone is inspired during a service, he or she will rise at the moment of inspiration and begin to sing, often with greater clarity and volume than usual. It is relatively easy to tell when a new verse is being introduced, even for members of the church whose repertoires are limited. A palpable grip takes hold of the old-timers, as if a pause button has been pushed so that concentration can be focused on the new sounds. Each time a new verse is aired in this way, its introduction is marked after the fact by the rationalization of its relevance to the proceedings. On the few occasions when I heard new verses, people spoke about them as perfectly suited to what had been going on at the moment of their debut. New verses are contributions to a conversation on the part of God; they are specific interventions that are also already paradigmatic elements of the True Bible because they are from heaven.

Verses inspired in dreams lack a sense of immediate relevance. They are understood as prophetic messages, the meanings of which a prophet must reveal. Dream verses are introduced during that part of a church service given over to testimonials and announcements from the congregation. Although they may not have immediate relevance to the proceedings, the congregation will devote five to ten minutes singing them in order to commit them to memory. After this, a prophet will provide a set of brief remarks about why the verse might be important for the future and the circumstances in which it might be sung.

We know from church history that prophets and prophets in the making can be inspired with new verses, either on the spot or in dreams. In the mid-1980s Nzira was used to introduce a series of new verses at Nyatsime that provided heavy artillery in the fight against witchcraft. (Verses are as displeasing to ancestral spirits and avenging spirits as they are pleasing to God.) It is important to note, however, that prophets are not more likely than ordinary members to be inspired in this way. In fact, I was told the majority of verses come through ordinary members. Divine channels are much more open when it comes to singing, which only lends to the sense of their importance among congregants.

Singing a verse under inspiration is understood as a sign of the Holy Spirit's presence. God is the agent at work, using the voice of an apostolic in much the same way that he uses the voice of a prophet for a sermon. The difference with inspired singing is that it does not result in the loss of a person's self-awareness. Sermonizers forget everything, but singers under inspiration are cognizant of "their" actions at all times. The presence of the Holy Spirit within someone inspired to sing is identifiable by nothing more than a sudden boost of confidence. "It was easy. It just happened like that," said one normally very shy man who introduced one of the new verses I managed to hear at Juranifiri Santa. The volume and clarity of his voice were taken as the signs of divine presence.

New verses spread among the congregations in one of two ways. I was told that some verses are introduced in all the congregations simultaneously—so that in effect they do not have to be spread. As Shimmer pointed out, this is "no problem" for God. Verses that are introduced through a single congregation, however, must be disseminated through the networks of members. Visitors to one congregation will bring any new verse they hear back to their own congregation, whereas members of the same congregation might take it on to others. Within several months a verse first heard in, say, Chiweshe ought to have reached all corners of the Masowe map.

The inspiration to sing is not limited to new verses. Apostolics are also inspired to sing the verses they already know. This second kind of inspiration is in fact much more common than the first. It is only rarely that a congregation receives a new verse, but during almost every service someone is inspired to sing. The character of the inspiration is the same in both cases. Compelled by the Holy Spirit, an apostolic will stand and deliver with uncharacteristic clarity. After one Juranifiri Santa service I spoke to a man who was inspired to sing "Runyararo" (Peace), one of the oldest-known verses. "It just came to me," he said. "I just did it." He had the glow of satisfaction. It was a moment in which the very principles of live and direct faith had been embodied through him. For this reason, singing will always retain an element of that which makes faith inalienable from the individual. Most of what an apostolic hears live and direct comes through the prophet, but there is always the possibility of this much more "direct," musical encounter.

It is in the limitless potential of music that apostolics feel confident in the superiority of verses to *chapter and verse,* a potential that is reinforced by the specific composition of their repertoire at any one moment, through which

God can make a direct intervention into the lives of the faithful. Verses provide a body of texts free from the trappings of physical form. Even more than the ritual speech of prophets, verses derive their authority from the quality of their entextualization. Like the *kiba* songs of Sotho-speaking migrants in South Africa, verses provide "comments on the immediacies of contemporary experience within a structure whose links with previous performance renders them durable and permanent" (James 1999, 71).

FROM INSPIRATION TO INITIATIVE

All verses come from heaven, but not all performances of them are inspired. Verses are a gift *(chipo)*, but it is incumbent on Christians to take the initiative in the realization of their potential. The apostolics are eager to please God and demonstrate the strength of their faith through the strength of their singing.

In every congregation there is a group of men and women called the *vaimbi* (sing., *muimbi*), or singers, whose primary task is to foster this dialectical exchange. Like a church choir, the vaimbi stand apart from the rest of the congregation. My friend Sirus, who served as a muimbi at Juranifiri Santa, explained the role: "The vaimbi are chosen by the Holy Spirit to sing. According to the Holy Spirit, in order for Him to come with power, He wants to be called with a strong voice—something like shouting even. A loud voice. It doesn't matter if it's men or women, but just serious singing. That's what vaimbi start." By providing "serious singing" during the services, vaimbi are able to work with prophets to shape a musical program, as it were, in order for the Holy Spirit "to come with power." One thing vaimbi do, then, is provide a model for the correct kind of singing.

Vaimbi also encourage ordinary members to take the lead. A good muimbi directs the singing only insofar as he or she encourages the congregants to take it on themselves. Vaimbi are supposed to downplay their position, because no apostolic should come off as a specially entitled performer. "Anyone can start a verse," said Sirus. "Even someone who has been a member for two months can start a verse. Anyone who is a member. But sometimes the problem is, you start it but you are not able to sing well. But you still love singing. We [vaimbi] can hear that you want to start but that you are failing, so we start singing it. I know that you love such-and-such a song but maybe you can't sing it out. That's what we can do." More than strong singers, the vaimbi must be good listeners. They can help the Holy Spirit hear what other apostolics might want to express.

Vaimbi are designated by the Holy Spirit, but they are not endowed with spiritual powers. They are not, therefore, more likely to receive divine inspiration to sing. Vaimbi are not even necessarily talented singers. Sirus, for one, was happy to admit that he would never have a career in the music business. But he took his calling seriously, practicing with the other vaimbi before the start of most services, so that, as he said, their "voices will become beautiful." The vaimbi even exercise in support of their duties: Sirus and some of the others at Juranifiri Santa ran together so they would not become short of breath in the middle of a service, when those around them needed them most.

Like other apostolics, Sirus often told me how much he liked to sing, and he kept a running tally of his favorite verses. When I visited him at work or at home, he might start to hum a verse in those moments when we were not conversing. Even without the grip of divine inspiration, Sirus, like others, found singing compelling. "Most of the time," he told me, "I sing for myself, because I want to sing the verses I love. So I must sing." Were the majority of apostolics to sing just what they "love," however, services would suffer from the weight of the resulting cacophony. While there is a degree of flexibility in the musical program of any one service, it is important for the apostolics to maintain a certain discipline and order. Vaimbi have a responsibility to structure the patterns of song performance. Certain verses have to be sung at certain times; others can be fit in as appropriate. Broadly speaking, there are three main kinds of verses, each of which deserves considered attention.

STANDARDS

There were about forty verses in regular circulation at Juranifiri Santa at any given time. Several of these are what I will call "standards."[10] Standards are heard at every sowe. They are important because they regulate the procession and pace of a church service. They are acoustic guides to performative competence. Their purpose is to provide routine.

Perhaps not surprisingly, standards are sung with less enthusiasm than other verses because of their routine flavor. (Standards do not often gravitate to the top of a member's "hit list.") No standard verse seems more routinized than "Musha Wedu," which is also called "the greeting verse." Somewhere near the beginning of a service, just after the visitors from other congregations have introduced themselves, an apostolic will begin the greeting verse:

Musha wedu wakanaka

Our home is good/welcoming

The congregation joins in, and a minute or two later it is over. It happens like clockwork—unless, of course, you happen to be a "Galatian."

Like most other standard verses, "Musha Wedu" elicited comments more about its function than its meaning. It signals the end of the period during which visitors announce themselves. When I pressed my friends for deeper associations they sometimes humored me with a remark about the duty of Christians to be welcoming to strangers. But really, they said, the verse is just a courtesy. I should not ask more of it than that. "Musha Wedu" is a polite formality.

"Musha Wedu" may not be the bright spark of live and direct faith, but it signals the healthy flow of a service. The employment of standard verses is one of the mechanisms that puts elders at ease about the integrity and perseverance of the Friday message. Marcus, for example, derived a good deal of comfort and assurance from the musical routines. In lieu of his written constitution, he could at least use verses as a gauge of the correctness of things. One of the ways he kept tabs on the happenings at Juranifiri Santa, for example, was to ask me, "What were they singing last week?" Standard verses are about the unity of the church. They are one way in which congregations can both keep on track and be kept track of.

There is one standard verse that is an exception to the rule. The "opening verse," called "Hossanah," still manages to light a spark in the hearts of the apostolics. As a congregation is settling down for worship after being called to the sowe by the elders, a muimbi will begin to sing:

Hossanah, Hossanah, Hossanah
Geroriah, Geroriah, Geroriah
Areruyah, Areruyah, Areruyah
A-yemeni

The verse slowly catches fire throughout the people and then quickly builds to full strength. It lasts for about five minutes only. The vaimbi will introduce harmonies into it along the way, but by the crescendo of the final "Amen" there is unity again. Like a fog—to borrow one of Geertz's images—the sounds of the opening verse engulf the congregation, transporting them into "another mode of existence" (Geertz 1973, 119–20). It is only after "Hossanah" has finished that a service is considered a service. And then, the apostolics say, they can get serious.

"Hossanah" stands out because it is the verse that Shoniwa-Johane first sang upon his transformation. It has a historical dimension that is analogically reproduced through its performance at the start of each service. More than this, however, "Hossanah" stands out because it cannot be reduced to its historicity. According to church elders, Johane heard it directly from the angels. They sang it for him on Marimba Hill. This method of transmission is otherwise unknown: all other verses have been introduced by the human voice. As one of my friends explained it, "Hossanah" is special because it came out of "thin air" in the voices of the angels. *And what does an angel sound like?* This question prompts no end of speculation, a speculation that is made possible through the commemoration of a moment in time. The regular performances of this verse, each of which produces a unique weaving of harmonies, is the always unfolding answer to that question. As Leroy Vail and Landeg White might argue, the "Hossanah" verse "draws its authority from the fact that everyone can refer back, specifically or by inference, to the occasion of its first performance. An historical intervention has become a reading of history and, hence, a way to transcend that history" (1991, 42). The performance of "Hossanah" always exceeds itself through the specificities of its entextualization. It is the exception to the rule that for singing, all you need is you.

FAVORITES

Most of the verses sung at Juranifiri Santa were the local "favorites." The favorite verses of one congregation are not necessarily those of other congregations, although most will be known and may be sung from time to time. Favorites are attributed to the influence of angels—they are not "Sirus's favorites," then, or those of any other individual member. Some angels like to hear particular verses and will convey these likes through apostolics by inspiring them to sing. Once a verse is recognized as an angel's favorite, the apostolics will take the initiative to sing it themselves. Favorite verses thus give each congregation a distinct stamp, according to which others can discern that congregation's reputation and strengths as a spiritual center.

The favorites at Juranifiri Santa accordingly emphasized its importance as a place of healing. Throughout 1999 "Tauya Baba" was a favorite that could be heard there almost every week:

Tauya Baba kuzopona

We come to the Father to be healed/saved

This verse would be sung near the beginning of a service. People always said there was serious healing on the days they sang it—especially if it had been inspired. "Tauya Baba" is a declaration of intention that sets a mood of hopeful expectation.

Other favorites at Juranifiri captured aspects of Pageneck's character. "Maboyi," the jibe about the cruelty of Africans, is one example; Pageneck used this because it was "tough."[11] Most of the character-revealing verses expressed the ferocity of Pageneck's spiritual warfare. Pageneck often cued the congregation to

Hondo iyo, hondo iyo
Haina mazana enyika

That war, that war
Its soldiers are not of this world / Its fruits are not of this world

During Saturday healing sessions, "Hondo iyo" and similar verses would be vigorously belted out, serving as a score for the drama that always unfolded between Pageneck and the possessed. These singing sessions were often singled out as some of the most rewarding by the apostolics. It is difficult to capture in words, but they are indeed the moments when singing can really make you flush; if it was not the transportation into another mode of existence, it was spectacular nonetheless. It was almost always in singing that I forgot my place as an anthropologist.

If standard verses stress the unity of the church, then favorites are testaments to its diversity. This is a good thing. In the fight against witchcraft, for example, having a range of verses from which to draw means the church can establish multiple fronts in the holy attacks. It keeps the vengeful spirits "guessing." Verses such as "Hondo iyo" are fight songs. They help to drive away witchcraft creatures and vengeful spirits. With every congregation using its own fight songs, the apostolics reckon, there is a greater chance of success in the spiritual war. They liken it to using both guns and grenades in a battle, as the guerrillas might have done in Zimbabwe's liberation war. Fight songs are phased in and out of use, disappearing from the repertoire only to be revived as a "surprise attack" several months or even years later.

Favorite verses are renditions of church history. Apostolics can trace a congregation's connection to other congregations through the favorites they sing. This is especially easy for old-timers, who might know where a verse first came from, or at least which verses are favorites in which groups. When I visited the congregation in Entumbane, Bulawayo, for example, I heard several verses that had been closely associated with Sandros and the Nyatsime group. This was an indication of the relationship between Gilbert, the prophet at Entumbane, and Sandros: Gilbert comes from Sandros. By contrast, at Nyamashesha, a small congregation in the Mondoro communal area, almost all the verses were favorites from Juranifiri Santa: Pageneck had started the Nyamashesha group. So above and beyond their religious importance, verses provide a map of history (cf. Bessant 1994; Vail and White 1991, 40–83). Within that history verses convey identities, genealogies, and allegiances; they are "history with the metaphysics included" (Vail and White 1991, 73).

A favorite verse at one sowe can be presented as a gift (chipo) to another. Because verses play a central role in the politics of group identification, a visitor can make friendly or at least diplomatic overtures in an effort to strengthen a set of intercongregational bonds. This happened several times at Juranifiri Santa. Once, a man from the Muzarabani congregation of the prophet Ezekiel announced himself and said he wanted to sing a verse. On behalf of his congregation, he said the verse was a gift ("our gift," chipo chedu):

Chengeta hwai dzaYesu

Look after Jesus' sheep

The visitor sang it three times through before several of the vaimbi joined in, and soon after that it was taken up by the entire congregation. "Hwai dzaYesu" is not unique to the Muzarabani sowe, and many of the apostolics at Juranifiri Santa had sung it before. But what mattered to them was the act of its presentation. In this case the gift was cementing an already tight bond; by 1999 Muzarabani was one of the few groups to which Nzira would travel. He often listened to Ezekiel's advice. "Hwai dzaYesu" was shared in recognition of the continuing importance of their relationship.

Although they capture the character of specific groups, favorite verses are not free from the stamp of routine. They may not be predictable in the way the opening and greeting verses are, but over several months they can certainly lose their edges of distinction. The messages they convey, the lessons they provide, and the ammunition they supply in spiritual warfare can all come to be taken for granted, repeated without reflection. Their occasional withdrawal from circulation helps to mitigate this effect, but they bear a mark of convention nevertheless. Next I want to explore verses that generate a different set of responses and expectations. In a concert of standards and favorites, there is always some improvisation.

ONE-OFFS

In between the standards and favorites of a service, apostolics sing a number of "one-off" verses (my term again). These verses are well known by a congregation as a whole, but individually they may not be sung very often. One-off verses are important because they address the lessons, themes, and events that unfold in a given service with a much higher degree of specificity than the standards and favorites. (One-off verses, it should be said, can become favorites and vice versa.) Because each service is unique, apostolics must be ready to respond, in song, to the needs and desires of other congregants, the prophet, or the Holy Spirit.

One-off verses are often used to reinforce aspects of a certain lesson or testimony. For example, one Sunday in July 1999 a man gave a testimonial of his faith by explaining how he came to the church:

> It was in 1989 that I first started getting beaten by *zvidhoma* [bloodthirsty witchcraft creatures]. I was staying in Masvingo at that time. This brought me all the way to Madzibaba Pageneck here in Chitungwiza. . . . During that period I was in darkness, smoking marijuana *[mbanje].* One day while sitting in the sowe Pageneck said, "I smell mbanje." The Holy Spirit started to look for the mbanje smoker, which was me. I just put my head between my legs and said to myself, "He won't find me." Then the people started singing, "Abruham, chiuya tironde" [Abraham, come! Let's look]. And then that Holy Spirit found me; I lifted up my head. I was caught by the troubles *[namokani]* in my heart *[moyo],* and I stood up, yelling at Pageneck, "Hey! Why are you trying to pick on me out of all these people?" And Pageneck said, "Your daughter is now troubled by zvidhoma." He even told me who sent the things. My daughter and I were treated and after that things were fine. Today I am standing up to thank the Holy Spirit for ten years of blessings.

Then the man sat down. His testimonial was of a fairly common variety. It reinforced the image of Juranifiri Santa as a place of healing. It highlighted not only Pageneck's power but also the impressive sphere of his influence (Masvingo is several hours' drive from Chitungwiza). This testimonial also suggests, as Howes (2003) would have us note, that the senses operate in relation to one another: Pageneck smelled mbanje; the man tried to hide by burying his head; the congregation responded by forcing the man to hear that, with the help of Abraham, they were looking for him. Abraham found the man through the verse, and the man revealed himself by speaking out with indignation. No single sense was enough to handle the problems caused by the witchcraft creatures.

It was the recollection of "Abruham Chiuya" that the man's July 1999 audience understood as the linchpin in his testimonial. Almost before the man had settled back down, a madzimai was on her feet, ringing out:

Mweya Mutsvene wemabasa
Baba Abruhama
Kuimbira Mweya Mutsvene

Holy Spirit of many works
Father Abraham
Is singing for the Holy Spirit

The congregation joined in. It was a sign of thanks *(kutenda)* to the Holy Spirit—an acknowledgment of the man's rescue from the zvidhoma. One-off verses are useful, then, because they go the extra step. In this case "Mweya Mutsvene weMabasa" highlights the important role that the angel Abraham played in the process of the man's transformation. In this rendition the verse signified not only thanks but also recognition of what the apostolics should be thankful for—the specific intervention of a specific angel.

More than favorites, and in a different way altogether from standards, the invocation of verses in one-off situations relies on human initiative. One-off verses are almost never inspired. When no inspiration takes hold, apostolics must draw something appropriate from their repertoire. "We have to help," I was once told. As a corpus of apostolic texts, verses can be used in testimonials and in their support as sources of confirmation and legitimacy, much as Scripture is used in other Christian contexts to bolster the authority of a particular speaker (see, e.g., Harding 2000, 26–28). Knowing what to sing can be like knowing what to cite. In the Masowe Church initiating one-off verses is evidence of having mutemo, of demonstrating the depth of faith.

There is a strong connection between singing and mutemo. Mutemo can be generated, articulated, and reinforced through verses. Strictly speaking, all standard verses are elements of mutemo; at its core "Musha Wedu" is not only an act of but also a lesson in hospitality. It is through one-off verses, however, that apostolics claim to learn the most about mutemo. This was once explained to me in terms of a one-off verse's "practicality." The man I was speaking with drew an analogy with learning how to fix cars. Anyone can take a course in auto mechanics, he said. In the classroom, a teacher can present you with diagrams and manuals. But if you really want to be an auto mechanic, it is best to work on something in the shop. The point was that nothing substitutes for hands-on experience. One-off verses provide that kind of experience: they are the tools put to use for a particular job. This kind of singing is not done in the abstract but always in relation to a particular case that teaches you something.

The dynamics between mutemo and singing often take on an urgent quality. When I first started attending apostolic services, I was struck by the frequency with which congregants interrupted speakers in order to sing (cf. Hoehler-Fatton 1996, 157; Kirsch 2002, 68)—excluding prophets filled with the Holy Spirit. No consideration is given to where speakers might be in making their points; speakers are often interrupted midsentence. Only rarely, however, do these actions cause offense. On the contrary, speakers often look pleased when forced to stop. If what you are saying prompts singing, that's a good thing.

Apostolics interrupt to sing when a speaker's point hits home—when they can reinforce through another register the importance of that point. On one occasion an elder at Juranifiri Santa was giving a lesson. He was focusing on the danger posed by spirit mediums and traditional healers (n'angas). He was saying that it is often tempting for people to consult with these figures because they might be able to help cure certain ailments. You can get medicine (muti) from a n'anga and it might clear up your troubles, but this is wrong. Healers are not of God, and whatever they do is against him because of the powers they rely on. Apostolics must resist consulting these figures, regardless of family pressure or the hope for a quick fix to a problem. The elder was still speaking when a woman stood up to sing:

Mbiri yese isingadzoke kudenga
haisi yaMwari

Any glory that cannot be traced to heaven
is not of God

The congregation joined in and sang the verse for about two minutes. (Interruptions are always short-lived; the point is to reinforce the speaker's main idea, not shift attention elsewhere.) Then the elder started up again, "Now, as I was saying . . . "

Interruptions like this are understood in two main ways. First, and most often, they are taken as pedagogical points. Singing teaches. A spoken lesson will sometimes make the same point over and over again. This is not necessarily a problem, but my friends could find that the repetition made it "difficult to hear" what was being said. A verse can inject new life into a lesson, providing a fresh perspective on the same concern. A one-off verse in this type of situation can refocus attention. Even when a speaker is compelling, however, there is scope for interruption. Whether in a dutiful monotone or a fiery torrent, the spoken word can be enhanced by its musical complement. Singing is a vital element in the lessons elders impart. In the context of a church service teaching mutemo is dependent on its completion through verse.

Interruptions are also understood as political maneuvers and metacommentaries on what others say. One-off verses raise the question of intention. Why did so and so introduce *that* verse at *that* moment? In most cases the question is easily answered; almost all one-off verses are taken as musical complements to a lesson, as in the case just described. But sometimes a verse is motivated by other concerns or at least is perceived to be motivated by other concerns.

Interruptions can certainly endow a singer with a measure of authority. Most apostolics do not initiate verses in this way but respect those who do because it takes such confidence and competence. There was one woman at Juranifiri Santa who captured the attention of others in this respect. Every few weeks at least she would sing something one-off. People thought she really knew something. Through singing, she commanded respect and was able to communicate not only her commitment to faith but also her mastery of mutemo-as-knowledge.

On occasion, however, one-off verses can overstep the thin line between pedagogy and pedantry. Singing can be showing off. As with any apostolic demonstration of knowledge, then, this practice has a dangerous edge. When a speaker is interrupted twice in quick succession, for example, the second interruption is often considered opportunistic and may peter out from lack of participation.

No one, of course, is perfect. If one-off verses sometimes smack of opportunism, of an immodesty unbecoming to the faith, they rarely mark an individual for long. And in some cases, the fact that someone's verse does not take hold is not attributed to showing off but to a sincere misunderstanding. Singers can get it wrong: they can introduce verses that do not complement what a speaker is saying, or which just do not "fit." When this happens an elder stops the singing with a wave of the hands. Once, for example, an elder was giving a lesson about the importance of using apostolic medicines (muteuro) exactly as instructed: if patients are told to use their muteuro morning, noon, and night, they must use it morning, noon, and night. As she was speaking a man got up and started to sing:

Gomo remutemo Esnai
Esnai, Esnai

Mountain of the Law, Sinai
Sinai, Sinai

Before the congregation could take it up, a second elder stopped the man. "Gomo reMutemo" was not an appropriate complement to what the first elder had been saying. Following instructions for muteuro is an aspect of mutemo, but "Gomo reMutemo" draws specific attention to the Ten Commandments. The man surely meant well but had overstated the connection in relation to the elder's point in the lesson. No one thought this was a case of showing off. It was, as one friend put it, an "honest mistake." By stopping the verse, the second elder was politely trying to preserve the focus of the lesson.

The examples presented thus far should not lead to the conclusion that lessons and testimonials are unquestionable. Speakers, like singers, can make mistakes. Christian truth can never be adequately captured by a person's words, because that truth is divine. Once in a while speakers might make controversial claims, misrepresent mutemo, or simply carry on too long. Verses help to redirect the service when these things happen, turning interruptions into interventions.

Most interventions are, like most interruptions, anodyne. Because everyone is encouraged to participate in services, it is not unusual for the occasional speaker to move off the message, or to offer points that do not add up to something coherent. At a service Lazarus and I attended in Chiweshe, for example, the congregation sat by as one man's confession morphed into something less recognizable. After confessing his sins, he praised the Holy Spirit with an unusual intensity and duration. Then he began thanking all the angels that came into his mind (*"thank you* Moses, *thank you* Gabriel, *thank you* . . . "). A muimbi intervened:

Mai Maria
Tivhenekere kune ino nyika
Nesimba raJesu

Mother Mary
Shed light on this land
Through the power of Jesus

This verse really had nothing to do with what the confessor had been saying. But as the congregation took it up, one of the elders got to his feet and, as the singing drew to a close, thanked the confessor. The elder said that hearing "Mai Maria" had prompted a point he wanted to make. The confessor conceded his position, and the elder delivered a lesson. This intervention was a polite way of redirecting the flow of the service.

Not all interventions are made with the feelings of the speaker in mind. When someone is saying something that strikes someone else as wrong, or offensive, the point is to shut the speaker down, and if the transition is not polite, then it is not polite. These open contestations of authority are rare; arguably, it is the possibility of an intervention that most effectively reins in the more firebrand speakers. But they do, on occasion, happen.

It is through interventions that the gendered dynamics of religious authority receive their most public airings. Women, especially vaimbi, were much more likely to intervene at Juranifiri Santa. Most of these interventions were made to disrupt lessons and testimonials in which women or images of womanhood came under fire. In one case, a male elder "warned" the congregation that many women are "snakes" *(nyoka).* It was not a flattering metaphor: snakes are omens of bad luck and are often used by witches as familiars. As Mukonyora has argued—and rightly so—Nzira's congregation in particular was subject to outbursts of "blatant sexism," even as women continually challenged "the excesses of male talk" (2000, 15). On the occasion in question, one woman refused to countenance the man's point. She stopped him by starting a verse that made it all but impossible for him to continue:

Regai vadiki vauya kwandiri
Musavarambidze kwandiri ndamureta

Let all the children come unto me
Do not forbid them

Often used as a verse to stress the virtues of equality, this intervention was an effective metacommentary. It was, simply, inappropriate for the elder to refer to women as snakes. He duly ended his "lesson." The woman who intervened tried to hide it, but she looked perfectly pleased that the man felt compelled to stop. It is in moments like this that the importance of a one-off verse is substantiated. Interventions add another dimension to the "directness" of live and direct faith; they empower members to shape the flow of ritual practice and suggest the extent to which the apostolics play an active role in articulating the content of Christianity.

Ritual performances often allow people to do and say things they might not be able to in other contexts. As Vail and White put it (taking cues from Max Gluckman), in these moments it "is *not* the performer who is licensed; it is the *performance*" (1991, 57; original emphasis). In the contest over women-as-snakes, it is telling that the singing won out over the speaking. In the hierarchy of performative genres, singing comes out on top because of the provenance of its authority. There are no verses about women as snakes, or, indeed, any verses that disparage womanhood specifically. The man thus had little ground on which to stand in making his point. The woman, moreover, was able to appeal to a verse that explicitly countered his claim. Contests over religious authority allow us to understand the purchase of singing. Verses are a privileged medium because they communicate the transcendental authority of God made live and direct in the voices of the congregation.

A LAST WORD ON LANGUAGE

Language is always situated in a semiotic ideology in which the medium of its transmission plays a signifying role. Language is never "just" words; it always has a material quality (Drucker 1994; Irvine 1989; Keane 1997b, 2003). For the Friday apostolics, its most desirable quality is its audibility. "Live and direct language" is language in sound, a presentation of the divine that eclipses a material form but which is nevertheless a materialization. As Dolar puts it, the voice is "something like the vanishing mediator" because "it makes the utterance possible, but disappears in it, it goes up in smoke" (2006, 15). The voice, like smoke, does a particularly good job of destabilizing the distinction between what is there and what is not there. For the apostolics, there is a metaphysics of sound, in which the voice is a presence that relies on its always impending absence. In this, it is an especially apt element in live and direct semiotics.

I have stressed in the previous two chapters that there is not one kind of live and direct language. In the Friday churches sermons and singing are each privileged registers of presence, exhibiting both like and unlike qualities. Sermons and singing are alike above all in that each is an oral discourse. They are also alike because the way in which those discourses become efficacious and authoritative is through the processes of their entextualization. Equally, both are subject to the risks that such processes entail. Prophets, for example, can "deaden" the message through its thingification in them, while verses can be deadened through the roteness of their invocation—such that the congregation hears but is not listening. Each of the live and direct registers has these potentials and problems.

In most other respects sermons and songs are unlike one another. Each may well be an oral discourse, for instance, but the qualities of the orality differ significantly. When the Holy Spirit fills a prophet it does not like to shout. The Spirit might speak so softly that congregants cannot properly hear and have to rely on the human megaphone. Singing needs no such amplification. It is loud enough on its own—and if it is not, then in most cases something is wrong. So what is it about the authoritative qualities of the voice? For the Holy Spirit to be quiet when speaking through a prophet is to focus itself on itself; close listening becomes the medium of recognition. Singing "almost like shouting" is a complementary move. High volume is a sign of sincerity and conviction, of expressing mutemo—and thus the presence of God—from deep within oneself.

The potentials of sound have other sociological effects and theological implications. I mentioned at the end of the previous chapter that when it comes through major prophets such as Pageneck, the live and direct message does not always seem very live and direct. In their roles as the Holy Spirit's channels, prophets are powerful mediators and become, in practice, empowered mediations. This aspect of live and direct faith is not something the apostolics would change; sermons provide an invaluable source of support, guidance, inspiration, and strength. What we learn in this chapter, however, is that sermons are only one kind of live and direct language and that the other major kind both decenters and complements the work done through prophets. Singing shifts the locus of live and direct language from prophet to congregant. It grounds the presence of the Holy Spirit in the community of practice, a grounding that must be acknowledged and acted on from within the religious subject—and all in a "racket" that the apostolics' fellow Zimbabweans have come to expect.

SEVEN

The Substance of Healing

TO WHAT EXTENT CAN RELIGION be given over to a project of immateriality? In 2003 the Victoria and Albert Museum in London mounted an exhibition, *Gothic: Art for England,* that provided something of an answer. One of the pieces in the show was a defaced church panel. Sometime in the sixteenth century the image on the panel had been scratched out. A verse from the Bible had been written in its place. The panel was an artifact of the Reformation; the Word had been used to destroy the evidence of Catholic idolatry. But if some English iconoclast had indeed purged the panel of its idolatrous nature, it was still, to the casual observer, an object. Whether or not its defacement was motivated by Edwards's idea that, as quoted in the introduction, "nothing spiritual can be present when there is anything material and physical," it could still be hung on the wall. Stripped of its theological and social dimensions (in a manner perhaps only museum exhibitions can accomplish) the materiality of the panel remained.

The destruction of Christian art in Gothic England suggests something of greater importance to the study of materiality in religious modes of signification. In a "vulgar" sense (see Miller 2005a, 7), it reminds us that a project of immateriality—as presenting the spiritual without the material and physical—is difficult to accomplish. The repudiation of the material is a selective process. What sustains projects of immateriality in religious practice is always the definition of what counts as materially dangerous.

Indeed, religion cannot do without material culture (see, e.g., Keane 1998; McDannell 1995; Tambiah 1984). The question posed at the outset of this chapter, then, becomes (cf. Keane 1998, 29), In what *sense* can religion be given over to a project of immateriality?

Miller has recently suggested that we can approach the commitment to immateriality best through "the messy terrain of ethnography" (2005a, 41). What matters in an exhibition documenting one strain of sixteenth-century iconoclasm is not the irreducible materiality of a church panel but how its defacement expresses a logic of spiritual transcendence. In any semiotic ideology we cannot assume that all material culture is valued in the same way. The task then becomes the recognition of how "relative" (Rowlands 2005) or "plural" (Myers 2005) materialities gain expression in practice.

Of all the "messes" that the apostolics' commitment to immateriality makes, healing might well be the biggest. More than any other aspect of their religious practice, healing challenges the coherence of the apostolics' repudiation of things. It is through the substance of healing, then, that the Friday apostolics face the problem of presence in its most consequential forms.

In this chapter I turn to a more explicit discussion of healing in the Friday churches. Its importance to the apostolics has been evident throughout the book: from the early days of Johane Masowe to its role in the making of major prophets to its valuation by ordinary members such as Shimmer and, even, the man castigated by Nzira for citing a passage from the Gospel of Luke. By bringing together a number of these shorter discussions, I want to analyze in more detail how the apostolic practices of healing and identification of potent "holy medicines" (muteuro) are situated in the wider field of therapeutics in Zimbabwe. Spiritual healing in Zimbabwe is big business, literally and figuratively. The Friday prophets have staked a significant corner in this market, but it is hardly theirs to control. A major concern in the Friday churches is the relationship between the circulation of therapeutic materiel (i.e., the objects and substances that prophets use in healing) and the meanings people associate with that materiel. This concern stems from the fact that Friday prophets and "traditional healers" both use material things, often the *same* things, in their healing practices. Defining the authority of objects in accordance with the terms of the Friday message is therefore a task of some importance. The commitment to immateriality makes what things the apostolics do use in religious life all the more important—not least when other healers want to define the qualities of those things in a different way. In the realm of healing, I argue, keeping the commitment to immateriality depends on the ability to define the significance and authority of objects. It depends on the ability to assert, through the elaboration of a semiotic ideology, a point highlighted in the introduction: some things are more material than others (Rowlands 2005, 80–84). There is a semiotics to therapeutics that tells us something important about how the Friday apostolics conceive a live and direct faith.

A STICKY SUBJECT

Like many anthropologists, I found my research was punctuated by a number of ailments, both real and imagined. I was fortunate in that the Friday apostolics always took a polite interest in my well-being. In an effort to maintain some critical distance from the churches, however, I tried to be careful about what I shared regarding my health, and also what I took from the prophets when they managed to extract a complaint or observe a symptom. This was not always easy, and on one occasion at Juranifiri Santa I found myself the recipient of one of their more significant preparations. It is called holy honey, the most effective spiritual medicine according to the Masowe. While primarily used to fight the ill effects of witchcraft, it was thought the honey might also relieve my this-worldly ailments.

Holy honey is not simply honey. Knowledge of the exact ingredients is guarded by the church's elders, but as I worked my way through two jars of the stuff over several weeks, I could detect in it hints of cooking oil and lemon juice. The honey is dark brown and viscous. It is sticky-sweet and has a tangy aftertaste (the lemons), with hints of smoke. Regardless of the ingredients or their preparation, however, I was told that what mattered was the blessing conferred on it by the Holy Spirit. Indeed, holy honey, like all apostolic medicines, is understood to be powerful because of its spiritual properties. As a substance it does not matter.

The apostolics' honey, perhaps like an Azande's *benge* (Evans-Pritchard 1976, 122–48) or a Thai Buddhist's amulet (Tambiah 1984, 243–57), derives its importance from what is considered an immaterial quality. Apostolics would always insist to me that the Holy Spirit can cure someone's afflictions without the benefit of medicine or blessed object. Nevertheless, holy honey occupies a privileged position in their religious imagination. In contrast to the other medicines they might receive, honey is characterized as something like a smart drug: it just makes you feel good. It gives you more energy throughout the day. It helps you think clearly. Some men told me it increased their sexual stamina. All things considered, and dutiful statements about the power of the Holy Spirit aside, if apostolics could have any healing treatment, it would be honey.

Yet there was something about holy honey that unsettled the apostolics. Although its properties were understood as the result of a spiritual blessing, in practice they sometimes treated it as if these properties were inherent. It was as if holy honey, qua honey, could do things. I got a clear sense of this the day I received a second jar in the course of my "treatment." It was immediately after one of the Wednesday early morning church services at Juranifiri, and I had promised to give a friend in the congregation a ride to his office in Harare. He knew I had the honey in the car, and he talked about it all the way into town, reminding me of its beneficial side effects and remarking on the fact that he was about to face a long and tiring day at work. As we pulled into the parking lot of his office he lingered for a moment. "Ah," he said. "Just one sip of that stuff might do me good." The prospect of a miserable day at work does not constitute an illness, as far as the Masowe are concerned. Moreover, apostolics claim that their medicines are only ever intended and effective for the persons to whom they are "prescribed." Nevertheless, by asking for a sip of the honey, my friend made it clear in that moment how easy it is to slip from the principle of the immaterial to the lure of the material.

One of the lessons in this awkward exchange is that material culture can play an important role in "spiritual" healing. In a sense, however, this point is so obvious that we might not think it warrants discussion. There has been a good deal of literature on medicines, witchcraft substances, and tools of divination in Africa. Evans-Pritchard's (1976) work on oracles among the Azande is an excellent case in point. In particular, his discussion of the poison oracle, or benge, made it clear that we need to pay attention to the context in which the cultural materiel of divination is used. Benge is a forest creeper vine that contains strychnine (Evans-Pritchard 1976, 228). Before "all occasions regarded by the Azande as dangerous or socially important" (1976, 122), benge is prepared according to a strict set of taboos and administered to a chicken. (An example of a "dangerous" occasion might include a long journey; a "socially important" occasion might be the marriage of one's child.) The results of the consultation are determined on the basis of whether or not the chicken dies after ingesting the benge. And yet Evans-Pritchard makes it clear to the reader that the Azande do not think of benge as poison. The creeper is not what kills chickens. For example, they would never think of using benge to kill a person, or indeed for anything other than an oracular consultation. Not only would it be a waste of the vine, it just would not make sense: "Properly speaking it is only this manufactured *benge* which is *benge* at all in Zande opinion. Hence Azande say that if it is deprived of its potency for some reason or other it is 'just an ordinary thing, mere wood'" (Evans-Pritchard 1976, 147). Putting aside the question of whether Evans-Pritchard's analysis suggests that the Azande operate within a closed system of thought (Horton 1967; cf. Appiah 1992), the discussion of benge is a reminder that material culture becomes meaningful in the activities of social life. One person's strychnine is another person's oracle.

My friend's request for a sip of the honey undercut the more general claim that apostolics make about healing substances. If God's blessing is what made honey a powerful spiritual medicine and if its use was inspired for individual cases, then for my friend it ought to have been just an ordinary thing, mere honey. Clearly, it was not. Its materiality mattered.

I want to use this vignette to frame a more general discussion of the apostolic disposition toward therapeutic things because it brings out so well the specificities of the relationship between material culture and immateriality in a live and direct semiotics. What makes my friend's request for honey interesting is the extent to which it highlights the emphasis on the immateriality of religious practice. Apostolics are wary of spiritual materiel; religious things are dangerous things and often betray shortcomings of faith. The manipulation of material culture is therefore a delicate matter in the church, and how the material and immaterial worlds are reconciled is a process fraught with pitfalls. As I hope to make clear at the end of this chapter, honey both challenges and confirms this logic in a poignant way. That morning in the car, it was a sticky subject for my friend. It made him feel awkward, even embarrassed, given his religious commitments. In treating the honey as a thing, he was undermining an important aspect of the semiotic ideology that as an apostolic he was supposed to uphold. Before explaining this further, however, let us revisit the ways in which the apostolics develop a systematic repudiation of the material. The discussion of healing allows us to bring these ways together into sharp focus.

DOING WITHOUT

In the context of this chapter there are two aspects of the apostolics' repudiation of material culture that I want to highlight. The first has to do with the mediums of religious authority and experience and brings us back, for a moment, to the themes explored in the introduction and the next two chapters of this book. The Friday apostolics say the Bible is unnecessary because they have a live and direct connection with God. They trace this connection to the coming of Johane. It is marked, in part, by stories of Johane burning the Bible, stories that have some parallel to what Johane "admits" in his statement to the police in November 1932.[1] I have already gathered this and several other narratives of church history into theological shape by focusing on the ways in which the apostolics instantiate their live and direct faith. The point I want to reinforce here is that rejection of the Bible is an indication of the apostolics' concern with material things—about what they can and cannot do. Books, in their view, cannot provide for a personal relationship with God, and they often serve to stand in the way.

Following Colleen McDannell's analysis in *Material Christianity*, we might say that the apostolics consider themselves "strong" Christians because they claim to "grasp spiritual truths directly" (1995, 8). In fact, even more than some of their Protestant forebears, the Masowe mean to do without things. Inasmuch as European iconoclasts moved away from images, they replaced those images—as evidenced in the Victoria and Albert Museum's *Gothic* exhibition—with the book (what Troeltsch would later call the "Lutheran Pope"). This practice of replacing objects one for the other is widespread in the history of the religion. In the United States, for example, "Protestants turned words into objects. During the nineteenth century, family Bibles became so lavish and encyclopedic that they functioned more like religious furniture than biblical texts" (McDannell 1995, 15). As I discussed at length in chapter 1, the British and Foreign Bible Society also turned words into objects—and not only for the African "heathens." The society's operators often spoke about the Bible as a thing in itself, something that had agency. Today the legacy of this ideology still shapes evangelism, providing men such as Gaylord Kambarami with the language to claim that "the Bible reads people." In this discussion, at least, the apostolics would want to claim that an object is an object. A Protestant's Bible is no less a material impediment to faith than a Catholic's icon. The apostolics see evidence of this throughout Zimbabwe, where people in other churches treat the Bible as an end in itself. Elsewhere the Bible will be wrapped in expensive leather bindings and displayed prominently in church services: the apostolics have no time for such "religious furniture."

The second aspect of the apostolics' concern with material culture brings us back to the main topic of this chapter. At this point I can expand on the discussions of healing in several earlier chapters by bringing them together in a consideration of apostolic etiology.

The anthropological literature on healing in central and southern Africa often emphasizes that healing is "fundamentally concerned with the reconstitution of physical, social, and spiritual order" (Comaroff 1980, 639; see also Janzen 1978; Janzen and Feierman 1992; Turner 1968b; West and Luedke 2006). For the apostolics, these social orders must be reconstituted as Christian and thus purged of the dangers of "African custom" or "culture." It is not that the apostolics deny the realities of witchcraft, then, or the sway of the ancestors. Indeed, as I have stressed in line with Matthew Schoffeleers, most African Independent churches in southern Africa "take belief in the power of witches, evil spirits and other mystical agents seriously and are for that reason, in the eyes of a large section of the public, able to provide help in cases where such agents are thought to be involved" (1991, 4). Healing, as discussed briefly in chapter 4, is what draws most people to the Friday churches. Shimmer did not go to Nzira because Nzira had rejected the authority of the Bible but because of his reputation as a healer. Nzira's claim, circulated through the patients who listened to his sermons, was that he offered something different: he would know what spiritual forces were maligning Shimmer, and he would know how to restore order in Shimmer's life because he had the full power of the Holy Spirit behind him to eradicate the effects of African jealousy.

Johane himself is remembered as a powerful healer—perhaps the most powerful of all, at least during the first few years of his mission. I was given several accounts of Johane's abilities. In each, the power of African Christian healing lay in its superiority to both Western biomedicine and traditional curative practices (spiritual and nonspiritual). Marcus once told me the story of how his grandmother came to Johane. The structure of the narrative is similar to Shimmer's: "According to her, when she joined Johane Masowe [in the early 1930s], one of her sons was very sick. And when she went to consult Johane, her son got better within three days. Yet she had moved around—she had gone to hospital and to other spiritual healers and to the n'anga without any joy, until in three days' time Johane Masowe prayed for him and the boy was up and running."

What made Johane such an effective healer, and what has fueled the success of Friday prophets since his time, was, in the opinion of Marcus and others, his focus on ridding the world of witchcraft medicines.

This is what Jesus asked him to do in the Gospel of God Church's account of his transformation. We might also recall that in his November 1932 statement to the police, Shoniwa-Johane states that the voice of God commanded him to "tell the natives to throw away their witchcraft medicines."[2] Whether they had been given these medicines, or whether they employed them to the benefit or detriment of others, the first step in the process of healing was to rid oneself of these things.

There is no exact term for "witchcraft medicines" in Shona, and we cannot be sure about the word Shoniwa used in his native chiManyika dialect. *Muti* is the most common word for "medicine" (it also means "tree"); another common term is *mushonga*. In Shona, however, *muti* and *mushonga* can have either positive or negative connotations. In other words, they can be used to signify what in English would be a difference between medicine and poison *(chepfu)*. But Shona speakers (and Zimbabweans generally) do not often describe what witches use as "medicines" at all; if anything they would be said to use poisons—or perhaps *bwanga*, "'black' medicine." What witches use is *uroyi*, although this term refers to both an essence (witchcraftness, as it were) and the objects and substances that witches employ. These objects and substances are usually organic matter: the blood and organs of humans or animals, for example, and the thorns and leaves from certain kinds of plants. Witches also use inorganic things in their "black medicines," such as coins and shards of glass.

Several of the "creatures" or "familiars" that witches use (in addition to snakes, hyenas, and owls) are constructed out of body parts and other things they can collect or steal. No one I met in Zimbabwe claimed to know exactly how this is done; witches keep their knowledge to themselves. "It's a mystery," Shimmer said. "Because the people who create those things, they never reveal. They never say *tinogadzira so-so-so* ["we assemble (them) like so"]. It's top secret." Despite this, most of the people I knew in Zimbabwe agreed on the general characteristics of the creatures in a witch's bestiary. A *chidhoma* (pl., *zvidhoma*), for example, is a dwarflike creature that feeds on the blood of humans. Shimmer told me that he had heard about one chidhoma that was constructed out of bits of skin sewn together into a humanlike form that was then stuffed with paper money. It was made for a man who wanted to succeed in business, and he had to give the chidhoma the blood of his relatives in yearly installments in exchange. A *chikwambo* (pl., *zvikwambo*) or *tokoloshi* (the Ndebele-language term that Shona speakers often use) can be made by witches but are more often "real" creatures—more like goblins, in other words, than homunculi.

Rutherford has pointed out that "European colonizers [in Zimbabwe] often lumped together diverse practices, moral concepts and person categories under the rubric of witchcraft and sorcery, drawing on their own European categories and history for these terms" (1999, 98). This often meant that spirit mediums and n'angas were spoken about as witches or "witch doctors," though they had nothing to do with the "occult." As I have explained, the Friday apostolics make similar lumpings. As far as they are concerned, the term *witchcraft medicines* should cover more than the substances and creatures manufactured by witches. Anything a spirit medium or traditional healer uses ought to be thought of in the same way. In theory, then, to an apostolic muti is more or less the same thing as uroyi.

In theory. According to Macheka Gombera, the apostolics have not always been so strict on this point. Gombera was a well-known healer who formed the African N'angas Herbalist Association in the 1950s. Like Weegirl, he was called to be a healer by an ancestral spirit (his paternal grandfather, or sekuru). His sekuru taught him how to mix several kinds of medicine in a series of dreams. Gombera also traveled throughout Mount Darwin and Chiweshe in the mid-1930s collecting mixtures from other spiritual healers. It was in that period that he ran into Johane's followers. "The climax of my knowledge came when it was announced that Johane had come and that he had ordered people to burn all the n'anga medicines," Gombera told the oral historian Dawson Munjeri. According to Gombera, some of Johane's followers agreed to sell "all the muti that was of medicinal value" to him rather than burn it as they had been instructed. Gombera "hated the Church" for calling for "a halt to n'anga belief." He saw his work as a benefit to the people and resented the all-or-nothing militancy of Johane's principles. But the betrayal of those principles, as Gombera makes clear to Munjeri, was both a hopeful sign that n'angas might continue and a telling indication that some apostolics might have a price, no matter how strong their rhetoric.[3]

The rejection of traditional curative and occult practices is one way in which the Masowe seek to differentiate themselves in a crowded field of practitioners. This difference is still represented in Johane's forceful image of the witchcraft medicines. Indeed, driven as it is by the desire for accumulation (see Englund 1996; Geschiere 1997; West 2001; see also Moore and Sanders 2001, 14–18), "witchcraft" is an apostolic's catch-all phrase of scorn, shorthand for the dangerous things produced by practitioners of spirit outside Christianity. As Gombera's experience suggests, however, it is not always easy to control the circulation of things, much less their meanings or the ways in which they are exchanged.

THE PLACES, ATTIRES, AND PRACTICE OF HEALING

The principles of healing bear resemblance to the places in which it is performed. The sowe is both everywhere and nowhere—a struggle against the fixed form (Mukonyora 1998a, 2000; Werbner 1985). While some of the major prophets now operate "hospital wards," these are built spaces in which to house patients during the course of their treatment. The increasing influence of architecture on the dynamics of church life is unmistakable. For all the ways in which the apostolics' "innovations in space" are becoming grounded in the physical world, however, it is telling that no prophets in the Friday churches have advocated holding church services or healing sessions under a roof. The "House of Jesus" is one thing; a house of worship is another. Resistance to the lure of the material is, in this sense, still quite strong. The actual healing takes place in a place that is in principle no place at all.

In the absence of church buildings, the white robes of the apostolics form a kind of phantom wall that define the perimeters of the ritual space. As Shimmer has suggested, these robes are important because they are material evidence of commitment to the faith. And yet the robes also mark a paradox: they are the material evidence of the apostolic commitment to immateriality. What makes them special is their simplicity—their leveling effect. In contrast to the expensive suits and dresses one might see in other churches, or the elaborate dress of a spirit medium or n'anga, apostolic fashion is an antifashion. The robes are another statement about why things should not matter in the religious life. They are supposed to be "insignificant in their materiality."

Other than the robes, the staffs *(tsvimbo)* that some men carry are the only other everyday artifacts of faith. However, not all prophets in the Friday churches ask the madzibabas in their congregations to keeps staffs; some, in fact, forbid them.[4] Like the robes, staffs give the men that carry them a sense of "having" faith, because they only carry them after becoming "full-fledged" members. Staffs are made of bamboo, which often grows in Zimbabwe by the banks of rivers and streams.[5] They are whittled down at either end to smooth them out but are not carved with elaborate heads, as are the staffs carried by men in other apostolics churches (the Maranke apostolics' staffs, for example, often have the figure of the cross carved into the top end). This is, of course, because they must be "plain" and "not special." Their not-specialness is another sign of the material commitment to immateriality, although there have been occasions on which staffs seem to have taken on undue significance. In August 1999, for example, it was clear that Nzira-Pageneck thought the men in his congregation were too invested in their staffs. Exactly why this was he did not say, but he demanded—as he could—that the men surrender them all; when they did so, he had the elders burn them.

Even with these places and ritual attires in mind, ritual and social life as a Friday apostolic is without question less materially saturated than in most other churches in Zimbabwe. The apostolics have no houses of worship, no elaborate altars, and only simple robes. They do not even have the Scripture of their scriptural religion. What is more, while prophets do not want to see their congregations live in poverty, being a successful and faithful Christian does not, in their view, require the accumulation of commodities and material riches. As strong Christians, those "who use objects or images in their devotional lives or who feel that certain places are imbued with special power are seen as needing spiritual help or crutches" (McDannell 1995, 8).

With these points in mind I want to move on to a more detailed description of the healing rituals that take place in masowe. Healing sessions vary in style from one Masowe congregation to the next, but there is a general pattern as to what one can expect. Shimmer's experience in 1991 has already provided a general outline. In most congregations healing sessions are held after the main services on Fridays and Sundays. The more influential prophets, such as Nzira, hold separate meetings on Saturday afternoons to accommodate the large numbers of people in attendance. When everyone has gathered in the grove or field, seated in a large circle with the men and women facing each other, the vaimbi begin to sing, perhaps "Tauya Baba." Their voices help to soothe the congregation's afflictions. The sounds are the call for, and of, the Holy Spirit. The singing might continue for an hour, interspersed with short monologues from a prophet about the power of God and the seriousness of the "battle" taking place. Other verses might be used to reinforce the overriding message that the spiritual war is "not of this world."

Eventually a prophet asks those who have come for healing to stand up in accordance with their particular illness. Can they not conceive a child? Are they estranged from their families? Have they lost their jobs? Do they have stomach pains? Are they "mentally ill"? When the sick have been accounted for, church elders call them off to one side of the main gathering. In many congregations, as the patients move off, they shuffle past the prophet, who touches their foreheads. The vaimbi stand around the prophet on either side, so that the patients move between them. I asked Sirus about the importance of the arrangement, he replied, "You see, even a doctor has got his consultation room. So that is [Pageneck's] consultation room. So each and every sick person has got to pass through that. And if [some]one has got zvikwambos and so forth, [that person] will not be able to pass through that consultation room without that chikwambo talking [i.e., making itself known to the prophet]. That place is serious. It's so serious." That place, of course, is no place at all. The walls of a "consultation room" are the robes of the vaimbi, and the room thus created is insulated by the sound of voices in song.

After patients pass through the consultation room, the elders arrange them in long rows. The people bend down on their knees, and over the course of the next hour or so they are given holy water and other blessings from God in the form of medicines. It is in these sessions that one could expect to receive holy honey. More commonly, however, each person is given a sip of holy water and something else—some object or substance—that has been blessed and which they take away as part of a prescribed treatment.

When apostolics talk about the stuff they receive for healing, they often refer to it, as I have, as "medicine." Indeed, the language of a healing session mirrors the language of a biomedical system. People come as patients, they are treated in weekly clinics and consultation rooms, and, if necessary, they are watched over by church elders in hospital wards. Not much is made of this mirroring; they do not see it as a threat to the specificities of their own practices. And, of course, today at least the Friday apostolics see no reason not to take advantage of medical science. Medicine is in fact considered a blessing from God of another kind; it can supplement the more important work of spiritual healing. This is not to say the apostolics think of aspirin as a spiritual treatment. They see it as entirely "natural." Medical doctors pose no problems theologically because they do not claim their authority from the spiritual world. In the apostolics' view, this is the key difference between a medical doctor and a n'anga or medium. Medical doctors present no cause for alarm because their material things carry no immaterial pretensions. And so when someone is suffering from witchcraft, or because of an angered ancestral spirit, biomedicine may help to relieve his or her symptoms. There is nothing inherently wrong with giving aspirin to a bewitched person. All the same, biomedicine will never get to the root of the problem. It will never provide a cure. For that, spiritual intervention is required.

Apostolics do not consider holy honey and aspirin substances of the same kind. The specific ways in which they refer to their spiritual medicines helps to make this differentiation clear. For apostolics, indeed, "the relation between material things and immaterial meanings . . . must be effected through speech" (Keane 1998, 28). This is especially important when those material things might ambiguate the immaterial meanings. Calling their spiritual medicines "muteuro" is a move against the dangers of materiality in no uncertain terms. As I mentioned in passing in chapter 4, the word *muteuro* means "prayer." In the context of this chapter and in light of the discussions of live and direct language, the force of this signification becomes clear. Holy medicines are not identified primarily as "things"; they are, rather, "words." Holy medicine is unlike other therapeutic substances because it is understood to have this language-like quality.

The most common type of muteuro are pebbles.[6] Any pebble or stone about the size of a marble (or smaller) will suit the purposes of the church. I saw elders collect pebbles in the dirt around the sowe in preparation for healing sessions. What patients are meant to do with the pebbles can vary. Each case is handled individually, and so when one receives muteuro in this form, one also receives instructions for its use. For example, if a patient is suffering from stomach pains—as Shimmer did—he or she may be asked to place the pebble in a glass of drinking water. The pebble conveys its spiritual blessing to the water, in effect creating holy water "on the spot," without the burden of providing someone with a week's supply of it. Similarly, someone might be asked to place the pebble in the tub or bucket of water with which one bathes each morning. The muteuro helps the water cleanse the body of any spiritual impurities or afflictions. But not every such spiritual remedy involves the manufacture of holy water. If someone has lost his job, or is looking for a job, he might be asked to place the muteuro in his wallet (although it should never touch money directly). When taking a school exam or a test at work, apostolics will keep the pebbles in their pockets, which can help them to remember what they have studied. In one of the more unusual testimonies I collected, a man was made redundant from a factory job in Bulawayo.

236   THE SUBSTANCE OF HEALING

Subsequently, he came to Harare to consult a certain Masowe prophet. The prophet gave him a pebble and told him to mail it to a friend back in Bulawayo. On instruction, this friend then took the pebble and threw it over the perimeter wall of the factory site. Within a few weeks the man was reinstated in his job.

What makes pebbles and small stones special is the fact that they are not special. Pebbles are free, easy to gather, and do not inspire envy or want—sentiments associated with witchcraft. Pebbles are also very practical. I was told water is an effective medium for healing, but it is difficult to carry, especially in large quantities. It can also be hard to come by for congregations that do not have easy access to a river, borehole, or tap. For this reason, water is used sparingly, and only in the course of an actual healing session, where one five-liter jug might last several weeks if doled out to the patients a sip at a time. Pebbles, on the other hand, are much easier to circulate. In most cases elders will pass them out during a healing session immediately after the sharing of the water. They are durable too. No material thing is foolproof, but pebbles come close. If you drop a pebble, you can pick it up. If you drop a cup of holy water, it might be gone forever—dissolving into the ground or spilling into a crack in the floor. Pebbles do not break or split easily. They maintain their integrity in the face of regular use (even as, in geological terms, they represent a process of gradual dissolution). Cloth and wood—long used in other Christian churches and in other healing rituals—might tear or splinter or break. And pebbles are easy for patients to keep track of. This is not always the case with other muteuro: think of how difficult it was for me to keep my honey to myself; that friend of mine put the pressure on for a sip. I doubt he would have been interested in my muteuro if it had been a pebble instead. In another incident, a friend of mine in the church was given muteuro in the form of a mango paste. He made the mistake of leaving it in the kitchen, and his brother used it as chutney for an evening meal.

Pebbles also have the distinct advantage of not sparking association with traditional African healing (either spiritual or medicinal).[7] The Friday apostolics might be comfortable using the language of biomedicine to describe their healing practices, but in their effort to break with African custom they would never use the language of a n'anga or spirit medium. N'angas and spirit mediums in Zimbabwe use a variety of objects and substances in their healing practices, but pebbles are not among them. The weChishanu have therefore made something significant out of something that had no prior meaning in the local social field of African therapeutics.

The paradox of the pebble is its being special because-it-is-not. In this context the pebble is, to borrow a description from Roland Barthes, the paradigmatic "mere signifier" (quoted in Drucker 1994, 34).[8] As a key symbol of Christianity it expresses the apostolics' systematic repudiation of the potential for religious representation through objects. At the same time it is the thing through which the value of the material might be saved. In many respects the pebble is the most important thing in the Friday churches. Some might argue that an apostolic's white robes are the best representation of faith; robes are indeed valued by their wearers as a sign of commitment to the church. But muteuro, especially the pebble, is an index of the spiritual power of God; it is what makes donning the robes significant. Pebbles are the tools of evangelization. Whereas most Christians place the Bible at the center of faith, the Masowe would want to stress their muteuro as the evidence of Christian success. Having rejected the Bible, the apostolics objectify their faith in something that in and of itself should have no social or cultural value. What better way to undercut the importance of material culture than to hold up as its archetype something you find in the dirt? As I suggested at the beginning of this section, the very word apostolics use to signify their ritual medicines is meant to shift attention away from the question of materiality. A pebble is a prayer. It is part of the live and direct relationship with God that strong Christians ought to possess, a claim that "signification offers the subject an escape from materiality" (Keane 2001, 87).

IMMATERIAL DISTINCTIONS

The emphasis on live and direct faith and the rejection of the Bible can lead apostolics to be dismissive of other Christian churches. When pressed, or in certain moods, they might indeed claim that they are the only "true" Christians because they have seen past the false security of the Book. But in practice, as the discussion of gospel music tapes in the previous chapter might suggest, they are not always concerned with Christian objects other than the Bible, and it would be an overstatement to say they spend most of their time deriding other Christians, even as they insist on the correctness of their own live and direct approach. Rather, as I have already alluded to in the discussion of witchcraft medicines, the apostolics direct their concern with objects toward traditional healers and spirit mediums. Muti is bothersome and dangerous, and the Masowe take pleasure in talking about it as such. What healers and mediums use in their practices always evokes dismissal, as much as the stuff of witch-craft. But muti also sparked anxiety because the apostolics are concerned that people might think prophets are simply another kind of spirit medium. The arguments of Weegirl and Gombera make them nervous because they are not so easy to dismiss.

Traditional healers and spirit mediums occupy distinct roles in the social field of Zimbabwean therapeutics. N'angas may or may not have relationships with spirits that help them in their vocation (Chavanduka 1994, 46). Most, in any case, undergo training for the collection and preparation of flora and fauna used as muti in treatments for patients (Reynolds 1996). These healers are neither good nor bad per se; some have reputations as being helpful, and others are said to be open to using their skills for malevolent purposes. Mediums, on the other hand, are normally viewed in a positive light and are, moreover, figures with duties to their communities (Fontein 2004; Spierenberg 2004). Weegirl might have wanted nothing to do with her spirits, but she had little choice. Indeed, the interventions of the ancestral spirits that speak through mediums are considered necessary for the maintenance of social order: "The most important quality of ancestral spirits is that they have the welfare of the people who live within their provinces at heart" (Lan 1985, 55). This is not to say that the authority of mediums goes uncontested (or that ancestral spirits will not reprimand the people who live in their provinces, when necessary). Both during and after the liberation war, for example, a number of mediums got caught up in politicized struggles over their authority and authenticity. In at least one high-profile case, involving the mhondoro Chaminuka, the medium ended up being shot to death (see Ranger 1982). Whether in spite of or because of these contestations, mediums are prominent players in local and sometimes national politics.

The Friday apostolics have never denied that healers can use their skills to help alleviate people's ills, and they are well aware of the important role that mediums have played in the past. The problem is that these figures are not Christian: whatever ends they achieve, the means are unacceptable. And because the "means" in most cases involve the significant use of ritual objects and substances, the weChishanu make an effort to distinguish their muteuro from the n'anga or medium's muti. If pebbles were the only muteuro, there might be little more to discuss on this point. But set against this normative "spiritual medicine" are a number of more specialized substances that do not have the benefit of being "mere signifiers." Many of the things prophets use are already meaningful. Of these, water and honey are two of the most important. Water and honey each highlight, in different ways, how apostolics try to differentiate the immateriality of muti and muteuro at the material level.

The studies of "traditional" healing in Zimbabwe have documented hundreds of plant and animal extracts used in the production of muti and the practice of divination (Gelfand et al. 1985; Reynolds 1996). Alongside these extracts water is probably the most prominent substance in the therapeutic imagination. Many healers claim to learn their skills underwater, at the bottom of rivers, and the most powerful healing spirits are the mermaids (njuzu) (Reynolds 1996, 158–60). More generally, rain is a key symbol of life and the social order; the significance of rain and the extent to which it defines idioms of the spirit has been the subject of important studies on mediums (Lan 1985) and the Mwari cults (Ranger 1999; Werbner 1989b). In my own research with mediums and n'angas, the importance of fluid substances in healing practices was particularly evident: millet beer, water, and liquids produced by adding water to botanical poultices, the ashes from fires, and other substances were commonly employed. The literature on Zimbabwe lends support to Christopher Taylor's argument, based on his research on healing in Rwanda, that in many Bantu cosmologies fluids mediate "notions of causality" (1992, 36). To control the proper flow of fluids (water, humors) is to control the course of life and social well-being.

Water, then, is not a substance that Masowe apostolics can claim as their own, despite its long-standing centrality to Christian symbolisms.[9] Almost any religious figure in Zimbabwe might claim to benefit from water's properties; there is nothing necessarily Christian about it. This made Weegirl especially angry about apostolic claims to have privileged access to the spiritual world. She used njuzu to cure the afflictions of the people who came to her, and she did not see why her reliance on these water spirits was any different from an apostolic prophet's reliance on holy water. She was also critical of Nzira in particular because Juranifiri Santa was positioned near Chitungwiza's municipal water tanks, and she claimed that Nzira was in all likelihood hiding mermaids in the tanks. When I mentioned these objections to informants in the church, they would laugh off her assertion of hidden mermaids, but more generally they always replied by saying that holy water was substantively different because it had God's blessing. Their answers suggested that water in and of itself did not have intrinsic qualities—that its meaning is imbued. This is the logic behind muteuro.

At the same time, however, I would argue that it was precisely because water is such a common element in religious symbolisms that the apostolics did not get too worked up about the accusations of their duplicity. Water is meaningful in so many different religious contexts that the apostolics were able to resolve their anxieties over any parallel between their use of it and that of a traditional healer or medium. In other words, the apostolics seemed to accept that water *did* have something of an intrinsic value, and so it hardly made sense to try to control the meanings people associated with it. Water's universal appeal made it both a lost cause and nothing to worry about. It is also worth pointing out how, above and beyond its ubiquity in symbolic schemes, the material properties of water might be understood to inform its significative potentials. Water is in some respects like smoke (and even the human voice). Its materiality is—literally—difficult to pin down. Water does not offer much resistance; you can move through it. And it is, in a sense, highly unstable; it tends to seep away, evaporate, and condense. In its materiality, then, it is not always very "material"—at least not like a book or a brick wall. But just as such, it can be dangerous. Like smoke, its not-very-material properties can become powerfully so, as for example when they fill one's lungs. Then their not-very-material properties are beside the point.

So, from the apostolic point of view, the symbolic and material meanings of water are the opposite of the pebble. This difference is what makes them similarly unproblematic and begins to suggest how apostolics understand some things as "more material than others." Both are safe because both are mundane. As poles in a spectrum of material culture, they anchor the constellation of value in therapeutic things. But as is often the case, it is not the extreme things that elicit the most interest and concern. Extremes are predictable because their associations are easier to control. That which lies between the poles is more disconcerting, because it embodies the potential problems in the substance of healing. For the apostolics, honey is the substance that best characterizes this tension, so I return to it here by way of conclusion.

A STICKY OBJECT

My friend who stressed the merits of honey on the way to work that Wednesday morning might have been the most enthusiastic proponent of its use, but he was not alone. Honey has been an important substance since the early days of Johane's mission. During his transformative illness, for example, through which he received the revelatory dreams on Marimba hill, Johane claims to have survived on wild honey.[10] Much was made of this point when I collected oral histories from the old-timers. Today, when describing the groves and fields in which they pray, apostolics often refer to them as their lands of milk and honey. In the masowe apostolics can be heard to sing a verse, the simplicity and directedness of which is difficult to miss:

Uchi, uchi
uchi, uchi, uchi

Honey, honey
honey, honey, honey

This verse is used to soothe people when they are possessed by ancestral spirits, avenging spirits, or witchcraft familiars. Apostolics also use honey as a simile to describe any place that is particularly prosperous. After a good rainy season, for example, one apostolic from the Chiweshe District said the farms looked like a land of milk and honey. Once a friend of mine in the church jokingly referred to a Mercedes Benz as a "honey car" *(motokari weuchi)*.

In the wider socioreligious field, however, the holiness of honey breaks down. Honey produces comfort, but it also produces anxiety. Its positive qualities, which are linked to explicitly Christian imageries, are balanced out by more troublesome associations. Unlike pebbles (which the apostolics can claim as their own) and water (which is so obviously salubrious), honey occupies a more ambiguous therapeutic role. Part of the problem is that mediums and n'angas also use honey, so the apostolics cannot claim it as their own. But honey does not have the common currency of water either. It is not *so* meaningful, in other words, that it becomes meaningless. Unlike water, a case has to be made for honey's meaning because the apostolics do not want to cede its value as something open to interpretation. While it is clear to them that the substance lends itself to Christian uses, there is nothing to stop a medium such as Weegirl from mounting a convincing case that it lends itself equally well to African "customary" uses. This state of affairs is exacerbated by the properties of honey as a substance, chiefly that it can be fermented. In fact, the process of fermentation is dependent on its dilution, which is precisely what prophets and elders do to make it "holy." Yet honey wine is one of the last things the apostolics would want to make: along with millet beer, it is one of the worst kinds of alcohol because it is used to propitiate and honor the ancestors—practices the apostolics hope to end. In their appropriation of this substance as a powerful channel for spiritual healing, the apostolics seem to be playing with fire.

The positive potential of honey helps to explain what drove my friend to ask for a sip of mine in the car that day. The negative potentials should give us a sense of why his request for some was a sticky subject. My friend was talking himself into temptation. He was allowing for the possibility that the honey carried inherent properties. In the car the honey did not represent a live and direct connection with God. What it represented— what it *was*—was a way of dealing with a long day in the office. The taste of honey was the hope for relief. In this instance my friend was treating it like aspirin or, worse yet, muti, not muteuro. He was suggesting that its materiality mattered in a way that cut against the grain of his faith.

From honey as a sticky subject of conversation, then, we come to see honey as a sticky object. In the realm of healing it becomes the practical channel through which the apostolics articulate an exception to the rule that a Friday faith should be immaterial. As a sticky object it represents the realization that even "strong" Christians cannot divorce themselves from the material. Holy honey is both the testament and the test of faith. As I hope to have shown in this chapter, the extent to which religious communities objectify their authority through the use of things deserves attention as much for what it tells us about the immaterial world as it does about the persistence of the material one. Apostolic religious practice is driven by a desire for immateriality, but this will always involve a process of objectification. More than this, however, what we add to our understanding of live and direct faith is that in any semiotic ideology specific forms of objectification become the processes through which immateriality can be both demonstrated and lost. How the apostolics talk about and use the substances of healing shows that materiality is a matter of degree and kind.

Turning now to the book's conclusion, I want to step back from the things that tempt apostolics in everyday life to reconsider, in its broad scope, the problem of presence. The discussion of healing has shifted attention away from the question of the text, but it has also reinforced the concern that motivates that question in the first place. Whether the Bible or a jar of honey, the problem is how to manage the meanings that become associated with objects and the authority those associations bear.

Conclusion

WERE THEY EVER TO MEET, it is doubtful that Gaylord Kambarami would think much of Godfrey Nzira's Christianity. Kambarami's understanding of Christianity emerges out of a tradition in which "the Bible, the whole Bible, and nothing but the Bible" is a clarion call. Kambarami wants to put a Bible in the hands of every Zimbabwean. The image that his goal brings to mind is animated by the palpable sense that Christianity can be quantified; the more Bibles there are, the more Christianity there is. For Kambarami, the Bible is not a representation but a presence. When Zimbabweans are joined together by the Book he will have what Crapanzano calls the coalescence of signifier and signified, which is what many conservative Protestantisms often work to produce. In his encouragement of his congregants to use the Bible as toilet paper, Nzira's threat to Kambarami's understanding of Christianity is clear.

It is not that Kambarami is above subjecting the Bible to physical defamation. For him, the materiality of the book can be sacrificed in the service of the change it is able to effect in those who read it. It is more important for the Word to "take change in you" than it is for it to maintain the integrity of its representing form. We learned this in the story of the headman in Murewa. Sending a Bible up in smoke may not be the *best* strategy for its successful dissemination, but in Kambarami's Bible-based semiotics this humble object is always also a humble subject, and that dimension of subjectivity should never be discounted. "In fact," as Kambarami might again remind us, "the Bible reads people." But of course even secure in the knowledge of the Bible's agency, Nzira's suggestions would never be welcome. As this study has shown, objects retain traces of significance even when significance is denied to them. Although a semiotic ideology might claim otherwise, there is no such thing as a mere thing.

More pointedly, however, Nzira's suggestions are a challenge to the authority of Kambarami's understanding of the nature of the Book. Kambarami and Nzira are working with distinct senses of the Bible's material and immaterial qualities. Kambarami cannot, despite the force he draws from the legacy of scriptural imperialism, fix the Bible's significance. The mounting number of Bibles in Zimbabwe is not, in and of itself, a sign of the Bible Society's success. In other words, we might say, the presence of evidence is not evidence of presence. The Friday apostolics remind us that objects are stable in neither form nor meaning. Their valuation is open to contestation.

And what would Nzira think of Kambarami's work? Perhaps not much either. Nzira might think of Kambarami as caught in a bibliolatry of his own making. For the Friday apostolics, the Bible is troublesome in at least three respects, none of which can be resolved by reading, or being "read." First, it is the tainted sign. In postcolonial Africa the Bible carries an indelible essence of white might. Second, and more important, the Bible causes trouble because of its nature as an object. Its materiality is a sign of its limitations. As a medium, texts are not only a barrier to the presence of the divine but also a reminder of the problem with a thingi-fied faith. Books can "fall apart," as Nzira said. They can take the focus away from what Christianity is really about, which is a live and direct relationship with God. The third troublesome aspect of the Book is not necessarily one the apostolics would highlight, but books are also trouble because they can be used to challenge the authority of prophets. When you have members of the congregation referring to the Gospel of Luke, you are leaving open an avenue of interpretive authority. Absence of the text is one way to focus attention on the presence of the prophet. The concern with "focus" has this double edge and forces us to consider how the problem of presence is never only theological but also an element in the struggle for social power.

One irony in this mutual disapproval—an irony that an ecumenicist might want to point out—is that all Christians might claim that, at some level, their faith is "live and direct." The particularities of this claim as explored in this book belong to the Friday apostolics, but the dynamics that animate it are not unique. Christian languages are shaped by vocabularies of distance and proximity. The proximity, or directness, may well be presented in other idioms and through other mediums: the pope, the preacher, the prophet, the saint, the Bible, the friend in Jesus, the Inner Light, imaginings of the Celestial Kingdom. But if we were to ask Kambarami, for example, in the most general terms, "Do you want a faith that is live and direct?" he would probably answer, "Yes."

The Friday message has been marked by the repudiation of the Bible from the outset. Johane suggested in some of his earliest work that the Bible is a very material thing. There is, however, much more to the live and direct faith than a repudiation of the Bible. On the messy terrain of ethnography we have encountered several ways in which the apostolics renounce material things. Alongside the Bible, Johane preached against traditional medicines and other such things. The dangers of "African culture" were as real as those of a misshapen Christianity. He also warned against the dangers of money, dangers that the elders are particularly keen to stress these days. "Church history" is also defined by a concern with things, and a commitment to immateriality. The major prophets are denied life after death as subjects and objects of veneration. Not knowing what Johane looked like is, as Tsitsi made clear to Lazarus and me, a point of pride; it demonstrates the extent to which the apostolics have resisted the idolatrous sway of the image and, thus, a particular form of religious representation. The instantiation of faith in the religious subject likewise resists thingification: mutemo is a process of becoming that can never be complete. This apostolic "law" is also a "knowledge" that unfolds. It does not conform to a form. These concerns with fixation and fixity are expressed as well in live and direct language, the essence of which obtains in the finely balanced processes of entextualization and inspiration that sermons and singing provide. Healing too is a move beyond objects. The materiel of therapeutics gain their potency through the idioms of prayer and through the rationalization of their material properties as "immaterial." So it is not only a question of the Bible. Everything discussed in this book suggests that the Masowe weChishanu are committed to a project of immateriality. They want a religion in which things do not matter.

Part of what makes ethnography a messy terrain, however, is that what people "want" is not always borne out in practice. The models by which people live their lives are only that. Objects are the obstacle to developing a live and direct relationship with God. But for every repudiation of the material we can catalog, that repudiation runs up against its own limits. Johane himself, after all, eventually took up the Book. While the Friday churches have reconciled themselves to Johane's falling off track, it nevertheless points to lingering questions about the inevitability of the written word. Will there ever be a church constitution, as Marcus hopes? Could such a document preserve the essence of the live and direct message? Is writing down church history, or recording aspects of mutemo, a dangerous prelude to stale faith? The influences and impacts of money are also being felt. It too has seeped into the churches. Emmanuel, Sandros, Nzira, and Hwimbo are only the better-known prophets who have shored up their religious positions through consolidations of capital. Each has implied his plenitude (or allowed others to do it) through the construction of things—be they "hospital wards" or the most solid houses in Africa. These moneyed places ground authority in space, which is antithetical to the Friday ideal. The same mixing of divine with earthly plans might well affect the character of the apostolics' music—if Marcus's children get their way and start to record the verses or if the more widespread popularity of collecting gospel tapes is an indication of things to come. Live and direct language poses other risks: it makes prophets over into objects of authority. However momentary these objectifications ought to be, the problem is that "human nature" can take prophets off track by compelling them to try to extend these moments into lasting states. And of all the "messes" that the commitment to immateriality makes, it seems the biggest has to do with the practice of healing. Muteuro can be a sticky subject because of the meanings that people invest in it as an object. Dispensing with the Bible, then, has not resolved the problems that materiality poses. A commitment to immaterial faith is realized, inasmuch as it can be, through the assertion that some things are more material than others. This is the assertion behind "live and direct semiotics."

It will probably come as little surprise that a church committed to the accessibility of the divine has produced a number of prophets who try to regulate that accessibility through themselves. Neither should it surprise us that in a church concerned with the degradation of religion through a wayward emphasis on things we find such savvy political and economic entrepreneurs. Any cosmological principle is vitalized by its opposite, when the spark turns from creative to destructive.

In this Godfrey Nzira may unfortunately be a case in point. On May 6, 2002, he was charged with nine counts of rape in the Chitungwiza

Magistrate's Court. The charges were brought against him by two women who had gone to Juranifiri Santa for help with their afflictions. The women claimed that Nzira told them they would be healed if they had sexual intercourse with him. The magistrate set bail at Z$10,000 and required Nzira to report to a local police station every Monday and Friday until his trial commenced.[1] Nzira was also told to remain at Juranifiri Santa at all times rather than at his home in a nearby Chitungwiza neighborhood.[2]

This was not, of course, the first time Nzira had been in the news. During the 2000 elections Juranifiri Santa had been used as a rallying ground for Madzibaba Border Gezi, ZANU(PF) governor of Mashonaland Central and parliamentary candidate for the town of Bindura. This was a controversial move that prompted other Friday congregations to condemn the use of church sites for political purposes, and for dragging the church into the press.

But the next year Nzira's public image only grew. He appeared in the papers twice more. On January 5, 2001, there was a report in the *Daily Mail* that seven members of a family from Ashdown Park in Harare were assaulted when they went to Juranifiri Santa to retrieve their father, a certain Dennis Mushope, who they said was being treated in one of Nzira's hospital wards for tuberculosis. One of the men's daughters alleged seeing an apostolic from the congregation driving her father's car in town. The family members then went to Juranifiri Santa to inquire what was happening, but, they said, they were told they could not see their father. The apostolic who spoke to the police about the incident claimed that the man's family had become abusive and violent and that it was only then that the apostolics defended themselves.[3] Three days later, in another *Daily News* story, Dennis Mushope was quoted as saying the report was untrue: "It has been twelve years since I last saw [my family] and I am not suffering from tuberculosis." Mushope maintained his commitment to the church. "We do not beat people up at our church," he said. "We heal people."[4]

On December 2, 2001, Juranifiri Santa was back in the news. According to a report in the *Sunday Mail*, a "clash between two opposing spiritual worlds" had erupted over the preceding weeks between Nzira and a local "witch hunter" *(tsikamutanda)* who had come to a village in the Seke Communal Lands (which border Chitungwiza) to perform a "cleansing ceremony." Local residents were reportedly asked to contribute money for the ceremony. The witch hunter then put wooden pegs *(hoko)* outside the homes of people who were witches or who used zvidhoma. Some of the homes that were pegged were those of apostolics from Juranifiri Santa.

"I told my followers to remove the pegs and bring them to my church," Nzira is quoted as saying. "What I saw was nothing but heaps of man-made strange items, some with beads around them as well as feathers. I ordered that these things be burnt." In the week after the pegging incident, nothing happened to the people whose houses had been marked, and the villagers are alleged to have demanded their money back from the tsikamutanda, who had disappeared in the meantime. Nzira and his elders were alarmed at the hostile reaction to the church. "When nothing happened to my followers after the burning of his goblins," Nzira went on, "Tsikamutanda's aides went around telling the villagers I had gone crazy following the burning of the items. This was all done to divert the villagers' attention from demanding their money back. I am not crazy, as you [the *Sunday Mail* reporter] can see. Nothing happened to me because I am a believer in God. I have proved to [the witch hunter] that he is going around cheating people."[5]

In their starkness, and in their own way, these two newspaper stories bring out something of the texture of a live and direct faith. Reading them as I did, two years after my fieldwork and thousands of miles from Zimbabwe, I could not help but notice how the controversy in each hinged on a notion of propriety: in the first, the propriety of relationships; in the second, the propriety of things. In each we find hints of why semiotic ideologies matter in the constitution of social life. In each the friction emerges out of the apostolics' commitment to realigning the values of "African culture" in more "Christian terms," of being able to define the significance and authority of things.

It would have been in the midst of the 2002 election campaign that Nzira raped the two women who came to Juranifiri Santa for healing. This was at another low point for Zimbabwe's democracy; the campaigning by ZANU(PF) in the run-up to the March 9 vote was brutal, with the opposition Movement for Democratic Change candidates and supporters being systematically targeted (see Melber 2002). Nzira was a staunch supporter of Mugabe, and he attended rallies on the ruling party's behalf. Terence Ranger, who was in Zimbabwe for most of the campaign, reported on one prayer rally at which apostolics from Juranifiri Santa sang a liberation war song and held up ZANU(PF) placards: "Baba Nzira announced a prophecy that Mugabe was 'a divinely appointed King of Zimbabwe and no man should dare challenge his office'" (2002, 8).

On March 17, 2003, Godfrey Nzira was convicted in the Harare Magistrate's Court on nine counts of rape:

Nzira Supporters Run Amok

By Angela Makamure and Brian Mangwende

Angered by the conviction of their leader, Godfrey Nzira, for rape, about 2,000 members of the Johane Masowe Apostolic Sect went haywire yesterday, beating up court officials, policemen on duty and smashing the entry doors of the Harare Magistrates' Courts. Betty Chidziva, the trial magistrate, reportedly escaped death by a whisker when some of the members pounced on her soon after she delivered the judgment. . . .

. . . "The situation was chaotic," a court official said. "All hell broke loose." (*Daily News*, March 18, 2003)

The next day, Magistrate Chidziva sentenced Nzira to thirty-two years. "You couldn't believe it," one of my friends told me on the phone. "A servant of the Lord doing a wonderful job. You can't believe it."

In the eyes of his supporters, Nzira has lost a battle but not the war. He is suffering for a reason. They do not know why the Holy Spirit let this happen, but many are convinced that Nzira will be back. "This is very difficult to know," I was told. "We miss that guy."

But not everyone misses Nzira. For elders like Marcus, who had long since suspected that Nzira had succumbed to "human nature," the conviction was a predictable end to the prophet's time. Regardless, it is felt, Nzira's court case brought the question of leadership to a new level—one that I think his supporters and detractors alike regret. By the time of Nzira's trial, he was a well-known national personality. (On the London Underground one day in October 2002, I ran into three Zimbabwean men on the Northern Line who knew all about Nzira, even though they were not from the Harare area.) "This isn't good for our church," said another friend on the phone. He pointed out to me that his congregation, a smaller Friday group in Harare, has been meeting since 1984 and has not suffered from such "'troubles." Indeed, most Friday congregations have never been through this kind of trial, literal or figurative. This is a point that needs to be stressed, especially as we near the end of this book.

Juranifiri Santa is still there. It is, in a sense, even "more" there than when I was conducting my fieldwork. In the period after 2000, as Nzira's public image grew, he had a wall built around the prayer site. Then, I am told, he put razor wire on top of the wall and ran power lines into the hospital wards. Even as he was contesting the legitimacy of the witch hunter through a denunciation of his wooden pegs—just a pile of "man-made strange items," according to a live and direct semiotics—Nzira was pegging himself in.

I'm not sure I will come to terms, personally, with what has happened to Godfrey Nzira, or what, it pains me to say, may have happened to the two women. There is no rule of law in Zimbabwe, so it is plausible that Nzira was sent to jail simply because he had fallen afoul of his ZANU(PF) cronies. It is plausible that the case was fabricated for political reasons—that something happened during the March 2002 election campaign that gave Mugabe or other officials in ZANU(PF) pause over Nzira's rising popularity. But I cannot say for sure. "Power can corrupt," as Marcus told me. I have to believe it corrupted Nzira. I think that he helped thousands of people over the course of his time at Juranifiri Santa, and I know that many hundreds, at least, still see him as a servant of God. But I think that over the years, as his popularity grew, Nzira fell off track—as the apostolics would put it (although for me it is a sociological point, not a religious one). As I have noted, my friend and colleague Bella Mukonyora saw this all too clearly in her visits to Juranifiri. I saw it too but not in full light until the courtroom trial.

It is difficult for me to write this—in part because Nzira is someone I came to care about and in part because I recognize that once it leaves my study, this story about Nzira may well be taken up by some as an example of what is "wrong" with Africa. The Western stereotype of Africans as corrupt is not one I want to reinforce. It is grossly misleading. Just as disturbing, in recent years a number of African churches have been portrayed in the Western media—when they are portrayed at all—as barbaric cults, devoid not only of Christianity (which many could take or leave) but also of a basic humanity.[6]

I hope the ethnography presented here is strong enough to counter the negative stereotypes of Africans and African Christians that Nzira's conviction might otherwise reinforce. This book is not a defense of—much less an apologetic for—any one vision of faith, even as I have tried to show that it is crucial for anthropologists to pay attention to what motivates the faithful. This ending to my project is the product of history, not fate. Nzira happened; the worst thing to do here would be to gloss that over.

"There were a lot of divisions after the incarceration," one of the elders recently told me on the phone. "But some, they are coming back." There is a new prophet at Juranifiri Santa now, a woman from Mutoko named Magdalene. "She is doing the same wonders that Nzira used to do if not more," wrote a friend in an e-mail. "This demonstrates to all of us that the real prophet that does wonders is not the human being that we see and talk to but someone from heaven."

The live and direct faith of the Friday apostolics represents a dynamic and ongoing engagement with one of the most fundamental questions posed by Christianity. How does God become present? As I acknowledged in the introduction, from the perspective of Christians this is, in an important sense, a "problem" that is already solved: it was (and will be) solved in the coming of Jesus Christ. In between the event and the return, however, the evidence of presence has been marshaled by Christians through what David Tracy has characterized as a host of "relatively adequate" signs. It is in their relative adequacy that these signs—the gifts of the Holy Spirit, the Eucharist, the icon, the Bible, a prophet—reveal themselves as the proper subject not only of theologians but also of social scientists (and students of philosophy, and of literature, and of art, and poets, and others) committed to the investigation of Christianity in its sociohistorical formations. As my friend seemed to recognize in the e-mail he sent me about the appearance of Magdalene at Juranifiri Santa, the apostolics are also well equipped to recognize this relative adequacy.

In this book I have tried to present a detailed historical and ethnographic picture of a small church in Africa. Equally, though, I have tried to stress how, at its most general level, the problem of presence is a problem of representation—of how words, objects, and actions get defined as such and, in the process, become significant. Any anthropology that concerns itself with questions of presence and representation has to take these processes into account.

NOTES

INTRODUCTION

1. The Masowe weChishanu Church is what most scholars of Christianity in Africa call an African Independent Church. This label, with roots in the pioneering and still-rewarding work of Bengt Sundkler (1961), has been given its basic definition by David Barrett: "The formation and existence . . . of an organized religious movement with a distinct name and membership that claims the title Christian in that it acknowledges Jesus Christ as Lord, and which has either separated by secession from a mission church, or has been founded outside the mission as a new kind of religious entity under African initiative and leadership" (1968, 50). Like most labels, it has been deployed with caution, ambivalence, and, on occasion, derision. There are, however, several helpful reviews that are sensitive to the limits of "the taxonomic imperative" (Fernandez 1978, 201) behind such labeling: Daneel 1987, 29–42; Fabian 1991a; Fernandez 1978; Meyer 2004; Ranger 1986.

2. *Madzibaba* is the term of address for males in the church; *madzimai* is the equivalent for females. These title prefixes translate very roughly as "elder," although they are used regardless of an apostolic's age or length of association with the church. In this sense they serve the function of leveling social differences that might obtain in other, nonapostolic relations.

3. Some people also commented on the staffs (called *tsvimbo* by the Friday apostolics) that men often carry; I say more about the staffs in chapter 7.

4. The Gospel of God Church—whose members were once known as the Korsten Basketmakers, after the neighborhood in Port Elizabeth, South Africa, where they lived for much of the 1940s and 1950s, selling baskets—is the subject of a monograph by the sociologist Clive Dillon-Malone (1978). Several other academics have written about the "Saturday" Masowe, including Bourdillon, Mashita, and Glickman (1976); Kileff and Kileff (1979); Mukonyora (1998a, 1998b, 2000); Ranger (1999a); Sundkler (1961); and Werbner (1985). These authors do not refer to the subjects of their studies as the "Saturday Masowe," but I use the label here because it was commonly accepted by the Gospel of God apostolics I met in the 1990s. Sometimes the Friday apostolics referred to the Saturday apostolics as "books" *(mabhuku).*

5. See National Archives of Zimbabwe (hereafter NAZ), S 138/22 vol. 2, 1931–33, statement by Native Detective Zakia.

6. John the Baptist imagery and the practice of baptism are important to Gospel of God apostolics. See, e.g., Dillon-Malone 1978; Mukonyora 1998b, 194; Sundkler 1961, 324–25.

7. I have come across at least two other academics who use the term "the problem of presence": the anthropologist Webb Keane (1997a, 51)—whose work I turn to in another capacity in a moment—and the Catholic historian of religion Robert Orsi (2006, 74).

8. Other texts in the anthropological literature on this point include Gell 1998; Irvine 1989; Keane 1997b, 2001, 2003; Latour 1993; Parmentier 1997; Tambiah 1984; Thomas 1991. See also many of the essays in the edited collections by Fred Myers (2001) and Daniel Miller (2005b). As I discuss later, the inspiration for much of this work comes from the writings of Charles Sanders Peirce.

9. Like Michael Lambek (2000, 309–10) and others, I recognize that demarcating "the anthropology of religion" as a subfield of the discipline raises issues of its own—even before we move on to staking out sub-subfields like the anthropology of Christianity, or Islam. While these terms highlight "religion" in one sense or another, I do not use them to sublate other topics or to suggest that they exist as stable objects.

10. This interest in Hebrew and Judaism is more widely evident in the African Christian imagination. In his work on Aladura Christianity in Nigeria, for example, Peter Probst has discussed the appeal of Kabbalah for Josiah Oshitelu, one of the church's prophets: "Especially appealing to his mind must have been the cabalistic idea that the Hebrew letters in which the sacred texts are written down are not just ordinary signs invented by man . . . but rather are reservoirs of divine power, symbols behind which the Biblical secrets are hidden" (1989, 487), while according to Cynthia Hoehler-Fatton (1996, 6), followers of Adolfo Mango in western Kenya refer to their churches as "synagogues." Father Ignatius Chidavaenze, a Catholic translator I met at Bible House in Harare, told me that Hebrew and Shona are related languages and that Africans (by which he meant

speakers of Bantu languages) were more "biblical" than Europeans. He kept a list of ninety-three Shona and Hebrew words that he claimed were cognates and planned to publish a paper on this topic.

11. While literacy is a linchpin in many of the discussions about the written word in Judeo-Christian history and while recognition of its ideological dimensions in anthropology has been important (Goody 1977, 1986; cf. Besnier 1995; Bloch 1998; Ewald 1988; Fuller 2001; Heath 1980; Janzen 1985; Parry 1986; Probst 1989; Schieffelin 1996, 2000; Schousboe and Larsen 1989; Scribner and Cole 1981; Street 1984), I do not think it is the most productive topic with which to frame the apostolics' rejection of the Bible. Johane's denunciations of the Bible were a move to "keep it oral," as David Guss (1986) says about the Yekuana in South America. But they were not denunciations of literacy per se. Today, in fact, most congregations push literacy as part of a social agenda. Nzira, for example, always congratulated those children who did well on their school exams, and he encouraged everyone in his congregation to take advantage of formal education if and when they could. Literacy, then, is not the issue: the issue is what one reads and toward what end. The apostolic view on reading confirms Brian Street's 1984 findings: the literate often differentiate between kinds of reading (cf. Boyarin 1993b; Heath 1980; Lambek 1991; Rutherford 2000; Schieffelin 1996; Scribner and Cole 1981). Reading is only a problem for the Friday apostolics when it is invested with faith-based significance; otherwise, it poses little concern.

12. It should not be forgotten that Henry VIII's and Edward VI's iconoclasm also benefited the royal treasury: precious metals in the religious art and objects destroyed were melted down and recast, and bishop's lands were confiscated by the crown; see Phillips 1973, 97–100.

13. Saussure defines semiology as "a science *which studies the role of signs as part of social life*" (1983, 15; original emphasis).

14. Semeiotic is "the formal doctrine of signs" (Liszka 1996, 1) and does not pertain only to language.

15. I attended services of the Apostolic Faith Mission (a Pentecostal church with which Johane Masowe once had close relations), the Maranke Apostolic Church, and the two main factions of the Saturday apostolics, the Gospel of God Church, headquartered near Shoniwa Masedza's childhood home in Gandanzara, Zimbabwe, and (with apologies for the confusion it invites) the Johane Masowe Church, which is based in Lusaka, Zambia, but has several large congregations in Zimbabwe, the main one of which is in Bulawayo.

16. Emerson, Fretz, and Shaw (1995, 41) suggest that ethnographers should not discuss fieldwork experiences with intimates until one's full notes are written up. I have to confess that I rarely followed this protocol. Lazarus and I almost always talked about what had happened at a service or an interview, especially if we faced a long car ride. From Juranifiri Santa, where we conducted

most of the research, we would often give two or three apostolics a ride into central Harare, and they too would participate enthusiastically in discussions of what had happened in church that day. However this might have compromised the texture of my full notes, I would also say it added valuable dimensions to the analysis I can present here.

17. This is not to suggest that Mwari is irrelevant; see Ranger 1999b for an example of how the Mwali cults in the Matopos Hills have played an important role in Zimbabwe's regional and national politics over the past century.

ONE. UP IN SMOKE

Epigraph: Isaac Hughes in a letter to Robert Moffat; quoted in Comaroff and Comaroff 1991, 215.

1. The Tongan writer Epeli Hau'ofa (1983) has written a story in which a man called Ti accidentally smokes a page from his Bible, only to be punished by Moses, Joshua, Samson, and, eventually, the Israeli Armed Forces for this original sin and the series of sins committed in the hope of penance for the initial act. It is only when Ti smokes Luke 23:34 (Then Jesus said, "Father forgive them, for they do not know what they are doing"), at the suggestion of his friend Manu, that the punishment stops, because, Manu says, "a sin can only be cancelled by an equal and opposite sin" (quoted in Hau'ofa 1983, 41). Ti's predicament also forces us to consider the tension between the materiality and immateriality of Scripture. Although this chapter focuses on the Bible in Africa, this is not to suggest that the arguments are only of relevance to Africanists.

2. See, e.g., the report by Justin Ukpong (2000) on popular readings of the Bible in contemporary Nigeria, which indicates that Catholic approaches to Bible reading at the individual level do not differ markedly from Protestant approaches.

3. See Howsam 1991 for a more detailed discussion of the BFBS and the Bible as a commodity.

4. See Comaroff and Comaroff 1991, 1997, for more detailed discussions of the relationships between Christianity and capitalism; and Fabian 1991a, 128–29, for an argument on the continuing phenomenon of the commodification of religion in postcolonial Africa.

5. Recent studies of mission education include Pels 1999 on the Catholic Holy Ghost Fathers in Tanganyika (197–236) and Summers 2002 on a number of Protestant stations in Southern Rhodesia, including those of the Dutch Reformed Church and the Wesleyan Methodists.

6. The Bible was not the only Christian text with a significant influence in this respect; as Isabel Hofmeyr (2004) has shown in probably the most comprehensive history of the book in Africa, John Bunyan's *The Pilgrim's Progress* was likewise so.

7. The CMS has never operated in Zimbabwe.

8. See Ranger 1995, for example, on the Samkange family and the "making of Methodism" in the interwar period.

9. A full Setswana Bible, with a print run of fifty copies, was not published until 1867, just three years before Moffat left Kuruman (Bradlow 1987, 29).

10. The philosophy of translation is not a topic I can adequately address here, so a lengthy endnote will have to do. According to Sanneh, "Translatability is the source of the success of Christianity across cultures" (1989, 51). "The task of the translator," Walter Benjamin has argued, "consists in finding that intended effect upon the language into which he is translating which produces in it the echo of the original" (1968, 76). In the Christian tradition, however, there is an added consideration. Translation is based on the principle that "culture is only an instrumental means at our disposal, rather than an end" (Sanneh 1989, 197). For the Christian, there is no corner of the linguistic and cultural map inaccessible to God's Word. Scripture is always original, always authentic in a way that secular texts cannot be; the Bible is therefore considered "unconditionally translatable" (Benjamin 1968, 82). This is not to say that missionaries faced no problems finding the intended effect to which Benjamin alludes or, indeed, that missionaries did not make ideological claims through their translation efforts—as I discuss presently in relation to Robert Moffat. Power and misunderstanding have always been constituent elements of missionary, colonial, and ethnographic encounters (Fabian 1995, 2000).

11. See Etherington 1983 for an alternative reading to Sanneh's. He argues that the Church of England did not become more racist at the end of the nineteenth century but rather "re-invigorated" by "individual Christian 'perfection' and selfless holiness" (Etherington 1983, 126) that shifted emphasis away from institution-building agendas.

12. The unintentional character of Shembe's mission is a common theme in narratives of religious transformation. I discuss this at greater length in chapter 2.

13. Jean Comaroff relates a similar case in her study of Tshidi Zionists, in which illiterate members "sought to regain command over an estranged world through the iconic manipulation of letters and newsprint" (1985, 143).

14. Details of the political history of Uganda in this paragraph are taken from Behrend 1999, 22–35; and Allen 1991.

15. Allen writes, "Establishing written regulations for a group is in fact common among the Acholi, and the HS rules are presented in a similar manner to the list of regulations established each year by farm work groups" (1991, 377).

16. After Alice's defeat new movements arose, including "Lakwena Part Two" and the Lord's Resistance Army. See Allen 1991; Van Acker 2004.

17. See Pieterse 2001 for a discourse analysis of Tutu's speeches and sermons. Pieterse shows that liberation theology is one of the most recurrent themes in Tutu's work.

18. This emphasis on the Bible should not be taken to mean that Tutu removed himself from this-worldly struggles. There are some indications in his speeches and sermons that armed resistance to apartheid was not inevitable: "If the government is determined to balkanise South Africa and to snatch away citizenship from Blacks then there won't be a peaceful solution, then they are declaring war on us. What are Blacks then expected to do in such a situation? Fold their hands?" (Tutu 1983, 43).

19. John de Gruchy calls Tutu "a true pastor and prophet amongst the politicians" (1996, 49).

TWO. THE EARLY DAYS OF JOHANE MASOWE

1. The quotations by Shoniwa in this and the following paragraph are taken from a statement in NAZ, November 1, 1932, S 138/22.

2. November 2, 1932, NAZ S 138/22.

3. ACNC, Goromonzi to CNC, September 10, 1934, NAZ S 1542/P10; ACNC to CNC, April 23, 1934, NAZ S 1542/P10.

4. I define transformation in the most elementary sense as change. The emergence of Johane Masowe is an indication of "fairly radical changes" (Fabian 1991b, 65) in the religious perspective of Shoniwa Masedza.

5. See Summers 2002 for a more general discussion of education in Southern Rhodesia after World War I.

6. The Land Apportionment Act of 1931 no doubt also had an effect on the attitude of potential converts in Makoni.

7. It is unlikely a Catholic priest would have been distributing Bibles in the 1930s. If Johane received any text from a Catholic priest, it was probably a catechism or religious booklet. Here again we see—as with Mzilikazi—the metonymic potential of the Book.

8. Statement by Shoniwa, November 1, 1932 NAZ S 138/22 (emphasis added).

9. Actually, from the Friday apostolics' point of view, it was not a spirit but an angel *(ngirozi)*—a distinction I address in chapter 5.

10. The accounts of those who witnessed Johane's mission in October 1932 are found in NAZ S 138/22 vol. 2, 1931–33. All of the quotations are taken directly from these documents.

11. See Hartley District Criminal Register, 1931–34, NAZ S 546.

12. This is mentioned by Andrea in his statement from NAZ S 138/22 vol. 2, 1931–33.

13. NC, Hartley to CNC, March 2, 1933, NAZ S 1032.

14. November 30, 1933, NAZ S 1542/M8.

15. Major Arthur Stoyle to CNC, April 30, 1934, NAZ S 1542/M8B vol. 1.

16. The certificate of Johane's position in the AFM is found in NAZ S 1542/M8B vol. 2.

17. April 23, 1934, NAZ S 1542/P10.

18. Sgt. Harold Jackson to CID, June 3, 1934, NAZ S 1542/M8B vol. 2.

19. To CNC, NAZ S 1542/M8B vol. 1.

20. NAZ S 318.

21. NAZ S 1542/P10.

22. Kraal head Nekario, under Chief Soswe, April 27, 1934, NAZ S 1542/M8B vol. 2.

23. If Johane initially spoke of kaffir beer and a return to the religion of the forefathers, by 1934 his rejection of "African culture" was increasingly apparent. As Ranger (1999a) argues, Johane's early disposition toward most European missionaries was hostile not because they were Christian but because they were not Christian enough in stamping out African practices; see also Engelke 2004a. Mukonyora (1998a) also discusses how the Saturday church threatened local-level systems of African political authority because of its rejection of "tradition."

24. Circular Minute 23, May 1934, NAZ S 1542/P10.

25. Chiefs at this time were empowered by the colonial state, an issue discussed in much of the historiography of Southern Rhodesia; see, e.g., Ranger 1970, 1983.

26. June 3, 1934, NAZ S 1542/P10.

27. There is not space to develop the point here, but see Crapanzano 2000, 41–44, for a discussion of the differences between Pentecostalism and fundamentalism.

28. Dawson Munjeri, NAZ oral histories AOH/4.

29. The description of events concerning Mudyiwa's activities in Goromonzi are found in a letter written to the CNC from the NC, Goromonzi in NAZ S 318.

THREE. THE QUESTION OF LEADERSHIP

1. I am using the term *genealogy* only very loosely; it is important to stress that the apostolics do not understand prophetism as "inherited" or as marking a "kinship" relation. See Bouquet 1996 for a discussion of how genealogy has functioned in the making of anthropology, with a particular focus on the genealogical diagram.

2. See, e.g., NAZ S 235/516 vol. 1, which contains annual reports for 1938. Any mention of the "wapostoli" or "Baba Johan" movement is positive. The native commissioner for Marandellas, for example, says, "There is much to be commended in their simple form of faith."

3. The historian Timothy Burke helps to contextualize the sentiments Philip was drawing on: "Western ideals of cleanliness, appearance, and bodily behavior became increasingly powerful within African communities, even

among non-elites, during the 1930s. New African elites and whites both publicly explained the growing power of these new behaviors as signs of the struggle between 'traditional' and 'modern' life, 'African' and 'European' ways, 'heathenism' and 'Christianity'" (1996, 43).

4. See NAZ S 2824/3. On July 24, 1962, the Basketmakers sent a letter to the minister of native affairs, H. J. Quinton: "The problem that exists between ourselves and your Government is the granting of a satisfactory location for our village. We have explained to you that we cannot accept the offer of the land at Seki. This distance from the city of Salisbury would make it quite impossible for us to carry on our community life and make a satisfactory living. You are aware that we have, for the past fifteen years, lived almost within the city of Port Elizabeth. We have become urbanized as a people and various trades depend upon our proximity to a large community where we may sell our wares. It would not be possible for us to overcome the handicap of living seventeen miles from the City of Salisbury and we hope that Government will recognise that in this matter we really have no choice at all. We must be located near a city."

5. The words to this song are in "ancient Hebrew," the details of which are discussed in chapter 5.

6. According to Ezra Chitando, in the midst of Zimbabwe's land crisis Nzira made his political allegiances clear: he "claimed that he had a vision during the liberation struggle in which God showed him Mugabe parceling out land to ululating land-hungry peasants" (2002, 9).

7. Gezi was killed in a car accident less than a year after the Juranifiri rally. Rumor has it that President Mugabe arranged the "accident" because Gezi was becoming too powerful within the party. In e-mails and over the telephone some apostolics suggested to me that perhaps the Holy Spirit gave Gezi what he deserved for falling off track.

FOUR. MUTEMO IN THREE PORTRAITS

1. See the work of Fabian (1971, 1991a, 1991b) and Keller (2004) for discussions of concepts similar to mutemo. Among the Jamaa movement in Zaire, Fabian found that people spoke about *mawazo* (ideas) as "the most important and most typical concept of Jamaa doctrine" (1971, 137). Mawazo, like mutemo, is akin to a process of becoming: it is realized through "gradual initiation, so much so that becoming Jamaa and being Jamaa, means and ends, became indistinguishable" (1991, 76). For the Seventh-day Adventists in Madagascar whom Keller worked with, the concept of *mazava* is akin to mutemo-as-knowledge. It is "a very powerful concept" (not only in the Adventist Church) which, for the Adventists, denotes "clarity of mind" and gives them "the intellectual potency to remove Satan's veil of deception" (Keller 2004, 101).

2. The intellectualist approach to conversion is associated most closely with the work of Robin Horton (1975a, 1975b). There are several discussions of Horton's work in the anthropological literature; see Hefner 1993, 20–25, for a thorough overview.

3. Talal Asad (1993) and Maurice Bloch (1989) have both made important cases against the surfeit of meaning in anthropological analyses of religion and ritual. It is not that they think meaning should play no role in anthropological analysis, but it is "misguided to argue, as so many anthropologists have done, that religion is an explanation, a speculation about such things as man's place in the world" (Bloch 1989, 37; see also Asad 1993, 33).

4. *Maboyi* (boy) is a term in Rhodesian "kitchen kaffir" used to infantilize African men. It is an offensive and derogatory label (as is the "kaffir" in "kitchen kaffir").

5. The local politics and discourse of whiteness for the Orokaiva and the Masowe apostolics differ in several respects; see Engelke 2001 for a more detailed look at this issue.

6. See Fabian 1991b, 77, on how the Jamaa spoke about mawazo in a similar way; the concept of mawazo is explained in note 1, above.

7. Dillon-Malone reports that the Basketmaker Church considers biomedicine a "defilement" because "the use of any physical medicines is looked upon as a failure to trust wholeheartedly in the power of God" (1978, 91). I discuss the Friday apostolics' arguments for accepting biomedicine in more detail in chapter 7 but might note here that the Maranke Church takes a stance similar to that of the Basketmaker Church. During my fieldwork in 1999, a group of Maranke apostolics made the news when they overturned a government truck carrying medicine to treat victims of a cholera epidemic in an area where the church had a significant following; see "Cholera Claims Six Johane Marange Sect Members," Zimbabwe *Herald*, November 19, 1999.

8. This was a concern in other congregations too—so much so that one elder at Nyatsime wrote a letter to the editor in the *Herald* explaining the problem: "We are seriously concerned about the confusion over the apostolic churches prefixed with the name Johane" (November 22, 1999).

9. I chose not to live with an apostolic family for two reasons. First, I did not want to be too closely associated with particular individuals. Second, in most cases my presence would have been a strain on household resources, even if I were to contribute to the household budget.

FIVE. LISTENING FOR THE TRUE BIBLE

1. Luther, for instance, stressed that "the Incarnation into humanity was also an incarnation into language" (Milbank 1997, 93). Saint Augustine argued that language is "the means of access to divine truth" (Cameron 1991, 66). And,

as Robert Alter notes, there is "a supreme confidence in an ultimate coherence of meaning through language that informs the biblical vision" (1981, 112) of the Old Testament.

2. Compare this with Tracy's 1981 discussion on the "relative inadequacy" of all signs other than the Christ, which I highlighted in the introduction.

3. Linguistic anthropologists have criticized the concept of the speech community on several grounds. Irvine and Gal, for example, have argued that while the foundational work in sociolinguistics put paid to the argument that linguistic diversity produces social disorder, it "only rarely examined the ways in which identity is produced by ideas of opposition between culturally defined groups, and by practices that promote exclusion, divergence, and differentiation" (2000, 75; see also Gal 1989, 349).

4. Not surprisingly, if a newcomer to the church spoke up during a service he or she might not begin with "rufaro kwamuri," much less incorporate the correct posture and bodily movements that complete the greeting. Ordinary members sitting around newcomers would point this out when they got the chance.

5. The metaphor of depth is commonly used to describe the formality of ritual speech elsewhere in Africa (see, e.g., Ashforth 2000, 59, 88; Bastian 1993, 59).

6. It is worth noting that apostolics would use ancient Hebrew words at the metalinguistic level; when I asked about ancient Hebrew they were quite comfortable listing the words they could remember having heard, and speculating on their possible meanings. But they never used the words in everyday conversation.

7. See the discussion in chapter 1 of Comaroff and Comaroff (1991, 218) and Musa Dube (1999) for a similar discussion on the Tswana term for ancestors (badimo), which missionaries used to refer to the Christian conception of demons.

8. Spirit mediums are often referred to as jars or containers by Shona speakers. For examples of water imagery in African and African Christian religious symbolism, see Bourdillon 1987, 68, 203; Comaroff 1985, 200–201; Ray 1993, 277–78; Sundkler 1961, 201, 206; Turner 1968b. I return to a discussion of water in chapter 7.

9. The plural here should be vamiriri vamweya—interpreters of the spirit—based on the noun class prefixes in standard Shona. Apostolics never used the plural, however, even when referring to more than one such individual. No one ever said so explicitly, but it was my sense that they did not use the plural because they considered "the interpreter" a performative role instantiated only in the act, such that there could never be more than one interpreter at a time. But in casual conversation those individuals who performed this duty were referred to as mumiriri wemweya even when not "at work."

10. When I asked why only men are mumiriri, most apostolics said they did not know. Some hazarded the guess that men's voices are stronger.

11. The apostolics who did not give either of these explanations offered no alternatives; they just said they did not know what had been significant about it.

12. Hatcliffe is a high-density suburb of Harare, about 30 kilometers from Juranifiri Santa in Chitungwiza.

13. The debate over Galatians 2:16 centers on how ἐάν μή should be translated: either "a person is justified not by the works of the law *but* through faith in Jesus Christ" or "a person is justified not by the works of the law *unless* through faith in Jesus Christ" (Das 2000; see also Dunn 1990; Räisänen 1985). The latter translation significantly alters the meaning of the verse by leaving room for the law as a legitimate aspect of Christian practice.

14. The elder's interpretation would probably be considered unorthodox by most Christians. Paul's rejection of the law is not considered an outright rejection of Scripture. "There is scarcely a basic element of Christian teaching that Paul does not refer to scripture" (Gamble 1995, 212). In fact, Paul uses Scripture in Galatians to build his case against the law, albeit a case that many scholars find unconvincing (Das 2000, 538; Goulder 1997, 490). What is more, elsewhere (e.g., in Romans) Paul presents an argument based on knowledge of the law, although exactly which law he is referring to (the Jewish or the Roman) is unclear; see Tomson 2003.

SIX. SINGING AND THE METAPHYSICS OF SOUND

Epigraph: Ong 1967, 12.

1. The quotations from the archival record in this paragraph are drawn from NAZ file S318, in a set of documents collected by the Goromonzi native commissioner, covering the period between March 26 and December 5, 1934.

2. Werbner's important study of Tswapong divination provides a counterexample to this emphasis on sound. He argues that divination "has to be seen and felt" and that for much of the time "little or nothing need actually be said. Instead, a silent language of objects is used for the presentation from the occult of felt realities, for interpretation, and for reflection" (1989a, 19).

3. As Ranger (1999b) shows, this emphasis on sound can be traced as well to the regionally based Mwari cults; in Zimbabwe and other parts of southern Africa, Shona speakers are not unique in their sensual emphases.

4. I attended five *mapira* during the course of my fieldwork: three in Harare, one in Gweru, and one in Chiweshe. Two of the *mapira* in Harare were organized by Weegirl. Not surprisingly, there were differences at each—not only in terms of process, but also of procedure. Each, however, involved the extensive use of music to call an ancestral spirit.

5. According to Berliner (1978, 188), drums are sometimes used in lieu of the mbira.

6. Note that ancestral spirits are tied to the material world in which humans live; in the invisible realm of the ancestors, the senses still matter.

7. One reason apostolics might feel drawn to gospel music is the character of its lyrics, many of which support the apostolic project to break with the past. According to Ezra Chitando, "True Christians, [gospel singers] maintain in their music, are those who are no longer bound to indigenous spirituality" (2002, 64).

8. In his discussion of the "linguistics of the voice," Dolar offers an interesting set of observations relevant here: "What singles out the voice against the vast ocean of sounds and noises, what defines the voice as special among the infinite array of acoustic phenomena, is its inner relationship with meaning. No doubt we can ascribe meaning to all kinds of sounds, yet they seem to be deprived of it 'in themselves,' independent of our ascription, while the voice has an intimate connection with meaning, it is a sound which appears to be endowed in itself with the will to 'say something,' with an inner intentionality" (2006, 14). But while illuminating, this is, of course, illuminating primarily to the extent that it reflects an argument about signification; it is made coherent by a semiotic ideology. The Kaluli people, for example, might not accept these observations.

9. Berliner (1978, 24) and Chitando (2002, 22) both mention that Shona verbal arts have long included singing styles based on humming and yodeling.

10. Several of the terms I use to organize the three kinds of verses are borrowed loosely—very loosely—from descriptives for jazz. I am not making an argument here and do not intend to imply a point-for-point connection between the structures of jazz music and apostolic verses.

11. I only heard "Maboyi" at Juranifiri Santa, although members of other congregations told me that they knew how to sing it.

SEVEN. THE SUBSTANCE OF HEALING

1. See "Statement by Shoniwa to Native Detective Zakia," November 1, 1932, NAZ S 138/22.

2. See NAZ S 138/22.

3. Munjeri's interviews with Gombera were conducted on February 8 and May 3, 1979. The quotes in this paragraph are taken from the corresponding NAZ file, AOH/49.

4. Although it was never explicitly mentioned, it may be that some prophets forbid the men to carry staffs because spirit mediums use them too.

5. The fact that bamboo grows near rivers and streams is important to note; as I discuss in more detail later in this chapter, water is an important kind of muteuro, and things that are associated with water are often invested with a spiritual significance.

6. I am using the word *pebble* here because this is how the apostolics referred to them. Technically, however, not all the "pebbles" they used were in fact pebbles (rounded stones shaped by flowing water); some were chips of rock, and some were little crystalline bits. However, I could not discern a pattern to their use that reflected a conscious differentiation of material properties at this level of specificity.

7. This would not be the case in West Africa, where stones do in fact play an important role in religious therapeutics; see Jackson 1989, and see also Keane 1998 on the ritual use of stones in Sumba and Parmentier 1987 on their use in Belau. As Terence Ranger (1999b) has shown, rocks are integral to the southern African religious imagination but more in terms of what they tell us about space and place than in their materiality per se. Bengt Sundkler, as well, has written of the Zionist prophet John Mtanti who, in the mid-1920s, found holy stones in a river with which to build "the new Jerusalem": "They looked like ordinary stones to ordinary people, but Mtanti discovered a message in them, or rather *on* them" (1976, 125). The message was a linguistic one; each stone was marked by a letter of the Roman alphabet, to be deciphered as a source of biblical revelation. This case is again different from that of the apostolics. For Mtanti, only particular stones were of interest, and only because they charted a predetermined "supernatural drama" (Sundkler 1976, 135), which he was in effect reading like the New Testament.

8. The literary critic John Frow uses the example of the pebble to make a similar point about its objective insignificance. He cites a poem by Zbigniew Herbert that describes the pebble as "filled exactly / with a pebbly meaning" (quoted in Frow 2001, 271) to highlight the more general problem of representing "things" in literature. "This is the paradox of the key fascination with the thingness of things: that things posited in themselves, in their distinctness from intention, representation, figuration, or relation, are thereby filled with an imputed interiority and, in their very lack of meaning, with a 'pebbly meaning' which is at once full and inaccessible" (Frow 2001, 272).

9. Another kind of muteuro that are closely associated with water, and that reinforce the Judeo-Christian imagery, are reeds. At Juranifiri Santa the elders tended a patch of water reeds that were used in healing services for the protection of children. The reeds were not given to the children, but the children were asked to pass through the reed patch at certain times of the year, usually before school exams. This was said to "hide" the children from witches and vengeful spirits that might be looking to disrupt their academic progress. In explaining the importance of this muteuro, several apostolics drew attention to the story of Moses being hidden from the Pharaoh in the bulrushes as a baby in Exodus 3. This was never explicitly remarked on in the course of the ritual "hidings" but serves as another example of how Bible knowledge was incorporated into church life (see chapter 5).

10. See NAZ S 138/22.

1. In May 2002 the official exchange rate of the Zimbabwe dollar was locked at 55:1 to the U.S. dollar, making the bail approximately $181. Although this was a significant amount of money for the average Zimbabwean, it would have been easily met by Nzira, who had many financial "well-wishers" in his congregation.

2. Nzira's case was covered widely in the local media throughout the period of the trial. See, e.g., *Daily News,* May 7, 2002, "Nzira Charged with Nine Counts of Rape," by Sam Munyavi; *Herald,* October 15, 2002, "Nzira Warned against Interfering with Witnesses"; *Daily News,* March 18, 2003, "Nzira Supporters Run Amok," by Angela Makamure and Brian Mangwende; *Herald,* March 18, 2003, "Nzira Convicted of Rape, Followers Turn Violent"; *Zambezi Times* Online (http://dinarfiles.zambezitimes.com), March 27, 2003 (accessed July 30, 2004), "Nzira's Followers Brain-washed."

3. See *Daily News,* January 5, 2001, "Church Group Attacks Family."

4. See *Daily News,* January 8, 2001, "Man Dismisses Family Report against Faith Healer."

5. The details and citations in this paragraph are taken from the *Sunday Mail* article by Emilia Zindi, published on December 2, 2001, "Disturbances as Witch-Hunter Tsikamutanda Descends on Seke."

6. For two recent examples of how African Christians make the news when involved in scandals, see *Daily Telegraph* (London), January 13, 2006, "Pastor Is Arrested after Inquiry into Claims of Cruelty to 'Child Witches,'" by Caroline Davies; and *Sunday Times* (London), February 5, 2006, "Torment of Africa's 'Child Witches,'" by Richard Hoskins. For a more general critique of African churches, see the two-part television documentary *God Is Black,* hosted by the Birmingham-based theologian Robert Beckford, which aired on Channel 4 in the United Kingdom in June 2004.

REFERENCES

ARCHIVAL SOURCES

National Archives of Zimbabwe, Harare

FILE NO.   DESCRIPTION

AOH/4   Interview with Amon Nengomasha and Jack Dzvuke.
                Conducted by Dawson Munjeri, February 17, March 3, 1977.

AOH/49   Interview with Macheka Gombera. Conducted by Dawson
                Munjeri, February 3, 1979.

AOH/51   Interview with Pauros Mugwagwa Musonza. Conducted by
                Dawson Munjeri, March, 2, 8, 29, and April 18, 1979.

GO 4/1/1   "Gospel of God Church," Historical Records.

GO 4/2/1   "Gospel of God Church," Historical Records.

S 138/22   Criminal Investigation Division statements, 1931–33. 2 vols.

S 210   Criminal Record Book, District Court, Marandellas, 1932–33.

S 235/514   Annual Reports, Department of Native Affairs, 1935.

S 235/515   Annual Reports, Department of Native Affairs, 1936.

S 235/516   Annual Reports, Department of Native Affairs, 1938.

S 235/518   Annual Reports, Department of Native Affairs, 1946.

S 289   Criminal Record Book, Umtali, 1932.

S 318   Correspondence, Native Affairs, Goromonzi District, 1930–34.

S 546	Criminal Record Book, Hartley District, 1931–34.
S 1032	Correspondence, Department of Native Affairs, 1932–33.
S 1542/M8	File "Apostolic Faith Mission."
S 1542/M8B	File "Apostolic Faith Mission." 2 vols.
S 1542/P10	File "Pseudo-Religious Movements."
S 2824	"Korsten Basket Makers," 1957–62. 3 vols.
S 3276	"The Spirit Index." 3 vols.

NEWSPAPER SOURCES

Daily News (Zimbabwe)

June 21, 2000, "Church Sect Demands Apology from Gezi."
January 5, 2001, "Church Group Attacks Family."
January 8, 2001, "Man Dismisses Family Report against Faith Healer."
May 7, 2002, "Nzira Charged with Nine Counts of Rape."
March 18, 2003, "Nzira Supporters Run Amok."

Herald (Zimbabwe)

March 30, 1993, "Church to Set up $2.5m Centre for Disabled."
November 19, 1999, "Cholera Claims Six Johane Marange Sect Members."
October 15, 2002, "Nzira Warned against Interfering with Witnesses."
March 18, 2003, "Nzira Convicted of Rape, Followers Turn Violent."

Independent (Zimbabwe)

June 16, 2000, "ZANU(PF)'s Election Mascot Says He Is Not for Hire."

Sunday Mail (Zimbabwe)

December 2, 2001, "Disturbances as Witch-Hunter Tsikamutanda Descends on Seke."

Zambezi Times Online

http://dinarfiles.zambezitimes.com.
March 27, 2003, "Nzira's Followers Brain-washed." (Accessed July 30, 2004)

Daily Telegraph (London)

January 13, 2006, "Pastor Is Arrested after Inquiry into Claims of Cruelty to 'Child Witches.'"

Sunday Times (London)

February 5, 2006, "Torment of Africa's 'Child Witches.'"

SECONDARY SOURCES

Alexander, Jocelyn, JoAnn McGregor, and Terence Ranger. 2000. *Violence and Memory: One Hundred Years in the "Dark Forests" of Matabeleland.* Portsmouth, NH: Heinemann.

Allen, John. 1994. The Divine Imperative. In *The Rainbow People of God: The Making of a Peaceful Revolution,* by Desmond Tutu. New York: Image Doubleday.

Allen, Tim. 1991. Understanding Alice: Uganda's Holy Spirit Movement in Context. *Africa* 61(3): 370–99.

Alter, Robert. 1981. *The Art of Biblical Narrative.* New York: Basic Books.

Anderson, Benedict. 1991. *Imagined Communities: Reflections on the Origin and Spread of Nationalism.* New York: Verso.

Appiah, Kwame Anthony. 1992. Old Gods, New Worlds. In *In My Father's House: Africa in the Philosophy of Culture.* New York: Oxford University Press.

Asad, Talal. 1993. *Genealogies of Religion: Discipline and Reasons of Power in Christianity and Islam.* Baltimore: Johns Hopkins University Press.

———. 1996. Comments on Conversion. In *Conversion to Modernities: The Globalization of Christianity,* edited by Peter van der Veer. London: Routledge.

Ashforth, Adam. 2000. *Madumo: A Man Bewitched.* Chicago: University of Chicago Press.

———. 2005. *Witchcraft, Violence, and Democracy in South Africa.* Chicago: University of Chicago Press.

Aston, Margaret. 1988. *England's Iconoclasts: Laws against Images.* Vol. 1. Oxford: Clarendon Press.

Augustine of Hippo. 1997 [ca. 397]. *The Confessions.* Translated by Maria Boulding. New York: Vintage.

Axelsson, Olof E. 1974. Historical Notes on Neo-African Church Music. *Zambezia* 3(2): 89–102.

Banana, Canaan. 1990. The Role of the Church in the Struggle for Liberation in Zimbabwe. In *Turmoil and Tenacity: Zimbabwe 1890–1990,* edited by Canaan Banana. Harare: College Press.

————. 1993. The Case for a New Bible. In *"Rewriting" the Bible: The Real Issues,* edited by Isabel Mukonyora, James Cox, and Franz Verstraelen. Gweru, Zimbabwe: Mambo Press.

Barnes, Terri, and Everjoyce Winn. 1992. *To Live a Better Life: An Oral History of Women in the City of Harare, 1930–1979.* Harare: Baobab Books.

Barrett, David. 1968. *Schism and Renewal in Africa: An Analysis of Six Thousand Contemporary Religious Movements.* Nairobi: Oxford University Press.

Bashkow, Ira. 2000. "Whitemen" Are Good to Think With: How Orokaiva Morality Is Reflected on Whitemen's Skin. *Identities* 7(3): 281–332.

Bastian, Misty. 1993. "Bloodhounds Who Have No Friends": Witchcraft and Locality in the Nigerian Popular Press. In *Modernity and Its Malcontents: Ritual and Power in Postcolonial Africa,* edited by Jean Comaroff and John L. Comaroff. Chicago: University of Chicago Press.

Bauman, Richard. 1983. *Let Your Words be Few: Symbolism of Speaking and Silence among Seventeenth-Century Quakers.* Cambridge: Cambridge University Press.

Beck, Roger. 1997. Monarchs and Missionaries among the Tswana and Sotho. In *Christianity in South Africa: A Political, Social, and Cultural History,* edited by R. Elphick and R. Davenport. Oxford: James Currey.

Behrend, Heike. 1999. *Alice Lakwena and the Holy Spirits: War in Northern Uganda, 1986–1997.* Athens: Ohio University Press.

Beidelman, Thomas O. 1974. Social Theory and the Study of Christian Missionaries in Africa. *Africa* 44: 235–49.

————. 1981. Contradictons between the Sacred and the Secular Life: The Church Missionary Society in Ukaguru, Tanzania, East Africa, 1876–1914. *Comparative Studies in Society and History* 23(1): 73–95.

————. 1982. *Colonial Evangelism.* Bloomington: Indiana University Press.

Belting, Hans. 1994. *Likeness and Presence: A History of the Image before the Era of Art.* Chicago: University of Chicago Press.

Benjamin, Walter. 1968. The Task of the Translator: An Introduction to the Translation of Baudelaire's *Tableaux Parisiens.* In *Illuminations.* New York: Schocken Books.

Berliner, Paul. 1978. *The Soul of Mbira: Music and Traditions of the Shona People of Zimbabwe.* Berkeley: University of California Press.

Bernstein, Charles. 1998. Introduction. In *Close Listening: Poetry and the Performed Word,* edited by Charles Bernstein. Oxford: Oxford University Press.

Besnier, Niko. 1995. *Literacy, Emotion, and Authority: Reading and Writing on a Polynesian Atoll.* New York: Cambridge University Press.

Bessant, Leslie. 1994. Songs of Chiweshe and Songs of Zimbabwe. *African Affairs* 93: 43–73.

Bloch, Maurice. 1989 [1974]. Symbols, Song, Dance, and Features of Articulation: Is Religion an Extreme Form of Traditional Authority? In *Ritual, History, and Power: Selected Papers in Anthropology.* London: Athlone.

————. 1998 [1989]. Literacy and Enlightenment. In *How We Think They Think: Anthropological Approaches to Cognition, Memory, and Literacy.* Boulder: Westview.

Bloom, Harold. 1996. *Omens of Millennium: The Gnosis of Angels, Dreams, and Resurrection.* New York: Putnam.

Boddy, Janice. 1988. *Wombs and Alien Spirits: Women, Men, and the Zār Cult.* Madison: University of Wisconsin Press.

Bouquet, Mary. 1996. Family Trees and Their Affinities: The Visual Imperative of the Genealogical Diagram. *Journal of the Royal Anthropological Institute* 2(1): 43–66.

Bourdillon, Michael. 1987. *The Shona Peoples.* 3d ed. Gweru, Zimbabwe: Mambo Press.

Bourdillon, M. F. C., T. Mashita, and M. Glickman. 1977. Traditional Religion and an Independent Church. In *Christianity South of the Zambezi,* vol. 2, edited by M. F. C. Bourdillon. Gweru, Zimbabwe: Mambo Press.

Boyarin, Daniel. 1993. Placing Reading: Ancient Israel and Medieval Europe. In *The Ethnography of Reading,* edited by Jonathan Boyarin. Berkeley: University of California Press.

Boyarin, Jonathan. 1993a. Voices around the Text: The Ethnography of Reading at Mesivta Tifereth Jerusalem. In *The Ethnography of Reading,* edited by Jonathan Boyarin. Berkeley: University of California Press.

————, ed. 1993b. *The Ethnography of Reading.* Berkeley: University of California Press.

Bradlow, Frank. 1987. *Printing for Africa: The Story of Robert Moffat and the Kuruman Press.* Kuruman: Kuruman Moffat Misssion Trust.

Brown, Bill. 2001. Thing Theory. *Critical Inquiry* 28(1): 1–22.

Brown, Duncan. 1995. Orality and Christianity: The Hymns of Isaiah Shembe and the Church of the Nazarites. *Current Writing* 7(2): 69–96.

Brown, Peter. 1967. *Augustine of Hippo: A Biography.* London: Faber & Faber.

————. 1981. *The Cult of the Saints: Its Rise and Function in Latin Christianity.* Chicago: University of Chicago Press.

Bucholtz, Mary. 1999. "Why Be Normal?" Language and Identity Practices in a Community of Nerd Girls. *Language in Society* 28: 203–23.

Bultmann, Rudolf. 1956. *Primitive Christianity in Its Contemporary Setting.* Translated by R. H. Fuller. London: Thames and Hudson.

Burke, Timothy. 1996. *Lifebuoy Men, Lux Women: Commodification, Consumption, and Cleanliness in Modern Zimbabwe.* Durham, NC: Duke University Press.

Cameron, Averil. 1991. *Christianity and the Rhetoric of Empire: The Development of Christian Discourse.* Berkeley: University of California Press.

Cannell, Fenella. 1999. *Power and Intimacy in the Christian Philippines.* Cambridge: Cambridge University Press.

———. 2005. The Christianity of Anthropology. *Journal of the Royal Anthropological Institute* 11(2): 335–56.

———. 2006. Introduction: The Anthropology of Christianity. In *The Anthropology of Christianity*, edited by Fenella Cannell. Durham, NC: Duke University Press.

Chavanduka, Gordon. 1994. *Traditional Medicine in Zimbabwe*. Harare: University of Zimbabwe Press.

Chitando, Ezra. 2002a. "Down with the Devil, Forward with Christ!" A Study of the Interface between Religious and Political Discourses in Zimbabwe. *African Sociological Review* 6(1): 1–13.

———. 2002b. *Singing Culture: A Study of Gospel Music in Zimbabwe*. Uppsala: Nordiska Afrikainstitutet.

Cohn, Bernard. 1985. The Command of Language and the Language of Command. In *Subaltern Studies*, edited by Ranajit Guha. New Delhi: Oxford University Press.

Coleman, Simon. 2000. *The Globalization of Charismatic Christianity: Spreading the Gospel of Prosperity*. Cambridge: Cambridge University Press.

———. 2006. When Silence Isn't Golden: Charismatic Speech and the Limits of Literalism. In *The Limits of Meaning: Case Studies in the Anthropology of Christianity*, edited by Matthew Engelke and Matt Tomlinson. New York: Berghahn.

Comaroff, Jean. 1980. Healing and the Cultural Order: The Case of the Barolong boo Ratshidi. *American Ethnologist* 7(4): 637–57.

———. 1985. *Body of Power, Spirit of Resistance: The Culture and History of a South African People*. Chicago: University of Chicago Press.

Comaroff, John L., and Jean Comaroff. 1991. *Of Revelation and Revolution: Christianity, Colonialism, and Consciousness in South Africa*. Vol. 1. Chicago: University of Chicago Press.

———. 1997. *Of Revelation and Revolution: The Dialectics of Modernity on a South African Frontier*. Vol. 2. Chicago: University of Chicago Press.

Crapanzano, Vincent. 2000. *Serving the Word: Literalism in America from the Pulpit to the Bench*. New York: New Press.

Csordas, Thomas. 1997. *Language, Charisma, and Creativity: The Ritual Life of a Religious Movement*. Berkeley: University of California Press.

Daneel, Martinus. 1987. *Quest for Belonging*. Gweru, Zimbabwe: Mambo Press.

Das, Andrew. 2000. Another Look at ἐάν μή in Galatians 2:16. *Journal of Biblical Literature* 119(3): 529–39.

de Gruchy, John. 1996. The Transfiguration of Politics. In *Archbishop Tutu: Prophetic Witness in South Africa*, edited by L. Hulley, L. Kretzschmar, and L. L. Pato. Cape Town: Human and Rousseau.

———. 1999. Remembering a Legacy. In *The London Missionary Society in Southern Africa: Historical Essays in Celebration of the Bicentennial of the LMS in Southern Africa, 1799–1999*, edited by John de Gruchy. Cape Town: David Philip.

de Gruchy, Steve. 1999. The Alleged Political Conservatism of Robert Moffat. In *The London Missionary Society in Southern Africa: Historical Essays in Celebration of the Bicentenial of the LMS in Southern Africa, 1799–1999*, edited by John de Gruchy. Cape Town: David Philip.

Dening, Greg. 1996. *Performances*. Chicago: University of Chicago Press.

Derrida, Jacques. 1974. *Of Grammatology*. Translated by Gayatri Spivak. Baltimore: Johns Hopkins University Press.

Dillon-Malone, Clive. 1978. *The Korsten Basketmakers: A Study of the Masowe Apostles*. Manchester: Manchester University Press.

Dirks, Nicholas. 2002. Annals of the Archive: Ethnographic Notes on the Sources of History. In *From the Margins: Historical Anthropology and Its Futures*, edited by Brian Keith Axel. Durham, NC: Duke University Press.

Dolar, Mladen. 2006. *A Voice and Nothing More*. Cambridge, MA: MIT Press.

Dorman, Sara Rich. 2003. NGOs and the Constitutional Debate in Zimbabwe: From Inclusion to Exclusion. *Journal of Southern African Studies* 29(4): 845–64.

Draper, Jonathan. 1996. "Was there no-one left to give glory to God except this foreigner?" Breaking the Boundaries in Luke 17:11–19. In *Archbishop Tutu: Prophetic Witness in South Africa*, edited by L. Hulley, L. Kretzschmar, and L. L. Pato. Cape Town: Human and Rousseau.

Drucker, Johanna. 1994. *The Visible Word: Experimental Typography and Modern Art, 1909–1923*. Chicago: University of Chicago Press.

———. 1998. The Art of the Written Image. In *Figuring the Word: Essays on Books, Writing, and Visual Poetics*. New York: Granary Books.

Dunn, J. D. G. 1990. *Jesus, Paul, and the Law: Studies in Mark and Galatians*. Louisville: Westminster/John Knox.

Ela, Jean-Marc. 1994. Christianity and Liberation in Africa. In *Paths of African Theology*, edited by Rosino Gibellini. Maryknoll, NY: Orbis Books.

Emerson, Robert, Rachel Fretz, and Linda Shaw. 1995. *Writing Ethnographic Fieldnotes*. Chicago: University of Chicago Press.

Engelke, Matthew. 2000a. An Interview with Edith Turner. *Current Anthropology* 41(5): 843–52.

———. 2000b. The Politics of Plumbing: The Culture of Toilets in Religious Movement. Paper presented at the Britain-Zimbabwe Research Seminar, St. Antony's College, Oxford, June 3.

———. 2001. ZANU(PF), Magical Injections, and the Children of Ham: Politics and Race in an African Apostolic Church. Paper presented at the annual meeting of the American Ethnological Society, Montreal, Canada, May 6.

———. 2003. The Book, the Church, and the "Incomprehensible Paradox": Christianity in African History. *Journal of Southern African Studies* 29(1): 294–303.

———. 2004a. Discontinuity and the Discourse of Conversion. *Journal of Religion in Africa* 34(1–2): 82–109.

————. 2004b. "The Endless Conversation": Fieldwork, Writing, and the Marriage of Victor and Edith Turner. In *Significant Others: Interpersonal and Professional Commitments in Anthropology*, edited by Richard Handler. History of Anthropology, vol. 10. Madison: University of Wisconsin Press.

————. 2006. Clarity and Charisma: On the Uses of Ambiguity in Ritual Life. In *The Limits of Meaning: Case Studies in the Anthropology of Christianity*, edited by Matthew Engelke and Matt Tomlinson. New York: Berghahn.

Engelke, Matthew, and Matt Tomlinson, eds. 2006. *The Limits of Meaning: Case Studies in the Anthropology of Christianity*. New York: Berghahn.

Englund, Harri. 1996. Witchcraft, Modernity and the Person: The Morality of Accumulation in Central Malawi. *Critique of Anthropology* 16(2): 257–79.

Erlmann, Veit. 2004. But What of the Ethnographic Ear? Anthropology, Sound, and the Senses. In *Hearing Cultures: Essays on Sound, Listening and Modernity*, edited by Veit Erlmann. Oxford: Berg.

Etherington, Norman. 1977. Social Theory and the Study of Christian Missions in Africa: A South African Case Study. *Africa* 47(1): 31–40.

————. 1978. *Peasants, Preachers, and Politics in Southeast Africa, 1835–1880: African Christian Communities in Natal, Pondoland, and Zululand*. London: Royal Historical Society.

————. 1983. Missionaries and the Intellectual History of Africa: A Historical Survey. *Itinerario* 7(2): 116–43.

Evans-Pritchard, E. E. 1976. *Witchcraft, Oracles, and Magic among the Azande*. Abridged ed. Oxford: Clarendon Paperbacks.

Ewald, Janet. 1988. Speaking, Writing, and Authority: Explorations in and from the Kingdom of Taqali. *Comparative Studies in Society and History* 30(2): 199–224.

Fabian, Johannes. 1971. *Jamaa: A Charismatic Movement in Katanga*. Evanston, IL: Northwestern University Press.

————. 1979. The Anthropology of Religious Movements: From Explanation to Interpretation. *Social Research* 46(1): 4–35.

————. 1986. *Language and Colonial Power: The Appropriation of Swahili in the former Belgian Congo*. Berkeley: University of California Press.

————. 1990. *Power and Performance: Ethnographic Explorations through Proverbial Wisdom and Theater in Shaba, Zaire*. Madison: University of Wisconsin Press.

————. 1991a [1981]. Six Theses Regarding the Anthropology of African Religious Movements. In *Time and the Work of Anthropology: Critical Essays, 1971–1991*. Amsterdam: Harwood Academic Publishers.

————. 1991b [1979]. Text as Terror: Second Thoughts about Charisma. In *Time and the Work of Anthropology: Critical Essays, 1971–1991*. Amsterdam: Harwood Academic Publishers.

————. 1993. Keep Listening: Ethnography and Reading. In *The Ethnography of Reading,* edited by Jonathan Boyarin. Berkeley: University of California Press.

————. 1995. Ethnographic Misunderstanding and the Perils of Context. *American Anthropologist* 97(1): 41–50.

————. 2000. *Out of Our Minds: Reason and Madness in the Exploration of Central Africa.* Berkeley: University of California Press.

Febvre, Lucien. 1976. Preface. In *The Coming of the Book: The Impact of Printing, 1450–1800.* New York: Verso.

Feierman, Steven. 1999. Colonizers, Scholars, and the Creation of Invisible Histories. In *Beyond the Cultural Turn: New Directions in the Study of Society and Culture,* edited by Victoria Bonnell and Linda Hunt. Berkeley: University of California Press.

Feld, Steven. 1990 [1982]. *Sound and Sentiment: Birds, Weeping, Poetics, and Song in Kaluli Expression.* 2d ed. Philadelphia: University of Pennsylvania Press.

Fenn, Eric. 1963. The Bible and the Missionary. In *The Cambridge History of the Bible: The West from the Reformation to the Present Day,* edited by S. L. Greenslade. Cambridge: Cambridge University Press.

Fernandez, James. 1978. African Religious Movements. *Annual Review of Anthropology* 7: 195–234.

————. 1982. *Bwiti: An Ethnography of the Religious Imagination in Africa.* Princeton: Princeton University Press.

Fernandez, Renate, and David Sutton, eds. 1998. *In the Field and at Home: Families and Anthropology.* (Special issue of *Anthropology and Humanism* 23[2].) Arlington, VA: American Anthropological Association.

Fontein, Joost. 2004. "Traditional Connoisseurs" of the Past: The Ambiguity of Spirit Mediums and the Performance of the Past in Southern Zimbabwe. Working Paper of the Centre of African Studies, University of Edinburgh.

Frei, Hans. 1974. *The Eclipse of Biblical Narrative: A Study in Eighteenth- and Nineteenth-Century Hermeneutics.* New Haven: Yale University Press.

Frow, John. 2001. A Pebble, a Camera, a Man Who Turns into a Telegraph Pole. *Critical Inquiry* 28(1): 270–85.

Frye, Northrop. 1981. *The Great Code: The Bible and Literature.* New York: Harcourt Brace Jovanovich.

Fuller, C. J. 1988. Hinduism and Scriptural Authority in Modern Indian Law. *Comparative Studies in Society and History* 30(2): 225–51.

Gadamer, Hans-Georg. 1989 [1960]. *Truth and Method.* 2d ed. Revised translation by Joel Weinsheimer and Donald Marshall. New York: Continuum.

Gal, Susan. 1989. Language and Political Economy. *Annual Review of Anthropology* 18: 345–67.

Gamble, Harry Y. 1995. *Books and Readers in the Early Church: A History of Early Christian Texts.* New Haven: Yale University Press.

Garbett, Kingsley. 1969. Spirit Mediums as Mediators in Valley Kore Kore Society. In *Spirit Mediumship and Society in Africa,* edited by John Beattie and John Middleton. London: Routledge.

Geertz, Clifford. 1973. Religion as a Cultural System. In *The Interpretation of Cultures.* New York: Basic Books.

Gelfand, Michael, et al. 1985. *The Traditional Medical Practitioner in Zimbabwe: His Principles of Practice and Pharmacopoeia.* Gweru, Zimbabwe: Mambo Press.

Gell, Alfred. 1998. *Art and Agency: An Anthropological Theory.* Oxford: Oxford University Press.

Geschiere, Peter. 1997. *The Modernity of Witchcraft: Politics and the Occult in Postcolonial Africa.* Charlottesville: University Press of Virginia.

Geurts, Kathryn Linn. 2002. *Culture and the Senses: Bodily Ways of Knowing in an African Community.* Berkeley: University of California Press.

Gibellini, Rosino, ed. 1994. *Paths of African Theology.* Maryknoll, NY: Orbis Books.

Gilmont, Jean-François. 1999. Protestant Reformations and Reading. In *A History of Reading in the West,* edited by Guglielmo Cavallo and Roger Chartier. Cambridge: Polity Press.

Goffman, Erving. 1981. *Forms of Talk.* Oxford: Basil Blackwell.

Goody, Jack. 1977. *The Domestication of the Savage Mind.* New York: Cambridge University Press.

———. 1986. *The Logic of Writing and the Organization of Society.* Cambridge: Cambridge University Press.

Gottlieb, Alma. 1995. Beyond the Lonely Anthropologist: Collaboration in Research and Writing. *American Anthropologist* 97(1): 21–26.

Goulder, Michael. 1997. The Pauline Epistles. In *The Literary Guide to the Bible,* edited by Robert Alter and Frank Kermode. London: Fontana.

Green, Maia. 1995. Why Christianity Is the "Religion of Business": Perceptions of the Church among Pogoro Catholics in Southern Tanzania. *Journal of Religion in Africa* 25(1): 25–47.

———. 2003. *Priests, Witches, and Power: Popular Christianity after Mission in Southern Tanzania.* Cambridge: Cambridge University Press.

Gumperz, John. 1972. The Speech Community. In *Language and Social Context,* edited by Pier Paolo Giglioli. London: Penguin.

Gunner, Elizabeth. 1979. Songs of Innocence and Experience: Women as Composers and Performers of *Izibongo,* Zulu Praise Poetry. *Research in African Literatures* 10(2): 239–67.

———. 1988. Power House, Prison House: An Oral Genre and Its Use in Isaiah Shembe's Nazaretha Baptist Church. *Journal of Southern African Studies* 14(3): 204–27.

———. 2002. *The Man of Heaven and the Beautiful Ones of God: Writings from Ibandla lamaNazaretha, a South African Church.* Leiden: Brill.

Guss, David. 1986. Keeping It Oral: A Yekuana Ethnology. *American Ethnologist* 13(3): 413–29.

Hallencreutz, Carl. 1984. *Daring in Order to Know: Studies in Bengt Sundkler's Contribution as Africanist and Missionary Scholar.* Uppsala: Swedish Institute of Missionary Research.

———. 1999. Religion in the City. In *Sites of Struggle: Essays in Zimbabwe's Urban History,* edited by Brian Raftopoulos and Tsuneo Yoshikuni. Harare: Weaver Press.

Hammar, Amanda, Brian Raftopoulos, and Stig Jensen, eds. 2003. *Zimbabwe's Unfinished Business: Rethinking Land, State, and Nation in the Context of Crisis.* Harare: Weaver Press.

Hampl, Patricia. 1997. Preface. In *The Confessions.* New York: Vintage.

Hanciles, Jehu. 2002. *Euthanasia of a Mission: African Church Autonomy in a Colonial Context.* London: Praeger.

Handler, Richard. 1988. *Nationalism and the Politics of Culture in Quebec.* Madison: University of Wisconsin Press.

———, ed. 2004. *Significant Others: Interpersonal and Professional Commitments in Anthropology.* History of Anthropology, vol. 10. Madison: University of Wisconsin Press.

Hanks, William. 1996a. Exorcism and the Description of Participant Roles. In *Natural Histories of Discourse,* edited by Greg Urban and Michael Silverstein. Chicago: University of Chicago Press.

———. 1996b. *Language and Communicative Practices.* Boulder: Westview.

Harding, Susan. 2000. *The Book of Jerry Falwell: Fundamentalist Language and Politics.* Princeton: Princeton University Press.

Harries, Patrick. 2001. Missionaries, Marxists and Magic: Power and the Politics of Literacy in South-East Africa. *Journal of Southern African Studies* 27(3): 405–27.

Hastings, Adrian. 1976. *African Christianity: An Essay in Interpretation.* London: Geoffrey Chapman.

———. 1994. *The Church in Africa, 1450–1950.* Oxford: Clarendon Press.

Hau'ofa, Epeli. 1983. *Tales of the Tikongs.* Honolulu: University of Hawaii Press.

Heath, Shirley Brice. 1980. The Function and Uses of Literacy. *Journal of Communication* 30(1): 123–33.

Hegel, Georg Wilhelm Friedrich. 1985. *Lectures on the Philosophy of Religion: The Consummate Religion.* Vol. 3. Translated by R. F. Brown et al. Berkeley: University of California Press.

Hefner, Robert. 1993. Introduction: World Building and the Rationality of Conversion. In *Conversion to Christianity: Historical and Anthropological Perspectives on a Great Transformation,* edited by Robert Hefner. Berkeley: University of California Press.

Hodgson, Peter. 1985. Editorial Introduction. In *Lectures on the Philosophy of Religion: The Consummate Religion*, by Georg Wilhelm Friedrich Hegel. Vol. 3. Translated by R. F. Brown et al. Berkeley: University of California Press.

Hoehler-Fatton, Cynthia. 1996. *Women of Fire and Spirit: History, Faith, and Gender in Roho Religion in Western Kenya*. Oxford: Oxford University Press.

Hofmeyr, Isabel. 1994. *"We Spend Our Year as a Tale That Is Told": Oral Historical Narrative in a South African Chiefdom*. Portsmouth, NH: Heinemann.

———. 2004. *The Portable Bunyan: A Transnational History of "The Pilgrim's Progress."* Princeton: Princeton University Press.

Horton, Robin. 1967a. African Traditional Religion and Western Science. Part I. *Africa* 37(1): 50–71.

———. 1967b. African Traditional Religion and Western Science. Part II. *Africa* 37(2): 155–87.

———. 1975a. On the Rationality of Conversion. Part I. *Africa* 45(3): 219–35.

———. 1975b. On the Rationality of Conversion. Part II. *Africa* 45(4): 373–99.

Howe, Nicholas. 1993. The Cultural Construction of Reading in Anglo-Saxon England. In *The Ethnography of Reading*, edited by Jonathan Boyarin. Berkeley: University of California Press.

Howes, David. 2003. *Sensual Relations: Engaging the Senses in Culture and Social Theory*. Ann Arbor: University of Michigan Press.

Howsam, Leslie. 1991. *Cheap Bibles: Seventeenth-Century Publishing and the British and Foreign Bible Society*. Cambridge: Cambridge University Press.

Hymes, Dell. 1974a. *Foundations in Sociolinguistics: An Ethnographic Approach*. Philadelphia: University of Pennsylvania Press.

———. 1974b. Ways of Speaking. In *Explorations in the Ethnography of Speaking*, edited by Richard Bauman and Joel Sherzer. New York: Cambridge University Press.

Irvine, Judith T. 1979. Formality and Informality in Communicative Events. *American Anthropologist* 81(4): 773–90.

———. 1989. When Talk Isn't Cheap: Language and Political Economy. *American Ethnologist* 16(2): 248–67.

Irvine, Judith T., and Susan Gal. 2000. Language Ideology and Linguistic Differentiation. In *Regimes of Language: Ideologies, Polities, Identities*, edited by Paul Kroskrity. Oxford: James Currey.

Isichei, Elizabeth. 1995. *A History of Christianity in Africa*. Trenton, NJ: Africa World Press.

Jackson, Michael. 1989. *Paths toward a Clearing: Radical Empiricism and Ethnographic Inquiry*. Bloomington: Indiana University Press.

James, Deborah. 1999. *Songs of the Women Migrants: Performance and Identity in South Africa*. Edinburgh: Edinburgh University Press.

Janzen, John. 1978. *The Quest for Therapy in Lower Zaire*. Berkeley: University of California Press.

———. 1985. The Consequences of Literacy in African Religion: The Kongo Case. In *Theoretical Explorations in African Religion,* edited by Wim van Binsbergen and Matthew Schoffeleers. London: Kegan Paul International.

Janzen, John, and Steven Feierman, eds. 1992. *The Social Basis of Health and Healing in Africa.* Berkeley: University of California Press.

Jasper, David, and Stephen Prickett, eds. 1999. *The Bible and Literature: A Reader.* Oxford: Blackwell.

Jeater, Diana. 1993. *Marriage, Perversion, and Power: The Construction of Moral Discourse in Southern Rhodesia, 1894–1930.* Oxford: Oxford University Press.

Jules-Rosette, Bennetta. 1975. *African Apostles: Ritual and Conversion in the Church of John Maranke.* Ithaca, NY: Cornell University Press.

Kalilombe, Patrick A. 1994. Spirituality in the African Perspective. In *Paths of African Theology,* edited by Rosino Gibellini. Maryknoll, NY: Orbis Books.

Katz, David. 2004. *God's Last Words: Reading the English Bible from the Reformation to Fundamentalism.* New Haven: Yale University Press.

Keane, Webb. 1997a. Religious Language. *Annual Review of Anthropology* 26: 47–71.

———. 1997b. *Signs of Recognition: Power and Hazards of Representation in an Indonesian Society.* Berkeley: University of California Press.

———. 1998. Calvin in the Tropics: Objects and Subjects at the Religious Frontier. In *Border Fetishisms: Material Objects in Unstable Spaces,* edited by Patricia Spyer. London: Routledge.

———. 2001. Money Is No Object: Materiality, Desire, and Modernity in an Indonesian Society. In *The Empire of Things: Regimes of Value and Material Culture,* edited by Fred Myers. Oxford: James Currey.

———. 2003. Semiotics and the Social Analysis of Material Things. *Language and Communication* 23(2–3): 409–23.

———. 2005. Signs Are Not the Garb of Meaning: On the Social Analysis of Material Things. In *Materiality,* edited by Daniel Miller. Durham, NC: Duke University Press.

———. 2007. *Christian Moderns: Freedom and Fetish in the Mission Encounter.* Berkeley: University of California Press.

Keller, Eva. 2004. Towards Complete Clarity: Bible Study among Seventh-day Adventists in Madagascar. *Ethnos* 69(1): 89–112.

———. 2005. *The Road to Clarity: Seventh-day Adventism in Madagascar.* New York: Palgrave.

Kiernan, James. 1990. African and Christian: From Opposition to Mutual Accommodation. In *Christianity amidst Apartheid: Selected Perspectives on the Church in South Africa,* edited by Martin Prozesky. London: Macmillan.

———. 1992a. The Herder and the Rustler: Deciphering the Affinity between Zulu Diviner and Zulu Prophet. *African Studies* 51(2): 231–42.

———. 1992b. The Ritual Looking Glass: An Analysis of the Girl's Puberty Ceremony in the Nazareth Church of Isaiah Shembe. *Journal of the Study of Religion* 5(1): 17–30.

Kileff, Clive, and Margaret Kileff. 1979. The Masowe Vapostori of Seki. In *New Religions of Africa,* edited by Bennetta Jules-Rosette. Norwood: Ablex.

Kipp, Rita Smith. 1995. Conversion by Affiliation: The History of the Karo Batak Protestant Church. *American Ethnologist* 22(4): 868–82.

Kirsch, Thomas. 2002. Performance and the Negotiation of Charismatic Identity in an African Indigenous Church in Zambia. *Paideuma* 48: 57–76.

———. 2004. Restaging the Will to Believe: Religious Pluralism, Anti-Syncretism, and the Problem of Belief. *American Anthropologist* 106(4): 699–709.

Koerner, Joseph. 2002. The Icon as Iconoclash. In *Iconoclash: Beyond the Image Wars in Science, Religion, and Art,* edited by Bruno Latour and Peter Weibel. Cambridge, MA: MIT Press.

Kriger, Norma. 1992. *Zimbabwe's Guerrilla War: Peasant Voices.* New York: Cambridge University Press.

Kuipers, Joel. 1990. *Power in Performance: The Creation of Textual Authority in Weyewa Ritual Speech.* Philadelphia: University of Pennsylvania Press.

Lambek, Michael. 1981. *Human Spirits: A Cultural Account of Trance in Mayotte.* New York: Cambridge University Press.

———. 1990. Certain Knowledge, Contestable Authority: Power and Practice on the Islamic Periphery. *American Ethnologist* 17(1): 23–40.

———. 1993. *Knowledge and Practice in Mayotte: Local Discourses of Islam, Sorcery, and Spirit Possession.* Toronto: University of Toronto Press.

———. 1995. Choking on the Quran: And Other Consuming Parables from the Western Indian Ocean Front. In *The Pursuit of Certainty: Religions and Cultural Formulations,* edited by Wendy James. London: Routledge.

Lan, David. 1985. *Guns and Rain: Guerrillas and Spirit Mediums in Zimbabwe.* Berkeley: University of California Press.

Last, Murray. 1992. The Importance of Knowing about Not Knowing: Observations from Hausaland. In *The Social Basis of Health and Healing in Africa,* edited by Steven Feierman and John Janzen. Berkeley: University of California Press.

Latour, Bruno. 1993. *We Have Never Been Modern.* Translated by Catherine Porter. Cambridge, MA: Harvard University Press.

Lave, Jean, and Etienne Wenger. 1991. *Situated Learning: Legitimate Peripheral Participation.* Cambridge: Cambridge University Press.

Leach, Edmund. 1969. *Genesis as Myth and Other Essays.* London: Cape.

Lessing, Doris. 1994. *Under My Skin: Volume One of My Autobiography, to 1949.* London: Flamingo.

Liszka, James Jacób. 1996. *A General Introduction to the Semeiotic of Charles Sanders Peirce.* Bloomington: Indiana University Press.

Luedke, Tracy, and Harry West, eds. 2005. *Borders and Healers: Brokering Therapeutic Resources in Southeast Africa*. Bloomington: Indiana University Press.

Luhrmann, Tanya. 2004. Metakinesis: How God Becomes Intimate in Contemporary U.S. Christianity. *American Anthropologist* 106(3): 518–28.

Malinowski, Bronislaw. 1965 [1935]. *Coral Gardens and Their Magic*. Vol. 2. Bloomington: Indiana University Press.

Mamdani, Mahmood. 2001. *When Victims Become Killers: Colonialism, Nativism, and the Genocide in Rwanda*. Princeton: Princeton University Press.

Mawerera, Ray. 1987a. Can This Man Be the Son of God? *Parade*, June 6–8.

———. 1987b. A Judas in the Court of "Christ." *Parade*, July 17–18.

Maxwell, David. 1998. Delivered from the Spirit of Poverty? Pentecostalism, Prosperity, and Modernity in Zimbabwe. *Journal of Religion in Africa* 28(3): 350–73.

———. 1999a. *Christians and Chiefs in Zimbabwe: A Social History of the Hwesa People, c. 1870s–1990s*. Edinburgh: Edinburgh University Press.

———. 1999b. Historicizing Christian Independency: The Southern African Pentecostal Movement, c. 1908–1960. *Journal of African History* 39(2): 243–64.

———. 2001. "Sacred History, Social History": Traditions and Texts in the Making of a Southern African Transnational Religious Movement. *Comparative Studies in Society and History* 43(3): 502–24.

Mbiti, John. 1994. The Bible in African Culture. In *Paths of African Theology*, edited by Rosino Gibellini. Maryknoll, NY: Orbis Books.

McDannell, Colleen. 1995. *Material Christianity: Religion and Popular Culture in America*. New Haven: Yale University Press.

McGann, Jerome. 1991. *The Textual Condition*. Princeton: Princeton University Press.

———. 1993. *Black Riders: The Visible Language of Modernism*. Princeton: Princeton University Press.

McLuhan, Marshall. 1962. *The Gutenberg Galaxy: The Making of Typographic Man*. New York: Signet Books.

Melber, Henning, ed. 2002. *Zimbabwe's Presidential Elections 2002: Evidence, Lessons, and Implications*. Uppsala: Nordiska Afrikainstitutet.

Merdinger, Jane. 1997. *Rome and the African Church in the Time of Augustine*. New Haven: Yale University Press.

Meredith, Martin. 2002. *Our Votes, Our Guns: Robert Mugabe and the Tragedy of Zimbabwe*. New York: Public Affairs.

Meyer, Birgit. 1998. "Make a Complete Break with the Past": Memory and Post-Colonial Modernity in Ghanaian Discourse. *Journal of Religion in Africa* 28(3): 316–49.

———. 1999. *Translating the Devil: Religion and Modernity among the Ewe in Ghana*. Trenton: Africa World Press.

————. 2004. Christianity in Africa: From African Independent to Pentecostal-Charismatic Churches. *Annual Review of Anthropology* 33: 447–74.

Mignolo, Walter. 1994. Signs and Their Transmission: The Question of the Book in the New World. In *Writing without Words: Alternative Literacies in Mesoamerica and the New World,* edited by Elizabeth Hill Boone and Walter Mignolo. Durham, NC: Duke University Press.

Milbank, John. 1997a. The Linguistic Turn as Theological Turn. In *The Word Made Strange: Theology, Language, Culture.* Oxford: Blackwell.

————. 1997b. The Second Difference. In *The Word Made Strange: Theology, Language, Culture.* Oxford: Blackwell.

Miller, Daniel. 1987. *Material Culture and Mass Consumption.* Oxford: Blackwell.

————. 2005a. Introduction: Materiality. In *Materiality,* edited by Daniel Miller. Durham, NC: Duke University Press.

————, ed. 2005b. *Materiality.* Durham, NC: Duke University Press.

Miller, Joseph. 1999. History and Africa / Africa and History. *American Historical Review* 104(1): 1–32.

Moffat, Robert. 1842. *Missionary Labours and Scenes in Southern Africa.* London: John Snow.

————. 1945a. *The Matabele Journals of Robert Moffat.* Vol. 1. Edited by J. P. R. Wallis. London: Chatto & Windus.

————. 1945b. *The Matabele Journals of Robert Moffat.* Vol. 2. Edited by J. P. R. Wallis. London: Chatto & Windus.

Mofokeng, Takatso. 1988. Black Christians, the Bible, and Liberation. *Journal of Black Theology* 2: 34–42.

Moore, Henrietta, and Todd Sanders. 2001. Magical Interpretations and Material Realities: An Introduction. In *Magical Interpretations, Material Realities: Modernity, Witchcraft, and the Occult in Postcolonial Africa,* edited by Henrietta Moore and Todd Sanders. New York: Routledge.

Morrison, J. H. 1969. *The Missionary Heroes of Africa.* New York: Negro Universities Press.

Mudimbe, V. Y. 1988. *The Invention of Africa: Gnosis, Philosophy, and the Order of Knowledge.* Bloomington: Indiana University Press.

Mukonyora, Isabel. 1998a. The Complementarity of Male and Female Imagery in Theological Language: A Study of the Valentinian and Masowe Theological Systems. Ph.D. diss., Faculty of Theology, University of Oxford.

————. 1998b. The Dramatization of Life and Death by Johane Masowe. *Zambezia* 25(2): 191–207.

————. 2000. Marginality and Protest in the Wilderness: The Role of Women in Shaping Masowe Thought Pattern. *Southern African Feminist Review* 4(2): 1–22.

Mukonyora, Isabel, James Cox, and Franz Verstraelen, eds. 1993. *"Rewriting" the Bible: The Real Issues.* Gweru, Zimbabwe: Mambo Press.

Muller, Carol Ann. 1997. "Written" into the Book of Life: Nazarite Women's Performance Inscribed as Physical Text in *Ibandla lamaNazareta. Research in African Literatures* 27(1): 3–14.

———. 1999. *Rituals of Fertility and the Sacrifice of Desire: Nazarite Women's Performance in South Africa.* Chicago: University of Chicago Press.

Munn, Nancy. 1986. *The Fame of Gawa: A Symbolic Study of Value Transformation in a Massim (Papua New Guinea) Society.* Cambridge: Cambridge University Press.

Murphree, Marshall. 1969. *Christianity and the Shona.* London: Athlone.

Myers, Fred. 2005. Some Properties of Art and Culture: Ontologies of the Image and Economies of Exchange. In *Materiality,* edited by Daniel Miller. Durham, NC: Duke University Press.

———, ed. 2001. *The Empire of Things: Regimes of Value and Material Culture.* Oxford: James Currey.

Ngũgĩ wa Thiong'o. 1986. *Decolonizing the Mind.* London: Heinemann.

Ong, Walter. 1967. *The Presence of the Word.* New Haven: Yale University Press.

Orsi, Robert. 2005. *Between Heaven and Earth: Religious Worlds People Make and the Scholars Who Study Them.* Princeton: Princeton University Press.

Owen, John. 1817. *The History and Origin of the First Ten Years of the British and Foreign Bible Society.* New York: James Eastburn & Co.

Palmer, Robin. 1977. *Land and Racial Domination in Rhodesia.* London: Heinemann.

Pape, John. 1999. *Chimurenga* in the *kia:* Domestic Workers and the Liberation Struggle in Zimbabwe. In *Sites of Struggle: Essays in Zimbabwe's Urban History,* edited by Brian Raftopoulos and Tsuneo Yoshikuni. Harare: Weaver Press.

Parmentier, Richard. 1987. *The Sacred Remains: Myth, History, and Polity in Belau.* Chicago: University of Chicago Press.

———. 1994. *Signs in Society: Studies in Semiotic Anthropology.* Bloomington: Indiana University Press.

———. 1997. *The Pragmatic Semiotics of Cultures.* (Special issue of *Semiotica* 106[1].) Berlin: Mouton de Gruyter.

Parry, Jonathan. 1986. The Brahmanical Tradition and the Technology of the Intellect. In *Reason and Morality,* edited by Joanna Overing. London: Tavistock.

Parry, Richard. 1999. Culture, Organization, and Class: The African Experience in Salisbury, 1892–1935. In *Sites of Struggle: Essays in Zimbabwe's Urban History,* edited by Brian Raftopoulous and Tsuneo Yoshikuni. Harare: Weaver Press.

Paul, Garrett E. 1991. Preface to the Translation. In *The Christian Faith,* by Ernst Troeltsch. Minneapolis: Fortress Press.

Peek, Philip. 1994. The Sounds of Silence: Cross-World Communication and the Auditory Arts in African Societies. *American Ethnologist* 21(3): 474–94.

Peel, J. D. Y. 1995. For Who Hath Despised the Day of Small Things? Missionary Narratives and Historical Anthropology. *Comparative Studies in Society and History* 37(3): 581–607.

———. 2000. *Religious Encounter and the Making of the Yoruba*. Bloomington: Indiana University Press.

Peirce, Charles Sanders. 1955. *Philosophical Writings of Peirce*. Selected and edited by Justus Buchler. New York: Dover.

Pels, Peter. 1999. *A Politics of Presence: Contacts between Missionaries and Waluguru in Late Colonial Tanganyika*. Amsterdam: Harwood Academic Publishers.

Phillips, John. 1973. *The Reformation of Images: Destruction of Art in England, 1535–1660*. Berkeley: University of California Press.

Pieterse, Hendrik J. C., ed. 2001. *Desmond Tutu's Message: A Qualitative Analysis*. Leiden: Brill.

Pitkin, Hanna Fenichel. 1967. *The Concept of Representation*. Berkeley: University of California Press.

Placido, Barbara. 2001 "It's All to Do with Words": An Analysis of Spirit Possession in the Venezuelan Cult of María Lionza. *Journal of the Royal Anthropological Institute* 7(2): 207–24.

Potts, Deborah. 2006. Restoring Order? The Interrelationships between Operation *Murambatsvina* in Zimbabwe and Urban Poverty, Informal Housing, and Employment. *Journal of Southern African Studies* 32(2): 273–91.

Raftopoulous, Brian. 1999. Nationalism and Labour in Salisbury, 1953–1965. In *Sites of Struggle: Essays in Zimbabwe's Urban History*, edited by Brian Raftopoulos and Tsuneo Yoshikuni. Harare: Weaver Press.

Raftopoulous, Brian, and Tsuneo Yoshikuni, eds. 1999. *Sites of Struggle: Essays in Zimbabwe's Urban History*. Harare: Weaver Press.

Räisänen, H. 1985. Galatians 2:16 and Paul's Break with Judaism. *New Testament Studies* 31: 543–53.

Ranger, Terence. 1970. *The African Voice in Southern Rhodesia, 1898–1930*. London: Heinemann.

———. 1981. Poverty and Prophetism: Religious Movements in Makoni District, 1929–1940. Paper read at the School of Oriental and African Studies, University of London.

———. 1982a. The Death of Chaminuka: Spirit Mediums, Nationalism, and the Guerrilla War in Zimbabwe. *African Affairs* 81: 349–69.

———. 1982b. Medical Science and Pentecost: The Dilemma of Anglicanism in Africa. In *The Church and Healing*, edited by W. J. Shiels. Oxford: Basil Blackwell.

———. 1985. *Peasant Consciousness and Guerrilla War in Zimbabwe*. London: James Currey.

———. 1986. Religious Movements and Politics in Sub-Saharan Africa. *African Studies Review* 29(2): 1–69.

———. 1987. Taking Hold of the Land: Holy Places and Pilgrimage in Twentieth-Century Zimbabwe. *Past and Present* 117: 158–94.

———. 1991. Missionaries, Migrants, and the Manyika: The Invention of Ethnicity in Zimbabwe. In *The Creation of Tribalism in Southern Africa,* edited by Leroy Vail. Berkeley: University of California Press.

———. 1999a. "Taking on the Missionary's Task": African Spirituality and the Mission Churches of Manicaland in the 1930s. *Journal of Religion in Africa* 29(2): 175–205.

———. 1999b. *Voices from the Rocks: Nature, Culture and History in the Matopos Hills of Zimbabwe.* Bloomington: Indiana University Press.

———. 2002. The Zimbabwe Elections: A Personal Experience. Paper read at the Oxford Centre for Mission Studies, March 19.

Ray, Benjamin C. 1993. Aladura Christianity: A Yoruba Religion. *Journal of Religion in Africa* 23(3): 266–91.

Reynolds, Pamela. 1996. *Traditional Healers and Childhood in Zimbabwe.* Athens: Ohio University Press.

Ricoeur, Paul. 1998. Thinking Creation. In *Thinking Biblically: Exegetical and Hermeneutical Studies,* by André LaCocque and Paul Ricoeur. Translated by David Pellauer. Chicago: University of Chicago Press.

Robbins, Joel. 2001. "God Is Nothing but Talk": Modernity, Language, and Prayer in a Papua New Guinea Society. *American Anthropologist* 103(4): 901–12.

———. 2003a. On the Paradoxes of Global Pentecostalism and the Perils of Continuity Thinking. *Religion* 33: 221–31.

———. 2003b. What Is a Christian? Notes toward an Anthropology of Christianity. *Religion* 33: 191–99.

———. 2004. *Becoming Sinners: Christianity and Moral Torment in a Papua New Guinea Society.* Berkeley: University of California Press.

Rowlands, Michael. 2005. A Materialist Approach to Materiality. In *Materiality,* edited by Daniel Miller. Durham, NC: Duke University Press.

Rutherford, Blair. 1999. To Find an African Witch: Anthropology, Modernity, and Witch-Finding in Northwest Zimbabwe. *Critique of Anthropology* 19(1): 89–109.

———. 2001. *Working on the Margins: Black Workers, White Farmers in Postcolonial Zimbabwe.* London: Zed Books.

———. 2004. Desired Publics, Domestic Government, and Entangled Fears: On the Anthropology of Civil Society, Farm Workers, and White Farmers in Zimbabwe. *Cultural Anthropology* 19(1): 122–53.

Rutherford, Danilyn. 2000. "The White Edge of the Margin": Textuality and Authority in Biak, Irian Jaya, Indonesia. *American Ethnologist* 27(2): 312–39.

———. 2006. The Bible Meets the Idol: Writing and Conversion in Biak, Irian Jaya, Indonesia. In *The Anthropology of Christianity,* edited by Fenella Cannell. Durham, NC: Duke University Press.

Sanneh, Lamin. 1989. *Translating the Message: The Missionary Impact on Culture.* Maryknoll, NY: Orbis Books.

———. 1994. Translatability in Islam and in Christianity in Africa. In *Religion in Africa: Experience and Expression,* edited by Thomas Blakeley. Portsmouth, NH: Heinemann.

Saunders, Christopher. 1999. Looking Back: 170 Years of Historical Writing on the LMS in South Africa. In *The London Missionary Society in Southern Africa: Historical Essays in Celebration of the Bicentenary of the LMS in Southern Africa, 1799–1999,* edited by John de Gruchy. Cape Town: David Philip.

Saussure, Ferdinand de. 1983. *Course in General Linguistics.* Translated by Roy Harris. LaSalle, IL: Open Court.

Schapera, Isaac. 1940. *Married Life in an African Tribe.* London: Penguin.

Schieffelin, Bambi. 1996. Creating Evidence: Making Sense of Written Words in Bosavi. In *Interaction and Grammar,* edited by Elinor Ochs, Emanuel Schegloff, and Sandra Thompson. New York: Cambridge University Press.

———. 2000. Introducing Kaluli Literacy. In *Regimes of Language: Ideologies, Polities, and Identities,* edited by Paul Kroskrity. Oxford: James Currey.

Schleiermacher, Friedrich. 1958 [1799]. *On Religion: Speeches to Its Cultured Despisers.* Translated by J. Oman. New York: Harper & Row.

———. 1977 [1805–33]. *Hermeneutics: The Handwritten Manuscripts.* Translated by J. Duke and J. Forstman. Edited by H. Kimmerle. Atlanta: Scholars Press.

Schoffeleers, Matthew. 1991. Ritual Healing and Political Acquiescence: The Case of the Zionist Churches in Southern Africa. *Africa* 60(1): 1–25.

Schousboe, Karen, and Mogens Trolle Larsen, eds. 1989. *Literacy and Society.* Copenhagen: Akademisk Forlag.

Schylter, Ann. 2003. *Multi-habitation: Urban Housing and Everyday Life in Chitungwiza, Zimbabwe.* Uppsala: Nordiska Afrikainstitutet.

Scott, Michael W. 2005. "I Was Like Abraham": Notes on the Anthropology of Christianity from Solomon Islands. *Ethnos* 79(1): 101–25.

Scribner, Sylvia, and Michael Cole 1981. *The Psychology of Literacy.* Cambridge, MA: Harvard University Press.

Shenk, Wilbert. 1983. *Henry Venn: Missionary and Statesman.* Maryknoll, NY: Orbis Books.

Shoaps, Robin. 2002. "Pray Earnestly": The Textual Construction of Personal Involvement in Pentecostal Prayer and Song. *Journal of Linguistic Anthropology* 12(1): 1–38.

Silverstein, Michael. 1976. Shifters, Verbal Categories, and Cultural Description. In *Meaning in Anthropology,* edited by Keith Basso and Henry Selby. Albuquerque: University of New Mexico Press.

————. 1979. Language Structure and Linguistic Ideology. In *The Elements: A Parasession on Linguistic Units and Levels*, edited by Paul Clyne, William Hanks, and Carol Hofbauer. Chicago: Chicago Linguistic Society.

————. 2003. *Talking Politics: The Substance of Style from Abe to "W."* Chicago: Prickly Paradigm Press.

Spierenberg, Marja. 2004. *Strangers, Spirits, and Land Reforms: Conflicts about Land in Dande, Northern Zimbabwe.* Leiden: Brill.

Stanley, Brian. 1990. *The Bible and the Flag: Protestant Missions and British Imperialism in the Nineteenth and Twentieth Centuries.* Leicester: Apollos.

Stock, Brian. 1990. *Listening for the Text: On the Uses of the Past.* Philadelphia: University of Pennsylvania Press.

————. 1996. *Augustine the Reader: Meditation, Self-Knowledge, and the Ethics of Interpretation.* Cambridge, MA: Harvard University Press.

Stoller, Paul. 1984. Sound in Songhay Cultural Experience. *American Ethnologist* 11(3): 559–70.

————. 1997. *Sensuous Scholarship.* Philadelphia: University of Pennsylvania Press.

Street, Brian. 1984. *Literacy in Theory and Practice.* New York: Cambridge University Press.

Sugirtharajah, R. S. 2001. *The Bible and the Third World: Precolonial, Colonial, and Postcolonial Encounters.* New York: Cambridge University Press.

Summers, Carol. 2002. *Colonial Lessons: Africans' Education in Southern Rhodesia, 1918–1940.* Oxford: James Currey.

Sundkler, Bengt. 1961 [1948]. *Bantu Prophets in South Africa.* 2d ed. Oxford: Oxford University Press.

————. 1976. *Zulu Zion and Some Swazi Zionists.* London: Oxford University Press.

Tambiah, S. J. 1968. The Magical Power of Words. *Man*, n.s., 3(2): 175–208.

————. 1981. A Performative Approach to Ritual. In *Proceedings of the British Academy for 1979.* London: Oxford University Press.

————. 1984. *The Buddhist Saints of the Forest and the Cult of the Amulets.* New York: Cambridge University Press.

Taylor, Christopher. 1992. *Milk, Honey, and Money: Changing Concepts in Rwandan Healing.* Washington, DC: Smithsonian Institution Press.

————. 1999. *Sacrifice as Terror: The Rwandan Genocide of 1994.* Oxford: Berg.

Thomas, Nicholas. 1991. *Entangled Objects: Exchange, Material Culture, and Colonialism in the Pacific.* Cambridge, MA: Harvard University Press.

Tomson, Peter. 2003. What Did Paul Mean by "Those Who Know the Law" (Rom. 7.1)? *New Testament Studies* 49: 573–81.

Tracy, David. 1981. *The Analogical Imagination: Christian Theology and the Culture of Pluralism.* London: SCM Press.

Troeltsch, Ernst. 1991 [1925]. *The Christian Faith*. Translated by Garrett E. Paul. Minneapolis: Fortress Press.

Turino, Thomas. 2000. *Nationalists, Cosmopolitans, and Popular Music in Zimbabwe*. Chicago: University of Chicago Press.

Turner, Edith. 1992. *Experiencing Ritual: A New Interpretation of African Healing*. Philadelphia: University of Pennsylvania Press.

Turner, Victor. 1961. *Chihamba, the White Spirit: A Ritual Drama of the Ndembu*. Manchester: Manchester University Press.

———. 1967a. Betwixt and Between: The Liminal Period in *Rites de Passage*. In *The Forest of Symbols: Aspects of Ndembu Ritual*. Ithaca, NY: Cornell University Press.

———. 1967b. Mukanda: The Rite of Circumcision. In *The Forest of Symbols: Aspects of Ndembu Ritual*. Ithaca, NY: Cornell University Press.

———. 1968a. *The Drums of Affliction*. Oxford: Oxford University Press.

———. 1968b. The Waters of Life: Some Reflections on Zionist Water Symbolism. In *Religions in Antiquity: Essays in Memory of Erwin Ramsdell Goodenough*, edited by Jacob Neusner. Leiden: Brill.

———. 1969. *The Ritual Process: Structure and Anti-Structure*. Ithaca, NY: Cornell University Press.

Tutu, Desmond. 1982. *Crying in the Wilderness: The Struggle for Justice in South Africa*. London: Mowbray.

———. 1983. *Hope and Suffering: Sermons and Speeches*. Johannesburg: Skotaville Publishers.

———. 1994. *The Rainbow People of God: The Making of a Peaceful Revolution.* New York: Image Doubleday.

Ukpong, Justin. 2000. Popular Readings of the Bible and Implications for Academic Readings. In *The Bible in Africa*, edited by Gerald West and Musa Dube. Leiden: Brill.

Vail, Leroy, and Landeg White. 1991. "Maps of Experience": Songs and Poetry in Southern Africa. In *Power and the Praise Poem: Southern African Voices in History*. Charlottesville: University Press of Virginia.

van Onselen, Charles. 1982. *Studies in the Social and Economic History of the Witwatersrand, 1886–1914*. Vol. 1. New York: Longman.

Venn, Henry. 1971. *To Apply the Gospel: Selections from the Writings of Henry Venn*. Edited by M. Warren. Grand Rapids, MI: Eerdmans.

Wacker, Grant. 2001. *Heaven Below: Early Pentecostals and American Culture*. Cambridge, MA: Harvard University Press.

Wagner, Roy. 1981. *The Invention of Culture*. Rev. ed. Chicago: University of Chicago Press.

Weiss, Paul, and Arthur Burks. 1945. Peirce's Sixty-six Signs. *Journal of Philosophy* 42(14): 383–88.

Werbner, Richard. 1985. The Argument of Images: Zion to the Wilderness. In *Theoretical Explorations in African Religion*, edited by Wim van Binsbergen and Matthew Schoffeleers. London: Kegan Paul International.

———. 1989a. Regional Cult of God Above: Achieving and Defending the Macrocosm. In *Ritual Passage, Sacred Journey: The Process and Organization of Religious Movement*. Washington, DC: Smithsonian Institution Press.

———. 1989b. Tswapong Wisdom Divination: Making the Hidden Seen. In *Ritual Passage, Sacred Journey: The Process and Organization of Religious Movement*. Washington, DC: Smithsonian Institution Press.

———. 1998. Beyond Oblivion: Confronting Memory Crisis. In *Memory and the Postcolony: African Anthropology and the Critique of Power*, edited by Richard Werbner. London: Zed Books.

West, Gerald. 2000. Mapping African Biblical Interpretation: A Tentative Sketch. In *The Bible in Africa*, edited by Gerald West and Musa Dube. Leiden: Brill.

West, Gerald, and Musa Dube, eds. 2000. *The Bible in Africa: Transactions, Trajectories, and Trends*. Leiden: Brill.

West, Harry. 2001. Sorcery of Construction and Socialist Modernization: Ways of Understanding Power in Postcolonial Mozambique. *American Ethnologist* 28(1): 119–50.

———. 2003. "Who Rules Us Now?" Identity Tokens, Sorcery, and Other Metaphors in the 1994 Mozambican Elections. In *Transparency and Conspiracy: Ethnographies of Suspicion in the New World Order*, edited by Harry West and Todd Sanders. Durham, NC: Duke University Press.

———. 2005. *Kupilikula: Governance and the Invisible Realm in Mozambique*. Chicago: University of Chicago Press.

West, Michael. 2002. *The Rise and Fall of an African Middle Class: Colonial Zimbabwe, 1898–1965*. Bloomington: Indiana University Press.

White, Landeg. 1987. *Magomero: Portrait of an African Village*. New York: Cambridge University Press.

Wiener, Annette, and Jane Schneider, eds. 1989. *Cloth and Human Experience*. Washington, DC: Smithsonian Institution Press.

Williams, C. Peter. 1990. *The Ideal of the Self-Governing Church: A Study in Victorian Missionary Strategy*. Leiden: Brill.

———. 2000. "Not Transplanting": Henry Venn's Strategic Vision. In *The Church Mission Society and World Christianity, 1799–1999*, edited by Kevin Ward and Brian Stanley. Richmond, U.K.: Curzon Press.

INDEX

Italicized page numbers refer to illustrations.

Bulawayo group, 118–19, 129, 215, 236–37
Bullock, Charles, 100–101
Bunyan, John, 256n6
Burke, Timothy, 259–60n3

Cameron, Averil, 172–73
Campbell, Melvin, 83
Campbell, Reverend, 92
car accidents, 149–50
Carbutt, C. L., 80, 102
Carlyle, J. D., 51–52
Catholicism, 7, 15–16, 25–26, 28, 52, 91,
    254–55n10; and Johane Masowe, 80,
    87, 89, 94, 103, 258n7; and mission-
    aries, 49–50, 55–56, 85, 256n2; and
    mutemo (law/knowledge), 151, 164
causality, 32, 240
cell phones, 35
certitude, 103, 106–7, 136
charismatic leaders, 96, 113, 118, 137
Chidaushe, Lazarus. See Lazarus
Chidavaenze, Ignatius, 254–55n10
Chigwada, Philip. See Philip
Chihuri, Augustine, 132–33, 149
chiManyika, 85, 89
chipo (gift), 210, 215
Chitando, Ezra, 260n6, 264n7
Chiweshe, Chief, 115–16
cholera epidemic, 261n7
Christianity, 11–15, 65, 254n9; and colonial
    history, 5–6, 173; early, 16–18; and
    language, 172–73; and missionaries,
    52–63; paradox of, 9, 172; and Prot-
    estantism, 20–28; and translations,
    57–59, 257n10; and vernacular Bibles,
    55–58, 61–64
Christianity and the Rhetoric of Empire
    (Cameron), 172
church buildings, 108, 116–17, 136, 233–35,
    247
church history, 44–45, 109–37, 147, 162,
    193, 215, 228
Church Missionary Society (CMS), 54–55,
    62, 66, 257nn7,11
church services: and fieldwork, 34–35,
    255n15; and language, 171–72, 174–78,
    262n4; and mutemo (law/knowl-

edge), 144, 155–58, 162–63, 167–70;
    and ritual life/speech, 181, 185–88,
    191–96; and vernacular Bibles, 64
Circular Minute No. 23 (May 1934),
    100–102
circumcision, 196
Clapham Sect, 53–54
Clay, 149, 151
Clinton administration, 121
close reading, 6
coherence of Bible, 173–74, 193, 198
Cohn, Bernard, 59
Coleman, Simon, 173
colloquialisms, 177–78
colonial Africa, 5–7, 20, 36, 45, 48; and
    apostolics, 99, 101, 104, 106, 109–10,
    125, 127, 259n25; and Emmanuel
    Mudyiwa, 104–5, 114; and indepen-
    dent churches, 65–66; and Johane
    Masowe, 79–80, 85, 87–90; and
    missionaries, 50–62, 77, 257n10; and
    postcolonial theologians, 72–73, 75;
    and scriptural imperialism, 50, 75,
    198; and white settlers, 42–43, 61, 90,
    114, 120
Comaroff, Jean, 59, 257n13
Comaroff, John L., 59
communal lands, 36, 106, 114–17, 120–25
community of practice, 174–78, 181–82,
    187–88, 194
Confessions (Augustine), 17, 81
confessions, public: and Apostolic Faith
    Mission (AFM), 98; and Johane
    Masowe, 88, 90, 94, 97; and language,
    176; and mutemo (law/knowledge),
    8, 148
Congregationalists, 57
conservative Protestantism, 20, 22–24, 83,
    244
conversion: and fundamentalism, 83–84;
    of Saint Augustine, 17–18, 81; of
    Shimmer, 139–52, 171; utilitarian vs.
    intellectualist approaches to, 140–41,
    143, 146–47. See also transformations,
    religious
conviction, religious, 83–84, 90, 94, 98,
    106–7

missionaries, 5–6, 48–63, 77, 147, 173, 183, 257n10; and apostolics, 98–101, 200; and education, 52–53; and independent churches, 64–66, 70–71; and Johane Masowe, 80, 85–88, 90, 108, 259n23; and "sheep stealing," 98–99; and vernacular Bibles, 36, 55–58, 61–64

Missionary Labours and Scenes in Southern Africa (Moffat), 57

Moffat, Robert, 53, 56–63, 77, 140, 173, 257n10

Mofokeng, Takatso, 72

money, 8; and church history, 121, 129, 136, 247; and healing, 159, 231, 236; and Isaiah Shembe, 65; and Johane Masowe, 95, 108, 159, 246–47; and mutemo (law/knowledge), 149, 159–61, 163; and Nzira's trial/conviction, 248, 266n1; and Welsh Bibles, 51; and witchcraft, 41, 231, 248–49

Moorhead, William G., 24

Mormonism, 96

Mosaic Law, 195–96

Moses, 19, 69–70, 90, 134, 190, 192, 256n1, 265n9

Movement for Democratic Change (MDC), 44, 249

Msodzi, 95

Msonza, 94

Mtanti, John, 265n7

Mudimbe, V. Y., 45

Mudyiwa, Emmanuel. *See* Emmanuel

Mudzimu Unoera, 114–17, 119, 129

Mugabe, Robert, 43–44, 74, 114, 124, 132, 249, 251, 260n7

muimbi. *See* vaimbi (singers)

Mukonyora, Isabel, 35, 167, 169, 221, 251, 259n23

Muller, Carol Ann, 66–67

mumiriri wemweya (interpreter of the spirit), 185–88, 197, 199, 262nn9,10

Munjeri, Dawson, 232, 264n3

Munn, Nancy, 31

Murphree, Marshall, 96

Museveni, Yoweri, 67–68, 70

"Musha Wedu" (verse), 211–12, 218

mushonga. *See* traditional medicines

Mushope, Dennis, 248

mutemo (law/knowledge), 8–9, 43, 45, 138–70, 246, 260n1; and language, 171, 176, 178; in Marcus's opinion as elder, 153–65, 261n8; and ritual life/speech, 168, 183, 192; in Shimmer's conversion narrative, 139, 146–50, 152; and singing, 207, 217–19, 223; and Vera, 165–69

muteuro (holy medicines), 144–46, 220, 225–28, 235–41, 243, 247, 264n5, 265nn6–9

muti. *See* traditional medicines

Muzarabani congregation, 215

Mwari, 38, 95, 191, 240, 256n17

"Mweya Mutsvene weMabasa" (verse), 217

Mzengeli, Charles, 87, 89, 97

Mzilikazi, king of Ndebele, 59–61, 63–64, 140, 258n7

Namwebonde, Eriah. *See* Eriah

Namwebonde, Sandros. *See* Sandros

n'angas. *See* traditional healers (n'angas)

Nash, Rebecca, 34, 165–69

National Archives of Zimbabwe, 34, 89, 99, 110

National Constitutional Assembly (NCA), 43–44

National Resistance Army (NRA), 67

native agency, 54–55, 62, 71

native commissioners, 80, 97, 100–102, 105, 114, 200, 259n2

Nazarite Baptist Church (NBC), 64–67, 71, 257n12

negativity, 82–85, 102, 108, 164

Nehanda, 39

Nengomasha, Amon, 104

New Testament: canonical texts of, 17, 75; fundamentalists' views on, 24; and independent churches, 66; and postcolonial theologians, 75; and ritual life/speech, 189, 195–97, 263nn13,14; translations of, 36, 47, 57–59, 62, 257n10; and uncertainty, 81

ngirozi. *See* angels

Ngũgĩ wa Thiong'o, 162

Nguni-speaking peoples, 49–50, 65–66

self-denigration, 144

self-discipline, 155, 168–69, 187–88, 204

self-identification, angelic, 192–93

self-sufficient religious community, 88, 106

semeiotic, 31–33, 255n14

semiology, 29–32, 255n12

semiotic ideologies, 9–12, 19, 28–33; and the Bible, 48, 50, 54–55, 58, 77, 198; and cosmological systems, 185, 194; and Friday apostolics, 27, 45; and language, 175, 178, 222; and materiality, 28, 225–26, 228; and missionaries, 85; and prophets, 135; and Protestantism, 20–21; and singing, 201, 206, 264n8

sensible presence, 14–15

separation, 12, 26, 29–30, 84, 96

Setswana New Testament, 57–58, 62

Seventh-day Adventists, 37, 110, 196, 260n1

sexism, 221–22. See also gender analyses

sexual intercourse, 8, 248

Sharpeville Six trial, 73

"sheep stealing," 98

Shembe, Isaiah, 64–67, 71, 77, 257n12

Shimmer, 8, 139–52, 159, 169–71; and healing, 141–45, 177, 225, 230–31, 233–34, 236; and language, 175, 193, 198; and singing, 209

Shoaps, Robin, 183

Shoniwa-Johane. See Masowe, Johane

Sibanda, Julius, 103

signs and signification, 9–11, 29–33, 255n12; and angels, 190; and the Bible, 24, 48–50, 62, 71, 74, 77, 244–45; and cosmological systems, 185; and creation, 21; and Friday apostolics, 78; and language, 175; and pebbles, 238; and prophets, 113; and singing, 264n8; and women's religious attire, 66–67

silent reading, 18

Silverstein, Michael, 31

singing, 35, 45, 200–223, 263n4, 264nn8–10; and church history, 117, 121–22, 130, 134, 260n5; and favorite verses, 213–16; and healing, 213–14, 216, 234–35; and initiative, 210–11; and jealousy, 143–44, 261n4; and language, 222–23; and maverse (verses), 206–10;

and mutemo (law/knowledge), 143–44, 151, 161, 164, 168, 261n4; and one-off verses, 216–22; sound and religious practice, 202–7, 263nn2,3; and standard verses, 211–13, 217–18; and vernacular Bibles, 64

sins, confession of. See confessions, public

Sirus, 118–19, 123, 129, 131, 210–11, 235

sixteenth-century iconoclasm, 20–22, 224–25, 229, 255n12

skepticism, 103, 108, 129

slave trade, abolition of, 52

Smith, Ian, 43

smoking. See tobacco

snakes, 221–22, 231

social justice, 61, 73–74

sola scriptura, 23–24

Songhay sorcery, 202

sound, metaphysics of, 201–7, 222, 263nn2,3

South African apartheid, 71–73, 257n17, 258nn18,19

South African Communist Party, 73

South African Council of Churches (SACC), 72–73

sowe (church site), 34, 142, 175–76, 178, 181, 233. See also names of church sites, e.g., Juranifiri Santa

speaking in tongues, 99

speech communities, 174–81, 262n3

Spinoza, Benedict de, 173–74

spirit mediums, 10–11, 34, 37–40; and church history, 112; and healing, 232–33, 235, 237–42, 264n4; and independent churches, 64, 69; and Johane Masowe, 90, 92, 95, 108, 258n9; and prophets, 90–93; and ritual life/speech, 184, 193, 262n8; and semiotic ideologies, 33; and singing, 218; and War of Independence (1966–1980), 43

spirits. See ancestral spirits; evil spirits; tribal spirits

staffs, 117, 233–34, 253n3, 264n4

Standard Shona Dictionary (Hannan), 203

Stewart, Lyman, 23

Stewart, Milton, 23

Stock, Brian, 17

Stoller, Paul, 202
strategic essentialisms, 37–38
Street, Brian, 255n11
strychnine, 227–28
Sugirtharajah, R. S., 75, 198
"Sunday Christians," 171
Sundkler, Bengt, 253n1, 265n7
Swiss Mission, 63, 140
symbols, 32
synagogues, 18

Tambiah, Stanley, 180
tape recorders, 35
"Tauya Baba" (verse), 213–14, 234
Taylor, Christopher, 76, 240
television commercial, 121
Ten Commandments, 8, 69–70, 146–47, 220
tension between distance and proximity, 23, 28, 33, 82, 84, 107, 180, 186, 188, 199, 246
terror of the text, 7, 82
therapeutic materiel, 225–28. *See also* mu-teuro (holy medicines)
thingification, 26–27, 45, 112, 136–37, 147, 164, 183, 223, 245–46
things, 3, 9–11; and healing, 243, 265n8; and presence of the Bible, 48; and Protestantism, 20–22, 25–28; and semiotic ideologies, 29–31, 33
Thomas, Nicholas, 78
tobacco, 8, 115–16, 141, 145, 151
toilet paper, Bible as, 2, 33, 45, 77, 181, 244
toilets, 160
Torah, 19
Tracy, David, 13, 15, 81, 252, 262n2
traditional culture. *See* African culture
traditional customs. *See* African custom
traditional healers (n'angas), 34, 37–38, 40; vs. apostolic healing, 218, 225, 230, 232–33, 235, 237–42; and mutemo (law/knowledge), 141, 159
traditional medicines, 40, 42, 69; and healing, 218, 230–32, 238–40, 243; and Johane Masowe, 92–93, 112; and mutemo (law/knowledge), 141, 143–44

traditional religion, 37–42, 90–91, 95–96, 99, 191
traditional spirits. *See* tribal spirits
transcendence, 13, 95–96, 173, 187, 193, 197, 213, 225
transformations, religious: of Johane Masowe, 1–2, 84–86, 88–90, 92–97, 103–8, 178, 184, 213, 231, 258nn4,7,9; and mutemo (law/knowledge), 140, 144, 146, 153; of Philip Chigwada, 123; and singing, 216–17; and uncertainty, 81, 84–85, 90
translations, 47, 57–59, 62, 257n10
transubstantiation, 28
tribal spirits, 38–40, 42–43, 91, 95–96; and church history, 115; and healing, 239; and independent churches, 68–70; and mutemo (law/knowledge), 141; and ritual life/speech, 183–85, 187
the Trinity, 148
Troeltsch, Ernst, 25–26, 29, 174, 229
True Bible, 2, 77, 107, 172–74, 182, 189–90, 193–94, 197, 208
Truth and Reconciliation Commission, 72
tsikamutanda (witch hunter), 248–49
Tsitsi, 109–11, 118, 128, 134–35, 154, 246
Tsur, Reuven, 206
tsvimbo. *See* staffs
Turner, Edith, 165
Turner, Victor, 83, 97
Tutsi, 75–76
Tutu, Desmond, 71–77, 257n17, 258nn18,19
typography, 30

"Uchi, uchi" (verse), 242
Uganda National Liberation Army (UNLA), 67
Ugandan civil war, 67–71
Ukpong, Justin, 256n2
uncertainty, 13, 80–85, 90–93, 96, 102–4, 107–8
United Presbyterians, 56
uroyi, 231–32
utilitarian approach to conversion, 140–41, 143, 146–47